Hermann D Wrage

Lehrbuch der englischen Sprache

Hermann D Wrage

Lehrbuch der englischen Sprache

ISBN/EAN: 9783744695541

Hergestellt in Europa, USA, Kanada, Australien, Japan

Cover: Foto ©Paul-Georg Meister /pixelio.de

Weitere Bücher finden Sie auf **www.hansebooks.com**

Lehrbuch

der

Englischen Sprache.

Von

Hermann D. Wrage, A. M.,

Lehrer der deutschen Sprache an den öffentlichen Schulen in New York.

New York:
Verlag von D. Appleton & Company,
549 & 551 Broadway.
1872.

Entered according to Act of Congress, in the year 1871, by
D. APPLETON & CO.,
In the Office of the Librarian of Congress, at Washington.

Vorwort.

Gewagt, wie es erscheinen dürfte, die Fluth von Lehrbüchern fremder Sprachen noch um ein neues zu vermehren, so kann es mir doch nicht einfallen, mich deswegen entschuldigen zu wollen, oder um die Nachsicht derer zu bitten, die sich bewogen finden möchten, mein Buch beim Unterricht in der englischen Sprache oder zum Selbststudium zu gebrauchen. Ist das Buch zweckdienlich, dann wird es sich schon selbst Bahn brechen; ist es das aber nicht, so werden alle Entschuldigungen und Bitten um Nachsicht ihm doch keine Lebensfähigkeit verleihen können.

Wir leben in einer Zeit, wo der internationale Verkehr mit jedem Tage größere Dimensionen annimmt. Die daraus naturgemäß hervorgehende Nothwendigkeit, sich fremde Sprachen anzueignen, tritt an einen Jeden und namentlich an das heranwachsende Geschlecht immer gebieterischer heran. Es ist heutzutage nicht mehr genug einige Phrasen aus einer fremden Sprache auswendig gelernt zu haben, und zur Noth mit gelegentlicher Hülfe eines Wörterbuches ein in fremder Sprache geschriebenes Buch verstehen zu können; nein, es ist heutzutage für den Arbeiter, den Commis, den Handwerker sowohl wie für den Gelehrten von der größten Wichtigkeit, um nicht zu sagen durchaus unerläßlich, sich vollständig in den Besitz wenigstens **einer** fremden Sprache zu setzen. Die Methode, nach der dieses Ziel in der kürzesten Zeit erreicht wird, ist die beste und richtigste.

Die Natur ist, wie überall, so auch hier, die beste Führerin. Allein, wenn heutzutage fast kein Lehrbuch einer fremden Sprache erscheint, das nicht dem Grundsatze huldigte: „Man lerne eine fremde Sprache, wie man seine Muttersprache gelernt hat," so ist damit noch lange nicht gesagt, daß, so richtig auch dieser Grundsatz an und für sich ist, derselbe nun auch gehörig verstanden und befolgt wird.

Auch ich bekenne mich zu diesem Grundsatze und fordere, daß er beim Sprachunterrichte in allen seinen Einzelheiten streng durchgeführt werde.

Ist dieser Grundsatz aber richtig, so folgt daraus, daß es grundfalsch ist, wenn man gleich beim Anfang des Sprachunterrichts grammatikalischen Unterricht mit dem Sprachunterricht verbinden will. Wenn es doch, wie allgemein zugestanden werden muß, die Aufgabe der Grammatik ist, den Schüler **richtig** sprechen und schreiben zu lehren, so folgt doch daraus wohl von selbst, daß der Schüler ü b e r h a u p t der Lautsprache, wie der Schriftsprache bis zu einem gewissen Grade mächtig sein muß, ehe ihm der Unterricht in der Grammatik von Nutzen sein kann.

Wie verkehrt müssen nach diesem Grundsatze demnach alle Lehrbücher fremder Sprachen erscheinen, die mehr als die Hälfte ihres Raumes mit grammatikalischen Regeln anfüllen, die dann in einzelnen mehr oder minder gelungenen Beispielen erläutert werden. So unzweifelhaften Werth, vom grammatikalischen Standpunkt betrachtet, einzelne dieser Bücher auch besitzen mögen, so ist ihr Werth, was die Sprache selbst betrifft, doch nur von sehr untergeordneter Natur.

Nach meiner Ansicht sollte aller Unterricht fremder Sprachen nur mündlicher Unterricht sein; mit andern Worten, ein Sprachlehrer sollte nur verwendet werden, um Unterricht in der Lautsprache zu geben. Die Gründe für diese meine Ansicht sind folgende: Wenn wir die große Anzahl der Unterrichtsgegenstände erwägen, in denen unsere Kinder in den heutigen Schulen unterrichtet werden, so liegt die Gefahr nahe, daß sie von Allem **e i n w e n i g** lernen, von keinem Ge-

genstande aber eine **gründliche** Kenntniß erhalten, kurz, daß sie Vielwisser werden, oder wie der Lateiner sich ausdrückt, multa lernen, aber nicht multum. Die sorgfältigste Sparsamkeit mit der Zeit ist daher eine der wichtigsten Pflichten des Lehrers.

Da es nun aber leicht nachgewiesen werden kann, wie der Schüler sich ohne Hülfe eines Lehrers vermittelst geeigneter Uebersetzungen in den Besitz einer fremden **Schriftsprache** setzen kann, so bleibt also nur die Lautsprache übrig, zu deren Erlernung ein Lehrer nothwendig ist. Das aber will ich hier betont wissen, daß zur Erlernung der Lautsprache ein Lehrer **unentbehrlich** ist, und daß alle noch so sinnreichen Versuche, durch Zeichen eine fremde Lautsprache zu lehren, Laute deutlich zu machen, die dem Schüler gänzlich unbekannt sind, nicht nur höchst absurd sind, sondern auch von üblen Folgen begleitet sein müssen. Es gibt eben nur zweierlei: eine richtige und eine falsche Aussprache; das höchste aber, was durch jene Versuche, eine fremde Lautsprache durch Schriftzeichen zu lehren, erreicht werden kann, ist, daß des Schülers Aussprache eine **annähernd** richtige wird. Annähernd richtig ist aber nicht richtig, sondern, man mag sich drehen, wie man will, falsch. Lieber verzichte der Schüler ganz und gar auf das Erlernen der Lautsprache, stehen ihm keine anderen Hülfsmittel zu Gebote als Bücher, und suche sich eine gründliche Kenntniß der Schriftsprache anzueignen; er wird finden, daß, hat er sich diese nur recht gründlich angeeignet, es nur sehr kurzer Zeit bedarf um, sobald er in den Verkehr der die Sprache sprechenden Eingebornen tritt, auch der Lautsprache Herr zu werden. Der Lehrer beschränke daher seinen Unterricht so viel als möglich auf die Lautsprache. Die Methode, die er hierbei einzuschlagen hat, ist in dem obenangeführten Grundsatze: „Man lerne eine fremde Sprache, wie man seine Muttersprache gelernt hat," enthalten.

Sein erstes Augenmerk muß also darauf gerichtet sein, seinen Schülern Unterricht im **Hören** zu geben; denn durch **Hören** lernen wir S p r e ch e n. Fangen die Schüler erst einmal an das zu ihnen Gesprochene zu verstehen, so kann der Unterricht im Sprechen beginnen, oder vielmehr das Sprechen kommt dann von selbst.

Es muß also als ganz falsch bezeichnet werden, wenn der Lehrer, wie das nur zu oft geschieht, gleich in der ersten Stunde und im Anfange des Unterrichtes den Schüler zum Sprechen und lauten Vorlesen anhält, indem er ihm Sätze vorspricht oder vorliest, und von ihm verlangt, er solle sie nachsprechen. Ein solches Verfahren mag man wohl ein A b richten, aber gewiß nicht ein U n t e r richten nennen.

Das Obengesagte scheint die Benutzung eines Lehrbuches beim Sprachunterricht gänzlich überflüssig zu machen. Doch das scheint nur so. Der mündliche Unterricht kann nur dann von praktischem Werth sein, wenn der Lehrer sich an das geschriebene Wort hält; mit andern Worten, es kann nicht viel nützen, wenn der Lehrer seinen Schülern Sätze vorspricht und übersetzt, wie sie ihm der Augenblick eingibt, weil es ja unmöglich ist diese Sätze, die doch öfters wiederholt werden müssen, so im Gedächtniß zu behalten, daß er sie in derselben Wortfolge wiedergeben kann. D a s l a u t e V o r l e s e n a u s d e m L e h r b u ch e m u ß d a h e r a n d i e S t e l l e d e s S p r e ch e n s t r e t e n. Hier hat der Lehrer den Buchstaben vor sich; er kann, so oft wie er will, oder wie es ihm nöthig scheint, den Satz, die Erzählung von vorn anfangen, ohne in Gefahr zu kommen bei der Wiederholung ein Wort auszulassen oder anders zu setzen, wie er es das erste Mal gethan. Die Erfahrung lehrt mich, daß bei fleißigen, aufmerksamen Schülern ein drei= bis viermaliges Vorlesen genügte, um sie das betreffende Stück gründlich verstehen zu machen. Das „Lehrbuch" hat aber noch den ferneren Nutzen, daß der Schüler, wenn er vermittelst des dem Stücke vorausgehenden Wörterverzeichnisses, oder der dem Lesestück angehängten Fußnoten, die betreffende Lektion zu Hause studirt hat, und zwar so, daß er sie versteht, wenn er sie sieht, dadurch weit besser vorbereitet ist und weit weniger Zeit gebraucht sie verstehen zu lernen, wenn er sie laut vorlesen hört, als wenn er jene Arbeit unterlassen hätte.

Mein Verfahren für den Anfang ist einfach folgendes: Ich lese den Schülern die betreffende Lektion Satz für Satz laut vor und übersetze im Weitergehen jeden Satz, wobei ich ihnen selbstverständlich die nöthigen Sacherklärungen gebe. Dann verlange ich von ihnen, daß sie die betreffende Lektion zu Hause durchnehmen, so daß, wenn die Unterrichtsstunde kommt, sie dieselbe verstehen, wenn sie sie im Buche vor sich sehen. Wenn sie so vorbereitet in die Schule kommen, dann lasse ich sie ihre Bücher zumachen. Ich lese ihnen dann die Lektion Satz für Satz laut vor und lasse sie dieselbe Satz für Satz übersetzen, wobei sie anfangs meiner Hülfe bedürfen. Sind sie recht aufmerksam, so ist ein zwei- bis dreimaliges Vorlesen genug. Beim dritten oder vierten Male des Vorlesens lasse ich sie nicht mehr übersetzen, sondern gebe ihnen am Ende jedes Satzes Zeit, mich nach der Bedeutung dieses oder jenes Wortes zu fragen, welches sie nicht verstanden haben, worauf ich den Satz nochmal lese. Sodann, wenn dies geschehen, lese ich ihnen das Stück zum Schluß noch einmal und zwar rascher und ohne Unterbrechung vor und ich habe gefunden, daß auf diese Weise alle Schüler, mit wenig Ausnahmen, in das Verständniß des Stücks eindringen. Es kann mir bei dem beschränkten Raum eines Vorwortes nicht einfallen weiter auf diesen Gegenstand einzugehen. Es bleibt immer der Individualität des Lehrers überlassen, wie er unterrichten will, aber ich glaube sagen zu dürfen, daß ich dem Lehrer, der nicht selber noch Schüler der Sprache sein muß, die er unterrichten will, ein gutes, praktisches Material geliefert habe, das er besser verwerthen kann, als dasjenige, welches er in den meisten andern Büchern findet.

Das Buch ist in zweiunddreißig Lektionen eingetheilt, welche die Hauptschwierigkeiten der englischen Sprache in logischer Reihenfolge behandeln. Ich habe mich ferner bemüht dem Buche einen streng progressiven Charakter zu geben und hoffe, daß es mir gelungen. Die Lesestücke, Geschichten, Anekdoten, Gespräche, ꝛc., sind ebenfalls mit großer Sorgfalt ausgewählt worden und bieten, sowohl ihrem Inhalt als ihrer Form nach, viel Lehrreiches und Interessantes.

Die in den „Uebungs=Aufgaben" vorkommenden Redensarten, die mit zu den Hauptschwierigkeiten der englischen Sprache gehören, sind fast ohne Ausnahme den der Lektion angehängten Lesestücken entnommen.

Die Fußnoten sind mit besonderem Fleiße ausgearbeitet und wird es dem Verfasser von verständigen Lehrern schwerlich zum Vorwurf gemacht werden können, daß er die Bedeutung eines und desselben Wortes öfters wiedergegeben, da doch die Forderung, der Schüler müsse die Bedeutung eines einmal vorkommenden Wortes, wenn es zum zweiten Male vorkommt, im Gedächtniß behalten können, pädagogisch ganz verkehrt sein würde.

Ein „Schlüssel" zu dem Buche, der in nächster Zeit erscheinen wird, dürfte namentlich denen erwünscht sein, die das Lehrbuch zum Selbststudium benutzen wollen.

Der Verfasser.

New-York, im November 1871.

Inhalts-Verzeichniß.

Lektion I.—Das Hauptwort in der Einzahl; der bestimmte und unbestimmte Artikel . . . 1
    Lesestück 1.—Sarah and her Kittens . . . 3
    Lesestück 2.—Sarah and her Kittens (Schluß) . . 4

Lektion II.—Geschlecht des Hauptwortes. Persönliches Fürwort 4
    Lesestück 1.—James and his Dog Dash . . . 7
    Lesestück 2.—James and his Dog Dash (Schluß) . 7

Lektion III.—Geschlecht des Hauptwortes. Fürwörter (Fortsetzung) 8
    Lesestück 1.—The Old Slate 11
    Lesestück 2.—The Old Slate (Schluß) . . . 12

Lektion IV.—Die Hülfszeitwörter to have und to be (Gegenwärtige Zeit) 14
    Lesestück 1.—The Central Park 16
    Lesestück 2.—Night and Day 17

Lektion V.—Das Hauptwort in der Mehrzahl. Unregelmäßige Mehrzahl 18
    Lesestück 1.—The Little Chimney-Sweep . . 20
    Lesestück 2.—The Little Chimney-Sweep (Schluß) . 21

Lektion VI.—Unbestimmte Fürwörter. Redensarten 23
    Lesestück 1.—Little Dick and the Giant . . 25
    Lesestück 2.—Little Dick and the Giant (Schluß) . 26

Lektion VII.—Das Eigenschaftswort (Adjectiv). Attribut. Prädikat 28
    Lesestück 1.—Jack Frost and the South-wind . 31
    Lesestück 2.—Jack Frost and the South-wind (Schluß) 32

Lektion VIII.—Redensarten 33
    Lesestück 1.—The Wishes' Shop . . . 35
    Lesestück 2.—The Wishes' Shop (Fortsetzung) . 38
    Lesestück 3.—The Wishes' Shop (Schluß) . . 41

Inhalts-Verzeichniß.

Lektion IX.—Das regelmäßige Zeitwort. Gegenwart. Vergangenheit. Redensarten 44
    Lesestück 1.—The Cadi's Decisions . . . 47
    Lesestück 2.—The Cadi's Decisions (Fortsetzung) . 49
    Lesestück 3.—The Cadi's Decisions (Schluß) . 52

Lektion X.—Hauptwort. Geschlecht. Ableitung des weiblichen Geschlechts vom männlichen . . 55
    Lesestück 1.—The Story of Can and Could . . 57
    Lesestück 2.—The Story of Can and Could (Schluß) . 61

Lektion XI.—Fürwörter. Demonstrative. Relative. Redensarten 64
    Lesestück 1.—The Crows and the Wind-mill . . 66
    Lesestück 2.—The Ant and the Cricket . . 70

Lektion XII.—Frage- und Verneinungssätze. Das Hülfszeitwort to do. Redensarten . . 72
    Lesestück 1.—The Hard Task 75
    Lesestück 2.—The Physician and the Student . 76

Lektion XIII.—Adjektivische Fürwörter. Redensarten 80
    Lesestück 1.—The Grateful Indian . . . 83
    Lesestück 2.—Knowledge is Power . . . 85

Lektion XIV.—Das regelmäßige Zeitwort. Vergangene Zeit. Gebrauch des Imperfekts. Redensarten 87
    Lesestück 1.—Death and Burial of Little Nell . 90
    Lesestück 2.—Death and Burial of Little Nell (Schluß) 93

Lektion XV.—Adverbien—der Zeit—des Ortes. Redensarten 97
    Lesestück 1.—The Youthful Witness . . . 101
    Lesestück 2.—The Young Shepherd . . . 104
    Lesestück 3.—The Young Shepherd (Schluß) . 107

Lektion XVI.—Zahlwörter—Cardinal—Ordinal. Redensarten 110
    Lesestück 1.—How Time is Measured . . 112
    Lesestück 2.—The Sayings of Poor Richard . 114
    Lesestück 3.—The Story of the Fairy's Ten Little Workmen 116

Inhalts-Verzeichniß.

xi

Lektion XVII.—Das regelmäßige Zeitwort. Seite
Zukünftige Zeit. Redensarten 120
   Lesestück 1.—The Use of the Beautiful . . 124
   Lesestück 2.—The Use of the Beautiful (Schluß) . 127

Lektion XVIII.—Das Adverb. Adverbien des
Grades und der Weise. Redensarten . . 130
   Lesestück 1.—The Venturesome Boy . . 131
   Lesestück 2.—The Venturesome Boy (Schluß) . 135

Lektion XIX.—Das Eigenschaftswort (Adjektiv).
Steigerung (Comparation). Redensarten . . 137
   Lesestück 1.—The Valley of Tears . . . 141
   Lesestück 2.—The Valley of Tears (Schluß) . 144

Lektion XX.—Fragende Fürwörter und Adver-
bien. Redensarten 146
   Lesestück 1.—A Wonderful Instrument . . 149
   Lesestück 2.—A Silent Partner . . 153
   Lesestück 3.—How to Use the Almanac . . 155

Lektion XXI.—Der Possessiv Casus. Redensarten 156
   Lesestück 1.—Out of the Way . . 159
   Lesestück 2.—Out of the Way (Fortsetzung) . 162
   Lesestück 3.—Out of the Way (Schluß) . . 166

Lektion XXII.—Das Adverb. Bildung des
Adverbs vom Adjektiv. Steigerung des Adverbs.
Redensarten 170
   Lesestück 1.—The Lost Camel . . 173
   Lesestück 2.—Who is a Gentleman . . 175

Lektion XXIII.—Präpositionen. Conjunktio-
nen. Redensarten 178
   Lesestück 1.—Prince Henry . . 182
   Lesestück 2.—Duke of Alba's Breakfast . . 184

Lektion XXIV.—Correlative Fürwörter. Re-
densarten 187
   Lesestück 1.—The Little Man in Black . . 190
   Lesestück 2.—The Little Man in Black (Schluß) . 195

Inhalts-Verzeichniß.

Lektion XXV.—Unregelmäßige Zeitwörter. Conjunktionen. Redensarten 200
 Lesestück 1.—A Child's Dream of a Star . . . 206
 Lesestück 2.—The Forgiven Debt 210

Lektion XXVI.—Unregelmäßige Zeitwörter. Präpositionen. Redensarten 214
 Lesestück 1.—An Indian Stratagem . . . 219
 Lesestück 2.—After Marriage 223

Lektion XXVII.—Unregelmäßige Zeitwörter. Conjunktionen. Redensarten 227
 Lesestück 1.—A Storm at Sea 232
 Lesestück 2.—A Storm at Sea (Schluß) . . 235

Lektion XXVIII.—Unregelmäßige Zeitwörter. Präpositionen. Conjunktionen. Redensarten . 238
 Lesestück 1.—The United States of America . 243
 Lesestück 2.—New York in the Dutch Times . 246

Lektion XXIX.—Reflexive Zeitwörter. Vergleichende Wörter und Sätze. Redensarten . . 249
 Lesestück 1.—A Good Investment . . . 253
 Lesestück 2.—A Good Investment (Schluß) . . 255

Lektion XXX.—Das Passivum. Redensarten . 258
 Lesestück 1.—The Pine-Tree Shilling . . . 263
 Lesestück 2.—The Pine-Tree Shilling (Schluß) . 265

Lektion XXXI.—Die Hülfszeitwörter des Modus. Redensarten 268
 Lesestück 1.—National Monument to Washington . 272
 Lesestück 2.—Liberty and Union . . . 275

Lektion XXXII.—Die progressive Form. Redensarten 278
 Lesestück 1.—Supposed Speech of Regulus to the Carthagenians 282
 Lesestück 2.—The English Language . . . 286

Lektion I.

Das Hauptwort in der Einzahl; der bestimmte und unbestimmte Artikel.

Wörter-Verzeichniß (Vocabulary).

boy, Knabe.
girl, Mädchen.
rose, Rose.
flower, Blume.
bee, Biene.
insect, Insekt.
table, Tisch.
round, rund.
knife, Messer.
sharp, scharf.
friend, Freund.
true, treu.
ink, Tinte.
black, schwarz.
chair, Stuhl.
high, hoch.
stool, Schemel.
low, niedrig.
door, Thür.
shut, zu.
man, Mann, Mensch.
stout, beleibt.
woman, Frau, Weib.
slender, schlank.
brother, Bruder.
sister, Schwester.

good, artig.
house, Haus.
old, alt.
eagle, Adler.
bird, Vogel.
pan, Pfanne.
hot, heiß.
pen, Feder.
sharp, spitz.
water, Wasser.
cold, kalt.
bed, Bett.
soft, weich.
garden, Garten.
large, groß.
handsome, schön.
dwarf, Zwerg.
ugly, häßlich.
dog, Hund.
watchful, wachsam.
beggar, Bettler.
poor, arm.
king, König.
rich, reich.
street, Straße.
wide, breit.

Lehrbuch der englischen Sprache.

Uebungs-Aufgabe 1.

Charles is a boy. Louisa is a girl. The rose is a flower. The bee is an insect. The table is round. The knife is sharp. A friend is true. The ink is black. The chair is high. The stool is low. The door is shut. The man is stout. The woman is slender. The brother and sister are good. The house is old. An eagle is a bird. The pan is hot. The pen is sharp. The water is cold. The bed is soft. The garden is large. The woman is handsome. The dwarf is ugly. The dog is watchful. The beggar is poor. The king is rich. The street is wide.

Wörter-Verzeichniß.

Gabel, fork.
blank, bright.
Topf, pot.
Milch, milk.
süß, sweet.
Stecknadel, pin.
spitz, sharp.
Apfel, apple.
sauer, sour.
Feder, feather.
weich, soft.
Kirche, church.
Schule, school.
geräumig, roomy.
Mütze, cap.
hübsch, pretty.
Kleid, dress.
zerrissen, torn.
Kragen, collar.
schmutzig, dirty.
Kopf, head.
rund, round.
Hemd, shirt.
weiß, white.
Aermel, sleeve.

kurz, short.
Trinkglas, tumbler.
leer, empty.
Krug, pitcher.
voll, full.
Knopf, button.
verloren, lost.
Auge, eye.
blau, blue.
Schiff, ship.
Fahrzeug, vessel.
Aal, eel.
Schlange, snake.
Reptil, reptile.
Schneider, tailor.
Handwerker, mechanic.
Fenster, window.
offen, open.
Zimmer, room.
schmal, narrow.
Nagel, nail.
rostig, rusty.
Schnee, snow.
Himmel, sky.
roth, red.

Das Hauptwort. 3

Uebungs-Aufgabe 2.

Die Gabel ist blank. Der Topf ist schwarz. Die Milch ist süß. Die Stecknadel ist spitz. Der Apfel ist sauer. Eine Feder ist weich. Die Kirche ist neu. Die Schule ist geräumig. Die Mütze ist hübsch. Das Kleid ist zerrissen. Der Kragen ist schmutzig. Der Kopf ist rund. Das Hemd ist weiß. Der Aermel ist kurz. Das Trinkglas ist leer. Der Krug ist voll. Der Knopf ist verloren. Das Auge ist blau. Das Schiff ist ein Fahrzeug. Der Aal ist ein Fisch. Eine Schlange ist ein Reptil. Der Schneider ist ein Handwerker. Das Fenster ist offen. Das Zimmer ist schmal. Der Nagel ist rostig. Der Schnee ist weiß. Der Himmel ist blau. Die Rose ist roth.

Lesestück 1 (Reading Lesson).

SARAH AND HER KITTENS (Sarah und ihre Kätzchen).

1. Sarah has[1] a cat which[2] has four[3] little[4] kittens. One[5] is white,[6] and the other three[7] are gray[8] and white.

2. Sarah has put[9] some[10] milk in a dish[11] and now[12] she sits[13] and looks at them[14] while[15] they lap it up.[16]

3. I have[17] a little kitten, too.[18] Its color[19] is a dark[20] gray, except[21] the tip[22] of[23] its nose[24] and one paw,[25] which are white.

4. When you take it up[26] kindly,[27] it begins[28] to pur[29] and lick[30] your[31] hand with[32] its rough[33] tongue.[34]

5. If you hold it still[35] for a while,[36] and gently[37] pass your hand[38] over[39] its back,[40] it will fold its paws,[41] and itself up,[42] and go to sleep.[43]

[1] hat, [2] welche, [3] vier, [4] klein, [5] eins, [6] weiß, [7] die drei übrigen, [8] grau, [9] gethan, [10] etwas, [11] Napf, [12] jetzt, [13] sitzt sie, [14] schaut sie an, [15] während, [16] sie sie auflecken, [17] ich habe, [18] auch, [19] seine Farbe, [20] dunkel, [21] ausgenommen, [22] Spitze, [23] von, [24] Nase, [25] Pfote, [26] wenn du es aufnimmst, [27] freundlich, [28] fängt es an, [29] zu spinnen, [30] lecken, [31] deine, [32] mit, [33] rauh, [34] Zunge, [35] wenn du es still hältst, [36] eine Zeitlang, [37] sanft, [38] mit der Hand führst, [39] über, [40] Rücken, [41] zieht es seine Pfoten ein, [42] rollt sich auf, [43] beginnt zu schlafen.

Lesestück 2 (Fortsetzung.)

1. It is a sprightly[1] little kitten when it is awake,[2] and will play[3] with pieces[4] of paper,[5] or[6] any thing[7] it finds[8] on[9] the floor.[10]

2. One day[11] it got[12] into[13] my[14] work-basket,[15] rolled[16] the ball of yarn[17] and spool[18] of thread[19] out[20] on the floor,[21] and then[22] pulled[23] the needles[24] and stitches[25] out of my work.[26]

3. If you tie[27] a string[28] to a ball of yarn, and then roll it around[29] on the floor,[30] the kitten will chase after it,[31] as though[32] it were[33] a mouse.

4. It is not old[34] enough[35] to catch[36] mice, but it will prick up its ears,[37] and look[38] very fierce,[39] when it hears[40] a sound[41] like[42] nibbling[43] or scratching.[44]

5. If a dog comes[45] into the room, it will crook up[46] its back,[47] and raise up[48] its hair,[49] as though it were very angry,[50] and getting ready[51] to fight.[52]

[1] munter, [2] wach, [3] und spielt, [4] Stücke, [5] Papier, [6] oder, [7] irgend etwas, [8] (was es) findet, [9] auf, [10] Fußboden, [11] eines Tages, [12] gerieth es, [13] in, [14] mein, [15] Arbeitskörbchen, [16] rollte, [17] Knäuel Garn, [18] Spule, [19] Zwirn, [20] hinaus, [21] Diele, [22] dann, [23] zog, [24] Nadeln, [25] Stiche, [26] Arbeit, [27] bindest, [28] Faden, [29] umher, [30] Fußboden, [31] jagt darnach, [32] als ob, [33] es wäre, [34] alt, [35] genug, [36] fangen, [37] aber es spitzt seine Ohren, [38] sieht aus, [39] wild, [40] hört, [41] Geräusch, [42] wie, [43] Nagen, [44] Kratzen, [45] kommt, [46] macht es einen krummen, [47] Buckel, [48] sträubt, [49] Haare, [50] zornig, [51] sich fertig macht, [52] zum Kampf.

Lektion II.

Geschlecht des Hauptwortes.—Persönliches Fürwort.

Wörter-Verzeichniß.

smells, riecht.
sweet, lieblich.
whose, wessen.
table, Tisch.

this, dies.
mine, der meinige.
I bought, ich habe gekauft.
yesterday, gestern

clock, Uhr.
strikes, schlägt.
twelve, zwölf.
too fast, zu früh.
wound up, aufgezogen.
I shall sell, ich werde verkaufen.
its, ihre.
hands, Zeiger.
broken, zerbrochen.
very, sehr.
bad, schlecht.
scratches, kratzt.
give me, geben Sie mir.
soup, Suppe.
I want to eat, ich will essen.
does—shine, scheint.
moon, Mond.
not yet, noch nicht.
out, heraus.
bright, hell.
sails, segelt.
where, wo.
corner, Ecke.
stove, Ofen.

stable, Stall.
color, Farbe.
did you buy? hast du gekauft?
made me a present of, hat mir geschenkt.
there is, da ist.
door, Thür.
what does she want? was will sie?
piece of bread, Stück Brot.
to her, ihr.
hungry, hungrig.
husband, Mann.
dead, todt.
must, muß.
beg, betteln.
alms, Almosen.
red, roth.
dark, dunkel.
eye, Auge.
mirror, Spiegel.
soul, Seele.
put, stelle.
hearth, Heerd.

Uebungs-Aufgabe 1.

The rose is a flower. It smells sweet. Whose table is this? It is mine. I bought it yesterday. The clock strikes twelve. It is too fast. It is not wound up. I shall sell it. Its hands are broken. This pen is very bad; it scratches. Give me the soup, I want to eat it. It is too hot; I do not like it so hot. Does the moon shine? No, it (she) is not out yet. The sun shines bright. It (he) is very large. The ship sails. It (she) is new. Where is my hammer? It is in the corner by the stove. Give it to me. The horse is in the stable. He is very large. His color is black. Did you buy him? I did not buy him. My uncle made me a present of him. There is a woman at the door. What does she want? She wants a piece of bread. Give it to her. She is hungry. Her husband is dead. She must beg alms. The ink is read. It is too dark. The eye is the mirror of the soul. The pan is hot. It is too small. Put it on the hearth.

Wörter-Verzeichniß.

gehört mir, is mine.
noch, still.
sehr, very.
jung, young.
Ohr, ear.
heiß, hot.
ranzig, strong.
ich will sie nicht essen, I don't want to eat it.
es ist, there is.
Loch, hole.
Krempe, rim.
was kostet? what is the price of?
billig, cheap.
er kostet, it costs.
nur, only.
zwanzig, twenty.
ich will ihn nicht kaufen, I don't want to bay it.
mir zu theuer, too dear for me.

gieb mir, give me.
Stock, stick.
Rock, coat.
ich will ausklopfen, I want to beat.
staubig, dusty.
Straße, street.
breit, broad.
auch, also.
Birne, pear.
hübsch, pretty.
Schirm, umbrella.
wo hast du gekauft? where did you buy?
willst du ihn haben? do you want it?
ich danke, thank you.
magst du leiden? do you like?
diese Hose, these pantaloons.
etwas hell, rather light.

Uebungs-Aufgabe 2.

Der Hund gehört mir; er ist noch sehr jung; seine Ohren sind spitz. Die Suppe ist gut; sie ist sehr heiß. Die Butter ist ranzig; sie ist nicht gut; ich will sie nicht essen. Ist das dein Hut? Er ist mir zu klein. Es ist ein Loch in seiner Krempe. Was kostet der Ofen? Er ist sehr billig; er kostet nur zwanzig Thaler. Ich will ihn nicht kaufen; er ist mir zu theuer. Gib mir den Stock; ich will meinen Rock ausklopfen; er ist sehr staubig. Die Straße ist sehr breit; sie ist auch lang. Was kostet dieser Apfel? Er kostet drei Cents. Und diese Birne? Sie kostet fünf Cents. Wo hast du diesen hübschen Schirm gekauft? Ich habe ihn im Broadway gekauft; er ist mir zu groß. Willst du ihn haben? Nein, ich danke; er ist mir auch zu groß. Magst du diese Hose leiden? Sie ist etwas hell.

Lesestück 1

JAMES AND HIS DOG DASH (Jakob und sein Hund Flink).

1. Mr. Morton was[1] a farmer,[2] and he kept[3] a large dog by the name of[4] Dash, to watch[5] his house at night.[6]
2. Dash was also[7] very[8] useful[9] in the day-time;[10] for[11] he churned[12] the cream,[13] and went[14] with[15] James to drive[16] the cows[17] to the pasture.[18]
3. There[19] was a large pond[20] (of water) in the pasture where[21] James and Dash used[22] to go[23] and play[24] together.[25]
4. James would take[26] a stick[27] and throw[28] it into[29] the water as far as[30] he could,[31] and then[32] tell[33] Dash to go and fetch[34] it.
5. Dash could plunge[35] into the water, seize[36] the stick in his mouth[37] and swim[38] with it[39] to the shore.[40]
6. Sometimes[41] James would throw a stone[42] into the water, and then bid[43] Dash go and fetch it.

[1] war, [2] Landmann, [3] hielt, [4] Namens, [5] bewachen, [6] bei Nacht, [7] auch, [8] sehr, [9] nützlich, [10] bei Tage, [11] denn, [12] butterte, [13] Rahm, [14] ging, [15] mit, [16] treiben, [17] Kühe, [18] Weide, [19] da, [20] Teich, [21] wo, [22] pflegten, [23] hinzugeben, [24] zu spielen, [25] zusammen, [26] nahm auch wohl, [27] Stock, [28] warf, [29] in's, [30] so weit als, [31] konnte, [32] dann, [33] hieß, [34] holen, [35] sprang, [36] ergriff, [37] mit dem Maule, [38] schwamm, [39] damit, [40] an's Ufer, [41] mitunter, [42] Stein, [43] hieß.

Lesestück 2.

JAMES AND HIS DOG DASH. (Fortsetzung.)

1. Dash would again rush[1] into the water and look around for[2] the stone; but would soon return[3] without[4] finding[5] it.

2. But James did not deceive⁶ Dash in this way⁷ more than⁸ two or three times;⁹ for, when¹⁰ he threw a stone into the water and told Dash to go and fetch it, the dog seemed¹¹ to say:¹² "No; you have¹³ deceived me before;¹⁴ and now¹⁵ I do not know¹⁶ when to believe you."¹⁷

3. If boys wish¹⁸ to have their dogs obey them,¹⁹ they must be careful²⁰ not to deceive them.²¹

4. It is wrong²² to practice deceit²³ even²⁴ in sport;²⁵ for it sometimes leads²⁶ to very sad results.²⁷

5. A bad²⁸ boy once,²⁹ in sport, told³⁰ a little girl³¹ to pick up³² a piece of iron³³ in a blacksmith's³⁴ shop.³⁵

6. The girl did not know³⁶ that the iron was hot,³⁷ and it burned³⁸ her hand³⁹ so badly,⁴⁰ that she lost⁴¹ the use⁴² of it.⁴³

¹ stürzte wiederum, ² sah sich um nach, ³ aber er kehrte bald um, ⁴ ohne, ⁵ zu finden, ⁶ hinterging nicht, ⁷ auf solche Weise, ⁸ mehr als, ⁹ zwei= bis dreimal, ¹⁰ als, ¹¹ schien, ¹² sagen, ¹³ du hast, ¹⁴ zuvor, ¹⁵ jetzt, ¹⁶ weiß ich nicht, ¹⁷ wann ich dir glauben soll, ¹⁸ wenn Knaben wollen, ¹⁹ daß ihre . . . ihnen gehorchen sollen, ²⁰ so müssen sie sich in Acht nehmen, ²¹ sie, ²² unrecht, ²³ Betrug zu üben (d. h. zu betrügen), ²⁴ selbst, ²⁵ Spaß, ²⁶ zieht nach sich, ²⁷ sehr traurige Folgen, ²⁸ böse, ²⁹ einmal, ³⁰ sagte, ³¹ Mädchen, ³² sie solle . . . aufheben, ³³ ein Stück Eisen, ³⁴ Grobschmied, ³⁵ Werkstätte, ³⁶ wußte nicht, ³⁷ heiß, ³⁸ verbrannte, ³⁹ ihr die Hand, ⁴⁰ so schlimm, ⁴¹ einbüßte, ⁴² Gebrauch, ⁴³ derselben.

Lektion III.

Geschlecht des Hauptwortes.—Fürwörter.
(Fortsetzung.)

Wörter=Verzeichniß.

sick, krank.
coat, Rock.
new, neu.
loves, liebt.
teacher, Lehrerin.
kind, freundlich.

difficult, schwer.
yonder, dort.
saw, sah.
told us to come in, sagte wir sollten hereinkommen.
is staying, weilt.

Geschlecht des Hauptwortes.

card, Adreßkarte.
it is no fault of yours, es ist Ihre Schuld nicht.
was lost, verloren ging.
cellar, Keller.
kitchen, Küche.
woods, Gehölz.
playmates, Spielkameraden.
pond, Teich.
I warned, ich warnte.
careful, vorsichtig.
bad, schlecht.
scratches, kratzt.
I shall throw away, ich werde wegwerfen.
Katy, Käthchen.
bonnet, Hut.
Joe, Joseph.
Jim (James) Jakob.
orchard, Obstgarten.
holiday, Feiertag.
pencil, Bleistift, Griffel.
Fred, Fritz.
do you see, siehst du.
church, Kirche.
Our Father, who, &c., Unser Vater, der du bist, ꝛc.

Uebungs=Aufgabe 1

I have a father and a mother. My brother and my sister are sick. My coat is new. This book is not mine, but those books are mine. My teacher loves me. We love our teacher; she is very kind. Our lesson is not difficult. This house is ours, and that yonder is yours. He saw us in the garden and told us to come in. A friend of mine is staying at our house. Will you give me your card? I tell you, it is no fault of yours that his dog was lost. He is in the cellar, she is in the kitchen. Where are the children? They are in the woods; their playmates are with them. Charles and Louisa and a cousin of theirs are in a boat on the pond. I warned them to be careful. That pen of yours is very bad; it scratches. I shall throw it away. Katy, where is that bonnet of yours? I gave mine to Clara, and she gave me hers. Joe and Jim are in the orchard. They have a holiday. Whose pencil is this? Is it yours, Fred, or is it your brother's? It is not mine, it is his. Do you see that church yonder? I see it. Our Father, who art in heaven, hallowed be thy name, thy kingdom come, thy will be done on earth as it is done in heaven; give us this day our daily bread, and forgive us our trespasses as we forgive those who trespass against us ; lead us not into temptation, but deliver us from evil, for thine is the kingdom and the power and the glory forever and ever.

Wörter-Verzeichniß.

hübsch, pretty.
ganz, quite.
Fenster, window.
Schüler, pupil.
von mir, of mine.
wohnt, lives.
größer, larger.
wo hast du gekauft? where did you buy?
Geschenk, present.
Besen, broom.
schläft das Kind noch? is the child still sleeping?
wacht, is awake.
warum, why.
ich glaube, I believe.
hungrig, hungry.
durstig, thirsty.
trägt der Baum? does the tree bear?
Frucht, fruit.
manchmal, sometimes.
immer, always.
schlage nicht, do not strike.
beißt, bites.
Federhalter, pen-holder.

Uebungs-Aufgabe 2.

Dies ist ein hübsches Haus; es ist ganz neu; seine Fenster sind sehr groß. Ist es das Ihrige? Nein, es gehört meinem Bruder. Dieser Knabe ist ein Schüler von mir. Ein Freund von mir wohnt in New York. Ist das ein Vetter von Ihnen? Nein, er ist mein Neffe. Diese Stadt ist sehr groß; sie ist größer als Berlin. Wo hast du diese Uhr gekauft? Sie ist ein Geschenk von einem guten Freunde von mir. Der Besen ist neu; er ist sehr gut. Schläft das Kind noch? Nein, es wacht schon. Warum weint es? Ich glaube, es ist hungrig und durstig. Trägt der Baum Früchte? Manchmal trägt er Früchte, aber nicht immer. Schlage den Hund nicht; er beißt. Gieb diesen Brief deiner Mutter; er kommt von deiner Tante. Wem gehört dieser Federhalter? Er gehört meinem Bruder.

Geschlecht des Hauptwortes.

Lesestück 1.

THE OLD SLATE (Die alte Schiefertafel).

1. "I have a great mind[1] to break[2] this stupid[3] old slate," said Charles one morning, as he sat,[4] with tears[5] in his eyes,[6] almost crying[7] over his first lesson in subtraction.[8]

"Why,[9] what has the poor slate done?"[10] asked[11] the pleasant voice[12] of his sister Helen behind[13] him.

2. "Nothing. That is just[14] what I complain of.[15] It won't make[16] the figures[17] in this lesson for me; and here it is[18] almost[19] school-time!"[20]

"What a wicked[21] slate, Charles!"

3. "So it is.[22] I mean[23] to throw[24] it out of the window,[25] and break it in pieces[26] on the stones."[27]

"Will that get your lesson for you,[28] Charley?"

"No: but if there were[29] no slates in the world,[30] I would have no such lessons to learn."

4. "Oh ho! indeed![31] But that does not follow by any means.[32] Did slates make arithmetic?[33] Would people[34] never[35] have to count[36] and calculate,[37] if there were[38] no slates? You forget[39] pens,[40] lead-pencils,[41] and paper; you forget all about oral arithmetic,[42] Charley!"

"Well, I don't like[43] to cipher,[44] that's all; but I do like to count."[45]

5. "And so,[46] you hasty[47] boy, you get angry[48] with the poor, harmless[49] slate, that is so convenient[50] when you make mistakes[51] and wish to rub them out.[52] This is the way with[53] a great many[54] thoughtless,[55] quick-tempered[56] people. They try[57] to find fault[58] with somebody[59] or something,[60] and get into a passion,[61] and perhaps do mischief;[62] when,[63] if they would reflect,[64] they would find that they themselves ought to bear[65] all the blame.[66] Now, Charley, let me see what I can do for you."

---

[1] große Lust, [2] zerbrechen, [3] dumm, [4] saß, [5] Thränen, [6] in den Augen, [7] fast weinend, [8] im Subtrahiren, [9] ei! [10] gethan, [11] fragte, [12] die freundliche Stim-

me, ¹³ hinter, ¹⁴ das ist's ja gerade, ¹⁵ worüber ich bös bin, ¹⁶ sie will nicht machen, ¹⁷ Zahlen, ¹⁸ es ist jetzt, ¹⁹ beinahe, ²⁰ Zeit zur Schule, ²¹ was für eine böse, ²² das ist sie auch, ²³ ich will, ²⁴ werfen, ²⁵ Fenster, ²⁶ Stücke, ²⁷ Steine, ²⁸ wirst du damit deine Lektion kriegen? ²⁹ wenn es gäbe, ³⁰ Welt, ³¹ wirklich! ³² das folgt durchaus nicht, ³³ die Rechnenkunst, ³⁴ Leute, ³⁵ niemals, ³⁶ zählen, ³⁷ berechnen, ³⁸ wenn es gäbe, ³⁹ vergißt, ⁴⁰ Federn, ⁴¹ Bleifedern, ⁴² Kopfrechnen, ⁴³ ich mag nicht, ⁴⁴ rechnen, ⁴⁵ ich mag gern zählen, ⁴⁶ deshalb, ⁴⁷ voreilig, ⁴⁸ wirst du böse, ⁴⁹ unschuldig, ⁵⁰ bequem, ⁵¹ Fehler, ⁵² und sie auswischen, ⁵³ so machen es, ⁵⁴ sehr viele, ⁵⁵ gedankenlos, ⁵⁶ hitzköpfig, ⁵⁷ sie bemühen sich, ⁵⁸ etwas auszusetzen, ⁵⁹ an Leuten, ⁶⁰ Dingen, ⁶¹ und gerathen in Hitze, ⁶² und vielleicht stiften sie sogar Unglück an, ⁶³ wohingegen, ⁶⁴ wenn sie nachdenken würden, ⁶⁵ sie selbst tragen sollten, ⁶⁶ allen Tadel.

Lesestück 2.

THE OLD SLATE. (Schluß.)

1. So Helen sat down in her mother's great easy-chair;¹ she tried² to look grave³ and dignified,⁴ like an old lady, though⁵ she was but eighteen. Charley came rather unwillingly,⁶ laid the slate on her lap,⁷ and began to play⁸ with the trimmings⁹ on her apron.¹⁰

"Why, what is this?" said she; "soldiers,¹¹ and cats, and dogs, and houses with windows of all shapes¹² and sizes?"¹³

2. Charley looked foolish.¹⁴ "Oh, the lesson is on the other side,"¹⁵ said he, turning the slate over.¹⁶

"Ah, silly boy!" said Helen; "here you have been sitting¹⁷ half an hour drawing pictures,¹⁸ instead of trying¹⁹ to learn your lesson. And now, which do you think ought to be broken,²⁰ you or your slate?" And she held the slate up high,²¹ as if²² she meant²³ to beat²⁴ his head with it.²⁵

3. Charley looked up,²⁶ with his hands at his ears,²⁷ but laughing²⁸ all the while,²⁹ for he knew³⁰ she was only playing³¹ with him. Presently,³² however,³³ she put on a serious face,³⁴ and said, "Now, my little man,³⁵ you must go to work³⁶ in good earnest,³⁷ to make up³⁸ for lost time."³⁹

4. "Oh, Helen, it wants only twenty minutes of nine;⁴⁰ I shall be late⁴¹ to school. Can't you, just this once,⁴² make the figures for me?"

"No," said Helen.

"Oh, do! just this once."

5. "No, Charley; there would be no kindness in that.[43] You would never learn arithmetic in that way.[44] If I do it once, you will find it harder [45] to be refused [46] to-morrow. I will do a much kinder thing.[47] I will just show you a little, and you may do all the work yourself."

6. So she passed [48] her arm gently [49] around [50] him; and though Charley pouted [51] at first,[52] and could hardly[53] see through his tears, she questioned [54] him about the rule,[55] and then began to show him the proper way [56] to get [57] his lesson.

When all was finished,[58] Charley was surprised [59] to find that he should still [60] be in season [61] for school.

7. "Now, to-morrow, Charley," said Helen, "do not waste[62] a moment, but [63] begin your lesson at once,[64] and you will find it a great saving,[65] not only of time,[66] but of temper.[67] I hope you will not get into a passion[68] again with this good old slate of mine.[69] It went to school with me when I was a little girl, and I should be sorry [70] if you had broken it for not doing [71] your work."

8. Away [72] ran Charles to school, thinking to himself,[73] "Well, I suppose [74] I was wrong,[75] and Helen is right.[76] I ought not have been making [77] pictures. I ought to have been getting [78] my lesson."

---

[1] Lehnstuhl, [2] versuchte, [3] ernst auszusehen, [4] würdevoll, [5] obschon, [6] fast widerstrebend, [7] Schooß, [8] spielen, [9] Besatz, [10] Schürze, [11] Soldaten, [12] Gestalten, [13] Größen, [14] albern, [15] Seite, [16] indem er die Tafel umkehrte, [17] hast du gesessen, [18] Bilder zeichnend, [19] statt zu versuchen, [20] sollte gebrochen werden, [21] in die Höhe, [22] als ob, [23] wollte, [24] schlagen, [25] damit, [26] blickte auf, [27] Ohren, [28] lachend, [29] in einem fort, [30] wußte, [31] sie scherzte nur, [32] plötzlich, [33] jedoch, [34] nahm sie eine ernsthafte Miene an, [35] Kerl, [36] mußt du an die Arbeit gehen, [37] ernstlich, [38] einzubringen, [39] die verlorene Zeit, [40] es sind nur zwanzig Minuten bis neun, [41] ich werde zu spät kommen, [42] nur dies eine Mal. [43] das würde nicht freundlich sein von mir, [44] auf diese Weise, [45] so wird es dir schwerer werden, [46] abschlägigen Bescheid zu erhalten, [47] etwas viel Besseres. [48] schlang sie, [49] sanft, [50] um, [51] maulte, [52] anfangs, [53] kaum, [54] fragte sie, [55] nach der Regel, [56] die richtige Weise, [57] zu lösen, [58] beendigt, [59] erstaunt, [60] noch, [61] zeitig genug, [62] vergeude, [63] sondern, [64] sogleich, [65] Ersparniß, [66] an Zeit, [67] Aerger,

⁶⁸ du wirst nicht wieder so in Harnisch gerathen über, ⁶⁹ von mir, ⁷⁰ es sollte mir leid thun, ⁷¹ dafür, daß sie nicht gethan, ⁷² fort, ⁷³ bei sich selbst denkend, ⁷⁴ ich vermuthe, ⁷⁵ ich hatte unrecht, ⁷⁶ hat recht, ⁷⁷ ich hätte nicht machen sollen, ⁷⁸ ich hätte machen sollen.

Lektion IV.

Die Hülfszeitwörter *to have* und *to be* (Gegenwärtige Zeit).

Wörter-Verzeichniß.

I have, ich habe.
you have, Sie (du) haben.
pencil, Bleistift.
he has, er hat.
slate, Tafel.
bonnet, Hut.
she has, sie hat.
also, auch.
veil, Schleier.
what, was.
child, Kind.
it has, es hat.
doll, Puppe.
we have, wir haben.
they have, sie haben.
watch, Uhr.
no pity, kein Mitleid.
where, wo.
umbrella, Regenschirm.
here, hier.
why, warum.
time, Zeit.
much sugar, viel Zucker.
I am, ich bin.
tired, müde.
are you? sind Sie (du)?
we are, wir sind.
young, jung.
but, aber.
you are, ihr (Sie) seid.
old, alt.
needle, Nähnadel.
on, auf.
floor, Fußboden.
handsome, hübsch.
she is, sie ist.
proud, stolz.
sick, krank.
now, jetzt.
cross, verdrießlich.
unhappy, unglücklich.
slippers, Pantoffeln.
they are, sie sind.
bedroom, Schlafzimmer.
give me, geben Sie mir.
key, Schlüssel.
door, Thür.

Geschlecht des Hauptwortes.

Uebungs-Aufgabe 1

I have a book, you have a pencil, and he has a slate. This girl has a bonnet; she has also a veil. What has the child? It (he or she) has a doll. We have a father and a mother. They have brothers and sisters. Has he the watch? No, he has not (got) it. We have no pity. Where have you (got) your umbrella? I have it here. Why have you no time? I have much sugar. I am tired. Are you tired? No, I am not tired. We are young, but you are old. Where is my needle? It is on the floor. This girl is handsome; she is very proud. Her brother is my friend; he is sick now. Why are you cross? I am not cross; I am unhappy. The dog and cat are not great friends. Where are your slippers? They are in my bedroom. Give me the key. It is in the door.

Wörter-Verzeichniß.

fein, no.
Nachbar, neighbor.
Pferd, horse.
viele, many.
Kühe, cows.
Sonnenschirm, parasol.
Kleid, dress.
Keller, cellar.
Holz, wood.
Kohlen, coal.
noch nicht, not yet.
reif, ripe.
Flecke, spots.
Spaten, spade.
Holzstall, wood-shed.
fleißig, diligent.
manchmal, sometimes.
faul, lazy.
glücklich, happy.
Großmutter, grandmother.
fertig, done.
aufmerksam, attentive.
unaufmerksam, inattentive.

Uebungs-Aufgabe 2.

Was hast du? Ich habe ein Messer und eine Gabel. Hast du auch einen Teller? Ich habe keinen Teller. Wir haben eine Katze und einen Hund, und unser Nachbar hat ein Pferd und viele Kühe. Was hat deine Schwester? Sie hat einen neuen Sonnenschirm. Hat sie auch ein neues Kleid?

Sie hat viele neue Kleider. Was habt ihr in eurem Keller? Wir haben Holz und Kohlen in unserem Keller. Diese Aepfel sind sehr groß; sie sind aber noch nicht reif; sie haben Flecke. Wo ist dein Spaten? Er ist in dem Holzstall. Bist du fleißig? Ich bin nicht immer fleißig; manchmal bin ich faul. Wir sind sehr glücklich. Wie alt ist deine Großmutter? Sie ist sehr alt. Sind meine Stiefel fertig? Sie sind noch nicht fertig. Ihr seid nicht aufmerksam; ihr seid unaufmerksam.

Lesestück 1.

THE CENTRAL PARK.

1. In the city[1] of New York there is[2] a very large park, called[3] *The Central Park.*

2. This park has been laid out[4] with great care,[5] so as to make it[6] a pleasant place for people to visit.[7]

3. The rocks[8] in many places[9] have been cut away,[10] and the ground[11] has been planted[12] with shrubs[13] and trees.

4. It has very fine roads[14] and gravel-walks,[15] leading[16] in different[17] directions,[18] so that[19] people[20] can ride[21] or walk[22] to any part[23] of it[24] they wish.[25]

5. The park is quite[26] uneven,[27] being made up of[28] many little hills[29] and valleys.[30]

6. Some[31] of the little valleys have been filled[32] with water, making[33] a number[34] of lakes or ponds.[35]

7. In the winter, when[36] these[37] ponds are frozen over, the boys and girls, and even[38] men[39] and women,[40] have fine sport,[41] skating[42] and sliding.[43]

8. When the weather[44] is pleasant,[45] and the skating is good, you may see[46] thousands of persons,[47] of almost[48] all ages,[49] all skating at the same time.[50]

9. In the summer-time you may see a number of large, white swans,[51] sailing around[52] in the water.

10. They were sent[53] to this country[54] as a present,[55] by the city[56] of Hamburg, in Europe.

11. It is a grand[57] sight[58] to see[59] them[60] curve[61] their long, slender[62] necks,[63] and float around on the water.

12. They spread out[64] their large wings[65] like[66] the sails[67] of a vessel[68] and the wind blows[69] them away.[70]

13. They are so tame,[71] that they will come and eat[72] corn or crumbs of bread[73] from[74] your hand.

14. Do you know[75] what we call[76] a young swan? Yes; a young swan is called[77] a cygnet. Like goslings,[78] they have very fine, soft[79] down,[80] till[81] they get to be[82] five or[83] six months[84] old.

¹ Stadt, ² es gibt, ³ genannt, ⁴ ist angelegt worden, ⁵ Sorgfalt, ⁶ um ihn zu machen zu, ⁷ angenehmer Erholungsort für's Volk, ⁸ Felsen, ⁹ Plätze, ¹⁰ sind aus dem Wege geschafft worden, ¹¹ Boden, ¹² ist bepflanzt worden, ¹³ Sträucher, ¹⁴ Straßen, ¹⁵ Nicswege, ¹⁶ führend, ¹⁷ verschiedene, ¹⁸ Richtungen, ¹⁹ daß, ²⁰ man, ²¹ fahren, ²² geben (zu Fuß), ²³ nach irgend einem Theile, ²⁴ desselben, ²⁵ (wohin) man will, ²⁶ ganz, ²⁷ uneben (hügelig), ²⁸ indem er besteht aus, ²⁹ Hügel, ³⁰ Thäler, ³¹ einige, ³² angefüllt, ³³ bildend, ³⁴ Anzahl, ³⁵ Seen, ³⁶ wenn, ³⁷ diese, ³⁸ zugefroren, ³⁹ sogar, ⁴⁰ Männer, ⁴¹ Frauen, ⁴² Vergnügen, ⁴³ Schlittschuh laufend, ⁴⁴ schurrend, ⁴⁵ Wetter, ⁴⁶ angenehm, ⁴⁷ kann man sehen, ⁴⁸ Menschen, ⁴⁹ beinahe, ⁵⁰ Altersstufen, ⁵¹ zu gleicher Zeit, ⁵² Schwäne, ⁵³ umhersegelnd, ⁵⁴ sie wurden geschickt, ⁵⁵ Land, ⁵⁶ Geschenk, ⁵⁷ Stadt, ⁵⁸ prächtig, ⁵⁹ Anblick, ⁶⁰ sehen, ⁶¹ sie, ⁶² biegen, ⁶³ schlank, ⁶⁴ Hälse, ⁶⁵ schwimmen, ⁶⁶ spreiten aus, ⁶⁷ Flügel, ⁶⁸ wie, ⁶⁹ Segel, ⁷⁰ Schiff, ⁷¹ treibt, ⁷² entlang, ⁷³ zahm, ⁷⁴ essen, ⁷⁵ Brodkrumen, ⁷⁶ aus, ⁷⁷ weißt du, ⁷⁸ nennen, ⁷⁹ wird genannt (heißt), ⁸⁰ Gössel, ⁸¹ weich, ⁸² Daunen, ⁸³ bis, ⁸⁴ werden, ⁸⁵ bis, ⁸⁶ Monate.

Lesestück 2.

NIGHT AND DAY (Tag und Nacht).

1. As¹ the light of the sun makes the day, when the sun sets² it is evening, which is soon³ followed⁴ by the darkness⁵ of night.

2. But when it is night here, is it night in all parts⁶ of the world?⁷ No; it is then day in some⁸ places; and when *we* see the sun setting, others, in a distant⁹ part of the world, see it rising.¹⁰ Our evening is their morning, and our midnight¹¹ is their noonday.¹²

3. Would you know¹³ the cause¹⁴ of these changes?¹⁵ The earth is a large globe¹⁶ or ball;¹⁷ and it turns¹⁸ on its axis,¹⁹ from west to east, once²⁰ in every twenty-four hours, at one time²¹ carrying²² us toward²³ the sun, and at another time²⁴ carrying us away from²⁵ it.

4. When we are carried²⁶ toward the sun, it is the

early²⁵ part of the day to us; and when we are carried away from it, the sun seems²⁶ to go down²⁹—down—until³⁰ it sets in the west, and at length³¹ night comes upon us. The sun *seems* to us to go round the earth; but it does not.

5. While³² we are on the side of the earth toward³³ the sun, there are other people who are on the opposite³⁴ side of the earth where it is night; and when we see the sun rising in *our* east, others see it setting in *their* west.

¹ wie, ² untergeht, ³ bald, ⁴ gefolgt, ⁵ Dunkelheit, ⁶ in allen Theilen, ⁷ Welt, ⁸ einige, ⁹ entfernt, ¹⁰ aufgeben, ¹¹ Mitternacht, ¹² Mittag, ¹³ möchtet ihr wissen, ¹⁴ Ursache, ¹⁵ Veränderungen, ¹⁶ Globus, ¹⁷ Kugel, ¹⁸ dreht sich, ¹⁹ um ihre Are, ²⁰ einmal, ²¹ das eine Mal, ²² tragend, ²³ nach—zu, ²⁴ das andere Mal, ²⁵ weg von, ²⁶ wenn wir getragen werden, ²⁷ früh, ²⁸ scheint, ²⁹ unter, ³⁰ bis, ³¹ endlich, ³² während, ³³ zugekehrt, ³⁴ entgegengesetzt.

Lection V.

Das Hauptwort in der Mehrzahl. — Unregelmäßige Mehrzahl.

Wörter-Verzeichniß.

lazy, faul.
diligent, fleißig.
where, wo.
do—come from, kommen—her.
from, aus.
Germany, Deutschland.
child, Kind.
cheerful, fröhlich.
man, Mensch, Mann.
mortal, sterblich.
lady, Dame.
gentleman, Herr.
are going, gehen.

many, viele.
church, Kirche.
minister, Prediger.
preaches, predigt.
congregation, Gemeinde.
hymn, Lied.
where, wohin.
people, Leute.
audience, das Auditorium.
applaud, applaudiren.
actor, Schauspieler.
how, wie.
knife, Messer.

Das Hauptwort in der Mehrzahl.

fork, Gabel.
do you want? wollen Sie haben?
I want, ich brauche.
five, fünf.
dentist, Zahnarzt.
pulls, zieht aus.
tooth, Zahn.
small, klein.
foot, Fuß.
leaf, Blatt.
on, auf.
tree, Baum.

faded, verwelkt.
here, hier.
which, welches.
caught, fing.
rat, Ratte.
mouse, Maus.
negro, Neger.
black, schwarz.
on board, an Bord.
we like, wir essen gern.
beef, Rindfleisch.
potato, Kartoffel.

Uebungs-Aufgabe 1.

This book is old. These books are new. The boy is lazy. The boys are diligent. The man and woman are in the garden. Where do these men and women come from? They come from Germany. A child is cheerful. All children are cheerful. Man is mortal. All men are mortal. Ladies and gentlemen are going to the concert. New York has many churches. The minister preaches and the congregation sing hymns. Where are these people going? They are going to the theatre. The audience applaud the actors. How many knives and forks do you want? I want five knives. The dentist pulls a tooth. He pulls many teeth. The lady has a very small foot; her feet are very small. The leaves on this tree are all faded. Here is a leaf which is not faded. The cat caught a mouse. Cats catch rats and mice. The negroes are black. Are all people on board? We like beef and potatoes.

Wörter-Verzeichniß.

Dieb, thief.
stehlen, to steal.
viele, many.

drei, three.
zwei, two.
ich habe mir den Fuß verrenkt, I have sprained my foot.

mir thun die Zähne weh, my teeth ache.
hohl, hollow.
Scheere, scissors.
es sind, there are.
zweiundzwanzig, twenty-two.
es gibt, there is, there are.
Stadt, city, town.
Dorf, village.
Land, country.
die größte, the largest.

Kartoffel, potato.
Gemüse, vegetables.
sie hatte, she had.
jetzt aber, but now.
nur noch, only.
gewaschen, washed.
Herr, gentleman.
Empfangszimmer, parlor.
Ratte, rat.
Maus, mouse.
Keller, cellar.

Uebungs-Aufgabe 2.

Der Dieb stiehlt. Die Diebe stehlen. Ich habe ein Messer; du hast viele Messer. Wie viele Häuser hat dein Vater? Mein Vater hat nur ein Haus. Er hat drei Brüder und zwei Schwestern. Dieses Kind hat sehr große Füße und Hände. Ich habe mir den Fuß verrenkt. Mir thun die Zähne weh; ich habe einen hohlen Zahn. Gib mir die Scheere; sie ist nicht scharf; sie ist stumpf. Wie viele Männer und Frauen sind in diesem Zimmer? Es sind zweiundzwanzig Männer hier, aber keine Frau. Es gibt Städte und Dörfer in allen Ländern. New York ist die größte Stadt in den Vereinigten Staaten. Was kosten die Kartoffeln? Kartoffeln und Gemüse sind sehr theuer. Wie viele Kinder hat diese Frau? Sie hatte drei Kinder; jetzt aber hat sie nur noch ein Kind. Hast du deine Hände gewaschen? Ich habe meine Hände und Füße gewaschen. Es sind zwei Herren im Empfangszimmer. Wir haben viele Ratten und Mäuse in unserm Keller.

Lesestück 1.

THE LITTLE CHIMNEY-SWEEP.[1]

1. Some years ago,[2] the good people of Dublin made[3] an effort[4] to have all the little sweeps of the city go[5] to a free[6] school, so that[7] they might be taught[8] to read.[9]

2. One of the sweeps who[10] went[11] to this school, was asked[12] by[13] his teacher,[14] if[15] he knew[16] his letters.[17]

3. "Yes, sir,"[18] said[19] the boy; "I know them[20] all."

4. "Do you know how to[21] read and spell?"[22] asked[23] the teacher.

5. "Yes, sir," answered[24] the lad;[25] "I learned[26] to read and spell some time ago."[27]

6. "What[28] book did you learn[29] to read from?"[30] the teacher asked again.[31]

7. "Oh, I never[32] had any[33] book!" said the little sweep.

8. "Will you tell me,[34] then," said the teacher, "how you learned[35] to read and spell?"

9. "Another[36] sweep who was a little[37] older than[38] I am, taught[39] me," answered the boy.

[1] Schornsteinfegerjunge, [2] vor mehreren Jahren, [3] machten, [4] Anstrengung, [5] gehen, [6] frei, [7] so daß, [8] sie unterrichtet werden möchten, [9] lesen, [10] welcher, [11] ging, [12] wurde gefragt, [13] von, [14] Lehrer, [15] ob, [16] er müßte, [17] Buchstaben, [18] ja, mein Herr! [19] sagte, [20] sie, [21] kannst du, [22] buchstabiren, [23] fragte, [24] antwortete, [25] Bursche, [26] lernte, [27] vor längerer Zeit, [28] was für ein, [29] hast du gelernt, [30] aus, [31] wieder, [32] niemals, [33] irgend ein, [34] willst du mir sagen, [35] du gelernt hast, [36] ein anderer, [37] ein wenig, [38] als, [39] unterrichtet.

Lesestück 2.

THE LITTLE CHIMNEY-SWEEP. (Schluß.)

1. "How[1] could he do it?"[2] asked[3] the teacher, "without[4] a book?"

2. "He did it by showing me[5] the letters[6] on the signs[7] over the shop-doors,[8] which[9] we read[10] as we went[11] through[12] the city," said the sweep.

3. The only[13] teacher this little boy had, was a sweep, like himself;[14] and his books were the signs over the doors of the shops and stores.[15]

4. If[16] this poor little sweep, who had never[17] been to school, had learned[18] to read[19] with such helps[20] as these, how much more[21] ought[22] children to learn who

have plenty²³ of good books, and teachers to instruct²⁴ them.

¹ wie, ² konnte er das, ³ fragte, ⁴ ohne, ⁵ indem er mir zeigte, ⁶ Buchstaben, ⁷ Schilder, ⁸ Thüren der Werkstätten, ⁹ welche, ¹⁰ lasen, ¹¹ gingen, ¹² durch, ¹³ einzig, ¹⁴ wie er selbst, ¹⁵ Läden, ¹⁶ wenn, ¹⁷ niemals, ¹⁸ gelernt, ¹⁹ lesen, ²⁰ Hülfe, ²¹ um wie viel mehr, ²² sollten, ²³ Ueberfluß an, ²⁴ unterweisen.

Lektion VI.

Unbestimmte Fürwörter.—Redensarten.

Wörter-Verzeichniß.

born, geboren.
equal, gleich.
about you, bei dir.
asked, stellte.
question, Frage.
to answer, beantworten.
I have spent, ich habe zuge=
bracht.
company, Gesellschaft.
no fault of mine, nicht meine
Schuld.
neighborhood, Nachbarschaft.
to be let, zu vermiethen.
hereabouts, hier herum.
thirsty, durstig.
I am very sorry, es thut mir
sehr leid.
ice, Eis.
ought to have brought, hätte
bringen sollen.
on register, auf der Liste.
absent, abwesend.
various, verschieden.
cause, Ursache.
in the country, auf dem Lande.
sick, krank.
pleasure, Vergnügen.
out fishing, Fischen gegangen.
caught, fingen.
there is no way of getting
along, es ist nicht fertig zu
werden.
fellow, Bursche.
to quarrel, streiten.
to fight, sich schlagen.
embarrassed, in Verlegenheit.
I would not bother myself,
ich würde mir keine grauen
Haare wachsen lassen.
importance, Bedeutung.
chickens, Hühner.
killed, umgebracht.
fortunate, glücklich.
happy, glücklich.
unfortunate, schade.
any sooner, früher.
to be introduced, vorgestellt
werden.

acquaintance, Bekanntschaft.
by no means, durchaus nicht.
to know how to, können.
to translate, übersetzen.
sentence, Satz.
to shut, zumachen.
to open, aufmachen.
draft, Zugwind.

another glass, noch ein Glas.
the other day, neulich.
troubles, Bemühungen.
to no purpose, vergebens.
in vain, umsonst.
to trouble one's self, sich Sorge machen um.
to alter, ändern.

Uebungs=Aufgabe 1.

All men are born free and equal. Have you any money about you? I have some, but not much. He asked many questions which I could not answer. I have spent many an hour in his company. That is no fault of mine. Do you know of any house in this neighborhood which is to be let? I know some houses that are to be let, but none hereabouts. I wish you would give me a little water, I am very thirsty. I am very sorry that I have no ice in the house; the iceman ought to have brought me some this morning. How many boys are in your class? I have forty on register, but to-day some are absent from various causes. Some are in the country, and a few are sick. I had a great deal of pleasure yesterday; we were out fishing and caught a great many fine, large fish. Do you want any? Thank you, I bought some this morning. There is no way of getting along with this fellow. He is always quarreling and fighting. I do not understand why you are embarrassed. In any case, I would not bother myself about things of so little importance. Where are all the chickens I bought for you? The cat has killed them all. All the people in this town are Germans. My brother has been very fortunate in his business, but he is not happy. It is very unfortunate that you did not come any sooner. There was a gentleman here who wished to be introduced to you. I should have been very happy to have made his acquaintance. People who are poor are by no means always unhappy. Do you know how to translate this sentence? Please to shut the door; I have opened the windows, and if the door is not shut there will be a draft. Give me another glass of water; I am very thirsty. Where were you the other day when I was at your house? Bear ye one another's burdens. Children should love each other. All my troubles have been to no purpose. It is in vain to trouble yourself about things which you cannot alter.

Wörter-Verzeichniß.

Mensch, man.
müssen, must.
sterben, to die.
vollkommen, perfect.
noch Suppe, any more soup.
noch etwas, some more.
giftig, poisonous.
ich auch nicht, I neither.
Feder, feather.
Flügel, wing.
fliegen, to fly.
vierzig, forty.
schlecht, bad.

er taugt etwas, is good for any thing.
wähle, choose.
schreiben, to write.
blaß, pale.
was fehlt Ihnen? what ails you?
Blume, flower.
entbehren, to spare.
gestern, yesterday.
Wien, Vienna.
Hauptstadt, capital.
Preußen, Prussia.
Oesterreich, Austria.

Uebungs-Aufgabe 2.

Alle Menschen müssen sterben; kein Mensch ist vollkommen. Hat Jemand mein Buch gesehen? Niemand hat dein Buch gesehen. Willst du noch Suppe? Gib mir noch etwas Fleisch. Manche Pflanzen sind giftig. Hast du viel Geld? Ich habe keins; hast du etwas? Ich auch nicht; wer hat Geld? Mein Bruder hat welches. Jeder Vogel hat Federn und Flügel; alle Vögel fliegen. Es sind vierzig Menschen in diesem Zimmer. Jeder hat ein Buch und eine Feder. Gib mir eine andere Feder; diese Feder ist schlecht; ich habe zwei Federn, aber keine von beiden taugt etwas. Hier sind zwei andere; wähle eine von beiden. Gib mir auch etwas Tinte. Mit solcher Tinte kann ich nicht schreiben; sie ist viel zu blaß. Manchen Tag bin ich in seinem Hause gewesen. Was fehlt Ihnen? Fehlt Ihnen etwas? Nein, mir fehlt auch nichts. Willst du mir einige von den Blumen geben? Ich kann keine entbehren. Dies ist derselbe Mann, den wir gestern sahen. Berlin und Wien sind große Städte. Jenes ist die Hauptstadt von Preußen, dieses ist die Hauptstadt von Oesterreich.

Lesestück 1.

LITTLE DICK AND THE GIANT (Der kleine [Dietrich] Fritz und der Riese).

1. "Now I will tell you a story[1]—and a true[2] story it is, too—about Little Dick and the Giant," said Uncle John; "and you must not ask me any questions about it,[3] until I get through."[4]

2. Little Dick was a happy[5] fellow.[6] He would sing and whistle[7] nearly[8] all day.[9] He was as merry[10] as a lark,[11] and scarcely[12] anything could make him sad.

3. One day[13] little Dick thought[14] he would have a ramble[15] in the forest,[16] at some distance[17] from his home. So off he went[18] in high spirits,[19] singing[20] and whistling[21] till[22] the woods[23] rang[24] with his music.[25]

4. At length[26] he reached[27] a clear[28] brook[29] that ran[30] through the woods; and being[31] very thirsty, he stooped down[32] to drink. But, just[33] at that moment, he was suddenly seized[34]—he scarcely[35] knew how[36]— and found himself in the hands of a fierce[37] ugly-looking[38] giant,[39] a hundred times[40] bigger[41] than himself.

5. For some time[42] the giant held[43] him in his big hands and looked at him[44] with great delight.[45] He then put[46] him into a large bag,[47] and carried[48] him away.[49]

6. Poor Dick, who was in great fear,[50] did all he could[51] do to escape[52] from his cruel[53] captor.[54] He screamed,[55] and he tried[56] to tear[57] the bag; but the giant only laughed[58] at him, and went on, holding him fast.

7. At last,⁵⁰ the giant came to his own house, unlike⁵⁹ any⁶¹ that Dick had ever⁶² seen before; for it was a gloomy⁶³ place⁶⁴—at least⁶⁵ it seemed so⁶⁶ to Dick—with a high wall⁶⁷ all around it,⁶⁸ and no trees, nor flowers.⁶⁹ When he went in, he shut⁷⁰ the door, and took⁷¹ Dick out of the bag.

8. The poor captive⁷² thought⁷³ the giant would now kill⁷⁴ him; for, when he looked⁷⁵ around, he saw a large fire, and before it were two victims⁷⁶ larger than himself, roasting⁷⁷ for the giant's dinner.⁷⁸ No wonder that Dick trembled⁷⁹ with fear!⁸⁰

¹ Geschichte, ² wahr, ³ darüber, ⁴ bis ich fertig bin, ⁵ glücklich, ⁶ Bursche, ⁷ er sang und pfiff, ⁸ fast, ⁹ den ganzen Tag, ¹⁰ lustig, ¹¹ Lerche, ¹² kaum, ¹³ eines Tages, ¹⁴ dachte, ¹⁵ er wollte umherstreifen, ¹⁶ Wald, ¹⁷ in einiger Entfernung, ¹⁸ fort ging's, ¹⁹ voll Lebenslust, ²⁰ singend, ²¹ pfeifend, ²² die, ²³ der Wald, ²⁴ wiederhallte, ²⁵ von seinem Gesange, ²⁶ endlich, ²⁷ kam er zu, ²⁸ klar, ²⁹ Bach, ³⁰ dahinfloß, ³¹ da er war, ³² bückte er sich nieder, ³³ gerade, ³⁴ wurde erplötzlich ergriffen, ³⁵ kaum, ³⁶ wußte, wie (ihm geschah), ³⁷ grimmig, ³⁸ häßlich, ³⁹ Riese, ⁴⁰ hundertmal, ⁴¹ größer, ⁴² eine Weile, ⁴³ hielt, ⁴⁴ betrachtete ihn, ⁴⁵ Entzücken, ⁴⁶ steckte er, ⁴⁷ Sack, ⁴⁸ trug, ⁴⁹ davon, ⁵⁰ Angst, ⁵¹ that alles was er konnte, ⁵² entwischen, ⁵³ grausam, ⁵⁴ Verfolger, ⁵⁵ schrie, ⁵⁶ versuchte, ⁵⁷ zerreißen, ⁵⁸ lachte, ⁵⁹ endlich, ⁶⁰ ganz anders wie, ⁶¹ irgend eines, ⁶² je, ⁶³ finster, ⁶⁴ Ort, ⁶⁵ wenigstens, ⁶⁶ kam es so vor, ⁶⁷ Mauer, ⁶⁸ ringsumher, ⁶⁹ Blumen, ⁷⁰ machte er zu, ⁷¹ holte, ⁷² Gefangene, ⁷³ dachte, ⁷⁴ umbringen, ⁷⁵ umherblickte, ⁷⁶ Schlachtopfer, ⁷⁷ bratend, ⁷⁸ Mittagessen, ⁷⁹ zitterte, ⁸⁰ vor Angst.

Lesestück 2.
LITTLE DICK AND THE GIANT. (Schluß.)

1. The giant, however,¹ did not mean² to kill Dick; but he put him into a prison³ which he had prepared⁴ for him. It was quite⁵ a dark⁶ room,⁷ with cross-bars⁸ all around it. The giant gave him a piece⁹ of dry¹⁰ bread and a cup¹¹ of water, and then left¹² him.

2. The poor captive¹³ was very wretched,¹⁴ for he had never before been deprived¹⁵ of his liberty.¹⁶ He beat¹⁷ his head against the iron¹⁸ bars,¹⁹ and dashed²⁰ backward²¹ and forward²² in his prison-house, but he could not escape.²³

3. The next day the giant came and looked at²⁴ Dick; and finding²⁵ that he had eaten none²⁶ of the

bread, he took him by the head²⁷ and crammed²⁸ some of the bread down²⁹ his throat.³⁰ Poor Dick, who was nearly³¹ choked to death³² by this rude³³ treatment,³⁴ was in too great a fright³⁵ to think of eating or drinking.

4. He was left alone³⁶ in his gloomy³⁷ prison another³⁸ day; and a sad day it was. The poor creature³⁹ thought of his own pleasant⁴⁰ home, his companions,⁴¹ the sunlight, the trees, the flowers, and the many nice⁴² things⁴³ he used⁴⁴ to eat; and then he screamed⁴⁵ and tried⁴⁶ to get out⁴⁷ between the iron bars;⁴⁸ but he only beat⁴⁹ and tore⁵⁰ himself, and all in vain.⁵¹

5. The giant came again, and wished Dick to sing,⁵² the same⁵³ as he did when he was in his own home, and was happy. "*Sing! sing! sing!*" said he, "*Why don't you sing?*" But Dick was too sad to sing. Who could sing in a prison!

6. At length the giant grew⁵⁴ very angry,⁵⁵ and took Dick out of his prison to make him sing. He shook⁵⁶ him, and his big hand almost⁵⁷ forced⁵⁸ the breath⁵⁹ out of Dick's body.⁶⁰ Dick gave⁶¹ a loud scream,⁶² plunged⁶³ and struggled,⁶⁴ and then sank dead⁶⁵ in the giant's hand!

7. "What a story that is!" said Henry. "Who believes there are any giants, or that they treat⁶⁶ little boys so!"

"Did I say⁶⁷ that Dick was a little boy, and that the giant was a big man? No, no. But I will tell you who they were. Poor Dick was a *little bird;* and that giant was a *cruel*⁶⁸ *boy.*" WILSON.

---

¹ jedoch, ² beabsichtigte nicht, ³ Gefängniß, ⁴ hergerichtet, ⁵ ganz, ⁶ dunkel, ⁷ Zimmer, ⁸ Gitter, ⁹ Stück, ¹⁰ trocken, ¹¹ Becher, ¹² verließ, ¹³ Gefangene, ¹⁴ unglücklich, ¹⁵ er war nie vorhem beraubt worden, ¹⁶ Freiheit, ¹⁷ schlug, ¹⁸ eisern, ¹⁹ Stangen, ²⁰ fuhr, ²¹ rückwärts, ²² vorwärts, ²³ entkommen, ²⁴ um zu sehen nach, ²⁵ und da er fand, ²⁶ nichts, ²⁷ nahm er ihn beim Kopf, ²⁸ stopfte, ²⁹ hinunter, ³⁰ Hals, ³¹ fast, ³² erstickte, ³³ roh, ³⁴ Behandlung, ³⁵ Angst, ³⁶ man ließ ihn allein, ³⁷ finster, ³⁸ noch einen, ³⁹ Geschöpf, ⁴⁰ freundlich, ⁴¹ Kameraden, ⁴² schön, ⁴³ Sachen, ⁴⁴ pflegte, ⁴⁵ schrie, ⁴⁶ versuchte, ⁴⁷ zu entwischen, ⁴⁸ eiserne Stangen, ⁴⁹ zerschlug, ⁵⁰ verwundete, ⁵¹ umsonst, ⁵² wollte daß Dick sänge, ⁵³ ganz so, ⁵⁴ wurde, ⁵⁵ zornig, ⁵⁶ schüttelte, ⁵⁷ beinahe, ⁵⁸ preßte,

⁵⁹ Athem, ⁶⁰ Leib, ⁶¹ stieß aus, ⁶² Schrei, ⁶³ schoß vorüber, ⁶⁴ zappelte, ⁶⁵ fiel todt nieder, ⁶⁶ behandeln, ⁶⁷ habe ich gesagt? ⁶⁸ grausam.

Lektion VII.

Das Eigenschaftswort. (Adjektiv).
Attribut.—Prädikat.

great, tall, large, big, little, short, small.

Wörter-Verzeichniß.

red, roth.
white, weiß.
I like, ich liebe.
naughty, unartig.
neighbor, Nachbar.
honest, bieder (ehrlich).
deaf, taub.
to hear, hören.
to speak, sprechen.
mute, stumm.
body, Leib.
mortal, sterblich.
spirit, Geist.
immortal, unsterblich.
knife, Messer.
sharp, scharf.
but, sondern.
blunt, stumpf.
to cut, schneiden.
hot, heiß.
cold, kalt.
what a, was für ein.
church, Kirche.
sometimes, mitunter.
to make, begeben.
mistakes, Fehler.
stupid, dumm.
leather, Leder.
tough, zähe.
brittle, spröde.
transparent, durchsichtig.
short, kurz.
earnest, ernst.
we shall stay, wir werden bleiben.
but, nur.
coat, Rock.
pair of pantaloons, Hosen.
vest, Weste.
obedient, gehorsam.
handsome, hübsch.
virtuous, tugendhaft.
orange, Apfelsine.
pleasant, angenehm.
taste, Geschmack.
great, groß.
tyrant, Tyrann.
difficulty, Schwierigkeit.
Cathedral, Münster.
tall, groß (d. h. hoch).
on the contrary, im Gegentheil.

short, klein (kurz).
I received, ich habe erhalten.
large, groß (bedeutend).
big, groß (dick).

suffer little, &c., lasset die
Kindlein zu mir kommen.
give me, geben Sie mir.
a little, ein wenig.

Uebungs=Aufgabe 1.

The rose is red; some roses are white. I like red and white roses. John is a good boy, and Louisa is a naughty girl. Our neighbor is an honest man. Not all men are honest. A person that cannot hear is deaf. A deaf man cannot speak; he is mute. Our bodies are mortal, but our spirits are immortal. The knife is not sharp but blunt. I cannot cut with a blunt knife. These knives are all blunt. Summer is hot, but winter is cold. What a beautiful church! it is very beautiful. Wise men sometimes make mistakes. Not all men are wise. This boy is very stupid. Leather is tough, glass is brittle and transparent. Life is short and earnest. We shall stay but a short time. I have a new coat and a new pair of pantaloons. My vest is old. Children must be obedient. We love obedient children. My mother is sick. We have a sick child. That is a handsome girl. Isn't she handsome? She is as virtuous as she is handsome. Oranges have a very pleasant taste. The weather is very pleasant. Nero was a great tyrant. Washington was as good as he was great. He speaks with great difficulty. The Strasburg Cathedral is very tall. Frederick the Great was not tall, but, on the contrary, very short. I received a large sum of money. Falstaff was a very big man. Suffer little children to come unto me. Give me a little bread and butter.

Wörter=Verzeichniß.

hübsch, pretty.
nicht so—als, not so—as,
arm, poor.
traurig, sad.

lesen, to read.
interessant, interesting.
lehrreich, instructive.
krank, sick.

Sohn, son.
kränklich, sickly.
Tochter, daughter.
immer, always.
als er scheint, as he seems.
Obst, fruit.
gesund, wholesome.
reif, ripe.
frisch, fresh.
gelb, yellow.
blau, blue.
grün, green.
bunt, party-colored.
warum trägst du? why do you wear?

bei, in.
Wetter, weather.
Kirsche, cherry.
angenehm, pleasant.
Geschmack, taste.
treu, true.
meide, shun.
Umgang, company.
böse, wicked.
leichtsinnig, careless.
böse Gesellschaft, evil company.
verderben, to spoil, corrupt.
Sitten, morals.

Uebungs-Aufgabe 2.

Diese Feder ist gut, aber jene ist schlecht. Ich kann nicht mit einer schlechten Feder schreiben. Dieser große Garten ist nicht so hübsch als jener kleine. Jener arme blinde Mann ist sehr traurig. Unser kleines Haus ist neu, aber dein großes Haus ist alt. Ich lese ein sehr interessantes Buch. Deine Bücher sind nicht so lehrreich als meine. Unser Nachbar hat einen kranken Sohn und eine kränkliche Tochter. Dieses Kind ist noch immer kränklich. Ein reicher Mann ist oft nicht so glücklich als er scheint, und ein armer Mann ist oft nicht so unglücklich als er scheint. Ist Obst gesund? Gutes, reifes Obst ist gesund, aber unreifes Obst ist ungesund. Haben Sie gute Butter? Meine Butter ist nicht gut; sie ist nicht frisch. Jener Vogel hat weiße, rothe, gelbe, blaue und grüne Federn. Er ist sehr bunt. Warum trägst du heute dieses schöne blaue Kleid bei diesem schlechten Wetter? Diese rothen Kirschen sind von angenehmen Geschmack. Neue Freunde sind nicht immer treue Freunde. Meide den Umgang böser und leichtsinniger Menschen; denn böse Gesellschaften verderben gute Sitten.

Das Eigenschaftswort.

Lesestück 1.

JACK FROST AND THE SOUTH WIND (Hans Frost und der Südwind.)

1. Jack Frost was a famous¹ king, who had come² a great way³ from the North. A long time he had ruled⁴ over the earth and over the streams;⁵ and every thing⁶ on which⁷ he laid⁸ his cold hands, he bound⁹ in icy chains.¹⁰

2. Jack Frost was a stern¹¹ old tyrant.¹² His locks¹³ were whitened with¹⁴ snow,¹⁵ so that he seemed¹⁶ to be very aged;¹⁷ and his beard¹⁸ was hung with¹⁹ icicles.²⁰ His voice²¹ was as harsh²² as the December-blast²³ that came howling²⁴ over the mountains;²⁵ he never smiled;²⁶ and it was said²⁷ of him that he never had any mercy on²⁸ the poor. They might starve²⁹ or freeze,³⁰ but little did Jack Frost care for³¹ their sufferings.³²

3. At length³³ there arose up³⁴ against him a great but very mild and gentle³⁵ king from the South, called³⁶ the South Wind. Unlike³⁷ Jack Frost, this king had a smiling³⁸ face,³⁹ a laughing⁴⁰ eye, and a voice⁴¹ soft⁴² and gentle.⁴³ He had flowing⁴⁴ auburn⁴⁵ locks, and his smooth⁴⁶ beardless⁴⁷ face was like that of a boy in the very⁴⁸ spring-time⁴⁹ of life.

4. When these two kings met,⁵⁰ "It is my time now to rule," ⁵¹ gently whispered⁵² the South Wind. "Pity⁵³ you are not more of a man," ⁵⁴ blustered⁵⁵ Jack Frost, as he looked⁵⁶ at the beardless face of his rival.⁵⁷

5. "Ah, well, to do as much good⁵⁸ as I can, is to do something," ⁵⁹ answered the South Wind. And in spite⁶⁰ of a chilling⁶¹ look⁶² of scorn⁶³ from Jack Frost, he went about⁶⁴ his work.

---

¹ berühmt, ² der gekommen war, ³ einen weiten Weg, ⁴ Regierung, ⁵ Ströme, ⁶ alles, ⁷ worauf, ⁸ legte, ⁹ schlug er, ¹⁰ eisige Ketten, ¹¹ finster, ¹² Tyrann, ¹³ Locken, ¹⁴ gebleicht von, ¹⁵ Schnee, ¹⁶ schien, ¹⁷ alt, ¹⁸ Bart, ¹⁹ hing voll von, ²⁰ Eiszapfen, ²¹ Stimme, ²² rauh, ²³ Sturm, ²⁴ der heulend daher kam, ²⁵ Berge, ²⁶ lächelte, ²⁷ man sagte, ²⁸ Erbarmen mit, ²⁹ sie mochten darben, ³⁰ erfrieren, ³¹ kümmerte sich um, ³² Leiden, ³³ endlich, ³⁴ erhob sich, ³⁵ sanft, ³⁶ genannt,

³⁷ ganz anders wie, ³⁸ lächelnd, ³⁹ Antlitz, ⁴⁰ heiter, ⁴¹ Stimme, ⁴² weich, ⁴³ sanft, ⁴⁴ flatternd, ⁴⁵ golden, ⁴⁶ glatt, ⁴⁷ bartlos, ⁴⁸ so recht mitten in, ⁴⁹ Blüthezeit, ⁵⁰ sich begegneten, ⁵¹ regieren, ⁵² flüsterte, ⁵³ wie Schade! ⁵⁴ mehr Mann, ⁵⁵ schnob, ⁵⁶ blickte, ⁵⁷ Nebenbuhler, ⁵⁸ so viel Gutes thun, ⁵⁹ heißt etwas thun, ⁶⁰ trotz, ⁶¹ kalt, ⁶² Blick, ⁶³ Hohn, ⁶⁴ begab er sich an.

Lesestück 2.

JACK FROST AND THE SOUTH WIND. (Schluß.)

1. First he unchained¹ the streams, and they ran off in a bound² rejoicing³ in their freedom. The miller hastened⁴ to his mill, and the fisher went for⁵ his rod.⁶

2. Next⁷ he breathed⁸ upon the snow-banks⁹ and they melted away;¹⁰ he loosened¹¹ the earth, and said to the grasses,¹² "Take courage."¹³ He swept¹⁴ through the forests,¹⁵ and he brushed¹⁶ over the orchards,¹⁷ starting¹⁸ the sap¹⁹ in the trees, and calling to²⁰ leaf, bud,²¹ and blossom,²² "Make ready!"²³

3. Wherever²⁴ he went, the birds followed²⁵ him with their songs,²⁶ and he bade²⁷ them have a thought for²⁸ their nests.

Then what a waking up²⁹ was there³⁰ in the farm-yard!³¹ The cows were heard to³² low,³³ the lambs to bleat,³⁴ and the hens to cluck;³⁵ the farmer began to bustle about,³⁶ and the housewife was all astir.³⁷

4. How kind, how cheerful is the South Wind! Though³⁸ he has a large realm³⁹ to rule over, and so much to do that he sometimes cannot help⁴⁰ puffing⁴¹ and blowing,⁴² he does not think it beneath him⁴³ to step aside⁴⁴ from his great out-door⁴⁵ work, and do *little things* to comfort⁴⁶ and to bless.⁴⁷

5. So he breaks gently into the chamber of sickness,⁴⁸ and whispers to the poor sufferer,⁴⁹ "Be of good cheer,⁵⁰ I bring you the promise⁵¹ of better things." Busy,⁵² busy, is the South Wind. "Every thing in its season,"⁵³ he says.

6. Already Jack Frost seemed to melt⁵⁴ a little, especially⁵⁵ when he looked around and saw what new

lite every thing had. "Talents differ,"⁵⁶ wheezed⁵⁷ he, "but it is hard to give up the rule."

7. "Remember,"⁵⁸ said the South Wind, kindly, "that of ourselves⁵⁹ we are nothing. We only do the bidding⁶⁰ of one Mightier than we, and we can serve⁶¹ him as much⁶² in *yielding*,⁶³ as in *doing*—as much in being *set aside*,⁶⁴ as in being *set up*."⁶⁵ "Well," sighed⁶⁶ Jack Frost, "perhaps it is so."⁶⁷ Tears ran down⁶⁸ his cheeks,⁶⁹ and he shrunk away.⁷⁰ WILSON.

¹ entfesselte, ² in Sprüngen, ³ fraß, ⁴ eilte, ⁵ holte herbei, ⁶ Angelruthe, ⁷ sodann, ⁸ hauchte er an, ⁹ Schneebänke, ¹⁰ zerschmolzen, ¹¹ machte frei, ¹² Gräser, ¹³ seid gutes Muthes, ¹⁴ fegte, ¹⁵ Wälder, ¹⁶ brauste, ¹⁷ Obstgärten, ¹⁸ belebend, ¹⁹ Saft, ²⁰ zurufend, ²¹ Knospe, ²² Blüthe, ²³ macht euch fertig, ²⁴ wohin immer, ²⁵ folgten, ²⁶ Lieder, ²⁷ hieß, ²⁸ denken an, ²⁹ Erwachen, ³⁰ gab es, ³¹ Bauernhof, ³² hörte man, ³³ brüllen, ³⁴ blöcken, ³⁵ gackern, ³⁶ sich geschäftig zu rühren, ³⁷ ganz Leben, ³⁸ obschon, ³⁹ Reich, ⁴⁰ nicht umhin kann, ⁴¹ pusten, ⁴² brausen, ⁴³ so hält er es doch nicht unter seiner Würde, ⁴⁴ bei Seite zu treten, ⁴⁵ außer dem Hause, ⁴⁶ trösten, ⁴⁷ segnen, ⁴⁸ Krankenstube, ⁴⁹ Leidender, ⁵⁰ sei gutes Muthes, ⁵¹ Verheißung, ⁵² rührig, ⁵³ alles zu seiner Zeit, ⁵⁴ schmelzen, ⁵⁵ besonders, ⁵⁶ die Gaben sind verschieden, ⁵⁷ pustete, ⁵⁸ bedenke, ⁵⁹ von uns selber, ⁶⁰ wir folgen dem Geheiß, ⁶¹ dienen, ⁶² ebenso sehr, ⁶³ im Unterlassen, ⁶⁴ darin daß wir zurückgesetzt werden, ⁶⁵ als darin daß wir emporgehoben werden, ⁶⁶ seufzte, ⁶⁷ dem mag so sein, ⁶⁸ flossen herab, ⁶⁹ Wangen, ⁷⁰ schmolz zusammen.

Lektion VIII.

Redensarten.

To like, to be fond of, to be right, wrong, to be sorry.

Wörter-Verzeichniß.

I am very fond of, ich bin ein großer Freund von.
to like, lieben, gern haben.
how do you like? wie gefällt dir?
dress, Kleid.
not at all, gar nicht.
a ride on horseback, Ritt.
ride in a carriage, Fahrt im Wagen.
bear, ausstehen.
do you like dancing? tanzest du gern?
would you like? möchtest du?

luscious, saftig.
pear, Birne.
and so forth, und so weiter.
when they should say, wo sie sagen sollten.
to be right, wrong, recht, unrecht haben.
undoubted, unzweifelhaft.
to dispose of, verfügen über.
property, Eigenthum.
to take advantage, zu Nutze machen.
misfortune, Unglück.
to ask me to, von mir zu verlangen, daß ich.
prepared, vorbereitet.
we are all fond of a sail, wir machen alle gern eine Wasserfahrt.
I am very sorry for this child, dieses Kind dauert mich.
are you sorry? thut es dir leid?
you neglected, du hast versäumt.
duty, Pflicht.
indeed, wirklich.

Uebungs-Aufgabe 1.

I am very fond of music and good books. What do you like? I like a good dinner and a bottle of wine. How do you like the color of this dress? I don't like it at all. I like nothing better than a ride on horseback. How do you like a ride in a carriage? I am not fond of riding in a carriage. I cannot bear it. Do you like dancing? Would you like to eat some of these luscious pears? Thank you, I never liked pears. What do you like best? I *love* a good child, but I *like* a faithful dog. Some people say that they *love* a dog, a cat, a flower, and so forth; when they should say, "we *like*," &c. Am I right in saying so? You are quite right. Now, which of these two boys is right, and which is wrong? You have an undoubted right to dispose of your own property, but you are wrong to take advantage of another person's misfortune. Do you like to speak English? I like it well enough, but I must first learn to understand it better when spoken. You would be wrong to ask of me to speak before I am better prepared to understand it. We are all fond of a sail. I am very sorry for this child. She has lost her mother. Are you sorry that you neglected your duty? Yes, sir, I am very sorry, indeed.

Redensarten.

Wörter-Verzeichniß.

das Reiten, riding on horseback.
rudern, rowing.
gar nicht, not at all.
lieber, better.
grau, gray.
tragen, to wear.
nie, never.
Farbe, color.
das Tanzen, dancing.
das Schwimmen, swimming.

das Reisen, traveling.
auf Eisenbahnen, by railroad.
Seereise, sea-voyage.
helfen, to help.
möglich, possible.
ungehorsam, disobedient.
Taugenichts, good-for-nothing.
nennen, to call.
so, thus.
glauben, to believe.

Uebungs-Aufgabe 2.

Sind Sie ein Freund vom Reiten? Ich reite sehr gern, rudern aber mag ich noch lieber. Mögen Sie meinen neuen Hut leiden? Ich mag ihn gar nicht leiden. Was magst du lieber leiden, einen schwarzen oder grauen Rock? Ich trage nur graue Röcke, denn ich mag die schwarze Farbe nicht. Mein Bruder ist ein großer Freund vom Tanzen und Schwimmen. Ich bin kein Freund vom Reisen auf Eisenbahnen; ich mag eine Seereise viel lieber. Es thut mir leid, daß ich dir nicht helfen kann; ich hätte dir gerne geholfen, aber es ist mir nicht möglich. Thut es dir leid, daß du ungehorsam gewesen bist? Es thut mir sehr leid. Habe ich nicht recht, wenn ich sage, daß du ein Taugenichts bist? Du hast unrecht, mich so zu nennen. Wer hat recht, du oder ich? Ich glaube, du hast recht.

Lesestück 1.

THE WISHES' SHOP (Der Wunschladen).

1. I had overworked my brain,[1] and was taken severely ill.[2] In vain[3] had my physician recommended[4] me to leave[5] business[6] for a while,[7] and seek[8] recreation[9] and health[10] in the country.[11] I wanted[12] health, but was unwilling[13] to make[14] the necessary[15] sacrifice[16] for it.

2. One day, while weary[17] and feverish[18] from the

toil[19] of examining[20] a long list of accounts,[21] I fell into a troubled[22] sleep. It seemed to me that I soon awoke,[23] and left my office[24] to seek relief[25] in the open air.[26] I wandered,[27] I scarcely[28] knew whither,[29] until my attention[30] was arrested,[31] in what seemed to be called[32] "Providence Street,"[33] by the following[34] notice[35] over the door of a modest[36] dwelling[37] opposite:[38] "Whoever wishes for any particular[39] object,[40] let him call here."[41]

3. Hurrying[42] across[43] the street, and entering[44] the door, I soon found myself in a large room, at the end of which,[45] on an elevated[46] platform,[47] was a table; and seated[48] behind it[49] was a little old gentleman in black,[50] who, I was told[51] on inquiry,[52] was Mr. Destiny[53] himself.

4. The room was filled[54] with persons who had come to make[55] their wants[56] known[55] to him; and as each applicant[57] for favors[58] came forward, the old gentleman repeated[59] to him the terms[60] on which he did business. "My principle[61] is, gentlemen," said he, "that whoever wishes any thing,[62] must give up something[63] of equal[64] worth[65] that he possesses."[66] Everybody nodded[67] assent[68] to the principle; but few seemed to realize[69] its full meaning.[70]

5. The first person who came forward was a lame man, who supported[71] himself with difficulty[72] on a crutch[73] and a cane. He wished to get rid[74] of his lameness,[75] and said he would give a great deal[76] if he could walk[77] as well as most people. "Very well," said Destiny, "will you give up your eyesight?"[78] "Certainly[79] not," said the lame man; "I will part with[80] none of the senses[81] to be rid of an infirmity.[82] *They* belong[83] to my soul;[84] *this* is only my body."[85]

6. Neither his eyesight nor his little property[86] would he part with; and so Destiny advised[87] him patiently[88] to bear[89] with the ills[90] he was accustomed to,[91] rather[92] than take up[93] with new ones.

"Yet I *should* like to *walk*," said the lame man.

7. "Ay,"[94] said Destiny, "but you don't seem will-

ing[95] to alter[96] your condition in any way,[97] except[98] that of getting rid of something very disagreeable.[99] If you wish to get a good thing, you must give up a good thing that you already possess. That's the principle of all trade,[100] is it not? Sorry,[101] sir, I can be of no use to you." [102]

8. "Thank you, sir. Well, I won't detain[103] you. Good morning." And the lame man took up his crutch and his cane, and hobbled[104] out of the room. He went away, thinking he might have had a greater affliction[105] than lameness.

9. Next came a woman, eagerly[106] pushing[107] through the crowd,[108] and with deep sobs[109] begging for the life of her son, a youth[110] of sixteen, who was dying of fever.

"It is a great thing you come for," said Mr. Destiny. "You must give a great thing for it. Will you give your own life?"

10. "Ay, twenty times!" said the mother, passionately.[111] "You have not twenty lives to give. You have one. Will you give that?"

"Yes, I will give my life," answered the mother, suddenly[112] sobered[113] from her passion[114] by the deep and calm[115] manner in which the question was asked.

11. "Very well; be it so.[116] Go home, and your wish will be bought[117] at that price." [118]

I saw the mother rise,[119] and go away with a face[120] of such calm[121] joy, that it seemed like the face of an angel,[122] returning[123] to heaven, after having faithfully accomplished[124] his mission[125] on earth.

---

¹ meine Nerven waren durch zu viel Arbeiten überreizt, ² ich wurde schwer krank, ³ vergebens, ⁴ empfohlen, ⁵ aufzugeben, ⁶ Geschäft, ⁷ eine Zeitlang, ⁸ suchen, ⁹ Erholung, ¹⁰ Gesundheit, ¹¹ auf dem Lande, ¹² bedurfte, ¹³ nicht Willens, ¹⁴ bringen, ¹⁵ nothwendig, ¹⁶ Opfer, ¹⁷ müde, ¹⁸ abgespannt, ¹⁹ Anstrengung, ²⁰ durchzusehen, ²¹ Rechnungsliste, ²² unruhig, ²³ aufwachte, ²⁴ Geschäftslokal, ²⁵ Erholung, ²⁶ im Freien, ²⁷ ich wanderte, ²⁸ kaum, ²⁹ wohin, ³⁰ Aufmerksamkeit, ³¹ gefesselt wurde, ³² zu heißen, ³³ Vorsichungsstraße, ³⁴ folgend, ³⁵ Bekanntmachung, ³⁶ bescheiden, ³⁷ Wohnhaus, ³⁸ gegenüber, ³⁹ besonderen, ⁴⁰ Gegenstand, ⁴¹ der möge hier versprechen, ⁴² eilend, ⁴³ über—hinüber, ⁴⁴ eintretend in, ⁴⁵ an dessen Ende, ⁴⁶ erhöhte, ⁴⁷ Plattform,

⁴⁸ sitzend, ⁴⁹ dahinter, ⁵⁰ schwarz, ⁵¹ wie man mir sagte, ⁵² auf meine Nachfrage, ⁵³ Schicksal, ⁵⁴ angefüllt, ⁵⁵ in Kenntniß zu setzen, ⁵⁶ Wünsche, ⁵⁷ Supplikant, ⁵⁸ Gunstbezeugungen, ⁵⁹ wiederholte, ⁶⁰ Bedingungen, ⁶¹ Grundsatz, ⁶² etwas, ⁶³ irgend etwas, ⁶⁴ gleich, ⁶⁵ Werth, ⁶⁶ besitzt, ⁶⁷ nickte, ⁶⁸ Zustimmung, ⁶⁹ zu fassen, ⁷⁰ Tragweite, ⁷¹ stutzte, ⁷² Mühe, ⁷³ Krücke, ⁷⁴ loszuwerden, ⁷⁵ Lahmheit, ⁷⁶ sehr viel, ⁷⁷ geben, ⁷⁸ Gesicht, ⁷⁹ gewiß, ⁸⁰ ich will mich trennen von, ⁸¹ Sinne, ⁸² Gebrechen, ⁸³ gehören, ⁸⁴ Seele, ⁸⁵ Körper, ⁸⁶ Vermögen, ⁸⁷ rieth, ⁸⁸ geduldig, ⁸⁹ zu tragen, ⁹⁰ das Uebel, ⁹¹ an das er gewöhnt war, ⁹² lieber, ⁹³ sich aufzuladen, ⁹⁴ ja wohl, ⁹⁵ willens, ⁹⁶ ändern, ⁹⁷ Weise, ⁹⁸ ausgenommen, ⁹⁹ Unangenehmes, ¹⁰⁰ Handel, ¹⁰¹ thut mir leid, ¹⁰² ich kann Ihnen nicht dienen, ¹⁰³ aufhalten, ¹⁰⁴ humpelte, ¹⁰⁵ Kreuz, ¹⁰⁶ begierig, ¹⁰⁷ sich drängend, ¹⁰⁸ Menge, ¹⁰⁹ Schluchzen, ¹¹⁰ Jüngling, ¹¹¹ leidenschaftlich, ¹¹² plötzlich, ¹¹³ ernüchtert, ¹¹⁴ Leidenschaft, ¹¹⁵ ruhig, ¹¹⁶ so sei's, ¹¹⁷ erkauft, ¹¹⁸ Preis, ¹¹⁹ sich erheben, ¹²⁰ Antlitz, ¹²¹ überirdische, ¹²² Engel, ¹²³ der zurückkehrt, ¹²⁴ nachdem er treu erfüllt hat, ¹²⁵ Mission.

Lesestück 2.

THE WISHES' SHOP. (Fortsetzung.)

1. The third applicant was a poor *gentleman;* a man of talent, refinement¹ and education.² "Sir," said he, "I have seven sons and one daughter, and have nothing wherewith to educate them."³

2. "Just the opposite⁴ to the rich man who lately⁵ called on me,⁶ and who had *no* children," said Mr. Destiny. "What a pity⁷ you and he could not have made a bargain!⁸ Well, sir, how can I serve you?"

"I wish for money," said he.

3. He was asked⁹ to give up his health;¹⁰ but he replied that he had not very much of that,¹¹ and none to spare.¹² "His principles,¹³ then?" He was very indignant¹⁴ at such a proposal.¹⁵ "Would he part with¹⁶ his talents, and be a fool?"¹⁷ Said he, "Of what good should I be to¹⁸ my family, then?"

4. "You have eight children, you say; people are very happy with two, or four, or even one. Suppose¹⁹ you give up *one* child. Can you part with the eldest?"

"Impossible!²⁰ He is just eleven, and so clever!²¹ He is full of talent²² and application.²³ With a book in his hand, he does not know whether one speaks to him or not."

5. "Then," said Destiny, "perhaps²⁴ you could more easily²⁵ part with the second."²⁶

"No, not the second—the second and third [27] are twins,[28] and to separate [29] them would be [30] to destroy [31] both. They are twin-cherries [32] on one stalk.[33] I can't part with *two*."

6. "And what do you say to parting with the *fourth?*" [34]

"A little fellow [35] of eight! [36] the most beautiful child—like his mother—and as gentle [37] as an angel! [38] He meets me [39] every day when I come home, and flings [40] himself into my arms. I could not be such a heartless [41] *brute!*" [42]

7. "I don't want to press you," [43] said Destiny. "But you have a girl. Let *her* go. Women [44] are often quite [45] useless,[46] and a heavy [47] weight [48] when you have to push them on in life." [49]

8. "Useless! My little Mary useless! Though [50] she is but [51] six, you should see her help her mother. She knows where every thing is to be found,[52] and will run [53] for it,[54] and back,[55] almost [56] before [57] you know you want it. And when anybody is ill,[58] how *still* she keeps,[59] and how *good* [60] she is. You should see how the baby [61] loves her!" [62]

9. "A baby, too? oh, let the baby go," said Destiny.

"What! the baby? No doubt [63] it cries, and keeps one awake; [64] but my wife [65] loves it better [66] than all the others.[67] Its slightest [68] illness [69] puts her in misery.[70] What would become of her,[71] if it should die!" [72]

10. "But there remain [73] two more.[74] Surely,[75] you can part with *them?*"

"No, no; the dear children! One can but just [76] speak, and the first word was my name. And the other—he is the only one [77] that is sickly; [78] he is always holding [79] by his mother's finger, or is carried [80] in my arms. Besides,[81] perhaps he will grow [82] stronger; [83] and then, how happy we shall be!"

11. "Really," [84] said Mr. Destiny, "you seem to be a very happy family, even if [85] you *are* poor; and your children are great comforts [86] to you; but of the *many*

things you so highly prize,⁸⁷ you seem unwilling to part with *any* of them for riches!"⁸⁸

12. "But I *should* like to be *rich*,"⁸⁹ said the poor man. "*Other* people are rich. My neighbor, Mr. Smith, has *twelve* children; yet he is *very* rich."

"Would you change⁹⁰ with him altogether?"⁹¹

"By no means."⁹²

"Why not?"

13. "For many very good reasons.⁹³ For example,⁹⁴ his children are very *inferior*⁹⁵ to mine. I should never be proud⁹⁶ of them; and I could never love them as I love my own. I should like to be⁹⁷ in his *situation*,⁹⁸ but would not be willing to be *himself*."⁹⁹

14. "Well," said Destiny, "I see you are like¹⁰⁰ other people. You wish to keep¹⁰¹ what you have, and to add¹⁰² something more. But that's not the bargain.¹⁰³ You may have something *else*,¹⁰⁴ but not something *more*."

"Then I must bear¹⁰⁵ my misfortunes¹⁰⁶ as I can. I see there's no help.¹⁰⁷ But I begin to think I am not so badly off¹⁰⁸ as I thought I was. Farewell,¹⁰⁹ sir."

---

¹ feine Manieren, ² Bildung, ³ um ihnen eine gute Erziehung zu geben, ⁴ das Gegentheil, ⁵ kürzlich, ⁶ bei mir vorsprach, ⁷ wie schade! ⁸ Geschäft, ⁹ er wurde gefragt, ob er wolle, ¹⁰ Gesundheit, ¹¹ davon, ¹² entbehren, ¹³ Grundsätze, ¹⁴ entrüstet, ¹⁵ Vorschlag, ¹⁶ sich trennen von, ¹⁷ Narr, ¹⁸ was würde ich nützen, ¹⁹ gesetzt, ²⁰ unmöglich, ²¹ gescheut, ²² talentvoll, ²³ fleißig, ²⁴ vielleicht, ²⁵ leichter, ²⁶ zweite, ²⁷ dritte, ²⁸ Zwillinge, ²⁹ trennen, ³⁰ hieße, ³¹ zerstören, ³² Kirschen, ³³ Stengel, ³⁴ vierte, ³⁵ Bursche, ³⁶ acht, ³⁷ sanft, ³⁸ Engel, ³⁹ kommt mir entgegen, ⁴⁰ fliegt, ⁴¹ herzlos, ⁴² Barbar, ⁴³ in Sie bringen, ⁴⁴ Weiber, ⁴⁵ ganz, ⁴⁶ nutzlos, ⁴⁷ schwer, ⁴⁸ Last, ⁴⁹ wenn man sie im Leben vorwärts bringen muß, ⁵⁰ obschon, ⁵¹ nur, ⁵² zu finden ist, ⁵³ läuft, ⁵⁴ darnach, ⁵⁵ zurück, ⁵⁶ fast, ⁵⁷ ehe noch, ⁵⁸ krank, ⁵⁹ sie sich verhält, ⁶⁰ artig, ⁶¹ das Kind in der Wiege, ⁶² sie liebt, ⁶³ freilich, ⁶⁴ wach, ⁶⁵ Frau, ⁶⁶ mehr, ⁶⁷ alle übrigen, ⁶⁸ geringste, ⁶⁹ Unwohlsein, ⁷⁰ macht sie ganz elend, ⁷¹ was würde aus ihr werden? ⁷² wenn es stürbe, ⁷³ bleiben übrig, ⁷⁴ noch zwei, ⁷⁵ gewiß, ⁷⁶ kann gerade eben, ⁷⁷ das einzige, ⁷⁸ kränklich, ⁷⁹ hält sich fest, ⁸⁰ getragen, ⁸¹ überdies, ⁸² werden, ⁸³ stärker, ⁸⁴ wirklich, ⁸⁵ wenn auch, ⁸⁶ Trost, ⁸⁷ die Sie so hoch schätzen, ⁸⁸ Reichthum, ⁸⁹ ich möchte aber doch gar zu gerne reich sein, ⁹⁰ tauschen, ⁹¹ ganz und gar, ⁹² bei Leibe nicht, ⁹³ Gründe, ⁹⁴ zum Beispiel, ⁹⁵ weit weniger begabt als, ⁹⁶ stolz, ⁹⁷ ich möchte sein, ⁹⁸ Lage, ⁹⁹ er selbst, ¹⁰⁰ wie, ¹⁰¹ behalten, ¹⁰² hinzufügen, ¹⁰³ Abrede, ¹⁰⁴ anderes, ¹⁰⁵ tragen, ¹⁰⁶ Unglück, ¹⁰⁷ Ausweg, ¹⁰⁸ es ist nicht so schlecht bestellt mit mir, ¹⁰⁹ leben Sie wohl.

Lejeſtück 3.

THE WISHES' SHOP. (Fortſetzung.)

1. Just at this moment a lady of wealth,¹ alighting² from her carriage, entered³ the door. Her footman⁴ officiously⁵ put aside⁶ the crowd,⁷ and she came forward, richly dressed,⁸ beautiful and graceful,⁹ with the conscious¹⁰ ease¹¹ of one who attracted¹² all eyes and disappointed¹³ none. What could that favored¹⁴ being¹⁵ wish for more? Was it possible that she could covet¹⁶ any thing farther?¹⁷

2. Mr. Destiny appeared to have some such ideas as these,¹⁸ for he inquired,¹⁹ "Is there any thing, madam, for which you can form²⁰ a wish?"

"I wish to be happy," said the lady.

"Alas!"²¹ said Destiny, "if *you* are not happy, who *can* be?"

"I do not come to *argue*²² the matter,"²³ said the lady; "I only state²⁴ my wish."

3. "True, madam, I beg your pardon,"²⁵ answered Mr. Destiny. "You seem to have every external²⁶ means²⁷ of happiness; but if you are *not* happy, what would you part with to be so?"²⁸

"With *every thing*," said the lady, really shedding tears,²⁹ and wiping³⁰ her eyes with a handkerchief³¹ trimmed³² with lace³³ at a guinea a yard.³⁴

4. "Then," said Destiny, "I will describe³⁵ a condition³⁶—that of an esteemed³⁷ acquaintance³⁸ of mine³⁹—and you may have a condition like hers and be happy. It is that of a little plain⁴⁰ woman, who is devotedly⁴¹ loved⁴² by her husband.⁴³ She has a dutiful⁴⁴ son, although he is rather⁴⁵ dull;⁴⁶ but she does not perceive⁴⁷ it. She reads a good book on Sundays; she has some pleasure in⁴⁸ putting on⁴⁹ her silk gown,⁵⁰ and a great deal⁵¹ in friendly gossip;⁵² she is busy⁵³ all day, and sleeps all night; she murmurs⁵⁴ an old song,⁵⁵ and is truly happy."

5. "It is all very well," said the lady, interrupting⁵⁶

him; "but it is not possible that *I* could be happy under those circumstances."[57]

"Only she *is*[58] happy," said Destiny; "and the bargain is that *you* shall be happy, if you will consent[59] to take[60] a condition like hers."

6. "Better be miserable[61] than be so ignorantly happy,"[62] said the lady, suddenly[63] rising.[64] "I prefer[65] my present[66] condition to *such* a change."[67]

"Just as you please,"[68] said Destiny. And with a graceful[69] and gracious[70] bend of the head[71] she rustled[72] through the shop, and entering[73] her elegant carriage, drove off.[74]

7. There were many more applicants who came with their wishes; but few of them were willing to part with what they had, for what they so much coveted; and most of those who came to terms,[75] seemed to me to make very poor bargains.[76]

8. One good-looking[77] young fellow's wish was to marry[78] an heiress.[79] Mr. Destiny was rather hard upon him.[80] "It is all fair[81] that you should marry an heiress," said he; "and if your wife has only money, what will you give?"

9. "Will you give up her beauty?"[82] "Yes." "Sense?"[83] "Yes." "Good temper?"[84] "Yes." "Your own way?"[85] "Oh! I'll manage[86] to get that."[87] "No, it is in the bargain that you shall not have it; will you give it up?" "Well, yes; I'll give up all for money." "You certainly deserve[88] a very rich bride, since[89] you lose[90] every thing else,"[91] said Destiny. "Have your wish,[92] then."

10. And now, as the interest[93] in others began to slacken[94] I thought I might as well[95] express[96] my own wishes; and approaching[97] Mr. Destiny, I told him that I wished for health.[98] A long dialogue[99] followed.[100] I was told[101] that I must give up half[102] of my successful[103] business, regain[104] half of my time, and give[105] that for health.

11. "Sir, I must think about it."[106]

"Don't think [107] too long," said he, "for fear [108] the opportunity [109] should pass." [110]

"Well, I dare say [111] you are right; [112] and to-morrow I will let you know." [113]

12. I reached [114] my office, somewhat confused [115] by what [116] I had seen and heard. I soon returned [117] home, and next morning, when I awoke in bed, I was in the chills [118] of a nervous fever. [119] Ideas [120] raced [121] through my brain [122] with a rapidity [123] which defied [124] my efforts [125] to catch [126] them. I talked, [127] but I knew not what I said. Sometimes [128] I cried; sometimes I laughed; and I remember [129] but little till complete exhaustion [130] seemed to sink [131] me into a profound [132] sleep, from which I awoke, and heard some one say, "He will live." [133]

13. And live I did. [134] I was frightened [135] at what [136] had happened. [137] It was only the fear of losing [138] life itself that prevailed; [139] and I *did* at length take measures [140] to exchange [141] a portion of my wealth [142] for health. I gave up one half of my business; I bought a horse, and took abundance of exercise. [143] I soon got [144] better, and was again a happy man; [145] but, what is remarkable, [146] although I went several times [147] in search [148] of "Providence Street," and "Mr. Destiny's Wishes' Shop," I never could find either. [149] In truth, the whole [150] now seems to me almost like a dream.

---

¹ Vermögen, ² aussteigend, ³ trat hinein in, ⁴ Bedienter, ⁵ dienstfertig, ⁶ schob bei Seite, ⁷ die Menge, ⁸ reich gekleidet, ⁹ anmuthig, ¹⁰ selbstbewußt, ¹¹ Leichtigkeit, ¹² die auf sich zieht, ¹³ täuscht, ¹⁴ bevorzugt, ¹⁵ Wesen, ¹⁶ begehren, ¹⁷ etwas weiter, ¹⁸ schien derartige Gedanken zu haben, ¹⁹ fragte, ²⁰ gegen, ²¹ ach Gott! ²² zu disputiren über, ²³ Sache, ²⁴ ich thue kund, ²⁵ bitte um Entschuldigung, ²⁶ äußerlich, ²⁷ Bedingungen, ²⁸ um es zu werben, ²⁹ Thränen vergießend, ³⁰ trocknend, ³¹ Taschentuch, ³² besetzt, ³³ Spitzen, ³⁴ yard (3 Fuß), ³⁵ beschreiben, ³⁶ Lage, ³⁷ geachtet, ³⁸ Bekannte, ³⁹ von mir, ⁴⁰ einfach, ⁴¹ mit Hingebung, ⁴² geliebt wird, ⁴³ Mann, ⁴⁴ gehorsam, ⁴⁵ eigentlich etwas, ⁴⁶ beschränkt, ⁴⁷ bemerkt, ⁴⁸ Freude daran, ⁴⁹ anzuziehen, ⁵⁰ Kleid (weites), ⁵¹ sehr viel Gefallen an, ⁵² freundschaftliches Geplauder, ⁵³ geschäftig, ⁵⁴ summt, ⁵⁵ Lied, ⁵⁶ unterbrechend, ⁵⁷ Umstände, ⁵⁸ sie ist aber doch, ⁵⁹ wenn Sie sich dazu verstehen wollen, ⁶⁰ anzunehmen, ⁶¹ besser unglücklich sein, ⁶² als Glück bei so großer Unwissenheit, ⁶³ plötzlich, ⁶⁴ sich erhebend, ⁶⁵ ich ziehe vor, ⁶⁶ gegenwärtig, ⁶⁷ Wechsel, ⁶⁸ ganz wie es Ihnen beliebt, ⁶⁹ graziös, ⁷⁰ gnädig, ⁷¹ Kopfverbeugung, ⁷² rauschte,

¹³ besteigend, ³⁴ fuhr sie davon, ⁷⁵ die auf die Bedingungen eingingen, ⁷⁶ schienen mir einen sehr erbärmlichen Kauf zu machen, ⁷⁷ von hübschem Aeußern, ⁷⁸ beirathen, ⁷⁹ reiche Erbin, ⁸⁰ stellte ihm harte Bedingungen, ⁸¹ nicht mehr als billig, ⁸² Schönheit, ⁸³ Verstand, ⁸⁴ sanftes Naturell, ⁸⁵ eigener Wille, ⁸⁶ ich will es schon fertig bringen, ⁸⁷ den durchzusetzen, ⁸⁸ Sie verdienen sicherlich, ⁸⁹ da, ⁹⁰ einbüßen, ⁹¹ alles andere, ⁹² Ihr Wunsch sei erfüllt, ⁹³ Interesse, ⁹⁴ nachzulassen, ⁹⁵ ich könnte eben so gut, ⁹⁶ ausdrücken, ⁹⁷ mich nähernd, ⁹⁸ Gesundheit, ⁹⁹ Zwiegespräch, ¹⁰⁰ folgte, ¹⁰¹ es wurde mir gesagt, ¹⁰² die Hälfte, ¹⁰³ einträglich, ¹⁰⁴ nehmen, ¹⁰⁵ widmen, ¹⁰⁶ ich muß das überlegen, ¹⁰⁷ besinnen Sie sich nicht, ¹⁰⁸ aus Furcht, ¹⁰⁹ Gelegenheit, ¹¹⁰ möchte vorübergehen, ¹¹¹ ich wage zu behaupten, ¹¹² Sie haben Recht, ¹¹³ will ich es Sie wissen lassen, ¹¹⁴ erreichte, ¹¹⁵ etwas verwirrt, ¹¹⁶ durch das, was, ¹¹⁷ kehrte zurück, ¹¹⁸ schüttelnder Frost, ¹¹⁹ Nervenfieber, ¹²⁰ Gedanken, ¹²¹ jagten sich, ¹²² Gehirn, ¹²³ Schnelligkeit, ¹²⁴ trotzte, ¹²⁵ Bemühungen, ¹²⁶ sie zu zügeln, ¹²⁷ sprach, ¹²⁸ bald, ¹²⁹ erinnere, ¹³⁰ Erschöpfung, ¹³¹ zu versenken, ¹³² tief, ¹³³ er wird am Leben bleiben, ¹³⁴ und ich blieb am Leben, ¹³⁵ erschrecken, ¹³⁶ über, das was, ¹³⁷ sich zugetragen hatte, ¹³⁸ zu verlieren, ¹³⁹ die Oberhand behielt, ¹⁴⁰ ich traf endlich wirklich Anstalten, ¹⁴¹ einzutauschen, ¹⁴² Reichthum, ¹⁴³ machte mir viel körperliche Bewegung, ¹⁴⁴ es ging mir bald, ¹⁴⁵ Mensch, ¹⁴⁶ merkwürdig, ¹⁴⁷ mehrmals, ¹⁴⁸ forschte nach, ¹⁴⁹ so konnte ich doch keines von beiden finden, ¹⁵⁰ das Ganze.

Lektion IX.

Das regelmäßige Zeitwort.—Gegenwart, Vergangenheit. Redensarten.

There is, there are. To take a walk. To have a mind.

Wörter-Verzeichniß.

too, auch.
when, als.
also, auch.
to praise, loben.
diligence, Fleiß.
we do so, wir thun es.
no longer, nicht mehr.
he wishes you to come, er wünscht, daß Sie (du) kommen.
to scold, schelten.
servant, Magd (Diener).
many a time, öfters.

to look, aussehen.
dirty, schmutzig.
to wait for, warten auf.
enough, genug.
to flog, prügeln.
an hour ago, vor einer Stunde.
when, wenn.
infant brother, Brüderchen.
to cry, schreien.
is to go, gehen soll.
to stop, anhalten.

Das regelmäßige Zeitwort.

will you stop your noise?
willst du (ihr) stille sein?
all he asked me, alles wonach
er mich gefragt hatte.
to depart, fortgeben.
to repeat, wiederholen.
question, Frage.
sentence, Satz.
twice, zweimal.
instructive, lehrreich.
to take a walk, spazieren gehen.
round, um.

to have a mind, Lust haben.
to accompany, begleiten.
really, wirklich.
to enter, eintreten in.
to travel, reisen.
to sail for, absegeln nach.
to escape, entlaufen.
master, Herr.
widow, Wittwe.
to die, sterben.
consumption, Schwindsucht.

Uebungs-Aufgabe 1.

I love my father and mother; they love me and my sister. My sister loves them, too. You love me and I love you. I loved this boy when he was diligent; his teachers loved him also. We praised him for his diligence, but we do so no longer. Thou knowest my downsitting and mine uprising, thou understandest my thought afar off. He wishes you to come to his house. I have scolded your servant many a time, she always looks so dirty. Will you wait for me? I have waited long enough, I can wait no longer. John flogged his dog an hour ago. He always flogs him when he has not obeyed. My infant brother always cries when he is to go to bed; he cried a whole hour yesterday. I stopped him in the street. Will you stop your noise? When I had answered all he had asked me I departed. Will you repeat my question? I repeated these sentences twice. There is no rose without thorns. There are many instructive books. I want to take a walk round the park. Have you a mind to accompany me? I accompanied you yesterday and to-day. I have really no mind to take a walk. Are there many cherries and plums in your garden? There are many cherries, but no plums. When I had just departed, my nephew entered my house. I have traveled many years in Europe and America. He has sailed for

Mexico. The slave has escaped his master. The poor widow has died; she died of consumption.

Wörter-Verzeichniß.

wohnen, to live, reside.
früher, formerly.
derselbe, the same.
zusammen, together.
was fehlt dir? what ails you?
suchen, to look for.
prächtig, splendid.
den ganzen Morgen, all the morning.
zu Hause, at home.
warten auf, to wait for.
wann, when.
zuletzt, last.
vor zwei Jahren, two years ago.
Abend, evening.

ausruhen, to rest.
undeutlich, indistinctly.
lauter, louder.
deutlicher, more distinctly.
wenn ich verstehen soll, if I am to understand.
vorgestern, day before yesterday.
als ich kam, while coming.
erzählte, told.
daß er gehen würde, that he would go.
Neuigkeit, news.
Börse, exchange.

Uebungs-Aufgabe 2.

Ich liebe deinen Bruder; er ist mein Freund. Er wohnte früher mit mir in demselben Hause; wir gingen oft spazieren zusammen. Was fehlt dir? Ich habe mein Messer verloren; willst du mir es suchen helfen? Gestern habe ich einen großen, prächtigen Elephanten gesehen. Wo hast du ihn gesehen? Wo bist du diesen Morgen gewesen? Ich war den ganzen Morgen zu Hause und wartete auf dich. Wann sind Sie zuletzt in Europa gewesen? Ich war vor zwei Jahren dort. Wie lange wohnen Sie (have you lived) in diesem Hause? Ich wohne (have lived) hier (schon seit) fünf Jahren. Ich habe den ganzen Abend geschrieben (I have been writing); jetzt muß ich ein wenig ausruhen. Du sprichst sehr undeutlich; sprich lauter und deutlicher, wenn ich dich verstehen soll. Ich sprach vorgestern deinen Bruder, als ich von der Arbeit kam. Er erzählte mir, daß er nach Californien gehen würde. Hast du schon unser neues Piano gesehen? Ich habe es noch nicht gesehen. Wo hast du diese Neuigkeit gehört? Ich hörte sie vor einer Stunde auf der Börse.

Lesestück 1.

THE CADI'S DECISION. AN ARABIAN TALE.
Der Richterspruch des Kadi. Eine arabische Geschichte.

1. Bon-Akas, at one time the Sheik[1] or chief ruler[2] of Algeria, having heard[3] that the cadi of one of his twelve tribes[4] administered[5] justice[6] in an admirable[7] manner, and pronounced decisions[8] in a style[9] worthy[10] of king Solomon himself, determined[11] to judge[12] from his own observation[13] of the truth[14] of the report.[15]

2. Accordingly,[16] dressed[17] like a private individual,[18] without[19] arms[20] or attendants,[21] he set out for[22] the cadi's town, mounted[23] on a docile[24] Arabian steed.[25] Having arrived there,[26] he was just entering[27] the gate,[28] when a cripple,[29] seizing[30] the border[31] of his garment,[32] asked him for alms[33] in the name of the prophet. Bon-Akas gave him money, but the cripple maintained his hold.[34]

3. "What dost thou want?"[35] asked the sheik. "I have already given thee alms."

"Yes," replied the beggar, "but the law[36] says not only, 'Thou shalt give alms to thy brother,' but also, 'Thou shalt do for thy brother whatsoever[37] thou canst.'"

"Well! and what can I do for thee?"

4. "Thou canst save[38] me—poor crawling[39] creature[40] that I am!—from[41] being trodden under the feet[42] of men, horses, mules,[43] and camels, which would certainly happen[44] to me in passing through[45] the crowded[46] square,[47] in which a fair[48] is now being held.[49]

"And *how* can I save thee?"

5. "By letting[50] me ride behind you, and putting me down[51] safely[52] in the market-place, where I have business."[53]

"Be it so,"[54] replied Bon-Akas. And stooping down,[55] he helped the cripple to get up[56] behind him;

a business.⁵⁷ which was not accomplished⁵⁸ without much difficulty.⁵⁹

6. The strangely-assorted riders⁶⁰ attracted⁶¹ many eyes as they passed⁶² through the crowded streets; and at length ⁶³ they reached the market-place.

"Is this where you wish to stop?"⁶⁴ asked Bon-Akas.

"Yes."

"Then get down."⁶⁵

"Get down yourself."

"What for."⁶⁶

7. "To leave⁶⁷ me the horse."

"To leave you my horse! What mean you by that?"⁶⁸

"I mean that he belongs to *me*. Know you not that we are now in the town of the just⁶⁹ cadi, and that, if we bring the case⁷⁰ before⁷¹ him, he will certainly decide in my favor?"⁷²

8. "Why should he do so,⁷³ when the animal⁷⁴ belongs to me?"

"Don't you think that, when he sees us two; you, with your strong, straight⁷⁵ limbs,⁷⁶ which Allah has given you for the purpose⁷⁷ of walking, and I with my weak⁷⁸ legs⁷⁹ and distracted⁸⁰ feet, he will decree⁸¹ that the horse shall belong to him who has most need of him?"⁸²

9. "Should he do so, he would not be the *just* cadi," said Bon-Akas.

"Oh, as to that,"⁸³ replied the cripple, laughing, "although⁸⁴ he is *just*, he is not *infallible*."⁸⁵

The sheik was greatly surprised.⁸⁶ "But," he thought to himself,⁸⁷ "this will be a capital opportunity⁸⁸ of judging⁸⁹ the judge." Then he said aloud,⁹⁰ "I am content,⁹¹ we will go before the cadi."

10. On arriving⁹² at the tribunal,⁹³ where the judge, according to the Eastern custom,⁹⁴ was publicly⁹⁵ administering justice,⁹⁶ they found that two trials⁹⁷ were already in waiting,⁹⁸ and would, of course,⁹⁹ be heard¹⁰⁰ before theirs.

Das gegenwärtige Zeitwort. 49

11. The first was between a *taleb*, or learned man,[101] and a peasant.[102] The point in dispute[103] was the *taleb's* wife, whom the peasant claimed[104] as his own.
12. The woman remained[105] obstinately[106] silent,[107] and would not declare[108] for either;[109] a feature[110] in the case[111] which rendered[112] its decision exceedingly[113] difficult. The judge heard both sides attentively,[114] reflected[115] for a moment, and then said, "Leave[116] the woman here, and return[117] to-morrow."

[1] Schah, [2] oberste Gebieter, [3] als er erfuhr, [4] Stämme, [5] verwaltete, [6] das Richteramt, [7] bewundernswürdig, [8] Richtersprüche fällte, [9] auf eine Art, [10] würdig, [11] beschloß, [12] zu urtheilen über, [13] aus eigener Beobachtung, [14] Wahrheit, [15] Gerücht, [16] demnach, [17] gekleidet, [18] Privatpersonen, [19] ohne, [20] Waffen, [21] Dienerschaft, [22] machte er sich auf den Weg nach, [23] reitend, [24] sanft, [25] Roß, [26] dort angekommen, [27] trat er gerade ein durch, [28] Thor, [29] Krüppel, [30] erfassend, [31] Saum, [32] Gewand, [33] Almosen, [34] hielt immer noch fest, [35] was wünschest du? [36] Gesetz, [37] was nur immer, [38] bewahren, [39] kriechend, [40] Geschöpf, [41] davor daß, [42] daß ich nicht komme unter die Füße, [43] Maulesel, [44] geschehen, [45] wenn ich ginge über, [46] gedrängt, [47] Marktplatz, [48] Jahrmarkt, [49] abgehalten wird, [50] indem du läßt, [51] mich niedersetzest, [52] wohlbehalten, [53] Geschäfte, [54] so sei's, [55] sich niederbeugend, [56] aufzusteigen, [57] Sache, [58] ausgeführt wurde, [59] Schwierigkeit, [60] das sonderbare Reiterpaar, [61] zog auf sich, [62] verbeißam, [63] endlich, [64] anzuhalten, [65] steige ab, [66] warum? [67] zu überlassen, [68] was meinst du damit? [69] gerecht, [70] Fall, [71] vor, [72] zu meinen Gunsten, [73] das thun, [74] Thier, [75] gerade, [76] Glieder, [77] in der Absicht, [78] schwach, [79] Beine, [80] verkrüppelt, [81] entscheiden, [82] es am meisten nöthig hat, [83] was das betrifft, [84] obschon, [85] unfehlbar, [86] höchst erstaunt, [87] dachte bei sich, [88] eine prächtige Gelegenheit, [89] zu prüfen, [90] laut, [91] zufrieden, [92] angelangt, [93] Richterstuhl, [94] nach orientalischer Weise, [95] öffentlich, [96] Recht sprach, [97] Prozesse, [98] bereits vorlagen, [99] natürlich, [100] vorkommen würden, [101] Gelehrter, [102] Bauer, [103] der streitige Punkt, [104] beanspruchte, [105] blieb, [106] eigensinnig, [107] still, [108] sich nicht erklären, [109] für Einen von Beiden, [110] Umstand, [111] Fall, [112] machte, [113] außerordentlich, [114] aufmerksam, [115] dachte nach, [116] lasset, [117] kommt wieder.

Lesestück 2.

THE CADI'S DECISIONS. (Fortsetzung.)

1. The learned man and the laborer[1] each bowed,[2] and retired;[3] and the next cause[4] was called.[5] This was a difference[6] between[7] a butcher[8] and an oil-seller.[9] The latter[10] appeared[11] covered[12] with oil, and the former[13] was sprinkled[14] with blood.

2. The butcher spoke first, and said: "I went to buy [15] some oil from this man, and, in order to [16] pay him for it,[17] I drew [18] a handful of money from my purse. The sight [19] of the money tempted [20] him. He seized me by the wrist.[21] I cried out, but he would not let me go; and here we are, having come before your worship,[22] I holding my money in my hand, and he still grasping [23] my wrist. Now, I assert [24] that this man is a liar,[25] when he says that I stole his money; for the money is truly [26] mine own."[27]

3. Then spoke the oil-merchant:
"This man came to purchase [28] oil from me. When his bottle was filled,[29] he said, 'Have you change [30] for a piece of gold?'[31] I searched [32] my pocket, and drew out [33] a handful of money, which I laid [34] on a bench [35] in my shop.[36] He seized it, and was walking off [37] with my money and my oil, when I caught [38] him by the wrist, and cried out, 'Robber!'"[39]

4. "In spite of my cries, however,[40] he would not surrender [41] the money; so [42] I brought him here, that your worship might decide the case. Now, I assert that this man is a liar, when he says that I want to steal his money; for it is truly mine own."

5. The cadi caused [43] each man to repeat [44] his story,[45] but neither [46] varied [47] one jot [48] from his original [49] statement.[50] He reflected for a moment, and then said, "Leave the money with me, and return to-morrow."

6. The butcher placed [51] the coins,[52] which he had never let go,[53] on the edge [54] of the cadi's mantle. After which,[55] he and his opponent [56] bowed to the tribunal, and departed.

It was now the turn [57] of Bou-Akas and the cripple.

7. "My lord cadi," said the former, "I came hither [58] from a distant [59] country, with the intention [60] of purchasing merchandise.[61] At the city gate I met [62] this cripple, who first [63] asked for alms, and then prayed [64] me to allow [65] him to ride behind me through the streets, lest [66] he should be trodden down in the crowd.

8. "I consented,⁶⁷ but, when we reached the market-place, he refused⁶⁸ to get down, asserting⁶⁹ that my horse belonged to him, and that your worship would surely adjudge⁷⁰ it to him who wanted⁷¹ it most. That, my lord cadi, is precisely⁷² the state of this case."⁷³

9. "My lord," said the cripple, "as I was coming on business to the market, and riding this horse, which belongs to me, I saw this man seated⁷⁴ by the road-side,⁷⁵ apparently⁷⁶ half dead from fatigue.⁷⁷ I kindly offered⁷⁸ to take him up behind me, and let him ride as far as the market-place,⁷⁹ and he eagerly⁸⁰ thanked me.

10. "But what was my astonishment,⁸¹ when, on our arrival,⁸² he refused to get down, and said that my horse was his. I immediately⁸³ required⁸⁴ him to appear before your worship, in order that⁸⁵ you might decide between us. That is the true state⁸⁶ of the case."

11. Having made each repeat⁸⁷ his statement, and having reflected for a moment, the cadi said, "Leave the horse here, and return to-morrow."

It was done,⁸⁸ and Bou-Akas and the cripple withdrew⁸⁹ in different directions.⁹⁰

¹ Arbeiter, ² verbeugten sich Beide, ³ traten ab, ⁴ Fall, ⁵ wurde aufgerufen, ⁶ Streit, ⁷ zwischen, ⁸ Fleischer, ⁹ Oelhändler, ¹⁰ Letzterer, ¹¹ trat vor, ¹² beschmiert, ¹³ Ersterer, ¹⁴ bespritzt, ¹⁵ ich kam um zu kaufen, ¹⁶ um—zu, ¹⁷ dafür, ¹⁸ zog ich, ¹⁹ Anblick, ²⁰ führte ihn in Versuchung, ²¹ Handgelenk, ²² Ehrwürden, ²³ festhaltend, ²⁴ behaupte ich, ²⁵ Lügner, ²⁶ wahrhaftig, ²⁷ mein Eigenthum, ²⁸ zu kaufen, ²⁹ gefüllt, ³⁰ Kleingeld, ³¹ Goldstück, ³² durchsuchte, ³³ zog hervor, ³⁴ legte, ³⁵ Bank, ³⁶ Laden, ³⁷ war im Begriff davon zu geben, ³⁸ ergriff, ³⁹ Räuber, ⁴⁰ jedoch, ⁴¹ herausgeben, ⁴² deswegen, ⁴³ ließ, ⁴⁴ wiederholen, ⁴⁵ Geschichte, ⁴⁶ keiner von Beiden, ⁴⁷ wich ab, ⁴⁸ ein Titelchen, ⁴⁹ anfänglich, ⁵⁰ Aussage, ⁵¹ legte, ⁵² Münzen, ⁵³ welche er keinen Augenblick losgelassen hatte, ⁵⁴ Saum, ⁵⁵ hierauf, ⁵⁶ Gegner, ⁵⁷ die Reihe war jetzt an, ⁵⁸ hierher, ⁵⁹ fern, ⁶⁰ Absicht, ⁶¹ Waaren, ⁶² begegnete ich, ⁶³ zuerst, ⁶⁴ bat, ⁶⁵ erlauben, ⁶⁶ damit nicht, ⁶⁷ willigte ein, ⁶⁸ weigerte er sich, ⁶⁹ indem er behauptete, ⁷⁰ zuerkennen, ⁷¹ bedürfe, ⁷² ganz genau, ⁷³ Sachlage, ⁷⁴ sitzend, ⁷⁵ am Wege, ⁷⁶ anscheinend, ⁷⁷ vor Ermattung, ⁷⁸ bot ihm freundlich an, ⁷⁹ bis zum Marktplatz, ⁸⁰ innig, ⁸¹ Erstaunen, ⁸² bei unserer Ankunft, ⁸³ sofort, ⁸⁴ verlangte, daß, ⁸⁵ damit, ⁸⁶ der wahre Verhalt, ⁸⁷ nachdem er einen Jeden hatte wiederholen lassen, ⁸⁸ es geschah, ⁸⁹ entfernten sich, ⁹⁰ nach verschiedenen Richtungen.

Lesestück 3.

THE CADI'S DECISIONS. (Schluß.)

1. On the morrow,[1] a number of persons besides[2] those immediately[3] interested[4] in the trials[5] assembled[6] to hear the judge's decisions. The *taleb* and the peasant were called first.

2. "Take away[7] thy wife," said the cadi to the former, "and keep[8] her." Then, turning[9] toward[10] an officer,[11] he added,[12] pointing[13] to the peasant, "Give this man fifty blows."[14] He was instantly obeyed,[15] and the taleb led[16] away his wife.

3. Then came forward the oil-merchant and the butcher. "Here," said the cadi to the butcher, "is thy money; it is truly thine, and not his." Then, pointing to the oil-merchant, he said to his officer, "Give this man fifty blows."

4. It was done,[17] and the butcher went away in triumph with his money. The third cause was then called, and Bou-Akas and the cripple came forward.

"Wouldst thou recognize[18] thy horse among twenty others?" said the judge to Bou-Akas.

5. "Yes, my lord."

"And thou?"

"Certainly, my lord," replied the cripple.

"Follow me," said the cadi to Bou-Akas.

6. They entered[19] a large stable,[20] and Bou-Akas pointed out[21] his horse among[22] the twenty which were standing side by side.[23]

"'Tis well," said the judge. "Return now to the tribunal, and send me thine adversary[24] hither."[25]

7. The disguised[26] sheik obeyed, delivered[27] his message,[28] and the cripple hastened[29] to the stable, as quickly[30] as his distorted limbs[31] could carry[32] him. He had quick eyes,[33] and a good memory,[34] so that he was able,[35] without the slightest hesitation,[36] to place[37] his hand on the right animal.

8. "'Tis well," said the cadi; "return to the tribunal."

His worship resumed [33] his place, and when the cripple arrived, judgment was pronounced.[39] "The horse is thine," said the cadi to Bou-Akas. "Go to the stable, and take [40] him." Then, turning to the officer, he said, "Give this cripple fifty blows." It was done, and Bou-Akas went to take his horse.

9. When the cadi, after concluding [41] the business of the day,[42] was retiring [43] to his house, he found Bou-Akas waiting for [44] him. "Art thou then discontented [45] with my award?" [46] asked the judge.

10. "No, quite the contrary," [47] replied the sheik. "But I want to ask by what means [48] thou hast rendered justice; [49] for I doubt [50] not that the other two causes were decided [51] as correctly [52] as mine. I am not a merchant; I am Bou-Akas, Sheik of Algeria, and I wanted to judge for myself of thy reported [53] wisdom."

11. The cadi bowed [54] to the ground,[55] and kissed his master's hand.

"I am anxious," [56] said Bou-Akas, "to know the reasons [57] which determined [58] your three decisions."

"Nothing, my lord, can be more simple. Your Highness saw that I detained,[59] for a night, the three things in dispute?" [60]

"I did."

12. "Well, early in the morning I caused the woman to be called,[61] and I said to her suddenly,[62] "Put [63] fresh ink [64] in my inkstand." [65] Like a person who had done the same thing a hundred times before,[66] she took the bottle, removed [67] the cotton,[68] washed them both, put in the cotton again, and poured [69] in fresh ink, doing it all [70] with the utmost neatness [71] and dexterity.[72]

13. "So I said to myself, 'A peasant's wife would know nothing about [73] inkstands; she must belong to the *taleb*.'"

"Good," said Bou-Akas, nodding his head.[74] "And the money?"

"Did your Highness remark that the merchant had his clothes and hands covered with [73] oil?"

"Certainly I did."

14. "Well, I took the money and placed [76] it in a vessel filled with water.[77] This morning I looked at it,[78] and not a particle of oil [79] was to be seen [80] on the surface [81] of the water. So I said to myself, 'If this money belonged to the oil-merchant, it would be greasy,[82] from the touch [83] of his hands; as it is not so, the *butcher's* story must be true.'"

15. Bou-Akas nodded [84] in token [85] of approval.[86] "Good," said he. "And my horse?"

"Ah! that was a different business; [87] and until this morning I was greatly puzzled." [88]

"The cripple, I suppose, did not recognize the animal?"

"On the contrary, he pointed him out immediately."

"How, then, did you discover [89] that he was not the owner?" [90]

16. "My object [91] in bringing you [92] separately [93] to the stable was, not to see if you would know the *horse*, but if the horse would know *you*. Now, when you approached him,[94] the creature [95] turned [96] toward you, laid back his ears,[97] and neighed [98] with delight; [99] but when the cripple touched [100] him, he kicked.[101] Then I knew you were truly his master."

17. Bou-Akas thought [102] for a moment, and then said, "Allah has given thee great wisdom. Thou oughtest [103] to be in my place, and I in thine. But I fear I could not fill [104] thy place as cadi!"

---

[1] am nächsten Morgen, [2] außer, [3] unmittelbar, [4] Betheiligte, [5] Gerichts=Verhandlungen, [6] versammelten sich, [7] führe hinweg, [8] behalte, [9] sich wendend, [10] gegen einen, [11] Gerichtsdiener, [12] setzte er hinzu, [13] indem er zeigte auf, [14] Hiebe, [15] man gehorchte ihm augenblicklich, [16] führte, [17] es geschah, [18] wiedererkennen, [19] traten ein, [20] Stall, [21] fand heraus, [22] unter, [23] die neben einander standen, [24] Gegner, [25] hierher, [26] verkleidet, [27] richtete aus, [28] Botschaft, [29] eilte, [30] so schnell, [31] Glieder, [32] tragen, [33] scharfes Auge, [34] Gedächtniß, [35] so daß er im Stande war, [36] ohne das mindeste Zögern, [37] legen, [38] nahm wieder ein, [39] wurde das Urtheil gefällt, [40] hole, [41] nach Beendigung, [42] Tagesgeschäfte, [43] im Begriff war sich zurückzubegeben, [44] wartend auf, [45] unzufrieden, [46] Zuerkennung, [47] ganz

Hauptwort. Geschlecht.

im Gegentheil, ⁴⁸ wodurch (es dir möglich war), ⁴⁹ Recht zu sprechen, ⁵⁰ ich zweifle, ⁵¹ entschieden, ⁵² richtig, ⁵³ berühmt, ⁵⁴ verneigte sich, ⁵⁵ Boden, ⁵⁶ begierig, ⁵⁷ Gründe, ⁵⁸ bestimmten, ⁵⁹ zurückbehielt, ⁶⁰ die drei streitigen Gegenstände, ⁶¹ ließ ich die Frau rufen, ⁶² plötzlich, ⁶³ gieße, ⁶⁴ Dinte, ⁶⁵ Dintengeschirr, ⁶⁶ zuvor, ⁶⁷ entfernte, ⁶⁸ Baumwolle, ⁶⁹ goß, ⁷⁰ und that dies Alles, ⁷¹ mit äußerster Sauberkeit, ⁷² Gewandtheit, ⁷³ von, ⁷⁴ mit dem Haupte nickend, ⁷⁵ voll von, ⁷⁶ that es hinein, ⁷⁷ in ein mit Wasser angefülltes Gefäß, ⁷⁸ sah ich nach, ⁷⁹ Oeltheilchen, ⁸⁰ war zu sehen, ⁸¹ Oberfläche, ⁸² fettig, ⁸³ Beruhigung, ⁸⁴ nickte, ⁸⁵ zum Zeichen, ⁸⁶ Zustimmung, ⁸⁷ eine ganz andere Sache, ⁸⁸ sehr in Verlegenheit, ⁸⁹ entdecktest du, ⁹⁰ Eigenthümer, ⁹¹ Zweck, ⁹² indem ich euch brachte, ⁹³ einzeln, ⁹⁴ als du dich ihm nähertest, ⁹⁵ Thier, ⁹⁶ wandte, ⁹⁷ legte die Ohren zurück, ⁹⁸ wieherte, ⁹⁹ vor Freuden, ¹⁰⁰ anrührte, ¹⁰¹ schlug es aus, ¹⁰² sann nach, ¹⁰³ du solltest, ¹⁰⁴ ausfüllen.

Lektion X.

Hauptwort. Geschlecht.—Ableitung des weiblichen Geschlechts vom männlichen.

Wörter-Verzeichniß.

husband, Mann (Ehemann).
brother-in-law, Schwager.
wife, Frau (Ehefrau).
sister-in-law, Schwägerin.
cock, Hahn.
to crow, krähen.
hen, Henne.
to cackle, gackern.
horse, männliches Pferd (Hengst).
mare, weibliches Pferd (Stute).
stable, Stall.
occupation, Geschäft.
actor, Schauspieler.
actress, Schauspielerin.
did you read? haben Sie gelesen?
pilot, Lootse.
to save, retten.
at the peril of her life, mit Gefahr ihres Lebens.
truly, in der That.
heroine, Heldin.
may be, kann sein.
lion, Löwe.
man-servant, Diener.
maid-servant, Magd.
cook, Koch, Köchin.
canary, Kanarienvogel.
male, Männchen.
female, Weibchen.
male department, Knabenklasse.
female department, Mädchenklasse.
are presided over, werden geleitet von.
about, ungefähr.
teacher, Lehrer (männlich und weiblich).
public, öffentlich.
the rest, die übrigen.

Uebungs-Aufgabe 1.

My sister's husband is my brother-in-law, and my brother's wife is my sister-in-law. I have two brothers-in-law and three sisters-in-law. My wife's mother is my mother-in-law and her husband is my father-in-law. The crown-prince of Prussia is Queen Victoria's son-in-law. Queen Victoria's daughter is King William I. daughter-in-law. King William I. is Emperor of Germany; his wife, Augusta, is the empress. The cock crows, the hen cackles. Our dog is old; we like him. There are two horses and one mare in our stable. Is not this a beautiful horse? he is seven years old. What is this man's occupation? He is an actor, and his wife is an actress. Did you read of the pilot's daughter who saved many people at the peril of her life? She was truly a heroine. A boy may be a hero and a girl a heroine. There is a lion and a lioness in the Central Park. My aunt has one man-servant and two maid-servants. Our cook is sick; she has a very bad cold. I have two canaries, a male and a female. The male bird is a year old and the female bird two. The male and female department of each school are presided over by a principal. The principal of the male department is a gentleman, and the principal of the female department is a lady. There are about three thousand teachers in the public schools of New York. More than two thousand of them are lady-teachers, the rest are male teachers.

Wörter-Verzeichniß.

Frau, woman, wife.
Amerikanerin, American.
hast du gekannt? did you know?
Schwager, brother-in-law.
Schwägerin, sister-in-law.
Großeltern, grand-parents.
am Leben, alive.
Schwiegersohn, son-in-law.
Königin, queen.
Magd, maid-servant.
reinlich, cleanly.
Jugend, youth.
ausgezeichnet, excellent.
Musiklehrer, music-teacher.
Componist, composer.

Piano-Virtuosin, performer on the piano.
nahm, took.
Unterricht, instruction.
Musiklehrerin, lady-teacher of music.
ein geborner Deutscher, a native of Germany.
Herr, gentleman.
Dame, lady.
Bekannte, acquaintances.
Landsleute, countrymen.
von uns, of ours.
Landsmännin, country-woman.
von mir, of mine.

Uebungs-Aufgabe 2.

Die Frau meines Bruders ist eine Amerikanerin. Hast du meinen Schwager gekannt? Ich habe deinen Schwager und deine Schwägerin gekannt. Meine Großeltern, Großvater und Großmutter, sind beide noch am Leben. Der Prinz von Wales ist der Schwiegersohn des Königs von Dänemark; seine Frau ist daher die Schwiegertochter der Königin von England. Unsere Magd ist sehr reinlich und fleißig. Ich hatte in meiner Jugend ausgezeichnete Lehrer. Mein Musiklehrer war ein großer Componist; seine Tochter war eine große Piano-Virtuosin. Meine Schwester nahm Unterricht bei einer Musiklehrerin. Unsere Nachbarin ist eine Freundin deiner Mutter; ihr Mann ist ein geborner Deutscher. Die Herren und Damen, die heute Abend kommen, sind alle alte Bekannte und Landsleute von uns. Die Frau, die gestern mit ihrem Manne bei mir war, ist eine Landsmännin von mir.

Lesestück 1.

THE STORY OF CAN AND COULD (Die Geschichte von „Kann" und „Könnte").

1. Once upon a time[1] *Could* went out to take a walk[2] on a winter's morning. He was very much out of spirits,[3] and he was made more so[4] by the necessity[5] under which he found himself,[6] of frequently[7] repeating[8] his own name. "Oh, if I *could*," and "Oh, if I were rich and great, for then I *could* do so and so."

2. About[9] the tenth time[10] that he said this, *Can*

opened the door of her humble [11] dwelling,[12] and set out [13] on an errand.[14] She went down [15] a back street,[16] and through a poor [17] neighborhood.[18] She was not at all [19] a grand [20] personage,[21] nor [22] was she so well dressed,[23] or so well lodged,[24] or so well educated [25] as Could. In fact,[26] she was altogether [27] more humble,[28] both in her own esteem [29] and in that of others. She went on [30] neither [31] sauntering [32] nor [33] looking about her,[34] for she was in a hurry.[35]

3. All on a sudden,[36] however,[37] this busy [38] little Can stopped,[39] and picked up [40] a piece of orange-peel.[41] "A dangerous [42] trick," [43] she observed,[44] "to throw orange-peel about,[45] particularly [46] in frosty weather,[47] and in such crowded [48] streets;" and she bustled on [49] till she overtook [50] a group [51] of little children who were scattering [52] it very freely.[53] They had been buying [54] oranges at a fruit-stand,[55] and were eating them as they went along.

4. "Well, it's little enough [56] that *I* can do," thought Can, "but certainly I can [57] *speak* to these children and try [58] to persuade [59] them to leave off [60] strewing [61] orange-peel."

5. Can stopped. "That's a pretty baby [62] that you have in your arms," she said to one of them; "how *old* is he?"

6. "He is fourteen months old," answered the little nurse,[63] "and he begins to walk. I teach him. He's my brother."

7. "Poor little fellow," [64] said Can; "I hope you are *kind* to [65] him. You know, if you were to let him fall,[66] he might never be able to walk any more." [67]

"I never let him drop," [68] replied the child; "I always take care [69] of the baby."

8. "And so do I," [70] "And so do I," repeated [71] other shrill [72] voices; [73] and two more [74] babies were thrust up [75] for Can's inspection.[76]

9. But if you were to slip down yourselves,[77] on this hard pavement,[78] you would be hurt; [79] and the baby would be hurt in your arms. Look! [80] how *can* you

be so careless⁸¹ as to throw all this peel about? Don't you see how slippery⁸² it is?"

10. "We always fling⁸³ it down," said one. "And I never slipped down but once⁸⁴ on a piece," remarked another.

"But was not that once too often?"

"Yes. I grazed⁸⁵ my arm very badly,⁸⁶ and broke⁸⁷ a cup⁸⁸ that I was carrying."⁸⁹

11. "Well, now, suppose⁹⁰ you pick up all the peel you can find; and to the one⁹¹ who finds most, when I come back, I will give a penny." They said they would do this, and setting about it⁹² very cheerfully,⁹³ promised⁹⁴ that they would never commit⁹⁵ this fault⁹⁶ again.

12. Can then went on; and it is a remarkable⁹⁷ circumstance that, just at that very moment,⁹⁸ as Could was walking in quite⁹⁹ a different part of the city, he also came to a piece of orange-peel which was lying in his path.¹⁰⁰

13. "What a shame!"¹⁰¹ he said, as he passed on. "What a disgrace¹⁰² it is to the city, that this practice¹⁰³ of sowing seed,¹⁰⁴ which springs up¹⁰⁵ into broken bones,¹⁰⁶ cannot be punished!¹⁰⁷ There is never¹⁰⁸ a winter that one or more accidents¹⁰⁹ does not arise¹¹⁰ from it! If *I* could only put a stop to it,¹¹¹ how glad¹¹² I should be! If I had the power¹¹³—"

14. "By your leave,¹¹⁴ sir," said a tall, strong man, with a heavy basket¹¹⁵ of coal¹¹⁶ on his shoulders.

15. Could, stepping aside,¹¹⁷ permitted the coal-carrier to pass him.¹¹⁸ "Yes," he continued,¹¹⁹ "if *I* had the power, I would punish everybody who throws orange-peel on the side-walk."¹²⁰ The noise¹²¹ of a heavy fall, and the rushing down¹²² as of a great shower of stones,¹²³ made Could turn hastily around.¹²⁴ The coal-carrier had fallen on the pavement, and the coal lay in heaps¹²⁵ around his head. Several¹²⁶ people¹²⁷ ran to him, and some were trying to raise¹²⁸ him. Could went near¹²⁹ enough to see that the man was stunned¹³⁰ and he also observed that a piece

of orange-peel was adhering [131] to the sole of his shoe.[132]

16. "How sad!"[133] said Could, as he passed along. "Now here is the bitter result [134] of this abuse.[135] If *I* had been in authority,[136] I could have prevented [137] this. Poor fellow! he is badly hurt,[138] and has a broken limb;[139] he is lamed,[140] perhaps for life. What the poet [141] says may be true enough:

'Of all the ills [142] that human kind [143] endure,[144]
Small is the part which *laws* [145] can cause [146] or cure.' [147]

"And yet I think *I* could frame [148] a law that would prevent [149] such accidents, or, at least,[150] that would punish the people who cause them."

---

[1] einstmals, [2] trat einen Spaziergang an, [3] er war bei sehr schlechter Laune, [4] wurde es noch mehr, [5] Nothwendigkeit, [6] in der er sich befand, [7] häufig, [8] zu wiederholen, [9] etwa, [10] das zehnte Mal, [11] bescheiden, [12] Wohnung, [13] ging aus, [14] Gewerbe, [15] hinab, [16] Seitengasse, [17] ärmlich, [18] Nachbarschaft, [19] ganz und gar, [20] wichtig, [21] Persönlichkeit, [22] auch nicht, [23] gut gekleidet, [24] noch wohnte sie so gut, [25] gebildet, [26] in der That, [27] in jeder Beziehung, [28] demüthiger, [29] in ihrer eigenen Schätzung, [30] ihres Wegs, [31] weder, [32] schlendernd, [33] noch, [34] um sich blickend, [35] in Eile, [36] auf einmal, [37] jedoch, [38] geschäftig, [39] blieb stillstehen, [40] hob auf, [41] Orangenschale, [42] gefährlich, [43] Streich, [44] bemerkte sie, [45] umherzuwerfen, [46] zumal, [47] Frostwetter, [48] belebt, [49] trippelte weiter, [50] einholte, [51] Schaar, [52] umherstreuten, [53] frei, [54] sie hatten gekauft, [55] Fruchtbude, [56] wenig genug, [57] aber ich kann doch, [58] versuchen, [59] überreden, [60] unterlassen, [61] streuen, [62] hübsches kleines Kind, [63] Wärterin, [64] Kerl, [65] gut gegen, [66] wenn du ihn fallen ließest, [67] so könnte er vielleicht nie wieder gehen, [68] ich lasse fallen, [69] ich gebe immer gut Acht, [70] ich auch, [71] wiederholten, [72] hell, [73] Stimmen, [74] noch zwei mehr, [75] emporgehoben, [76] Besichtigung, [77] wenn ihr selbst niederfielet, [78] Pflaster, [79] so würdet ihr euch weh thun, [80] seht her! [81] leichtsinnig, [82] schlüpfrig, [83] werfen, [84] einmal ausgenommen, [85] ich habe geschunden, [86] schlimm, [87] zerbrach, [88] Tasse, [89] ich trug, [90] wie wäre es, wenn, [91] demjenigen, [92] an's Werk gehend, [93] munter, [94] versprachen, [95] begeben, [96] Fehler, [97] merkwürdig, [98] in dem nämlichen Augenblick, [99] ging, [100] Pfad, [101] welche Schande! [102] Schmach, [103] Gewohnheit, [104] Samen zu säen, [105] aufgebt, [106] Knochen, [107] bestraft werden, [108] es gibt nie, [109] Unglücksfälle, [110] entstehen, [111] wenn ich dem nur einen Riegel vorschieben könnte, [112] froh, [113] Macht, [114] mit Ihrer Erlaubniß, [115] Korb, [116] Kohlen, [117] bei Seite tretend, [118] ließ den Kohlenträger vorbeigehen, [119] fuhrer fort, [120] Trottoir, [121] Geräusch, [122] Herunterpoltern, [123] Steinschauer, [124] ließ hastig umdrehen, [125] Haufen, [126] mehrere, [127] Leute, [128] aufzuheben, [129] nahe, [130] betäubt, [131] hing, [132] Schuhsohle, [133] beklagenswerth, [134] Frucht, [135] Unfug, [136] wenn ich zu befehlen gehabt hätte, [137] ich hätte verhindern können, [138] schlimm verletzt, [139] Glied, [140] gelähmt, [141] Dichter, [142] Uebel, [143] das Menschengeschlecht, [144] erduldet, [145] Gesetze, [146] verursachen, [147] heilen, [148] einrichten, [149] verhindern, [150] wenigstens.

Hauptwort. Geschlecht.

Lesestück 2.
THE STORY OF CAN AND COULD. (Schluß.)

1. Could soon got [1] into an omnibus, and as he was riding along [2] he was thinking of [3] how much good he could do, if he only had the means.[4] "Now there," said he to himself, "is a 'Home for Consumptive Patients.'[5] What a fine building,[6] and pleasant grounds! [7] How I would like to be [8] the founder [9] of such a noble institution, if I only had the means. But it is my lot [10] to sigh [11] over the troubles [12] of mankind,[13] without being able [14] to relieve [15] them; for, alas! with only small [16] means, I can do no more than provide [17] for my *own* wants.[18] I cannot gratify [19] my benevolent [20] wishes; but how willingly [21] I would, if I could."

2. The omnibus stopped,[22] and a pale-faced [23] man, in clean working-clothes,[24] inquired [25] if there was a seat inside.[26]

"No, there is not one," said the conductor, as he looked in. Most of the passengers were women. Would any gentleman," he asked, "like to go outside?"[27]

3. "Like!" thought Could with a laugh.[28] "Who would like to ride outside in such a wind as this! Thank Heaven,[29] I never take cold,[30] but I don't want a blast [31] like this to air [32] the lining [33] of my waistcoat,[34] and chill [35] the very shillings [36] in my pocket!"

4. "Because," [37] continued the conductor, "if any gentleman would like to go outside, here is a person who has been ill,[38] and would be very glad of [39] a place within." No answer came from within.

5. "I must ride outside, then," said the man, "for I have not much time for waiting." [40] So he got up with the driver,[41] and as the omnibus rumbled on,[42] a hollow [43] cough,[44] now and then,[45] was heard [46] from the sick man, which told [47] very plainly [48] that he [49] was not likely [50] to trouble [49] any one long.

6. After telling you [51] so much about *Could*, his

kind [52] wishes, and grand [53] projects, and regrets [54] that he could not do some great good, [55] I am almost ashamed [56] to mention [57] *Can* to you again. However, [58] I think I will venture, [59] though, poor little thing, her hopes and wishes are very humble, and she scarcely [60] knows what a *project* means. [61]

7. So you must know that, having finished [62] most of her business, she entered [63] a shop [64] to purchase [65] something for her dinner; [66] and while she waited to be served [67] a child entered, carrying [68] a basket much too heavy for her strength, [69] and having a shawl folded [70] upon her arm.

8. "What have you in your basket?" asked Can.

"Potatoes for dinner," said the child.

"It is very heavy for you," remarked Can, observing [71] how she bent [72] under the weight [73] of it.

9. "Mother is ill, and there is nobody to go [74] to the shop but me," [75] replied the child, setting down [76] the basket, and blowing [77] her numbed [78] fingers.

"No wonder you are cold," said Can; "why [79] don't you put your shawl *on*, [79] instead of [80] carrying it *so*?"

10. "It's so big," said the child in a piteous voice. [81] "Mother put a pin [82] in it, and told me to hold it up; but I can't, the basket's so heavy; and I trod on it, [83] and fell down."

11. "It's enough to give the child her *death* of cold," [84] said the mistress [85] of the shop, "to go crawling [86] home in this bitter wind, with nothing on but that thin frock." [87]

12. "Come," said Can, "I think I can tie [88] a child's shawl so as not to throw her down." [89] So she made [90] the little girl hold out her arms, and drawing [91] the garment [92] closely [93] around her, knotted it securely [94] at her back. [95] "Now, then," she said, having inquired where she lived, [96] "I am going your way, so I can help you to carry your basket."

13. Can and the child went out together, while Could, having reached [97] his comfortable home, sat down be-

fore the fire, and made[98] a great many reflections; and he thought over[99] a great many projects for doing good on a grand scale.[100] He made reflections on baths,[101] and wash-houses, and model lodging-houses for the poor. He made castles in the air;[102] and when, in imagination,[103] he had made a great many people happy, he felt that a benevolent disposition[104] is a great blessing,[105] and fell asleep[106] by the fire.

14. Can was too busy to make projects; she only made two things: when she had helped to carry the child's basket, she kindly made her sick mother's bed, and then she went home to make a pudding.

JEAN INGELOW.

[1] stieg, [2] wie er so dahin fuhr, [3] sann er darüber nach, [4] die Mittel, [5] Asyl für Schwindsüchtige, [6] Gebäude, [7] Anlagen, [8] wie gern möchte ich sein, [9] Grünter, [10] Loos, [11] seufzen, [12] Leiden, [13] Menschheit, [14] ohne zu können, [15] abhelfen, [16] gering, [17] sorgen, [18] eigene Bedürfnisse, [19] befriedigen, [20] wohlgemeint, [21] gerne, [22] hielt an, [23] blaß aussehend, [24] Arbeitszeug, [25] fragte, [26] drinnen, [27] draußen auf, [28] Lachen, [29] dem Himmel sei Dank, [30] ich erkälte mich nie, [31] Sturm, [32] auszulüften, [33] Unterfutter, [34] Weste, [35] erfrieren zu machen, [36] sogar die Schillinge, [37] weil, [38] krank, [39] froh über, [40] zu warten, [41] Kutscher, [42] dahinrollte, [43] hohl, [44] Husten, [45] von Zeit zu Zeit, [46] hörte man, [47] zu erkennen gab, [48] sehr deutlich, [49] daß er lästig fallen würde, [50] wahrscheinlich, [51] nachdem ich euch erzählt habe, [52] freundlich, [53] großartig, [54] Klagen, [55] ein großes, gutes Werk, [56] schäme ich mich beinahe, [57] erwähnen, [58] jedoch, [59] wagen, [60] kaum, [61] bedeutet, [62] nachdem sie besorgt hatte, [63] trat sie ein in, [64] Laden, [65] kaufen, [66] Mittagessen, [67] bis man sie bedienen würde, [68] welches trug, [69] Kraft, [70] gefaltet, [71] sehend, [72] gebeugt ging, [73] Gewicht, [74] der gehen könnte, [75] als ich, [76] niedersetzend, [77] pustend, [78] erstarrt, [79] warum ziehst du nicht an? [80] statt zu, [81] in kläglichem Tone, [82] Stecknadel, [83] ich habe darauf getreten, [84] es ist genug, das Kind tödtlich zu erkälten, [85] Eigenthümerin, [86] kriechend, [87] Röckchen, [88] binden, [89] daß sie nicht niederfällt, [90] ließ sie, [91] ziehend, [92] Tuch, [93] dicht, [94] knotete sie es fest, [95] Rücken, [96] wohnte, [97] als er erreicht hatte, [98] anstellte, [99] überdachte, [100] in großartigem Maßstabe, [101] Bäder, [102] Luftschlösser, [103] Einbildung, [104] Gesinnung, [105] Segen, [106] schlief ein.

Lektion XI.

Fürwörter.—Demonstrative, relative.
Redensarten.

Never mind, no matter, to borrow, to lend, to chance.

Wörter-Verzeichniß.

do you want? willst du?
sharp, scharf.
blunt, stumpf.
to live, wohnen.
stocking, Strumpf.
to knit, stricken.
worn-out, abgetragen.
interesting, interessant.
always, immer.
instructive, lehrreich.
gentleman, Herr.
to trust, trauen.
writer, Schriftsteller.
to live, leben.
by birth, von Geburt.
to intend, beabsichtigen.
two years ago, vor zwei Jahren.
subject, Gegenstand.
does concern you, geht Sie an.
not in the least, ganz und gar nichts.
lazy, faul.
sluggard, Faulpelz.
the very person, gerade die Person.
to perceive, bemerken.
yonder, jener.

rook, Krähe.
mineral wealth, Mineralreichthum.
inexhaustible, unerschöpflich.
to rely on, sich verlassen auf.
once, ehedem.
to own, besitzen.
well, wohl.
to remember, sich entsinnen.
to beg a person's pardon, Jemanden um Verzeihung bitten.
never mind, schadet nichts.
it is no matter, es ist einerlei.
I shall not suffer him to, ich werde nicht dulden, daß er.
disrespectfully, ehrenrührig.
to give trouble, Mühe machen.
as to, was betrifft.
to depend upon, sich verlassen auf.
to beg leave, um Erlaubniß bitten.
to introduce, einführen.
I chanced to meet, ich traf zufällig.
to lend, leihen.
to borrow, borgen.

Fürwörter.

Uebungs-Aufgabe 1.

This man is my brother; this girl is my sister; and this house is my father's (that of my father). Do you want this knife or that? This one is sharp, but that one is blunt. Where do these people live? They live in Houston Street. Where are those stockings that I have knitted for you? They are worn out. Books that are interesting are not always instructive. Whose dog is this? It is that of the gentleman whose little daughter goes to our school. A man whom I cannot trust is not my friend. Shakespeare, than whom no greater writer ever lived, was an Englishman by birth. I intend to sell the farm (that) I bought two years ago. The subject we are speaking of does not in the least concern you. Socrates was one of the wisest men that ever lived. A man who is always lazy is called a sluggard. You are the very person I was thinking of. The birds whose nest you perceive in yonder high tree are rooks. California, whose mineral wealth is inexhaustible, is a State of the United States. Do you think he is a man I can rely on? I once owned a dog whose name was Hector. I well remember the subject we were talking about last week. I beg your pardon for having broken your umbrella. Never mind; it was an old one. It is no matter what you think about this man; he is a friend of mine, and I shall not suffer him to be spoken of disrespectfully. I am afraid Joseph will give you much trouble; but as to Henry, he will be all right, you may depend upon. I would beg leave to introduce this young man to you. I chanced to meet him at the theatre. Can you lend me fifty dollars? I am sorry to say no! for I want to borrow some money myself. I borrowed thirty dollars from a friend. He lent me his umbrella.

Wörter-Verzeichniß.

geben Sie mir, give me.
Pult, desk.
liegen, to lie.
kennen, to know.
dort auf der Bank, on yonder bench.
der sitzt, who is sitting.
zufrieden, contented.
brauchen, to need.
heißen, are called.
Folgen, consequences.
Betragen, behavior.
umgeben, to associate.
freundlich, friendly.
gegen, toward.
verläumden, to slander.
Rücken, back.
drehen, to turn.
können, to be able.
Beschäftigung, employment.
hübsch, pretty.
Ohrringe, ear-rings.
Geschenk, present.
vorige Woche, last week.
zum Besuch, on a visit.
erblicken, to see.
Dreieinigkeitskirche, Trinity Church.
Bemerkung, remark.
Bezug nehmen auf, to refer to.

Uebungs-Aufgabe 2.

Geben Sie mir jene Bücher, die auf meinem Pulte liegen. Kennen Sie jenen Mann, der dort auf der Bank unter jenem großen Baume sitzt? Es gibt wenig Leute, die zufrieden sind mit dem, was sie haben. Es gibt viele Leute, die mehr Geld haben, als sie brauchen; diese heißen Reiche. Dies sind die Folgen deines schlechten Betragens. Wer einmal stiehlt ist ein Dieb. Ich gehe nicht gern um mit solchen, die freundlich sind so lange sie bei dir sind; aber dich verläumden, sobald du den Rücken gedreht hast. Diejenigen die arbeiten können, werden bald Beschäftigung finden. Wo hast du diese hübschen Ohrringe gekauft? Ich habe sie nicht gekauft; sie sind ein Geschenk der Dame, die vorige Woche bei uns zum Besuch war. Die Kirche, welche du am Ende jener Straße erblickst, heißt die Dreieinigkeitskirche. Die Bemerkung, auf die ich Bezug nehme, wurde von deinem Bruder gemacht.

Lesestück 1.

THE CROWS AND THE WIND-MILL. A FABLE.
(Die Krähen und die Windmühle).

1. It seems there was once a wind-mill—history[1] does not tell us exactly[2] where, and I suppose[3] it is not

much matter¹ where it was—which went round and
round,⁵ day after day.⁶ It did no harm⁷ to anybody.
It never knocked anybody down,⁸ unless⁹ he got¹⁰
under it, within¹¹ reach¹² of its great arms. What
if it did use the air!¹³ It did not hurt¹⁴ the air any,
for the air was just as good for breathing¹⁵ after it
had turned¹⁶ the mill, as it was before.¹⁷

2. But there was a flock¹⁸ of crows in the neighborhood,¹⁹ that took quite a dislike²⁰ to the innocent²¹
mill. They said there must be some mischief about
it.²² They did not at all like its actions.²³ The swinging²⁴ of those long arms, for a whole day at a time,²⁵
really looked suspicious.²⁶ And, besides²⁷ that, it was
rumored,²⁸ in the crow-village,²⁹ that a good-natured³⁰
crow once went to look at³¹ the wind-mill, and that the
great thing hit him a knock³² with one of its arms,
and killed him on the spot.³³

3. Some half a dozen³⁴ of the flock of crows that
felt so much alarmed,³⁵ were talking together at one
time, when the conversation³⁶ turned³⁷ as was generally the case,³⁸ upon the giant³⁹ mill. After talking a
while,⁴⁰ it was thought best⁴¹ to call⁴² a council⁴³ of
all the crows in the country, to see if⁴⁴ some means
could not be hit upon,⁴⁵ by which⁴⁶ the dangerous⁴⁷
thing could be got rid of.⁴⁸

4. The meeting⁴⁹ was called,⁵⁰ and the council met⁵¹
in a corn-field. Such a cawing⁵² and chattering⁵³ was
never before heard in that neighborhood. They appointed⁵⁴ a chairman⁵⁵—perhaps we ought to say⁵⁶ a
chair-*crow*⁵⁷—and other officers,⁵⁸ and proceeded⁵⁹ to
business.

5. As is usual⁶⁰ in public meetings,⁶¹ of this nature,⁶²
there were many different⁶³ opinions⁶⁴ as to⁶⁵ the
question, "What is best to be done⁶⁶ with the windmill?" Most of the crows thought⁶⁷ the wind-mill a
dangerous thing—a *very* dangerous thing indeed—but
then, as to the best mode⁶⁸ of getting rid of it, that
was not so easy a matter to decide.⁶⁹

6. There were some crows at the meeting who were

for going [70] at once [71] right [72] over to the wind-mill—all the crows in a body [73]—and destroying [74] the thing on the spot. [75] In justice [76] to the crow-family in general, [77] however, [78] it ought to be stated, [79] that those who talked about this warlike [80] measure [81] were rather young. [82] Their feathers were not yet fully grown, [83] and they had not seen so much of the world as their fathers had.

7. After there had been much loud talking [84] all over and around [85] the great elm-tree [86] where the council was held, one old crow said he had a few questions to ask. [87] He had a plan to recommend, [88] too—perhaps—and perhaps not. It would depend upon [89] the answers to his questions, whether [90] he gave any advice [91] or not.

8. He would beg leave [92] to inquire, [93] he said, through the chairman, if the wind-mill had ever been known to go away [94] from the place [95] where it was then standing, and to chase [96] crows around the fields, for the purpose [97] of killing them.

9. It was decided [98] that such conduct [99] on the part [100] of the giant had never been heard of. [101] Even [102] the oldest inhabitant, [103] who had heard, from his grandfather, the story about the unhappy fate [104] of the crow that perished [105] by a blow [106] from the giant's arms, did not remember [107] to have heard that the wind-mill had ever made such warlike visits. [108]

10. "How then," the speaker wished to know, "was that crow killed in old times?" The answer was, "By venturing [109] too near the mill."

11. "And is that the only way that any of us are likely to get killed by the wind-mill?" "Yes," the *scare-crow* [110] said, "that is the way, I believe."

And the crows generally [111] nodded [112] their heads, [113] as much as to say, [114] "Certainly, of course." [115]

12. "Well, then," said the old crow who asked the questions, "*let us keep away* [116] *from the mill.* That is all I have to say."

At this [117] the whole council set up a noisy laugh of

approbation.¹¹⁸ The meeting broke up.¹¹⁹ The general opinion was that the advice of the last speaker was, on the whole,¹²⁰ the safest¹²¹ and best that could be given.

13. There are some things,¹²² very harmless¹²³ in themselves,¹²⁴ and very useful too in their proper places,¹²⁵ that will be very apt¹²⁶ to injure¹²⁷ us if we go too near them.¹²⁸ In such cases,¹²⁹ remember¹³⁰ the advice of the wise crow, and *keep away from the mill.*

¹ Die Geschichte, ² genau, ³ ich denke, ⁴ es liegt auch nicht viel daran, ⁵ sich um und um drehte, ⁶ Tag für Tag, ⁷ Leid, ⁸ schlug nieder, ⁹ wenn .... nicht, ¹⁰ gerieth, ¹¹ innerhalb, ¹² Bereich, ¹³ Was lag daran wenn sie auch die Luft benutzte, ¹⁴ that nicht weh, ¹⁵ zum Athmen, ¹⁶ nachdem sie gedreht hatte, ¹⁷ als vorher, ¹⁸ Schaar, ¹⁹ Nachbarschaft, ²⁰ die einen ordentlichen Widerwillen faßten, ²¹ unschuldig, ²² es wäre irgend etwas nicht ganz richtig dabei, ²³ Bewegungen, ²⁴ Schwingen, ²⁵ in Einem fort, ²⁶ verdächtig, ²⁷ überdies, ²⁸ es ging ein Gerücht, ²⁹ Krähendorf, ³⁰ gutmüthig, ³¹ sich anzuziehen, ³² ihr einen Schlag versetzte, ³³ auf der Stelle, ³⁴ etwa ein halbes Dutzend, ³⁵ beunruhigt, ³⁶ Unterhaltung, ³⁷ sich drehte, ³⁸ wie das gewöhnlich der Fall war, ³⁹ Riese, ⁴⁰ nachdem sie eine Weile geschwatzt hatten, ⁴¹ hielt man es fürs Beste, ⁴² zusammenzurufen, ⁴³ Rath, ⁴⁴ ob, ⁴⁵ nicht irgend ein Mittel ausfindig gemacht werden könnte, ⁴⁶ wodurch, ⁴⁷ gefährlich, ⁴⁸ man los werden könnte, ⁴⁹ Versammlung, ⁵⁰ berufen, ⁵¹ kam zusammen, ⁵² Quarken, ⁵³ Schnattern, ⁵⁴ ernannten, ⁵⁵ Vorsitzender, ⁵⁶ wir sollten wohl eigentlich sagen, ⁵⁷ Krähen-Präsidentin, ⁵⁸ Beamte, ⁵⁹ nahmen vor, ⁶⁰ wie es gewöhnlich ist, ⁶¹ bei öffentlichen Versammlungen, ⁶² Art, ⁶³ verschiedene, ⁶⁴ Meinungen, ⁶⁵ mit Bezug auf, ⁶⁶ was thut man am Besten, ⁶⁷ hielten für, ⁶⁸ was die beste Weise betraf, ⁶⁹ das war nicht so leicht zu bestimmen, ⁷⁰ die dafür waren .... zu gehen, ⁷¹ sofort, ⁷² grade, ⁷³ in corpore, ⁷⁴ zu zerstören, ⁷⁵ auf der Stelle, ⁷⁶ zur Rechtfertigung, ⁷⁷ im Allgemeinen, ⁷⁸ jedoch, ⁷⁹ muß bemerkt werden, ⁸⁰ kriegerisch, ⁸¹ Maßregel, ⁸² noch etwas sehr jung, ⁸³ noch nicht ganz ausgewachsen, ⁸⁴ nachdem viel lautes Geschwätz stattgefunden hatte, ⁸⁵ ringsum, ⁸⁶ Ulmbaum, ⁸⁷ zu stellen, ⁸⁸ zu empfehlen, ⁸⁹ es käme an auf, ⁹⁰ ob, ⁹¹ Rath, ⁹² sie möchte so frei sein, ⁹³ zu fragen, ⁹⁴ ob man wüßte, daß die Windmühle je weggegangen wäre, ⁹⁵ Stelle, ⁹⁶ und gejagt hätte, ⁹⁷ in der Absicht, ⁹⁸ man entschied, ⁹⁹ Verfahren, ¹⁰⁰ von Seiten, ¹⁰¹ man nie gehört hätte, ¹⁰² selbst, ¹⁰³ Einwohner, ¹⁰⁴ Schicksal, ¹⁰⁵ umgekommen, ¹⁰⁶ Schlag, ¹⁰⁷ erinnerte nicht, ¹⁰⁸ feindselige Nachstellungen, ¹⁰⁹ dadurch, daß sie sich wagte, ¹¹⁰ einschüchternde Krähe (Vogelscheuche), ¹¹¹ sammt und sonders, ¹¹² nickten, ¹¹³ mit den Köpfen, ¹¹⁴ als wollten sie sagen, ¹¹⁵ natürlich, ¹¹⁶ laßt uns fern bleiben, ¹¹⁷ hierauf, ¹¹⁸ gab lachend seine Zustimmung, ¹¹⁹ löste sich auf, ¹²⁰ im Ganzen genommen, ¹²¹ sicherste, ¹²² Manches, ¹²³ harmlos, ¹²⁴ an sich, ¹²⁵ am geeigneten Platze, ¹²⁶ geeignet, ¹²⁷ schaden, ¹²⁸ wenn wir ihm zu nahe kommen, ¹²⁹ Fällen, ¹³⁰ denke an.

Lesestück 2.

THE ANT AND THE CRICKET. A FABLE IN PROSE.

Die Ameise und die Grille.—Eine Fabel in Prosa.

1. On the approach[1] of winter a company[2] of ants were busily[3] employed[4] in collecting[5] a supply[6] of food,[7] which they kept,[8] for a time,[9] at the doors of their country dwelling,[10] and then stored away[11] in chambers[12] below ground.[13]

2. A cricket, who had chanced to outlive[14] the summer, and was now, wet[15] and shivering with cold,[16] ready to starve with hunger,[17] approached[18] the ants with great humility,[19] and begged[20] that they would relieve her wants[21] with one mouthful[22] of food, and give her shelter[23] from the storm.[24]

3. "But how is it,"[25] said one of the ants, "that you have not taken pains[26] to provide[27] yourself a house, and to lay in[28] a supply of food for the winter, as we have done?"

4. "Alas,[29] friends," said she, "I needed[30] no house to live in in summer; and I passed away[31] the time merrily[32] and pleasantly,[33] in drinking, singing, and dancing, and never once[34] thought of winter."

5. "If that be the case,"[35] replied the ant, laughing, "all I have to say, is, that they who drink, sing, and dance all summer, must starve[36] in winter. We ants never borrow,[37] and we never lend."[38]

6. Moral.—Do not, like the silly[39] cricket, waste[40] all your time in play and idle amusement, but store your mind with knowledge,[41] which, like the hoard[42] of the industrious ants, will be of use[43] to you in the winter of adversity.[44]

7. "Go to the ant, thou sluggard; consider her ways, and be wise; which, having no guide, overseer, or ruler, provideth her meat in the summer, and gathereth her food in the harvest."[45]

THE ANT AND THE CRICKET. A Fable in Verse.

1. A silly young cricket, accustomed [46] to sing
Through the warm sunny months of gay [47] summer and spring,
Began to complain, [48] when he found that, at home,
His cupboard [49] was empty, [50] and winter was come:
Not a crumb [51] to be found [52]
On the snow-covered [53] ground;
Not a flower could he see,
Not a leaf on a tree:
"Oh! what will become," [54] says the cricket, "of me?" [55]

2. At last, by starvation [56] and famine [57] made bold,
All dripping with wet, [58] and all trembling with [59] cold,
Away he set off [60] to a miserly [61] ant,
To see if, to keep him alive, [62] he would grant [63]
Him shelter from rain,
And a mouthful [64] of grain, [65]
He wished only to borrow;
He'd repay [66] it to-morrow;
If not, he must die of starvation and sorrow. [67]

3. Says the ant to the cricket, "I'm your servant [68] and friend,
But we ants never borrow; we ants never lend.
But tell me, dear cricket, did you lay nothing by [69]
When the weather was warm?" Quoth [70] the cricket,
"Not I!
My heart was so light [71]
That I sang day and night,
For all nature looked gay."
"You sang, sir, you say?
Go then," says the ant, "and dance winter away."

4. Thus ending, [72] he hastily lifted the wicket, [73]
And out of the door turned [74] the poor little cricket.
Folks call this a *fable:* I'll warrant [75] it *true:*
Some crickets have *four* legs, and some have but *two*.

¹ Beim Herannahen, ² Schaar, ³ eifrig, ⁴ beschäftigt, ⁵ zu sammeln, ⁶ Vorrath, ⁷ Lebensmittel, ⁸ aufbewahrten, ⁹ eine Zeit lang, ¹⁰ Landhaus, ¹¹ aufspeicherten, ¹² Kammern, ¹³ unter der Erde, ¹⁴ welche zufällig überlebt hatte, ¹⁵ naß, ¹⁶ vor Kälte zitternd, ¹⁷ nahe daran zu verhungern, ¹⁸ näherte sich, ¹⁹ sehr demüthig, ²⁰ bat, ²¹ man möchte ihre Noth lindern, ²² Mundvoll, ²³ Schutz, ²⁴ vor dem bösen Wetter, ²⁵ wie geht es zu? ²⁶ daß du dir keine Mühe gegeben hast, ²⁷ dir ein Haus einzurichten, ²⁸ einzulegen, ²⁹ ach! ³⁰ brauchte, ³¹ brachte ... hin, ³² lustig, ³³ vergnügt, ³⁴ nicht einmal, ³⁵ wenn das der Fall ist, ³⁶ darben, ³⁷ borgen nie (von Andern), ³⁸ leihen (Andern) nie, ³⁹ thöricht, ⁴⁰ verschwende, ⁴¹ sammle für deinen Geist Kenntnisse, ⁴² Vorrath, ⁴³ von Nutzen, ⁴⁴ Unglück, ⁴⁵ Sprüche Sal. 6, 6—8, ⁴⁶ gewohnt, ⁴⁷ heiter, ⁴⁸ klagen, ⁴⁹ Küchenschrank, ⁵⁰ leer, ⁵¹ Krume, ⁵² zu finden, ⁵³ schneebedeckt, ⁵⁴ werden, ⁵⁵ aus mir, ⁵⁶ Darben, ⁵⁷ Hungersnoth, ⁵⁸ triefend von der Nässe, ⁵⁹ zitternd vor, ⁶⁰ machte sich auf den Weg, ⁶¹ geizig, ⁶² sich am Leben zu erhalten, ⁶³ gewähren, ⁶⁴ Mundvoll, ⁶⁵ Korn, ⁶⁶ wiederbezahlen, ⁶⁷ Noth, ⁶⁸ Diener, ⁶⁹ hast du nichts zurückgelegt? ⁷⁰ sprach, ⁷¹ leicht, ⁷² so schließend, ⁷³ öffnete das Thürchen, ⁷⁴ warf hinaus, ⁷⁵ wette.

Lektion XII.

Frage- und Verneinungssätze. Das Hülfszeitwort to do.—Redensarten.

To look like, to take care, to be about, to be going, to be pleased.

Wörter-Verzeichniß.

painter, Maler.
to paint, malen.
picture, Bild.
two, zwei.
last, vorig.
week, Woche.
when, wann.
them, sie.
why, warum.
saw, sah.
kitchen, Küche.
a little while ago, vor Kurzem.

to see, sehen.
to know how to, können.
to speak, sprechen.
yet, noch.
to begin, anfangen.
to understand, verstehen.
when spoken, wenn es gesprochen wird.
he does not want me to speak, er will nicht, daß ich spreche.
before, ehe.

Frage- und Verneinungssätze.

to buy, kaufen.
clothes, Kleider.
ready made, fertig.
to order, auf Bestellung.
how do you like? wie gefällt Ihnen?
suit, Anzug.
not at all, gar nicht.
not either, auch nicht.
what a taste! welch ein Geschmack!
I do declare! ich bitte dich
to tell, sagen.
soap, Seife.
bad, schlecht.
toothache, Zahnweh.
never, niemals.

to hope, hoffen.
to look like rain, aussehen nach Regen.
to look like, ähnlich sehen.
to take care of, in Acht nehmen.
to spoil, verderben.
to be about, beabsichtigen.
to grow weary, müde werden.
task, Aufgabe.
to impose upon, auferlegen.
to carry, bringen.
complaint, Klage.
to take leave, sich verabschieden.
not the less, nichtsdestoweniger.
to go on, fortfahren.

Uebungs-Aufgabe 1.

The painter paints. What does the painter paint? He paints a picture. He painted two pictures for me last week. When did he paint them? Last week. Where is Charles? Why does not he (don't he) come? I saw him in the kitchen a little while ago. Where did you see him? Do you know how to speak English? I do not know how to speak it yet, but I begin to understand it when spoken to me by my teacher. He does not want me to speak before I understand it better when spoken. Where do you buy your clothes? Do you buy them ready made or to order? How do you like this suit? I do not like it at all. Do you? No, I don't, either. What a taste! I do declare! Fred, go, wash your hands! Didn't I tell you to wash your hands? I did wash them, but the soap is bad. Do you know what toothache is? I do not, I never did, and I hope I never will. Does it look like rain to-day, or do you think the weather will be pleasant? Does not he look very much like his mother? I think he looks more like his father than his mother. Why don't you take care of your health? If you don't take better care of it, you will lose it. I lost my watch because I did not take care of it. Take care, or you will spoil your dress. What are you about to do with your boy? I am going to send him to school in Germany. Some people easily grow weary of a hard task imposed upon them. Why don't you carry your complaints before a magistrate? I did. Well, what did the judge say? He told me that there was no prospect of any good coming out of it. So I took my leave. But it is not the less true that I am right and that I have sufficient ground of complaint. Will you be pleased to see who is at the door? Go on with your reading; I understand every word you say.

Wörter-Verzeichniß.

wie viele, how many.
Sprache, language.
nicht weniger als, no less than.
französisch, French.
dänisch, Danish.
wenn es gesprochen wird, when spoken.
trinken Sie gern? do you like?
Kaffee, coffee.
Thee, tea.
gefällt Ihnen besser? do you like better?
bist du gewesen? were you?
heute Morgen, this morning.
zum Baden, bathing.
ich kann nicht, I do not know how to.
schwimmen, to swim.
zuletzt, last.
Frankreich, France.

das genaue Datum, the exact date.
Ankunft, arrival.
die jüngste Nachricht, the latest news.
Kriegsschauplatz, theatre of war.
geschlagen, defeated.
tapfer, bravely.
gekämpft, fought.
Sieg, victory.
errungen, gained.
fragt nicht viel darnach, does not care much about it.
zerrissen, torn.
bleibt, stays.
erinnerst du? do you remember?
Aussprache, pronunciation.

Uebungs-Aufgabe 2.

Hast du meinen Bruder gesehen? Nein, ich habe ihn nicht gesehen. Wie viele Sprachen sprechen Sie? Ich spreche nicht weniger als vier Sprachen, Deutsch, Englisch, Französisch und Dänisch. Sprechen Sie auch Spanisch? Ich spreche nicht Spanisch, aber ich verstehe es, wenn es gesprochen wird. Trinken Sie gern Kaffee und Thee? Ich trinke gern Kaffee, aber den Thee liebe ich nicht. Welche Sprache gefällt Ihnen besser, die Deutsche oder die Englische? Bist du heute Morgen auf dem Markte gewesen? Ich bin nicht da gewesen. Willst du mit mir zum Baden gehen? Ich kann nicht schwimmen. Wann seid ihr zuletzt in Frankreich gewesen? Ich weiß nicht das genaue Datum unserer Ankunft dort. Hast du die jüngsten Nachrichten vom Kriegsschauplatz gelesen? Haben die Deutschen die Franzosen geschlagen? Die Franzosen haben tapfer gekämpft, aber sie haben nicht einen einzigen Sieg errungen. Hören Sie gern Musik? Ich höre sie sehr gern, aber meine Schwester fragt nicht viel darnach. Wissen Sie, daß Sie Ihren Rock zerrissen haben? Ich weiß nicht, wo die Magd bleibt. Erinnerst du, was ich dir sagte über die Aussprache der englischen Sprache? Ich erinnere nicht Alles.

Lesestück 1.

THE HARD TASK (Die schwere Aufgabe).

Henry. Father, my teacher wishes me to draw[1] the branch[2] of a rose-bush, with one rose on it;[3] but I can not do it.

Father. My son, I do not think[4] your teacher would ask you[5] to do any thing[6] you can not do.

Henry. Well, I have tried[7] and tried to draw it; but it[8] does not look at all like the pattern.[8] I wish you would draw it for me.

Father. Do you think[9] it would be right[10] for me to draw your picture,[11] when your teacher expects[12] you to do it?[13]

Henry. No, sir; but I can never [14] draw that [15] rose like [16] the pattern. I know [17] I can not.

Father. Try again,[18] and then [19] it may not be [20] as difficult [21] as you now [22] think it is. Give it one more trial,[23] and then let [24] me see it.

Henry. Father, I have done [25] it! I have done it! It now looks [26] almost [27] as well as the pattern.

Father. Yes, Henry; you have done [28] it very well. And now, do you not feel much better [29] than you would have felt [30] if I had drawn [31] it for you?

Henry. Yes, father; and now I think I shall know how to [32] draw another [33] picture much better than I have done this.

Father. Yes; every task [34] you perform [35] by your own [36] skill [37] and labor,[38] enables [39] you to perform [40] still [41] greater ones. And remember,[42] my son, that any thing which does not cost you *time,*[43] *thought,*[44] or *labor,* is of little [45] worth.[46]

[1] wünscht, daß ich zeichne, [2] Zweig, [3] darauf, [4] ich denke nicht, [5] würde von dir verlangen, [6] irgend etwas, [7] versucht, [8] es sieht der Vorschrift durchaus nicht ähnlich, [9] meinst du, [10] recht, [11] Bild, [12] erwartet, [13] das du es thust, [14] nie, [15] diese, [16] wie, [17] ich weiß, [18] versuch noch einmal, [19] dann, [20] ist es vielleicht nicht, [21] schwierig, [22] jetzt, [23] mach noch einen Versuch, [24] laß, [25] fertig, [26] sieht aus, [27] beinahe, [28] gemacht, [29] ist dir nicht weit besser zu Muthe, [30] als dir zu Muthe gewesen sein würde, [31] gezeichnet, [32] ich werde—können, [33] noch ein, [34] Aufgabe, [35] du fertig bringst, [36] eigen, [37] Geschicklichkeit, [38] Anstrengung, [39] setzt dich in den Stand, [40] zu verrichten, [41] noch, [42] merke dir, [43] Zeit, [44] Nachdenken, [45] gering, [46] Werth.

Lesestück 2.

THE PHYSICIAN AND THE STUDENT.

Der Arzt und der Student.

1. I was awakened [1] by a hand taking mine, and, opening my eyes, the doctor stood before me.

2. After having felt [2] my pulse, he nodded [3] his head, sat down [4] at the foot of the bed, and looked at me, rubbing [5] his nose with his snuff-box.[6] I have since [7]

learned⁸ that this is always, with him, a sign of satisfaction.⁹

3. "Well! well! what a hurry you were in¹⁰ to leave¹¹ us!" said the doctor, in his half-joking,¹² half-scolding¹³ way. "Why,¹⁴ it was necessary to hold you back with both arms, at least!"

4. "Then you had given up¹⁵ all hope in my case,¹⁶ doctor?" asked I, rather alarmed.¹⁷

5. "Not at all," replied the old physician; "we can't give up that which we have not; and I make it a rule¹⁸ never to hope—but to trust.¹⁹ We are but²⁰ instruments²¹ in the hands of Providence,²² and each of us should say, with Father Ambrose, 'I tend²³ him; God cures him.'"

6. "May He be blessed,²⁴ as well as you," cried I, "and may my health²⁵ come back with the New Year!"

7. The doctor shrugged²⁶ his shoulders. "Begin by asking yourself for its return,"²⁷ resumed²⁸ he, bluntly.²⁹ "God has given it to you, and it is your good sense,³⁰ not chance,³¹ that must keep it for you. One would think, to hear people talk, that sickness comes upon us like the rain or the sunshine, without our having³² a word to say in the matter.³³ Before we complain³⁴ because we are ill, we should feel assured³⁵ that we have done our best to be well."

8. I was about³⁶ to smile, but the doctor looked angry.³⁷ "Ah! you think I am joking,"³⁸ resumed he, raising his voice;³⁹ "but tell me, then, which of us gives his health the same attention that he gives to his business? Do you take the same care of³⁹ your strength as of your money? Do you avoid⁴⁰ excess⁴¹ and imprudence⁴² in the one case, with the same care⁴³ that you do extravagance⁴⁴ and foolish speculations in the other?

9. "Let me ask you farther.⁴⁵ Do you keep as regular accounts of your mode of living as of your income? Do you consider,⁴⁶ every evening, what has been wholesome⁴⁷ or unwholesome for you? You may

smile; but have you not brought this illness upon yourself by a thousand indiscretions?"[48]

10. I began to protest against this, and asked him to point out these indiscretions. The old doctor spread out[49] his fingers, and began to reckon[50] upon them, one by one.

11. "*First*," cried he, "want of exercise.[51] You live here like a mouse in a cheese, without air, motion,[52] or change.[53] Consequently,[54] the blood circulates badly; the muscles,[55] being inactive, do not receive their share[56] of nutrition;[57] the stomach[58] flags;[59] and the brain grows weary.

12. "*Second:* Irregular food. Caprice[60] is your cook—your stomach a slave, who must accept what you give it, but who presently[61] takes a sullen[62] revenge, like all slaves.

13. "*Third:* Sitting up late. Instead of using the night for sleep, you spend it in reading: your bedstead is a book-case,[63] your pillow[64] a desk! At the time when the wearied brain asks[65] for rest, you impose[66] the severest[67] labors upon it; and you are surprised to find it the worse[68] for them the next day.

14. "*Fourth:* Luxurious habits. Shut up[69] in your attic,[70] you insensibly[71] surround[72] yourself with a thousand enervating[73] indulgences.[74] You must have list[75] for your door, a blind for your window, a carpet for your feet, an easy-chair[76] stuffed with wool for your back, your fire lit[77] at the first sign of cold, and a shade[78] to your lamp, and thanks to all these precautions,[79] the least draught of air[80] makes you take cold;[81] common chairs give you no rest, and you must wear spectacles[82] to aid your near-sightedness[83] or to support[84] the light of day. You have thought you were acquiring[85] comforts, and you have only contracted[86] infirmities.[87]

"*Fifth:*—"

15. "Ah! enough, enough, doctor!" cried I. "Pray, do not carry[88] your examination farther. Do not attach[89] a sense of remorse[90] to each of my plea-

sures." The old doctor rubbed his nose with his snuff-box. He was evidently⁹¹ pleased that I felt the rebuke.⁹²

16. "You see," said he more gently, and rising at the same time, "you would escape⁹³ from the truth. You shrink from⁹⁴ inquiring⁹⁵—a proof that you are guilty. But, my friend, do not go on⁹⁶ laying the blame⁹⁷ on Chance or Time."

17. Thereupon he again felt my pulse, and took his leave,⁹⁸ declaring that his duties were at an end, and that the rest depended upon myself. When the doctor had gone, I set about⁹⁹ reflecting upon what he had said.

18. Although his words were, perhaps, too sweeping,¹⁰⁰ they were not the less true in the main.¹⁰¹ How often we accuse chance of an illness, the origin of which¹⁰² we should seek in ourselves! And are not we equally¹⁰³ neglectful¹⁰⁴ of what is far more important— the proper means¹⁰⁵ of preserving the health of the soul? It is, indeed, true that our diseases, whether of mind or of body, are generally the fruit of our follies or vices,¹⁰⁶ and every one of us, within the narrow limits¹⁰⁷ of human capability,¹⁰⁸ himself makes his own disposition,¹⁰⁹ character, and permanent¹¹⁰ condition.

SOUVESTRE.

---

¹ Wurde erweckt, ² nachdem er gefühlt hatte, ³ nickte, ⁴ setzte sich nieder, ⁵ reizend, ⁶ Schnupftabacksdose, ⁷ seitdem, ⁸ erfahren, ⁹ Zufriedenheit, ¹⁰ in welcher Eile waren Sie, ¹¹ verlassen, ¹² halb scherzend, ¹³ halb ernst (scheltend), ¹⁴ ei! ¹⁵ so hatten Sie also aufgegeben, ¹⁶ Fall, ¹⁷ fast erschrocken, ¹⁸ ich mache es mir zur Regel, ¹⁹ vertrauen, ²⁰ nur, ²¹ Werkzeuge, ²² Vorsehung, ²³ pflege, ²⁴ gepriesen, ²⁵ Gesundheit, ²⁶ zuckte, ²⁷ Wiederkehr, ²⁸ fuhr fort, ²⁹ barsch, ³⁰ Verstand, ³¹ Zufall, ³² ohne daß wir hätten, ³³ Sache, ³⁴ wir uns beklagen, ³⁵ versichert, ³⁶ im Begriff, ³⁷ zornig, bös, ³⁸ mit gebebener Stimme, ³⁹ geben sie ebenso gut Acht auf, ⁴⁰ meiden, ⁴¹ Ausschweifung (Uebermaß), ⁴² Unvorsichtigkeit, ⁴³ Sorgfalt, ⁴⁴ Verschwendung, ⁴⁵ weiter, ⁴⁶ denken Sie nach über, ⁴⁷ gesund, ⁴⁸ Unvorsichtigkeiten, ⁴⁹ streckte aus, ⁵⁰ rechnen, ⁵¹ Mangel an Bewegung, ⁵² Bewegung, ⁵³ Abwechselung, ⁵⁴ folglich, ⁵⁵ Muskeln, ⁵⁶ Antheil, ⁵⁷ vom Ernährungsproceß, ⁵⁸ Magen, ⁵⁹ arbeitet träge, ⁶⁰ Laune, ⁶¹ plötzlich, ⁶² finster, ⁶³ Bücherschrank, ⁶⁴ Korkkissen, ⁶⁵ verlangt nach, ⁶⁶ legen Sie ihm auf, ⁶⁷ die hartesten, ⁶⁸ um so viel schlimmer, ⁶⁹ eingesperrt, ⁷⁰ Dachstube, ⁷¹ unvermerkt, ⁷² umringen, ⁷³ entnervend, ⁷⁴ Gewohnheiten, ⁷⁵ Luchegge, ⁷⁶ Lehnstuhl (Sorgenstuhl), ⁷⁷ angezündet, ⁷⁸ Schirm, ⁷⁹ Vorsichtsmaßregeln, ⁸⁰ Luftzug, ⁸¹ macht, daß Sie sich erkäl-

ten, ⁸² Brille, ⁸³ Kurzsichtigkeit, ⁸⁴ erträglich zu machen, ⁸⁵ Sie hätten sich erworben, ⁸⁶ zugezogen, ⁸⁷ Schwächen, ⁸⁸ führen, ⁸⁹ fügen Sie nicht hinzu, ⁹⁰ Gewissensbisse, ⁹¹ offenbar, ⁹² Vorwurf, ⁹³ Sie möchten entwischen, ⁹⁴ Sie schrecken zurück vor, ⁹⁵ Untersuchung, ⁹⁶ fahren Sie nicht fort, ⁹⁷ die Schuld aufzuladen, ⁹⁸ nahm Abschied, ⁹⁹ schickte ich mich an, ¹⁰⁰ weitgreifend, ¹⁰¹ Hauptsache, ¹⁰² deren Veranlassung, ¹⁰³ gleicherweise, ¹⁰⁴ nachlässig, ¹⁰⁵ die geeigneten Mittel, ¹⁰⁶ Laster, ¹⁰⁷ Grenzen, ¹⁰⁸ Jahigkeit, ¹⁰⁹ Gemüthsstimmung, ¹¹⁰ bleibend.

Lektion XIII.

Adjektivische Fürwörter.—Redensarten.

To favor, to go for, to send for, to object to.

This, these. That, those. This one, that one. Every, every one, every body, every thing. Each, each one. Some, some one, some body, some thing. Any, any one, any body, any thing. No one, nobody, none, nothing. All. Much, many. Little, few.

Wörter-Verzeichniß.

umbrella, Regenschirm.
to buy, kaufen.
razor, Rasirmesser.
take, bringe.
make it your rule, mache es dir zur Regel.
one thing, Eins.
at a time, zur Zeit.
everything, Jedes.
in its time, zu seiner Zeit.
every word you say, jedes Wort, das Sie sagen.
prone, geneigt.
evil, Böses.
stupid, dumm.
mortal, sterblich.

is studying, studirt.
certain, gewiß.
inalienable, unveräußerlich.
right, Recht.
cane, Spazierstock.
do you want? wollen Sie?
how to appreciate, zu schätzen.
blessing, Segnung.
health, Gesundheit.
lost, verloren.
easier, leichter.
parlor, Empfangszimmer.
will you favor us with? wollen Sie uns zum Besten geben?
lively, lebhaft.

Adjektivische Fürwörter.

at my aunt's, bei meiner Tante.
brothers and sisters, Geschwister.
received, erhielt.
interest in, Interesse an.
cloth, Tuch.
a yard, die Elle.
left, übrig.
difficult, schwierig.
to learn to speak, sprechen zu lernen.
foreign, fremd.
when spoken, wenn sie gesprochen wird.

question, Frage.
really, wirklich.
to go for, holen.
meat, Fleisch.
to send for, holen lassen.
I do not wish you to, ich wünsche nicht, daß Sie.
I dislike, ich mag nicht.
to smoke, rauchen.
if you have no objection, wenn Sie nichts dagegen haben.
I do not object at all, ich habe durchaus nichts dawider.

Uebungs-Aufgabe 1.

This umbrella is not so good as that one. Where did you buy that razor? Take these boots and those shoes to the shoemaker. Make it your rule: One thing at a time, and every thing in its time. I understand every word you say. All men are prone to do evil. Some men are wise, some are stupid, but all are mortal. We are fifty people in this room. Each one of us is studying his lesson. Every body has certain inalienable rights. Not every one knows every thing. Have you any friends in this town? I have some. Did any one of you see my cane? Nobody has seen your cane. Do you want some bread and butter? I do not want any bread, I want some milk. None know better how to appreciate the blessings of health than those who have lost it. Can any one of you tell me which way I must go to Hamilton Ferry? Nothing is easier than this. There was somebody in the parlor. Did you see anybody? Will you favor us with some music? Let us have something lively. I don't understand anything you say. I was at my aunt's with my brothers and sisters; each one of us received a present. No one takes more interest in this young man than I do. How much does this cloth cost a yard?

There is not much left. It is much more difficult to learn to speak a foreign language than to learn to understand it when spoken. How many lessons can you give me? How much time will it take me to learn English? That is a difficult question to answer. Some learn it with but little difficulty, but some find it very difficult. There are but few people who are really happy. Will you go for some meat? I went for a doctor yesterday; there was some one sick in our house. I shall send for some beer, if you wish any. I do not wish you to send for any; I dislike beer. I shall smoke a cigar, if you have no objection. I do not object at all. I have no objection whatever.

Wörter-Verzeichniß.

Kamm, comb.
Bürste, brush.
gehören mir, are mine.
Halstuch, necktie.
hübsch, pretty.
Hosenträger, suspenders.
gefallen mir, suit me.
Nachricht, news.
gießen, to pour.
Flasche, bottle.
Krug, pitcher, jug.
diese beiden, these two.
der ältere, the elder.
ebenso, just as.
Pflicht, duty.
Nächster, neighbor.
beistehen, to help.
ist verkehrt gegangen, has gone wrong.
hast du gemacht, did you do?
befehlen, to tell.
eine Handvoll, a handful of.
sich erfreuen, to enjoy.
Gesundheit, health.
wüßte, knew.

thät, would do.
manchmal, sometimes.
Ehre, honor.
wünschen Sie? do you want?
noch mehr, some more.
darf ich Sie bitten um? may I ask you for?
es hat mir Jemand gesagt, somebody told me.
daß du wolltest, that you wanted to.
Paket, package.
errathen, to guess.
was willst du anfangen? what are you going to do?
das geht dich nichts an, that's none of your business.
sogenannt, so-called, would-be.
Welt, world.
lange, for a long time.
Kummer, sorrow.
Feind, enemy.
Himmel, heaven.

Uebungs-Aufgabe 2.

Dieser Ball ist nicht so gut wie jener. Diese Kämme und jene Bürsten gehören mir. Dies Halstuch ist nicht hübsch, aber jene Hosenträger gefallen mir. Wo hast du diese Nachricht gehört? Gieße den Wein in diese Flaschen und das Bier in jene Krüge. Welcher von diesen beiden Knaben ist der ältere? Dieser ist ebenso alt, als jener. Es ist eines jeden Menschen Pflicht, seinem Nächsten beizustehen. Ein Jeder ist sich selbst der Nächste. Alles ist verkehrt gegangen. Hast du alles so gemacht, wie ich es dir befohlen habe? Ich habe einem jeden von diesen Kindern zwei Aepfel und eine Handvoll Nüsse gegeben. Ein Jeder von uns erfreut sich guter Gesundheit. Wenn mancher Mann wüßte, wer mancher Mann wär', thät mancher Mann manchem Mann manchmal mehr Ehr'. Wünschen Sie noch mehr Milch in Ihrem Kaffee? Darf ich Sie bitten um den Zucker? Hat Jemand meinen kleinen Hund gesehen? Es hat mir Jemand gesagt, daß du dein Haus verkaufen wolltest. Ist dem so? Was hast du in dem Paket? Etwas sehr Schönes, was Niemand von euch errathen kann. Was willst du mit all diesen Messern anfangen? Das geht dich nichts an. Es gibt viele sogenannte Freunde in der Welt, aber nur wenig treue. Weißt du etwas von Heinrich? Ich habe lange nichts von ihm gehört. Er hat nur wenig Geld und wenig Freunde, aber viel Kummer und viele Feinde. Alle Menschen sind Kinder eines Vaters im Himmel.

Lesestück 1.

THE GRATEFUL INDIAN (Der dankbare Indianer).

1. Many years ago, when there were but few white men in this country, an Indian went, in the dusk[1] of the evening, to a public-house[2] in a small village[3] called Wilton. He asked the woman to give him some drink and a supper. At the same time, he said he could not pay for them, as he had had no success[4] in hunting.[5] He promised, however, to pay her soon.

2. The woman told him that she had nothing for

him; called him a lazy, good-for-nothing⁶ fellow,⁷ and said she did not work so hard, to throw away⁸ her earnings⁹ upon such creatures¹⁰ as he was.

3. A gentleman who was sitting by, observed¹¹ that the Indian was suffering¹² from hunger and fatigue.¹³ As the Indian turned¹⁴ to leave the house, the gentleman told the woman to supply¹⁵ him with what he needed,¹⁶ and said that he would pay her himself. She did so.

4. When the Indian had finished¹⁷ his supper, he turned to the gentleman, thanked him, and told him that he should remember¹⁸ his kindness,¹⁹ and whenever he was able, would repay²⁰ him.

5. Some years after, the gentleman set out²¹ to visit a city at some distance from Wilton. In order to reach it,²² he was obliged to²³ pass through a wilderness. In the woods,²⁴ he was taken captive²⁵ by an Indian party,²⁶ and carried²⁷ to Canada.

6. When they arrived there, some of the Indians advised²⁸ that he should be put to death,²⁹ and others, that he should be kept as a prisoner. In the meantime,³⁰ he was bound, and kept safely³¹ until they should decide³² what to do with him.

7. One day, when most of the Indians were out hunting, one of them came to him and unbound³³ him. He then gave him a musket and some powder,³⁴ and a bag³⁵ with food³⁶ in it, to strap³⁷ on his back. Having done this, the Indian told him to follow him.

8. They traveled³⁸ for many days toward the south. The Indian preserved³⁹ all the time perfect silence. In the day-time they shot such game⁴⁰ as came in their way for food, and at night they kindled⁴¹ a fire by which they slept.

9. After a journey⁴² of many days, they came one morning to the top⁴³ of a hill,⁴⁴ from which they could see a number of houses, forming⁴⁵ quite a village. The Indian asked the man if he knew that place. He replied, very eagerly,⁴⁶ that it was Wilton.

10. His guide⁴⁷ then reminded⁴⁸ him, that many

years before he had relieved⁴⁹ the wants⁵⁰ of a weary and hungry Indian at a public-house in that place, and added,⁵¹ "I that Indian; now I pay you; go home."

11. Having said this, the Indian left him, and the man joyfully⁵² returned to his home.

¹ Dämmerung, ² Wirthshaus, ³ Dorf, ⁴ Glück, ⁵ auf der Jagd, ⁶ nichtsnutzig, ⁷ Geselle, ⁸ zu verschwenden an, ⁹ Verdienst, ¹⁰ Geschöpfe, ¹¹ bemerkte, ¹² litt, ¹³ Ermattung, ¹⁴ sich wandte, ¹⁵ zu versehen, ¹⁶ nöthig hatte, ¹⁷ beendigt, ¹⁸ erinnern, ¹⁹ Güte, ²⁰ wiedervergelten, ²¹ machte sich auf den Weg, ²² dahinzugelangen, ²³ mußte er, ²⁴ Wald, ²⁵ wurde er zum Gefangenen gemacht, ²⁶ Bande, ²⁷ geschleppt, ²⁸ riethen, ²⁹ daß er hingerichtet werden sollte, ³⁰ inzwischen, ³¹ in sicherem Gewahrsam gehalten, ³² entscheiden, ³³ löste seine Fesseln, ³⁴ Schießpulver, ³⁵ Tasche, ³⁶ Lebensmittel, ³⁷ schnallen, ³⁸ reisten, ³⁹ beobachtete, ⁴⁰ Wild, ⁴¹ zündete an, ⁴² Reise, ⁴³ Gipfel, ⁴⁴ Berg, ⁴⁵ die bildeten, ⁴⁶ freudig erregt, ⁴⁷ Führer, ⁴⁸ erinnerte, ⁴⁹ abgeholfen, ⁵⁰ Noth, ⁵¹ fügte hinzu, ⁵² froh.

Lesestück 2.

KNOWLEDGE IS POWER (Wissen ist Macht).

1. "What an excellent thing is¹ knowledge,"² said a sharp-looking, bustling³ little man, to one who was much older than himself. "Knowledge is an excellent thing," repeated⁴ he. "My boys know more at six and seven years old⁵ than I did at twelve.⁶ They can read all sorts⁷ of books, and talk on⁸ all sorts of subjects.⁹ The world¹⁰ is a great deal¹¹ wiser than it used¹² to be. Everybody knows something of everything now. Do you not think, sir, that knowledge is an excellent thing?"

2. "Why, sir," replied the old man, looking gravely,¹³ "that depends¹⁴ entirely¹⁵ upon the use¹⁶ to which it is applied.¹⁷ It may be a blessing¹⁸ or a curse.¹⁹ Knowledge is only an increase of power,²⁰ and power may be a bad as well as a good thing." "That is what I cannot understand," said the bustling little man. "How can power be a bad thing?"

3. "I will tell you," meekly²¹ replied the old man; and thus he went on:²² "When the power²³ of a horse is under restraint,²⁴ the animal²⁵ is useful²⁶ in bearing

burdens,²⁷ drawing loads,²⁸ and carrying his master;²⁹ but when that power is unrestrained,³⁰ the horse breaks³¹ his bridle,³² dashes to pieces³³ the carriage³⁴ that he draws, or throws³⁵ his rider." "I see," said the little man.

4. "When the water of a large pond³⁶ is properly³⁷ conducted³⁸ by trenches,³⁹ it renders⁴⁰ the fields around⁴¹ fertile;⁴² but when it bursts through⁴³ its banks,⁴⁴ it sweeps everything before it,⁴⁵ and destroys⁴⁶ the produce⁴⁷ of the fields." "I see!" said the little man; "I see!"

5. "When the ship is steered aright,⁴⁸ the sail⁴⁹ that she hoists⁵⁰ enables⁵¹ her sooner to get into port;⁵² but if steered wrong,⁵³ the more⁵⁴ sail she carries,⁵⁵ the further⁵⁶ will she go out of her course." "I see!" said the little man; "I see clearly!"⁵⁷

6. "Well, then," continued the old man, "if you see these things so clearly, I hope⁵⁸ you can see, too,⁵⁹ that knowledge, to be⁶⁰ a good thing, must be rightly applied. God's grace⁶¹ in the heart will render⁶² the knowledge of the head⁶³ a blessing,⁶⁴ but without this, it may prove to us⁶⁵ no better⁶⁶ than a curse." "I see! I see!" said the little man; "I see!"

---

¹ Was für eine herrliche Sache es ist um, ² das Wissen (Kenntnisse), ³ flink, ⁴ wiederholte, ⁵ wenn sie sechs bis sieben Jahre alt sind, ⁶ mit zwölf, ⁷ Arten, ⁸ sprechen über, ⁹ Gegenstände, ¹⁰ Welt, ¹¹ bedeutend, ¹² pflegte, ¹³ mit ernstem Blick, ¹⁴ kommt an, ¹⁵ ganz, ¹⁶ Gebrauch, ¹⁷ angewendet wird, ¹⁸ Segen, ¹⁹ Fluch, ²⁰ eine Machterweiterung, ²¹ sanftmüthig, ²² fuhr folgendermaßen fort, ²³ Kraft, ²⁴ (unter Zügelung) d. i. gezügelt, ²⁵ Thier, ²⁶ nützlich, ²⁷ (im Tragen von, 2c.) d. i. dadurch, daß es Lasten trägt, ²⁸ Lasten zieht, ²⁹ seinen Herrn trägt, ³⁰ ungezügelt, ³¹ zerreißt, ³² Zügel, ³³ schlägt in Stücke, ³⁴ Wagen, ³⁵ wirft ab, ³⁶ Teich, ³⁷ gehörig, ³⁸ geleitet wird, ³⁹ Abzugskanäle, ⁴⁰ macht, ⁴¹ rings umher, ⁴² fruchtbar, ⁴³ durchbricht, ⁴⁴ Ufer, ⁴⁵ reißt es Alles mit sich fort, ⁴⁶ zerstört, ⁴⁷ (Ertrag) Segen, ⁴⁸ richtig gesteuert wird, ⁴⁹ Segel, ⁵⁰ aufhißt, ⁵¹ setzt in den Stand, ⁵² Hafen, ⁵³ wenn es verkehrt gesteuert wird, ⁵⁴ jemehr, ⁵⁵ trägt, ⁵⁶ desto weiter, ⁵⁷ deutlich, ⁵⁸ hoffe, ⁵⁹ ebenfalls, ⁶⁰ um zu sein, ⁶¹ Gnade, ⁶² macht, ⁶³ Kopf, ⁶⁴ zum Segen, ⁶⁵ mag sich für uns erweisen, ⁶⁶ nicht besser.

Lektion XIV.

Das regelmäßige Zeitwort. Vergangene Zeit. Gebrauch des Imperfekts.—Redensarten.

To lay, lie; to favor with, to be in need of, to vent on, to call to mind, to be drowned, to take a seat, to sit down.

Wörter-Verzeichniß.

this morning, heute Morgen.
picking, pflückend.
when, wann.
did you buy? haft du gekauft?
I bought, ich habe gekauft.
last year, voriges Jahr.
I saw, ich sah.
advertised, angezeigt.
papers, Zeitung.
in, zu Hause.
she went out, sie ist ausgegangen.
an hour ago, vor einer Stunde.
he left for, er ging nach.
he was standing, er stand.
by the window, am Fenster.
passed, vorübergiug.
letters, Briefe.
day before yesterday, vorgestern.
barked, bellte.
told, sagte.
to be quiet, ihr solltet ruhig sein.
read, gelesen.
interesting, interessant.
never, niemals.
ever, je.
in the open air, im Freien.
rained, geregnet.
a week ago to-day, heute vor einer Woche.

insured, versichert.
carriages, Wagen.
riders on horse-back, Reiter.
chickens, Hühner.
do you like? magst du?
I used, ich pflegte.
not... any longer, nicht mehr.
tried, versucht.
difficult, schwer.
nonsense! Unsinn!
not at all, ganz und gar nicht.
play, spielen.
butcher, Fleischer.
brought, gebracht.
to lay, legen.
to lie, liegen.
to be in the habit of, die Gewohnheit haben zu.
coffin, Sarg.
to favor with, beehren mit.
to be in need of, nöthig haben.
to vent, auslassen, freien Lauf lassen.
anger, Zorn.
to call to mind, sich erinnern.
incident, Vorfall.
to cling to, sich anklammern an.
capsized, umgeschlagen.
to be drowned, ertrinken.
to listen to, zuhören.

Uebungs-Aufgabe 1.

Charles, where were you this morning? I was in the garden picking flowers. When did you buy this house? I bought it last year. I saw it advertised in the papers. Is your mother in? No sir, she went out an hour ago. He left for Europe last week. He was standing by the window when I passed. I have written three letters; day before yesterday I wrote only one. Our dog barked very loud last night. I told you this minute to be quiet. I have read many interesting books, but I never read one so interesting as this. Did you ever sleep in the open air? I often slept in the open air when I was a soldier. It has rained for more than two days. It rained a week ago to-day. He has insured his life in New York. I insured my life yesterday. I was in the Central Park this morning. There were many carriages and riders on horseback. We bought two chickens in Fulton Market. Do you like fish? I used to like them, but I do not like them any longer. I have tried to learn this lesson, but it is too difficult. Nonsense! You did not try at all. I saw you play with your brother. The butcher has brought the meat. When did he bring it? He brought it an hour ago.

Redensarten.—Where did you lay my book? It lies (is lying) on the table near the stove. A person that is in the habit of telling lies (stories) is called a liar. The two children lay side by side in their coffin. Will you favor me with your company? I was favored by her with one of her sweetest songs. What are you in need of? We are in need of money. It is wrong thus to vent your anger on an innocent creature. He sat down by his mother's side, and gave free vent to his tears. I call to mind an incident of my life which I shall never forget. In sailing down the Elbe river I saw two people who clung to the keel of their boat, which was capsized. A boat was dispatched immediately to save them; but before it could reach them, the two unfortunate persons let go their hold, and were drowned. If you want me to tell you a story you must listen to me attentively. Please to take a seat. Be seated. Sit down in this chair.

Wörter-Verzeichniß.

pflücken, to pick.
nicht weniger, no less.
Pfirsich, peach.
vor einer Stunde, an hour ago.
heute Abend, this evening.
könnte, could.
früh, early.
bitten, to ask.
mittheilen, to inform.
sein würde, would be.
Prediger, minister.
predigen, to preach.
glauben, to believe.
über den Text, on the text.
der verlorene Sohn, the prodigal son.
erfahren, to learn.

wenn ihr wollt, if you want.
vergangene Nacht, last night.
unangenehm, disagreeable.
Traum, dream.
es träumte mir, I dreamed.
Dach, roof.
fallen, to fall.
Hals, neck.
brach, broke.
Portemonnaie, pocket-book.
gefunden, found.
wonach, for which.
liegen, to lie.
es lag, it lay.
Schublade, drawer.
unter, among.
Hemd, shirt.

Uebungs-Aufgabe 2.

Wie viele Birnen hast du gepflückt? Ich habe einen ganzen großen Korb voll gepflückt. Gestern habe ich nicht weniger als zehn Körbe voll von Pfirsichen gepflückt. Was hat deine Schwester dir vor einer Stunde gesagt? Sie hat mir gesagt, daß sie heute Abend nicht zu dir kommen könnte. Hast du meinen Bruder gesehen? Ich habe ihn heute Morgen früh gesehen; er bat mich dir mitzutheilen, daß er zum Mittagessen zu Hause sein würde. Hast du deine Lektion gelernt? Ich habe sie noch nicht gelernt. Welcher Prediger hat heute Morgen gepredigt? Ich glaube, Herr N.; er predigte über den Text vom verlorenen Sohn. Was hast du gesagt, als du diese Nachricht erfuhrst? Sagten Sie etwas? Ich sagte, ihr müßtet fleißiger sein, wenn ihr etwas lernen wollet. Ich habe in vergangener Nacht einen sehr unan=

genehmen Traum gehabt. Es träumte mir, daß ich vom Dache meines Hauses fiel und den Hals brach. Ich habe dein Portemonnaie gefunden, wonach du so lange gesucht hast. Wo hat es gelegen? Es lag in deiner Schublade unter deinen Hemden.

Lesestück 1.

DEATH AND BURIAL OF LITTLE NELL (Tod und Begräbniß der kleinen Nelly).

1. By little and little [1] the old man had drawn back [2] toward the inner chamber, [3] while these words were spoken. He pointed [4] there, as he replied, with trembling [5] lips,
"You plot among you [6] to wean [7] my heart from her. You will never do that—never, while [8] I have life. I have no relation [9] or friend but her [10]—I never had—I never will have. She is all in all to me. It is too late to part [11] us now."

2. Waving them off [12] with his hand, and calling softly to her [13] as he went, he stole [14] into the room. They who were left behind, [15] drew close together, [16] and after a few whispered [17] words—not unbroken [18] by emotion, [19] or easily uttered [20]—followed him. They moved [21] so gently [22] that their footsteps made no noise; [23] but there were sobs [24] from among the group [25] and sounds [26] of grief [27] and mourning. [28]

3. For she was dead. There, upon her little bed, she lay at rest. The solemn [29] stillness [30] was no marvel [31] now. Yes, she was dead. No sleep so beautiful and calm, [32] so free from trace of pain, [33] so fair to look upon. [34] She seemed a creature [35] fresh [36] from the hand of God, and waiting for [37] the breath [38] of life; not one who had lived and suffered [39] death.

4. Her couch [40] was dressed [41] with here and there some winter-berries [42] and green leaves, gathered [43] in a spot [44] she had been used to favor. [45] "When I die, put near me [46] something that has loved the light, and

always had the sky⁴⁷ above it."⁴⁸ These were her words.

5. She was dead. Dear, gentle, patient,⁴⁹ noble⁵⁰ Nell was dead. Her little bird—a poor, slight thing⁵¹ the pressure³² of a finger would have crushed⁵³—was stirring⁵⁴ nimbly⁵⁵ in its cage;⁵⁶ and the strong heart of its child-mistress⁵⁷ was mute⁵⁸ and motionless⁵⁹ forever!⁶⁰

6. Where were the traces of her early cares,⁶¹ her sufferings,⁶² and fatigues?⁶³ All gone. Sorrow⁶⁴ was dead, indeed, in her; but peace⁶⁵ and perfect happiness were born; imaged⁶⁶ in her tranquil⁶⁷ beauty⁶⁸ and profound⁶⁹ repose.⁷⁰

7. And still⁷¹ her former self⁷² lay there, unaltered⁷³ in this change.⁷⁴ Yes; the old fire-side⁷⁵ had smiled⁷⁶ on that sweet face which had passed,⁷⁷ like a dream, through haunts⁷⁸ of misery⁷⁹ and care. At the door of the poor schoolmaster, on the summer-evening, before the furnace-fire,⁸⁰ upon the cold, wet⁸¹ night, at the still bedside of the dying boy, there had been the same mild, lovely look.

8. The old man held one languid⁸² arm in his, and kept the small hand tight⁸³ folded⁸⁴ to his breast for warmth.⁸⁵ It was the hand she had stretched out⁸⁶ to him with her last smile,⁸⁷ the hand that had led⁸⁸ him on through all their wanderings.⁸⁹ Ever and anon⁹⁰ he pressed it to his lips; then hugged⁹¹ it to his breast again; murmuring⁹² that it was warmer now; and as he said it, he looked in agony⁹³ to those who stood around, as if imploring them⁹⁴ to help her.

9. She was dead, and past⁹⁵ all help or need⁹⁶ of it. The ancient⁹⁷ rooms she had seemed to fill with life,⁹⁸ even⁹⁹ while her own was ebbing fast¹⁰⁰—the garden she had tended¹⁰¹—the eyes she had gladdened¹⁰²— the noiseless¹⁰³ haunts of many a thoughtless hour¹⁰⁴— the paths¹⁰⁵ she had trodden,¹⁰⁶ as it were,¹⁰⁷ but yesterday¹⁰⁸—could know her no more.¹⁰⁹

10. "It is not," said the schoolmaster, as he bent down¹¹⁰ to kiss her on the cheek,¹¹¹ and gave his tears

free vent,[112] "it is not in *this* world that heaven's justice[113] ends.[114] Think[115] what earth is, compared[116] with the world to which her young spirit[117] has winged its early flight,[118] and say, if one deliberate[119] wish, expressed[120] in solemn terms[121] above this bed, could call her back to life, which of us would utter[122] it."

11. They were all about her at the time she died, knowing that the end was drawing nigh.[123] She died soon after daybreak.[124] They had read and talked to her in the earliest portion[125] of the night, but as the hours crept on[126] she sank to sleep. They could tell,[127] by what[128] she faintly[129] uttered in her dreams, that they were[130] of her journeyings[131] with the old man; they were of no painful[132] scenes, but of those who had helped them, and used[133] them kindly; for she often said, with great fervor,[134] "God bless you!" Waking,[135] she never wandered in her mind[136] but once,[137] and that was at the sound[138] of beautiful music which she said was in the air. God knows. It may have been.

12. Opening her eyes, at last, from a very quiet sleep, she begged that they would kiss her once again.[139] That done,[140] she turned[141] to the old man, with a lovely smile upon her face[142]—such, they said, as they had never before seen, and never could forget—and clung[143] with both her arms about his neck.[144] They did not know that she was dead, at first.

13. For the rest,[145] she had never murmured[146] or complained;[147] but, with a quiet mind, and manner quite unaltered—save[148] that she every day became more earnest and more grateful to them—she had faded away[149] like the light upon the summer's evening.

---

¹ allmälig., ² hatte sich zurückgezogen, ³ nach dem innern Gemache, ⁴ zeigte, ⁵ bebend, ⁶ ihr schmiedet Pläne unter euch, ⁷ (entwöhnen) losreißen, ⁸ so lange, ⁹ Verwandte, ¹⁰ als sie, ¹¹ trennen, ¹² sie abwehrend, ¹³ ihr sanft rufend, ¹⁴ stahl er sich (sichlich er), ¹⁵ die zurückblieben, ¹⁶ traten einander näher, ¹⁷ geflüstert, ¹⁸ ununterbrochen, ¹⁹ innerer Bewegung, ²⁰ hervorgebracht, ²¹ bewegten sich, ²² leise, ²³ Geräusch, ²⁴ Schluchzen, ²⁵ unter dem Häuflein,

Regelmäßiges Zeitwort. Vergangene Zeit. 93

²⁶ Töne, ²⁷ Trauer, ²⁸ Wehklagen, ²⁹ feierlich, ³⁰ Stille, ³¹ Wunder, ³² ruhig, ³³ von Spuren des Schmerzes, ³⁴ so lieblich anzuschauen, ³⁵ Wesen, ²⁶ jüngst (hervorgegangen), ³⁷ wartend auf, ³⁸ Odem, ³⁹ erlitten, ⁴⁰ Lager, ⁴¹ geschmückt, ⁴² Beeren, ⁴³ gepflückt, ⁴⁴ Stelle, ⁴⁵ die ihr besonders lieb gewesen war, ⁴⁶ leget neben mich, ⁴⁷ Himmel, ⁴⁸ über sich, ⁴⁹ geduldig, ⁵⁰ edel, ⁵¹ kleines Wesen (welches), ⁵² Druck, ⁵³ zerdrückt, ⁵⁴ bewegte sich, ⁵⁵ bebend, ⁵⁶ Käfig, ⁵⁷ liebliche Herrin, ⁵⁸ stumm, ⁵⁹ bewegungslos, ⁶⁰ auf immer, ⁶¹ frühe Sorgen, ⁶² Leiden, ⁶³ Mühsale, ⁶⁴ das Leid, ⁶⁵ Friede, ⁶⁶ eingeprägt, ⁶⁷ (ruhig) friedlich, ⁶⁸ Schönheit, ⁶⁹ tiefe, ⁷⁰ Ruhe, ⁷¹ doch, ⁷² ihr früheres Selbst, ⁷³ unverändert, ⁷⁴ Wechsel, ⁷⁵ heimathliche Stätte, ⁷⁶ hatte angelächelt, ⁷⁷ sich bewegt hatte, ⁷⁸ Schlupfwinkel, ⁷⁹ Elend, ⁸⁰ Kaminfeuer, ⁸¹ (naß) regnerisch, ⁸² leblos, ⁸³ fest, ⁸⁴ gefaltet, ⁸⁵ um sie zu erwärmen, ⁸⁶ ausgestreckt, ⁸⁷ Lächeln, ⁸⁸ geführt, ⁸⁹ Wanderungen, ⁹⁰ immer auf's Neue, ⁹¹ drückte liebkosend, ⁹² flüsternd, ⁹³ ängstlich, ⁹⁴ als ob er sie anflehen möchte, ⁹⁵ überhoben, ⁹⁶ Noth, ⁹⁷ alt, ⁹⁸ zu beleben, ⁹⁹ sogar, ¹⁰⁰ schnell dahin schwand, ¹⁰¹ gepflegt, ¹⁰² erfreut, ¹⁰³ still, ¹⁰⁴ Mußestunde, ¹⁰⁵ Pfade, ¹⁰⁶ betreten, ¹⁰⁷ gleichsam, ¹⁰⁸ gestern noch, ¹⁰⁹ kannten sie nicht mehr, ¹¹⁰ wie er sich niederbeugte, ¹¹¹ Wange, ¹¹² seinen Thränen freien Lauf ließ, ¹¹³ Gerechtigkeit, ¹¹⁴ ihren Abschluß findet, ¹¹⁵ bedenket, ¹¹⁶ verglichen, ¹¹⁷ Geist, ¹¹⁸ seinen frühen Flug genommen hat, ¹¹⁹ wohlüberlegt, ¹²⁰ ausgedrückt, ¹²¹ mit feierlichen Worten, ¹²² aussprechen, ¹²³ herannahte, ¹²⁴ Tagesanbruch, ¹²⁵ im Beginne, ¹²⁶ dahinschlichen, ¹²⁷ schließen, ¹²⁸ aus dem, was, ¹²⁹ leise, ¹³⁰ daß diese handelten, ¹³¹ Wanderungen, ¹³² schmerzlich, ¹³³ behandelt, ¹³⁴ Innigkeit, ¹³⁵ im wachenden Zustande, ¹³⁶ phantasirte sie nie, ¹³⁷ ausgenommen einmal, ¹³⁸ bei dem Klange, ¹³⁹ noch einmal, ¹⁴⁰ als dies geschehen, ¹⁴¹ wandte sie sich, ¹⁴² Antlitz, ¹⁴³ klammerte sich, ¹⁴⁴ bald, ¹⁴⁵ im Uebrigen, ¹⁴⁶ gemurrt, ¹⁴⁷ geklagt, ¹⁴⁸ ausgenommen, ¹⁴⁹ dahingeschwunden.

Lesestück 2.

DEATH AND BURIAL OF LITTLE NELL. (Schluß.)

1. The child who had been her little friend, came there, almost as soon as it was day, with an offering[1] of dried[2] flowers, which he begged them to lay upon her breast.[3] He told[4] them of his dream[5] again, and that it was[6] of her being restored to them,[7] just as she used to be.[8] He begged hard[9] to see her—saying that he would be very quiet,[10] and that they need[11] not fear his being alarmed;[12] for he had sat[13] alone by his younger brother all day long[14] when he was dead, and he had felt glad[15] to be so near him. They let him have[16] his wish; and, indeed, he kept[17] his word, and was, in his childish[18] way,[19] a lesson[20] to them all.

2. Up to that time[21] the old man had not spoken

once,²² except²³ to her, nor stirred²⁴ from the bedside. But, when he saw her little favorite,²⁵ he was moved²⁶ as they had not seen him yet; and he made²⁷ as though²⁸ he would have²⁹ the lad³⁰ come nearer.³¹ Then, pointing³² to the bed, he burst³³ into tears for the first time; and they who stood by, knowing that the sight³⁴ of this child had done him good, left them alone together.

3. Soothing³⁵ him with his artless³⁶ talk³⁷ of her, the child persuaded³⁸ him to take some rest,³⁹ to walk abroad,⁴⁰ to do as he desired him.⁴¹ And, when the day came on which they must remove⁴² her, in her earthly shape,⁴³ from earthly eyes forever,⁴⁴ he led⁴⁵ the old man away, that he might not know⁴⁶ when she was taken from him. They were to⁴⁷ gather⁴⁸ fresh leaves and berries for her bed.

4. And now the bell⁴⁹—the bell she had so often heard by night and day, and listened to⁵⁰ with solemn pleasure,⁵¹ almost as a living voice,⁵² rung⁵³ its remorseless⁵⁴ toll⁵⁵ for her, so young, so beautiful, so good. Decrepit⁵⁶ age,⁵⁷ and vigorous⁵⁸ life, and blooming⁵⁹ youth,⁶⁰ and helpless infancy⁶¹ poured forth⁶²— on crutches,⁶³ in the pride⁶⁴ of strength and health, in the full blush⁶⁵ of promise,⁶⁶ in the mere dawn⁶⁷ of life—to gather⁶⁸ round her tomb.⁶⁹ Old men were there, whose eyes were dim⁷⁰ and senses⁷¹ failing⁷²— grandmothers who might have died⁷³ ten years ago, and still⁷⁴ been old—the deaf, the blind, the lame, the palsied,⁷⁵ the living dead⁷⁶ in many shapes⁷⁷ and forms, to see the closing⁷⁸ of that early⁷⁹ grave.

5. Along⁸⁰ the crowded⁸¹ path they bore⁸² her now, pure⁸³ as the new-fallen⁸⁴ snow that covered⁸⁵ it, whose day on earth had been as fleeting.⁸⁶ Under the porch,⁸⁷ where she had sat when Heaven in its mercy⁸⁸ brought her to that peaceful⁸⁹ spot, she passed again, and the old church received⁹⁰ her in its quiet shade.

6. They carried her to one quiet nook,⁹¹ where she had many and many a time sat musing,⁹² and laid their

burden⁹³ softly on the pavement.⁹⁴ The light streamed on it⁹⁵ through the colored⁹⁶ window—a window where the boughs⁹⁷ of trees were ever rustling⁹⁸ in the summer, and where the birds sang sweetly all day long. With every breath of air⁹⁹ that stirred¹⁰⁰ among those branches in the sunshine, some trembling,¹⁰¹ changing¹⁰² light would fall upon her grave.

7. Earth to earth—ashes¹⁰³ to ashes—dust¹⁰⁴ to dust. Many a young hand dropped in its little wreath¹⁰⁵—many a stifled sob¹⁰⁶ was heard. Some—and they were not few—knelt down.¹⁰⁷ All were sincere¹⁰⁸ and truthful¹⁰⁹ in their sorrow.¹¹⁰

8. The service done,¹¹¹ the mourners¹¹² stood apart,¹¹³ and the villagers¹¹⁴ closed round¹¹⁵ to look into the grave before the pavement-stone should be replaced.¹¹⁶ One called to mind¹¹⁷ how he had seen her sitting on that very spot, and how her book had fallen on her lap,¹¹⁸ and she was gazing¹¹⁹ with a pensive face¹²⁰ upon the sky.

9. Another told how he had wondered much¹²¹ that one so delicate¹²² as she should be so bold;¹²³ how she had never feared to enter the church alone at night, but had loved to linger¹²⁴ there when all was quiet, and even¹²⁵ to climb¹²⁶ the tower-stair¹²⁷ with no more light than that of the moon's rays¹²⁸ stealing¹²⁹ through the loopholes¹³⁰ in the thick, old walls.

10. A whisper went about¹³¹ among the oldest there, that she had seen and talked with angels;¹³² and when they called to mind how she had looked,¹³³ and spoken, and her early death, some thought it might be so indeed.¹³⁴ Thus coming to the grave in little knots,¹³⁵ and glancing¹³⁶ down, and giving place¹³⁷ to others, and falling off¹³⁸ in whispering groups of three or four, the church was cleared,¹³⁹ in time,¹⁴⁰ of all but¹⁴¹ the sexton¹⁴² and the mourning friends.

11. They saw the vault¹⁴³ covered, and the stone fixed down. Then, when the dusk¹⁴⁴ of evening had come on, and not a sound disturbed¹⁴⁵ the sacred¹⁴⁶ stillness of the place—when the bright moon poured

in [147] her light on tomb and monument, on pillar,[148] wall, and arch,[149] and, most of all (it seemed to them), upon her quiet grave—in that calm [150] time, when all outward things [151] and inward thoughts [152] teem [153] with assurances [154] of immortality,[155] and worldly hopes and fears are humbled in the dust [156] before them—with tranquil [157] and submissive [158] hearts, they turned away, and left the child with God.

DICKENS.

[1] Liebesgabe, [2] getrocknet, [3] Brust, [4] erzählte, [5] Traum, [6] daß er davon handelte, [7] daß sie ihnen wiedergegeben sei, [8] gerade so, wie sie früher war, [9] dringend, [10] still, [11] brauchten, [12] daß er sich erschrecken würde, [13] gesessen, [14] den ganzen Tag, [15] hatte sich gefreut, [16] sie gaben nach, [17] hielt, [18] kindlich, [19] Weise, [20] Lehre, [21] bis dahin, [22] einmal, [23] ausgenommen, [24] noch sich entfernt, [25] Liebling, [26] bewegt, [27] that, [28] als ob, [29] er haben wollte, daß, [30] der kleine Bursche, [31] näher, [32] weisend, [33] brach er aus, [34] Anblick, [35] beruhigend, [36] ungekünstelt, [37] Gespräch, [38] überredete, [39] sich etwas Ruhe zu gönnen, [40] fortzugehen, [41] was er von ihm haben wollte, [42] wegschaffen, [43] irdische Hülle, [44] für immer, [45] führte, [46] damit er nicht erfahre, [47] sie sollten, [48] sammeln, [49] die Glocke, [50] der sie gelauscht hatte, [51] mit innigem Vergnügen, [52] Stimme eines Lebenden, [53] ließ erschallen, [54] herzlos (ohne Gewissensbisse), [55] Geläute, [56] hinfällig, [57] Greisenalter, [58] kraftvoll, [59] blühend, [60] Jugend, [61] Kindheit, [62] strömten herbei, [63] Krücken, [64] in der Fülle (Stolz), [65] Blüthe, [66] Verheißung, [67] Morgen, [68] sich zu schaaren, [69] Grab, [70] trüb, [71] Sinne, [72] am Schwinden, [73] hätten sterben können, [74] doch, [75] gichtbrüchig, [76] Lebendigtodte, [77] Gestalten, [78] das Schließen, [79] früh, [80] längs, [81] dichtgedrängt, [82] trugen, [83] rein, [84] frischgefallen, [85] bedeckte, [86] ebenso rasch dahingeschwunden war, [87] Vorhalle, [88] Barmherzigkeit, [89] friedlich, [90] nahm auf, [91] Winkel, [92] in Sinnen vertieft, [93] Bürde, [94] Fliesen, [95] ergoß sich darauf, [96] bunt, [97] Zweige, [98] stets rauschten, [99] Luftzug, [100] sich regte, [101] zitternd, [102] schwankend, [103] Asche, [104] Staub, [105] Kranz, [106] unterdrücktes Schluchzen, [107] knieten nieder, [108] aufrichtig, [109] wahr, [110] Trauer, [111] als die Feierlichkeit vorüber war, [112] Leidtragende, [113] traten beiseite, [114] Dorfbewohner, [115] schlossen sich zusammen, [116] wieder an seinen Platz gelegt, [117] erinnerte sich, [118] Schooß, [119] angeschaut hatte, [120] mit sinnenden Augen, [121] wie er sich sehr gewundert habe, [122] zart, [123] muthig, [124] weilen, [125] sogar, [126] zu erklimmen, [127] Thurmtreppe, [128] Mondstrahlen, [129] die sich stahlen, [130] Ritzen, [131] Ein Geflüster ging rings umher, [132] Engel, [133] ausgesehen, [134] es könne sich wohl so verhalten, [135] Gruppen, [136] blickend, [137] Platz machend, [138] sich entfernend, [139] wurde leer, [140] allmälig, [141] bis auf, [142] Küster, [143] Gewölbe, [144] Dämmerung, [145] unterbrach, [146] feierlich, [147] ergoß, [148] Pfeiler, [149] Spitzbogen, [150] ruhig, [151] Außendinge, [152] innern Gedanken, [153] erfüllt sind (fluthen), [154] Gewißheit, [155] Unsterblichkeit, [156] in den Staub gedemüthigt sind, [157] ruhig, [158] ergeben.

Lektion XV.
Adverbien—der Zeit—des Ortes.

Redensarten: *in time, to remember to, to afford, to earn, to deserve, to be sorry, never mind, no matter, to borrow, to lend, to take pains, to succeed in.*

Wörter-Verzeichniß.

sometimes, mitunter.
less, weniger.
difficult, schwierig.
to be silent, schweigen.
business, Geschäft (Arbeit).
pleasure, Vergnügen.
frank, offen, aufrichtig.
we should, wir sollten.
to despair, verzagen.
people, Leute.
reverse of fortune, Glückswechsel.
to be pitied, zu bedauern.
seldom, selten.
happens, passirt.
that I am cheated, daß ich betrogen werde.
ever, je.
such a noise, solch einen Lärmen.
to trust, trauen.
to betray, verrathen.
ever and again, wiederholt.
to take pains, sich Mühe geben.
to find fault with, etwas auszusetzen finden an. [werden.
to be disappointed, getäuscht
you will come and see us, du wirst uns bald besuchen.
we shall be happy, wir werden uns freuen.
to receive, empfangen.
once, einst.

jump a fence, über eine Einfriedigung springen.
at your house, bei Ihnen.
to-morrow morning, morgen
last, zuletzt. [früh.
to neglect, versäumen.
to improve, sich ausbilden.
to get, bekommen.
a chance, eine Gelegenheit.
please, bitte.
I want, ich will.
at once, sofort.
to obey, gehorchen.
under the most peculiar circumstances, unter den eigenthümlichsten Umständen.
to be lost, zu verlieren.
in time, zu rechter Zeit.
to start, aufbrechen.
train, Zug.
it is I, ich bin's.
to open, aufmachen.
far, weit.
Vienna, Wien. [mir.
Remember me to, grüße von
near and dear, lieb und werth.
neither, keine von beiden.
so do I, ich auch.
neither do I, ich auch nicht.
I like to go, ich gehe gern.
to afford, ausführen.
to earn, verdienen.

than they deserve, als ihnen zukommt.
eulogy, Lobrede.
bestowed, gespendet.
merited, verdient.
supply, Angebot.
hardly, kaum.
demand, Nachfrage.
honesty is the best policy, ehrlich währt am längsten.
rogues, Spitzbuben.
to fall out, sich entzweien.
will get their own, kommen zu dem Ihrigen.
to rise, aufstehen.
wealthy, wohlhabend.
in need, in der Noth.
pitcher, Krug.
I could not help it, ich konnte nicht dafür.
never mind, schad't nichts.
anyhow, doch nur.
long ago, schon lange.
to lend, leihen (Jemandem).

to borrow, leihen (von Jemandem).
tell him to buy, sage ihm, daß er kaufe.
desk, Pult.
no matter, einerlei.
you cannot, Sie dürfen nicht.
seat, Sitz.
occupied, besetzt.
I don't care, es ist mir gleichviel.
to take pains, sich Mühe geben.
to finish, beendigen, fertig machen.
task, Aufgabe.
I did not succeed, es gelang mir nicht.
he succeeds in all, es gelingt ihm Alles (was).
to undertake, unternehmen.
to persuade, überreden.
to abandon, verlassen.
wicked, böse, gottlos.
companion, Gefährte.

Uebungs-Aufgabe 1.

It is sometimes less difficult to speak than to be silent. Children sometimes wish for what is not good for them. First business, then pleasure. My friends always told me that I was too frank. We should never despair. People who always despair after every little reverse of their fortune are to be pitied. It seldom happens to me that I am cheated. Did you ever hear such a noise? I never trusted a man who has betrayed his friend. I told you ever and again that if you do not take more pains, you will never learn English. We often find fault with our friends. It often happens that you will be disappointed. I hope you will soon come and see us. We shall always be happy to receive you. There was once a time when I could jump a fence six feet high. I shall be at your house early to-morrow morning. When did you see John? I saw him last in Berlin. Now is the time to learn. If you neglect now to improve, you will never get a chance again. Please, tell Frank that I want to see him at once. I already told him; but you know he never obeys. When I was in Europe last, it was under the most peculiar circumstances.

Redensarten.—There is no time to be lost; if you want to be in time for the train, you must start now. Who is there? It is I. Please, open the door. I have no time now to see you. How far is it from Berlin to Vienna? It is farther than from Berlin to Rome. Remember me to all that are near and dear to me. Here is an orange and a banana; which do you want? I want neither. I do not want either. My brother wants to learn Spanish, and so do I. He does not understand Spanish, neither do I. I like to go to the opera, but I cannot always afford it. How much money does a painter earn? They sometimes earn more than they deserve to earn. The eulogy bestowed upon this boy was well merited. There is a great supply of coal in the market, but there is hardly any demand. Honesty is the best policy. When rogues fall out, honest men will get their own. Early to bed and early to rise, makes a man healthy, wealthy and wise. A friend in need is a friend indeed. I have broken your pitcher; I am very sorry, but I could not help it. Never mind, it was an old one, anyhow. I wanted to buy another long ago. I want to borrow some money. Can you lend me ten dollars? I cannot. Tell him to buy a desk for me, no matter how much it may cost. You cannot take this seat; it is already occupied. I don't care; I shall take another, then. Where there is a will, there is a way. If you want to learn English, you must take pains. I took great pains to finish my task in time, but I did not succeed. He succeeds in all he undertakes. Did you succeed in persuading him to abandon his wicked companions.

Wörter-Verzeichniß.

Niagarafall, Niagara Falls.
Spaziergang, walk.
begleiten, to accompany.
Augenblick, moment.
begießen, to water.
lange her, a long time ago.
Vaterstadt, native town.
sich verändern, to change.
sehr, very much.
schneller, faster.
zu andern Zeiten, at other times.
naß, wet.
gesund, healthy.
gräßlich, awful, terrible.
Unglück, calamity.
vorig, last.
passirt ist, has happened.
Kessel, boiler.
explodiren, to explode.
nicht weniger, no less.
ums Leben kommen, to perish.
wurden verwundet, were wounded.
Unglücksfall, accident.
sich ereignen, to occur.
beendigen, to finish.
fertig, done.
wenn auch, even though.
Versprechen, promise.
holen, to fetch.
Ort, place.
liegt, is situated.
der letztere, the latter.
getrennt, separated.

Uebungs-Aufgabe 2.

Haben Sie je den Niagara Fall gesehen? Ich habe ihn oft gesehen, aber mein Bruder nie. Willst du mich jetzt auf einem Spaziergang begleiten? Ich habe jetzt diesen Augenblick keine Zeit; ich muß erst meine Blumen begießen. Es ist lange her, daß ich meine Vaterstadt gesehen habe; als ich sie zuletzt sah, hatte sie sich sehr verändert. Bisweilen arbeite ich viel schneller, als zu andern Zeiten. Die nassesten Sommer sind nicht immer die gesündesten. Hast du schon von dem gräßlichen Unglück gehört, das vorigen Sonntag passirt ist? Der Kessel eines Dampfbootes explodirte, und nicht weniger als zweihundert Menschen kamen dabei ums Leben oder wurden verwundet. Solche Unglücksfälle ereignen sich hier nicht selten. Wann werden Sie Ihre Arbeit beendigt haben? Ich werde eher damit fertig sein, als Sie denken. Wenn ich auch manchmal Etwas vergesse, so vergesse ich doch nie ein gegebenes Versprechen. Hier hast du einen Thaler und da ist ein Korb; nun gehe hin und hole mir fünf Pfund von dem besten

Beefsteak beim Schlachter. Wie weit ist es bis zu dem Ort, der dort vor uns liegt. Die Stadt Brooklyn liegt ganz nahe bei New York; sie ist von der letzteren nur durch den East River getrennt.

Lesestück 1.

THE YOUTHFUL WITNESS (Der jugendliche Zeuge).

1. A little girl, nine years of age,[1] was offered[2] as a witness in a court of justice,[3] against a prisoner who was on trial[4] for a crime[5] committed[6] in her father's house.

2. "Now, Emily," said the counsel[7] for the prisoner, "I desire[8] to know if you understand the nature[9] of an oath."[10] "I don't know what you mean," was the simple reply.[11] "There,"[12] said the counsel, addressing[13] the judge,[14] "is anything farther necessary[15] to show[16] that this witness should be rejected?[17] She does not understand the nature of an oath."

3. "Let us see," said the judge. "Come here, my daughter." Encouraged[18] by the kind tone and manner[19] of the judge, the child stepped[20] toward him,[21] and looked[22] confidingly[23] up in his face with a calm,[24] clear[25] eye, and in a manner so artless[26] and frank, that it went straight[27] to the heart.

4. "Did you ever take an oath?"[28] inquired[29] the judge. The little girl stepped back[30] with a look of horror,[31] and the red blood came up in a blush all over her face[32] and neck,[33] as she answered, "No, sir." She thought[34] he intended to[35] inquire if she had ever blasphemed![36]

5. "I do not mean that," said the judge, who saw her mistake;[37] "I mean, were you ever a witness before?" "No, sir; I never was in court before;" was the answer.

6. He handed[38] her the Bible open.[39] "Do you know that book, my daughter?" She looked[40] at it, and answered, "Yes, sir; it is the Bible." "Can you

tell me what the Bible is?" inquired the judge. "It is the word of the great God," she answered.

7. "Well," said the judge, "place [11] your hand upon this Bible, and listen to what [12] I say;" and he repeated,[13] slowly [14] and solemnly,[15] the following oath: [16] "Do you swear [17] that, in the evidence [18] which you shall give [19] in this case,[50] you will tell the truth, the whole truth, and nothing but the truth, and that you ask God to help you?" "I do," she replied.

8. "Now," said the judge, "you have sworn as a witness; will you tell me what will befall you [51] if you do not tell the truth?" "I shall be shut up [52] in the State prison," [53] answered the child. "Anything else?" [54] asked the judge. "I shall never go to heaven,"[55] she replied.

9. "How do you know this?" asked the judge again. The child took the Bible, turned [56] rapidly [57] to the chapter [58] containing [59] the commandments,[60] and pointing to the one [61] which reads,[62] "Thou shalt not bear false witness against thy neighbor," [63] said, "I learned that before [64] I could read."

10. "Has any one talked with you about your being [65] a witness in court [66] here against this man?" inquired the judge. "Yes, sir;" she replied, "my mother heard they wanted me to be [67] a witness, and last night [68] she called[69] me to her room and asked me [70] to tell [71] her the Ten Commandments; and then we kneeled down [72] together; and she prayed [73] that I might understand how wicked [74] it was to bear false witness against my neighbor, and that God would help me, a little child, to tell the truth. And when I came here with father, she kissed me, and told me to remember [75] the ninth commandment, and that God would hear every word that I said."

11. "Do you believe this?" asked the judge, while a tear glistened [76] in his eye, and his lip quivered [77] with emotion.[78] "Yes, sir;" said the child, with a voice and manner that showed her full belief [79] in its truth. "God bless [80] you, my child," said the judge, "you

have a good mother. The witness is competent," he
continued, turning³¹ to the prisoner's counsel. "Were
I on trial ⁸² for my life,⁸³ and innocent ⁸⁴ of the charge ⁸⁵
against me, I would pray God for such a witness as
this. Let her be examined." ⁸⁶

12. She told her story with the simplicity ⁸⁷ of a
child, as she was; but there was that in her manner
and voice which carried conviction of her truthfulness
to every heart.⁸⁸ The counsel for the prisoner asked
her a multitude ⁸⁹ of ingenious ⁹⁰ questions; but in
nothing did she vary ⁹¹ from her first statement.⁹²

13. The truth, as spoken by that little child, was
sublime.⁹³ Falsehood ⁹⁴ and perjury,⁹⁵ on the part ⁹⁶ of
the prisoner, had preceded ⁹⁷ her testimony,⁹⁸ and villainy⁹⁹ had made up ¹⁰⁰ for him a sham defense.¹⁰¹ But
by her testimony falsehood was scattered ¹⁰² like chaff.¹⁰³
The little child, for whom a mother had prayed for
strength to be given her ¹⁰⁴ to speak the truth as it
was before God, broke the cunning ¹⁰⁵ devices ¹⁰⁶ of
matured¹⁰⁷ villainy to pieces, like a potter's ¹⁰⁸ vessel.¹⁰⁹
The strength that her mother prayed for was given
her; and the sublime and terrible ¹¹⁰ simplicity ¹¹¹ with
which she spoke, terrible to the prisoner and his associates,¹¹² was like ¹¹³ a revelation ¹¹⁴ from God himself.

S. H. HAMMOND.

¹ alt, ² wurde vorgeführt, ³ Gerichtshof, ⁴ vor Gericht, ⁵ Verbrechen, ⁶ begangen, ⁷ Anwalt, ⁸ wünsche, ⁹ Bedeutung, ¹⁰ Eid (unter Umständen auch „Fluch"), ¹¹ Antwort, ¹² da haben wir's, ¹³ anredend, ¹⁴ Richter, ¹⁵ bedarf es noch eines Weiteren, ¹⁶ zeigen, ¹⁷ abgewiesen werden sollte, ¹⁸ ermuthigt, ¹⁹ Benehmen, ²⁰ schritt, ²¹ auf ihn zu, ²² blickte, ²³ vertrauensvoll, ²⁴ ruhig, ²⁵ offen, ²⁶ ungezwungen, ²⁷ direkt, ²⁸ hast du je einen Eid geleistet? (kann aber auch heißen: hast du je geflucht), ²⁹ fragte, ³⁰ trat einen Schritt zurück, ³¹ mit einem Ausdruck von Abscheu, ³² eine tiefe Röthe ergoß sich über ihr Antlitz, ³³ Hals, ³⁴ meinte, ³⁵ wollte, ³⁶ gelassen, ³⁷ Irrthum, ³⁸ reichte, ³⁹ aufgeschlagen, ⁴⁰ betrachtete, ⁴¹ lege, ⁴² höre auf das, was, ⁴³ wiederholte, ⁴⁴ langsam, ⁴⁵ feierlich, ⁴⁶ die folgende Eidesformel, ⁴⁷ schwörst du, ⁴⁸ Zeugniß, ⁴⁹ ablegen wirst, ⁵⁰ Rechtsfall, ⁵¹ was deiner wartet, ⁵² eingeschlossen werden, ⁵³ Staatsgefängniß, ⁵⁴ sonst noch etwas, ⁵⁵ Himmel, ⁵⁶ suchte, ⁵⁷ schnell, ⁵⁸ Kapitel, ⁵⁹ enthaltend, ⁶⁰ Gebote, ⁶¹ weisend auf dasjenige, ⁶² lautet, ⁶³ du sollst nicht falsch Zeugniß reden wider deinen Nächsten, ⁶⁴ ehe, ⁶⁵ darüber, daß du sein solltest, ⁶⁶ Gericht, ⁶⁷ man wollte,

ich sollte sein, ⁶⁸ gestern Abend, ⁶⁹ rief, ⁷⁰ forderte mich auf, ⁷¹ aufzusagen, ⁷² knieten nieder, ⁷³ betete, ⁷⁴ gottlos, ⁷⁵ sagte mir, ich solle denken an, ⁷⁶ glänzte, ⁷⁷ zitterte, ⁷⁸ vor Bewegung, ⁷⁹ Glaube, ⁸⁰ seyne, ⁸¹ sich wendend, ⁸² wäre ich angeklagt, ⁸³ auf Tod und Leben, ⁸⁴ unschuldig, ⁸⁵ Anklage, ⁸⁶ man examinire sie, ⁸⁷ Einfalt, ⁸⁸ welches jedes Herz von ihrer Wahrhaftigkeit überzeugte, ⁸⁹ Menge, ⁹⁰ verwickelt, ⁹¹ wich sie ab, ⁹² Aussage, ⁹³ erbaben, ⁹⁴ Lüge, ⁹⁵ Meineid, ⁹⁶ von Seiten, ⁹⁷ waren vorausgegangen, ⁹⁸ Zeugniß, ⁹⁹ Schurkerei, ¹⁰⁰ zu Stande gebracht, ¹⁰¹ elende Schein-Vertheidigung, ¹⁰² zerstob, ¹⁰³ Syrcu, ¹⁰⁴ daß ihr Kraft gegeben werden möchte, ¹⁰⁵ listig, ¹⁰⁶ Anschläge, ¹⁰⁷ abgefeimt, ¹⁰⁸ Töpfer, ¹⁰⁹ Gefäß, ¹¹⁰ schrecklich, ¹¹¹ Einfalt, ¹¹² Spießgesellen, ¹¹³ wie, ¹¹⁴ Offenbarung.

Lesestück 2.

THE YOUNG SHEPHERD (Der junge Schäfer).

1. Sha-Abbas, king of Persia, being on his travels,¹ withdrew ² from his retinue,³ in order to visit the country, and there, without being known,⁴ to behold ⁵ mankind ⁶ in all their native ⁷ freedom. He took with him only one of his officers,⁸ as an attendant.⁹

2. "I am weary," ¹⁰ said he, "of living among ¹¹ sycophants,¹² who take all occasions ¹³ to overreach,¹⁴ while they flatter ¹⁵ me. I am determined ¹⁶ to visit husbandmen ¹⁷ and shepherds, who know nothing of me."

3. He traveled with his confidant ¹⁸ through several¹⁹ villages ²⁰ where the peasants ²¹ were dancing, and was overjoyed ²² to see that his subjects,²³ though at such a distance from court, had their diversions,²⁴ and those so ²⁵ innocent and inexpensive.²⁶

4. After refreshing himself ²⁷ in a cottage,²⁸ he crossed ²⁹ a meadow,³⁰ enameled ³¹ with flowers, which decked ³² the borders ³³ of a limpid ³⁴ stream.³⁵ Here he spied ³⁶ a young shepherd, playing on his pipe ³⁷ beneath ³⁸ a shady elm,³⁹ while his flocks ⁴⁰ were grazing ⁴¹ around him.

5. The king accosts ⁴² him, surveys him closely,⁴³ finds his aspect ⁴⁴ agreeable, and his air,⁴⁵ though easy ⁴⁶ and natural, yet graceful ⁴⁷ and majestic.⁴⁸ The simple habit ⁴⁹ in which the shepherd was clad,⁵⁰ did not in the least diminish ⁵¹ the agreeableness of his

person.[52] The king supposed him[53] at first to be a youth[54] of illustrious birth,[55] who had disguised[56] himself; but he learned[57] from the shepherd that his parents dwelt[58] in an adjacent[59] village, and that his name was Alibeg.

6. The more[60] questions[61] the king put[62] to him, the more[63] he admired[64] the strength[65] and solidity[66] of his genius.[67] His eyes were lively,[68] and beaming[69] with intelligence; his voice was sweet and melodious; his features[70] were not rude,[71] neither[72] were they soft and effeminate.[73] The shepherd, though sixteen years of age, did not seem conscious[74] of those perfections[75] which were conspicuous[76] to others. He imagined[77] that his thoughts, his conversation, and his person were not unlike[78] those of his neighbors.

7. The king frequently smiled[79] at the innocent freedom[80] of the youth, who gave him much information about the state[81] of the people. He gave the officer who accompanied[82] him a private[83] signal[84] not to discover[85] that he was the king, for fear[86] that Alibeg, if he once knew with whom he conversed, would lose in an instant[87] his wonted[88] freedom, and all his native graces.[89]

8. "I am now convinced,"[90] said the prince to his attendant, "that nature is as beautiful in the lowest state[91] as in the highest. No monarch's son was ever born with nobler faculties[92] than this young shepherd. I should think[93] myself infinitely[94] happy, had I a son equally[95] handsome, intelligent and ingenuous.[96] I will have him educated[97] at my own court."

9. The king, accordingly, took Alibeg away with him; and the youthful shepherd was much surprised[98] to find that a prince should be so pleased[99] with his conversation. Taken to court, he was instructed[100] by proper tutors[101] in all the graces[102] which add[103] to manly beauty, and in all the arts[104] and sciences which adorn[105] the mind.[106].

10. The grandeur[107] of the court, and a sudden change of fortune[108] in some measure[109] influenced[110]

the temper[111] of Alibeg. His crook,[112] his pipe, and shepherd's dress were now forsaken;[113] and instead of them[114] he appeared in a purple robe,[115] embroidered[116] with gold, and a turban enriched[117] with jewels. Alibeg was handsomer than any other man at court. He was qualified[118] to transact[119] the most important affairs;[120] and his master, placing the utmost[121] confidence[122] in his integrity,[123] soon conferred[124] on him the post of jewel-keeper[125] and treasurer[126] of his household.

11. During the whole reign[127] of the great Sha-Abbas, Alibeg's reputation[128] daily increased.[129] But as he advanced in years, he frequently recalled to mind[130] his former state of life,[131] and always with regret.[132] "Oh, happy days!" would he whisper[133] to himself; "oh, innocent days! days wherein I tasted[134] true joys without danger; days since which I never saw one so pleasant; shall I not see you any more? He who has deprived[135] me of you, by making me thus great, has utterly undone[136] me."

12. Alibeg, after a long absence,[137] revisited[138] his native village.[139] Here he gazed[140] with fondness[141] on those places where he had formerly danced, sung, and tuned[142] his pipe with his fellow-swains.[143] He made presents to all his friends and relations;[144] but advised[145] them, as they valued[146] their peace of mind,[147] never to resign[148] their rural[149] pleasures, never to expose[150] themselves to the anxieties[151] and misfortunes of a court. Alibeg felt the weight[152] of those misfortunes soon after the death of his good master Sha-Abbas.

---

[1] als er sich auf Reisen befand, [2] zog sich zurück, [3] Gefolge, [4] ohne erkannt zu werden, [5] zu sehen, [6] Menschheit, [7] angeboren, [8] Officier (Beamter), [9] Begleiter, [10] müde, [11] unter, [12] Schmarotzer, [13] die alle Gelegenheit wahrnehmen, [14] zu übervortheilen, [15] schmeicheln, [16] entschlossen, [17] Ackerbauer, [18] Vertrauter, [19] mehrere, [20] Dörfer, [21] Bauern, [22] äußerst erfreut, [23] Unterthanen, [24] Vergnügungen, [25] und die noch dazu, [26] billig, [27] nachdem er sich erfrischt hatte, [28] Hütte, [29] schritt er über, [30] Wiese, [31] umkränzt von, [32] schmückten, [33] Ufer, [34] klar, [35] Bach, [36] erblickte, [37] Flöte, [38] unter, [39] einem schattigen Ulmbaum, [40] Heerde, [41] weideten, [42] redet an, [43] faßt ihn fest in's Auge, [44] Aeußeres,

⁴⁵ Mienen, ⁴⁶ gefällig, ⁴⁷ anmuthig, ⁴⁸ gebietend, ⁴⁹ Gewand, ⁵⁰ gekleidet, ⁵¹ that nicht den mindesten Abbruch, ⁵² seiner angenehmen Persönlichkeit, ⁵³ hielt ihn für, ⁵⁴ Jüngling, ⁵⁵ von edler Abkunft, ⁵⁶ verkleidet, ⁵⁷ erfuhr, ⁵⁸ wohnten, ⁵⁹ benachbart, ⁶⁰ je mehr, ⁶¹ Fragen, ⁶² richtete, ⁶³ desto mehr, ⁶⁴ bewunderte er, ⁶⁵ Kraft, ⁶⁶ Fülle, ⁶⁷ Geist, ⁶⁸ lebhaft, ⁶⁹ strahlend vor, ⁷⁰ Gesichtszüge, ⁷¹ gemein, ⁷² auch nicht, ⁷³ weibisch, ⁷⁴ schien sich nicht bewußt zu sein, ⁷⁵ Vorzüge, ⁷⁶ in die Augen fallend, ⁷⁷ er meinte, ⁷⁸ unähnlich, ⁷⁹ lächelte, ⁸⁰ Ungezwungenheit, ⁸¹ Lage, ⁸² begleitete, ⁸³ geheim, ⁸⁴ Zeichen, ⁸⁵ zu entdecken (verrathen), ⁸⁶ aus Furcht, ⁸⁷ auf der Stelle, ⁸⁸ gewohnt, ⁸⁹ natürliche Anmuth, ⁹⁰ überzeugt, ⁹¹ im niedrigsten Stande, ⁹² Eigenschaften, ⁹³ schätzen, ⁹⁴ unendlich, ⁹⁵ gleich, ⁹⁶ geistreich, ⁹⁷ ich werde ihn erziehen lassen, ⁹⁸ erstaunt, ⁹⁹ einen solchen Gefallen finden sollten an, ¹⁰⁰ unterrichtet, ¹⁰¹ von passenden Lehrern, ¹⁰² seiner Anstand, ¹⁰³ erhöhen (hinzufügen zu), ¹⁰⁴ Künste, ¹⁰⁵ zieren, ¹⁰⁶ Geist, ¹⁰⁷ Pracht, ¹⁰⁸ plötzlicher Glückswechsel, ¹⁰⁹ bis zu einem gewissen Grade, ¹¹⁰ wirkte auf, ¹¹¹ Gemüth, ¹¹² Stab, ¹¹³ abgelegt, ¹¹⁴ statt deren, ¹¹⁵ Purpurgewand, ¹¹⁶ gestickt, ¹¹⁷ verziert, ¹¹⁸ geschickt, ¹¹⁹ zu leiten, ¹²⁰ Angelegenheiten, ¹²¹ größte, ¹²² Vertrauen, ¹²³ Ehrlichkeit (Unbescholtenheit), ¹²⁴ übertrug, ¹²⁵ Juwelenbewahrer, ¹²⁶ Schatzmeister, ¹²⁷ Regierung, ¹²⁸ Ruf, ¹²⁹ stieg, ¹³⁰ rief in's Gedächtniß, ¹³¹ Lebenslage, ¹³² Bedauern, ¹³³ flüsterte er, ¹³⁴ schmeckte, ¹³⁵ der mich eurer beraubt hat, ¹³⁶ hat mich gänzlich vernichtet, ¹³⁷ Abwesenheit, ¹³⁸ besuchte wieder, ¹³⁹ Dorf seiner Geburt, ¹⁴⁰ blickte, ¹⁴¹ mit inniger Freude, ¹⁴² gespielt, ¹⁴³ Kameraden, ¹⁴⁴ Verwandte, ¹⁴⁵ rieth, ¹⁴⁶ wenn sie werthschätzen, ¹⁴⁷ ihren Seelenfrieden, ¹⁴⁸ aufzugeben, ¹⁴⁹ ländlich, ¹⁵⁰ sich auszusetzen, ¹⁵¹ dem unruhigen Treiben, ¹⁵² Gewicht.

Lesestück 3.

THE YOUNG SHEPHERD. (Schluß.)

1. Sha-Sephi succeeded[1] his father. Some envious,[2] artful[3] courtiers[4] found means[5] to prejudice[6] the young prince against him. "He has," said they, "betrayed[7] the trust reposed in him[8] by the late[9] king. He has hoarded up[10] immense treasures,[11] and embezzled[12] valuable[13] effects."[14]

2. Sha-Sephi was young and a monarch; which was more than sufficient[15] to make him credulous[16] and inconsiderate.[17] He had, besides,[18] the vanity[19] to think himself qualified to reform his father's acts,[20] and to judge[21] of things better than the latter[22] had done. To have some plea[23] for removing[24] Alibeg from his post, he commanded him to produce[25] the cimeter,[26] set[27] with diamonds of an immense value, which his royal grandsire[28] used to wear[29] in battle.[30] Sha-Abbas had formerly[31] ordered them to be taken

off;[32] and Alibeg brought witnesses to prove [33] that they were so removed long before his promotion.

3. When Alibeg's enemies found this scheme [34] too weak to effect [35] his ruin, they prevailed [36] on Sha-Sephi to give him strict orders [37] to produce an exact [38] inventory [39] of all the rich furniture [40] intrusted [41] to his care.[42] Alibeg opened the doors, and showed every thing committed [43] to his charge.[44] No one article was missing;[45] each was in its proper [46] place, and preserved [47] with great care.[48]

4. The king, surprised to see such order [49] everywhere observed,[50] began to entertain [51] a favorable [52] opinion of Alibeg, till he espied [53] at the end of a long gallery an iron [54] door, with three strong locks.[55] "There it is," whispered [56] the envious courtiers in his ears,[57] "that Alibeg has concealed [58] all the valuable effects which he has purloined." [59] The king now angrily [60] exclaimed, "I will see what is in that room. What have you concealed there? Show it me." Alibeg fell prostrate at his feet,[61] beseeching [62] him not to take from him all that he now held valuable upon earth.

5. Sha-Sephi now took it [63] for granted [64] that Alibeg's ill-gotten [65] treasure lay concealed within.[66] He commanded the door to be opened. Alibeg, who had the keys [67] in his pocket,[68] unlocked [69] the door. Nothing, however, was found there but his crook, his pipe, and the shepherd's dress which he wore [70] in his youth.[71]

6. "Behold,[72] great sir," said he, "the remains [73] of my former [74] felicity;[75] which neither fortune [76] nor your majesty have taken from me. Behold my treasure, which I reserve [77] to make me rich when you shall think proper [78] to make me poor. Take back every thing besides; but leave [79] me these dear pledges [80] of my rural station.[81] These are my substantial [82] riches [83] which will never fail [84] me.

7. "These, O king! are the precious,[85] yet innocent possessions [86] of those who can live contented [87] with

the necessaries[83] of life, without tormenting themselves[89] about superfluous enjoyments.[90] These are riches which are possessed[91] with liberty and safety;[92] riches which never give me one moment's disquiet.[93] Oh, ye dear implements[94] of a plain[95] but happy life! I value[96] none but you; with you I will live, and with you die. I here resign,[97] great sir, the many favors[98] which your royal bounty[99] has bestowed[100] upon me."

8. The king, convinced of Alibeg's innocence, instantly[101] banished[102] his accusers[103] from court. Alibeg became[104] his prime minister, and was intrusted[105] with the most important secrets.[106] He visited, however, every day his crook, his pipe, and rural habits,[107] that he might remember them, should fickle fortune[108] deprive[109] him of a monarch's favor. He died in a good old age,[110] without wishing to have his enemies punished,[111] or to increase[112] his possessions; and left[113] his relations no more than what would maintain[114] them in the station of shepherds, which he always thought the safest and most happy. FENELON.

[1] folgte, [2] neidisch, [3] verschlagen, [4] Häflinge, [5] Mittel und Wege, [6] einzunehmen, [7] verrathen, [8] das in ihm gesetzte Vertrauen (das Vertrauen, gesetzt in ihn), [9] verstorben, [10] zusammengescharrt, [11] ungeheure Schätze, [12] unterschlagen, [13] werthvoll, [14] Güter, [15] welches mehr als genügte, [16] leichtgläubig, [17] unüberlegt, [18] außerdem, [19] Eitelkeit, [20] Handlungen, [21] urtheilen, [22] Letzterer, [23] Vorwand, [24] zu entfernen, [25] herbeizuschaffen, [26] Krummsäbel, [27] eingefaßt, [28] Ahnherr, [29] zu tragen pflegte, [30] Schlacht, [31] ehedem, [32] diese wegnehmen lassen, [33] um zu beweisen, [34] Plan, [35] herbeizuführen, [36] vermochten sie es über, [37] gemessene Befehle, [38] genau, [39] Inventar, [40] Hausgeräth, [41] anvertraut, [42] Obhut, [43] übergeben, [44] Obhut, [45] fehlte, [46] bestimmt, [47] aufbewahrt, [48] Sorgfalt, [49] Ordnung, [50] beobachtet, [51] hegen, [52] günstig, [53] bis er gewahrte, [54] eisern, [55] Schlösser, [56] flüsterten, [57] ihm in's Ohr, [58] versteckt hält, [59] veruntreut, [60] zornig, [61] fiel ihm zu Füßen, [62] anflehend, [63] hielt es, [64] ausgemacht, [65] übelerworben, [66] drinnen, [67] Schlüssel, [68] Tasche, [69] schleß auf, [70] trug, [71] Jugend, [72] Siehe, das sind, [73] Ueberbleibsel, [74] ehemalig, [75] Glück, [76] Schicksal, [77] welchen ich aufbewahrt habe, [78] wenn du es für gut hältst, [79] lasse mir, [80] Pfänder, [81] meines ländlichen Standes, [82] wirklich, [83] Reichthümer, [84] im Stiche lassen, [85] köstlich, [86] Besitzthümer, [87] zufrieden, [88] nothwendigste Bedürfnisse, [89] ohne sich zu plagen, [90] um überflüssige Genüsse, [91] die man besitzt, [92] Sicherheit, [93] Unruhe, [94] Geräthschaften, [95] einfach, [96] schätze, [97] entsage ich, [98] Gunstbezeugungen, [99] Güte, [100] überschüttet, [101] augenblicklich, [102] verbannte, [103] Ankläger, [104] wurde, [105] betraut, [106] Geheimnisse, [107] Gewand, [108] das wankelmüthige Glück, [109] berauben, [110] in hohem Alter, [111] daß seine Feinde bestraft werden möchten, [112] zu mehren, [113] hinterließ, [114] ernähren.

Lektion XVI.

Zahlwörter—Cardinal, Ordinal.

Redensarten—*What o'clock is it? What day of the month? It is one o'clock. It is half past one, a quarter past one. It is (wants) ten minutes to one.*

Wörter-Verzeichniß.

how many are? wie viel ist?
if you take, wenn man nimmt.
remain, bleiben übrig.
sum, Summe.
subtracted, subtrahirt.
leaves, bleibt.
for remainder, als Rest.
add, addire.
to divide, dividiren.
you will get, du erhältst.
number, Zahl.
is divided, dividirt wird.
is called, heißt.
dividend, Dividendus.
result, Resultat.
obtained, was sich ergibt.
is to be multiplied, multiplicirt werden soll.
to multiply, multipliciren.
multiplier, Multiplicator.
answer, Antwort.
part, Theil.
year, Jahr.

we are in, worin wir sind.
to write, schreiben.
January, Januar.
month, Monat.
last, letzt.
what day of the month is it? was schreiben wir?
what o'clock? wie viel Uhr?
a quarter past five, ein Viertel nach fünf.
too fast, zu früh.
too slow, zu spät.
only, erst.
ten minutes of, zehn Minuten vor.
I shall start, ich werde abreisen.
precisely, präcis.
half past eight, halb neun.
I rise, ich stehe auf.
I go to bed, ich gehe zu Bett.
last night, gestern Abend.
a quarter to, ein Viertel vor.
late, spät.

Uebungs-Aufgabe 1.

Two and three are five. One, six and seven are fourteen. How many are ten and twelve? Twenty-two. If you take four from nine, how many remain?

Five. The sum of thirty-six and ten is forty-six. Fifty subtracted from one hundred and two leaves fifty-two for remainder. Add four dollars to seventy-five, and you have seventy-nine. Divide forty-five by five, and you will get nine. The number which is divided is called the dividend, and the number by which we divide, the divisor. The result obtained is called the quotient. Twice two are four; once ten are ten. Ten times ten are one hundred, and ten times one hundred are one thousand. The number which is to be multiplied is called the multiplicand, while the number by which we multiply is called the multiplier. The result obtained is called the product. The product of twenty-five times thirty is seven hundred and fifty. Twice two and a half are five. What is the sum of four, one third and five seven-twelfths? Four is one twenty-fifth part of one hundred. The year we are in is eighteen hundred and seventy-one, and we write it A. D. 1871. January is the first month, February the second, March the third, April the fourth, and December the twelfth or last month. What day of the month is it to-day? It is the twenty-fourth of May. Can you tell me what o'clock it is? It is a quarter past five. Our clock is always too fast. My watch is too slow. It is only ten minutes of five. I shall start precisely at half past eight o'clock in the morning. I rise at six and go to bed at eleven. Last night I went to bed at a quarter to twelve. What time is it? It is too late to go to church; it is a quarter to eleven.

Wörter-Verzeichniß.

bereits, already.
spätestens, at the latest.
geht ab, will start.
präcise, precisely.
es nimmt uns, it will take us.
wenigstens, at the least.
sich aufhalten, to stay.

erst, only.
verkehrt, wrong.
zu früh, too fast.
ei! why!
merkwürdig, queer.
daß sie sein sollte, that it should be.

sonst, formerly,
zu spät, too slow.
die Hälfte, one half.
Ente, duck.
höchstens, at most.

ein Dutzend, a dozen.
abziehen, to subtract.
bleiben, to remain.
dividirt durch, divided by.
macht, are.

Uebungs-Aufgabe 2.

Wie viel Uhr ist es? Es ist bereits zwölf. Wann müssen wir gehen? Wir müssen spätestens um halb zwei Uhr von hier fortgehen; das Boot geht präcise um halb drei Uhr ab; und es nimmt uns wenigstens drei Viertel Stunden dahinzukommen. Ich kann mich nicht länger aufhalten als bis zehn Minuten vor neun. Es ist erst ein Viertel nach acht. Ist es schon so spät? Nein, Ihre Uhr geht verkehrt; sie ist wenigstens eine halbe Stunde zu früh. Ei! das ist doch merkwürdig, daß sie zu früh sein sollte; sonst ging sie immer zu spät. Willst du mir die Hälfte von deinen Enten verkaufen? Ich kann dir zwei oder drei verkaufen, aber nicht die Hälfte; denn ich habe höchstens ein Dutzend. Wie viel ist zwölf mal zwölf? Antwort: hundertundvierundvierzig. Wenn du nun vierundzwanzig von hundertundvierundvierzig abziehst, wie viele bleiben noch? Antwort: hundertundzwanzig. Einundachtzig dividirt durch neun macht neun.

Lesestück 1.

HOW TIME IS MEASURED (Wie man die Zeit mißt).

1. Clocks[1] and watches[2] are used[3] to measure time.

2. It would be[4] a hard[5] task[6] to measure time without[7] the aid[8] of clocks or watches.

3. On[9] the face[10] of the clock there are[11] twelve numbers,[12] which[13] are placed[14] at[15] equal[16] distances[17] from each other.[18]

4. Between[19] each[20] of these numbers there are five small[21] dots,[22] making[23] in all[24] sixty dots for the sixty minutes in an hour.[25]

5. The long hand[26] moves[27] from one figure[28] to another,[29] in five minutes; and it[30] moves from XII to XII, all around[31] the face of the clock, in one hour.

Zahlwörter.

6. The short hand [32] moves only from one number to another in the same time; and, therefore, it takes [33] the short hand twelve hours to move all round the face of the clock.

7. It is twenty minutes of twelve o'clock [34] when the long hand points [35] to [36] eight and the short hand is near [37] twelve.

8. The long hand is called the *minute* hand,[38] and the short hand is called the *hour* hand.[39]

9. When the hour hand points to I, and the minute hand points to XII, the clock strikes [40] *one;* and it is then [41] one o'clock.

10. When the hour hand points to II, and the minute hand points to XII, the clock strikes *two;* and it is then *two o'clock.*

11. When the hour and minute hands both [42] point to XII, the clock strikes *twelve times,*[43] and it is then twelve o'clock.

12. Sixty seconds [44] make one minute; sixty minutes make one hour; twenty-four hours make one day; seven days make one week; four weeks make one month; twelve months make one year. Ten years are called a decade,[45] and one hundred years make a century.[46]

13. We should always [47] make a proper [48] use [49] of our time; since [50] time is of all things [51] we may possess [52] the most precious.[53] "Time is money" is a poor [54] proverb;[55] for, money that is lost [56] may be recovered,[57] but time once [58] lost, never [59] returns.[60]

---

[1] Uhren (große, als: Wanduhren, Tafeluhren, 2c.), [2] Uhren (Taschenuhren), [3] man braucht, [4] es würde sein, [5] schwierig, [6] Aufgabe, [7] ohne, [8] Hülfe, [9] auf, [10] Zifferblatt, [11] gibt es, [12] Zahlen, [13] welche, [14] angebracht sind, [15] in, [16] gleich, [17] Zwischenräume, [18] einander, [19] zwischen, [20] jeder, [21] klein, [22] Punkte, [23] machend, [24] in Allem, [25] Stunde, [26] der große Zeiger, [27] bewegt sich, [28] Ziffer, [29] zur andern, [30] er, [31] rings um—herum, [32] der kleine Zeiger, [33] gebraucht, [34] vor zwölf Uhr, [35] zeigt, [36] auf, [37] nahe bei, [38] Minutenzeiger, [39] Stundenzeiger, [40] schlägt, [41] dann, [42] beide, [43] mal, [44] Secunden, [45] Jahrzehnt, [46] Jahrhundert, [47] stets, [48] gut, [49] Gebrauch, [50] da, [51] Dinge, [52] besitzen, [53] kostbar, [54] elend, [55] Sprichwort, [56] verloren, [57] wiedergewonnen, [58] einmal, [59] niemals, [60] kehrt wieder.

Lesestück 2.

THE SAYINGS OF POOR RICHARD (Sprüche des armen Richard).

1. Would it not be thought[1] a bad government that should tax[2] its people one tenth part of their time, to be employed[3] in its service?[4] But *Idleness*[5] taxes many of us much more; and *Sloth*,[6] by bringing on[7] disease,[8] absolutely[9] shortens[10] life.

2. "Sloth, like rust,"[11] says the proverb,[12] "consumes[13] faster[14] than labor[15] wears,[16] while the used[17] key is always bright."[18] And again,[19] the proverb asks, "Dost thou love life? Then do not squander[20] *time*, for *that* is the stuff life is made of."[21] How much more than is necessary[22] do we spend[23] in sleep! forgetting that "the sleeping fox[24] catches[25] no poultry,"[26] and that "there will be sleeping enough in the grave."[27]

3. If time be[28] "of all things the most precious,"[29] wasting time[30] must be, as has been well said, "the greatest prodigality;"[31] since, as we are again told,[32] "Lost[33] time is never found again; and what we call *time enough*, always proves[34] little enough." Let us, then, be up and doing,[35] and be doing to the purpose;[36] so, by diligence, shall we do more with less perplexity.[37]

4. Sloth makes all things difficult, but industry makes all things easy. It is an old saying,[38] that "he that riseth[39] late must trot[40] all day, and shall scarce[41] overtake[42] his business at night;"[43] and again, "Laziness[44] travels[45] so slowly, that poverty[46] soon overtakes him." Drive[47] thy business; let not thy business drive thee.

5. So what is the use[48] of *wishing* and *hoping* for[49] better times? We may make the times better, if we better ourselves.[50] As has been said,[51] "The industrious man will not stand still to *wish;* and he that lives upon[52] hope alone will always be fasting.[53] There are no gains[54] without pains."[55] Then let the poor man say, "Help, hands,[56] for I have no hands."[57] But let me tell him, "He that hath a trade,[58] hath an es-

tate;⁵⁹ and he that hath a calling,⁶⁰ hath an office⁶¹ of profit and honor."

6. But, then, the trade must be *worked at*⁶² and the calling *well followed*,⁶³ or neither the estate nor the office will enable⁶⁴ us to pay our taxes. If we are industrious, we shall never starve.⁶⁵ It has been well said, "At the working-man's⁶⁶ house hunger looks in,⁶⁷ but dares not enter,⁶⁸ for Industry *pays debts*,⁶⁹ while Despair⁷⁰ increaseth⁷¹ them."

7. What! Though you have found no treasure, and though no rich relation has left⁷² you a legacy,⁷³ is not Diligence the mother of good luck." ⁷⁴ Ay.⁷⁵ God gives all things to industry. Then, "plough⁷⁶ deep, while sluggards⁷⁷ sleep, and you shall have corn to sell⁷⁸ and to keep." ⁷⁹ Work⁸⁰ while it is called⁸¹ to-day, for you know not how much you may be hindered to-morrow; and farther,⁸² "never put off⁸³ till to-morrow, what you can do to-day."

8. If you were a servant, would you not be ashamed⁸⁴ that a good master should catch⁸⁵ you idle? But are you not your *own* master? You should be ashamed, then, to catch *yourself* idle, where there is so much to be done⁸⁶ *for* yourself, your family, and your country.⁸⁷

9. Handle⁸⁸ your tools⁸⁹ without mittens;⁹⁰ remember⁹¹ that "the cat in gloves⁹² catches⁹³ no mice." It is true, there is much to be done, and, perhaps, you have none to help you; but work steadily,⁹⁴ and you will see great effects;⁹⁵ for "a constant dropping⁹⁶ wears away⁹⁷ stones;" and "by diligence⁹⁸ and patience the mouse ate in two⁹⁹ the cable." ¹⁰⁰

FRANKLIN.

---

¹ würde man das nicht halten für, ² besteuern, ³ um beschäftigt zu werden, ⁴ Dienst, ⁵ der Müssiggang, ⁶ Faulheit, ⁷ dadurch, daß sie herbeiführt, ⁸ Krankheit, ⁹ jedenfalls, ¹⁰ verkürzt, ¹¹ Rost, ¹² Sprichwort, ¹³ verzehrt, ¹⁴ schneller, ¹⁵ Arbeit, ¹⁶ ermüdet, ¹⁷ gebraucht, ¹⁸ blank, ¹⁹ wiederum, ²⁰ verschwende nicht, ²¹ woraus das Leben gemacht ist, ²² nothwendig, ²³ bringen wir zu, ²⁴ Fuchs, ²⁵ fängt, ²⁶ Huhn (Geflügel), ²⁷ Grab, ²⁸ ist, ²⁹ das Kostbarste, ³⁰ Zeit vergeuden, ³¹ Verschwendung, ³² wie man uns ferner sagt, ³³ verloren, ³⁴ erweist sich, ³⁵ auf dann! und an's Werk! ³⁶ Ziel (um ein Ziel zu erreichen), ³⁷ Schwierigkeit, ³⁸ Sprichwort, ³⁹ aufsteht, ⁴⁰ traben, ⁴¹ kaum, ⁴² einholt, ⁴³ ehe es Nacht

wird, ⁴⁴ Trägheit, ⁴⁵ geht, ⁴⁶ Armuth, ⁴⁷ treibe, ⁴⁸ was hilft es zu, ⁴⁹ auf, ⁵⁰ wenn wir uns fleißig rühren, ⁵¹ wie gesagt worden ist, ⁵² von, ⁵³ darben, ⁵⁴ Gewinn, ⁵⁵ Anstrengung, ⁵⁶ hilf, Hand, ⁵⁷ denn ich habe kein Land, ⁵⁸ Geschäft, ⁵⁹ Gut, ⁶⁰ Beruf, ⁶¹ Amt, ⁶² betrieben, ⁶³ man muß des Amtes warten, ⁶⁴ in den Stand setzen, ⁶⁵ darben, ⁶⁶ Arbeitsmann, ⁶⁷ blickt hinein, ⁶⁸ aber wagt nicht hineinzutreten, ⁶⁹ Schulden, ⁷⁰ Verzagtheit, ⁷¹ mehrt, ⁷² vermacht hat, ⁷³ Erbe, ⁷⁴ des Glückes, ⁷⁵ ja wohl, ⁷⁶ pflüge, ⁷⁷ Faulpelze, ⁷⁸ verkaufen, ⁷⁹ zu behalten, ⁸⁰ arbeite, ⁸¹ so lange es heißt, ⁸² weiter, ⁸³ schiebe nie auf, ⁸⁴ würdest du dich nicht schämen, ⁸⁵ ertappen, ⁸⁶ zu thun, ⁸⁷ Vaterland, ⁸⁸ greife an, ⁸⁹ Werkzeug, ⁹⁰ Handschuhe, ⁹¹ bedenke, ⁹² Handschuhe, ⁹³ fängt, ⁹⁴ mit Ausdauer, ⁹⁵ Folgen, ⁹⁶ Tröpfeln, ⁹⁷ höhlt aus, ⁹⁸ Fleiß, ⁹⁹ fraß entzwei, ¹⁰⁰ das Ankertau.

Lesestück 3.

THE STORY OF THE FAIRY'S TEN LITTLE WORKMEN.

(Die Geschichte von den zehn kleinen Arbeitern der Fee).

1. This story, kind friends, is not one for whose exact[1] truth I can vouch;[2] but something very nearly like it[3] is said[4] to have happened[5] to our Grandmother Charlotte, whom Martin remembers[6] as a woman of great strength of character,[7] and remarkable industry.

2. The Grandmother Charlotte had been young once on a time,[8] although[9] it was difficult to believe it when one looked at her silvery locks,[10] and hooked[11] nose almost meeting[12] her pointing[13] chin; but those of her own age[14] said that, in her youth,[15] no young girl had a more charming[16] countenance[17] or a greater love[18] of fun[19] and gayety.[20]

3. Unfortunately,[21] Charlotte was left alone[22] with her father, at the head[23] of a large farm, more burdened[24] with debts[25] than profits,[26] so that labor succeeded[27] labor; and the poor girl, who was not fitted[28] for so great a care,[29] often fell into despair,[30] and while vainly seeking[31] some means[32] to accomplish[33] everything, ended by[34] doing nothing.

4. One day, as she was sitting on the door-step,[35] her hands under her apron,[36] and her head bent forward[37] with a weary air,[38] she began to say to herself in a low voice,[39]

5. "Heaven pardon me! but my cares [50] are too great for so young a girl to bear! Even though I were [41] as prompt as the sun, as untiring [42] as the waves [43] of the sea, and as potent [44] as fire, I could not accomplish [45] all the work of the house. Oh! why is the good Fairy Bountiful [46] no longer in the world! If she could but hear and aid [47] me, perhaps we might escape; [48] I from the cares, and my father from his anxiety." [49]

6. "Be satisfied, then, for here I am!" inturrupted [50] a voice. And Charlotte saw before her the Fairy Bountiful looking at her attentively, [51] as she leaned [52] upon her little crutch [53] of holly-wood. [54]

7. At first the young girl felt afraid, [55] for the fairy was very old, wrinkled, [56] and ugly, and she wore [57] a costume seldom seen in that country.

8. Nevertheless, [58] Charlotte recollected herself [59] quickly, and asked the fairy, in a trembling but respectful voice, in what manner she could be of service to her. [60]

9. "It is I [61] who come to serve *you*, my child," replied the old woman. "I have heard your complaint, [62] and bring you that which shall relieve [63] you from all your sorrows." [64]

10. "Ah! are you in earnest, [65] good mother?" eagerly [66] cried Charlotte, having quite forgotten her embarrassment. [67] "Do you come to give me a piece of your wand, [68] with which I may render [69] all my labor easy?"

11. "Better than that," replied the fairy; "I bring you ten little workmen, who will obey [70] all your commands." [71]

"Where are they?" cried the young girl.

"You shall see them directly," [72] was the answer. The old woman opened her cloak, [73] and ten dwarfs [74] of different sizes [75] passed out. [76]

12. The first two were very short, [77] but strong and robust. "These," said the fairy, "are the most vigorous; [78] they will aid you in all your work, and supply [79]

in strength what they lack [80] in dexterity.[81] The two you see following them are taller,[82] and more skillful; they know how to [83] draw out the flax from the distaff,[84] and apply themselves to [85] all the work of the house.

13. "Their two brothers, next to them, are remarkable for their great height; [86] and while they are both useful in a variety of ways,[87] one is particularly[88] skillful in using [89] the needle, for which reason [90] I have crowned [91] him with a little steel thimble.[92]

14. "The next two, one of whom, you perceive,[93] has a ring for a girdle, are less active,[94] but still valuable [95] for the aid they render [96] the others. As for [97] the last two, their small size,[98] and want of [99] strength, render them of little use; [100] but they are entitled [101] to esteem,[102] nevertheless, on account of [103] the good will and sympathy they manifest.[104] You find it difficult to believe, I venture [105] to say, that the whole ten [106] can be of much importance; but you shall see them at their work, and then you can judge."

15. At these words the old woman made a sign, and the ten dwarfs glided [107] quickly away to the performance [108] of their various [109] duties. Charlotte saw them accomplish successfully,[110] and with equal facility,[111] the roughest [112] and coarsest,[113] as well as the most delicate [114] kinds of work. They hesitated [115] at nothing; they sufficed [116] for everything. Charlotte uttered [117] a cry of astonishment and delight,[118] and stretching her arms toward the fairy, exclaimed:

16. "Oh, good Mother Bountiful, lend me these ten brave workmen, and I shall have nothing more to desire."

"I will do better than that," replied the fairy, "I will give them to you; only, as [119] you would find it troublesome [120] to take them everywhere with you, I shall order each one to hide [121] himself in one of your ten fingers."

17. "You know now what a treasure [122] you possess," said the fairy, when this was accomplished;

"all will depend [123] now on the use you make of your knowledge. [124] If you do not know how to govern [125] your little servants, if you allow them to become enfeebled [126] through idleness, you will receive no benefit [127] from them; but direct [128] them always aright, [129] and for fear that they should sleep, never leave your fingers in repose, [130] and the work you so much dread, [131] you will find done as if by enchantment." [132]

18. Whether [133] the fairy's visit were reality, [134] or whether, as I am inclined [135] to believe, sleep overpowered [136] the young girl, as she sat on the doorstep, and it was all a dream, this much [137] is certain: our grandmother profited by her counsels, [138] and managed [139] the household so well that she not only enabled [140] her father to pay off [141] the debts of the farm, but aided him in gaining [142] a small competence, [143] which was left to her at his death, after she had been for some years happily married. [144]

19. She was thus enabled to bring up [145] her eight children in comfortable circumstances; and there is a tradition among us, that she has transmitted [146] the skillful workmen of the Fairy Bountiful to all the women of the family; and that, with a little care [147] and diligence, they are early set in motion, so that we all derive [148] great profit from them. Thus, we have a saying in our family, that in the movement [149] of the ten fingers of the housewife lies all the prosperity, [150] all the comfort, and all the joy of the household.

---

¹ voll (genau), ² verbürgen, ³ etwas ganz Aehnliches, ⁴ soll, ⁵ passirt sein, ⁶ deren Martin sich entsinnt. ⁷ Charakterstärke, ⁸ einst, ⁹ obschon, ¹⁰ Silberlocken, ¹¹ gebogen, ¹² berührend, ¹³ spitz, ¹⁴ Altersgenossen, ¹⁵ Jugend, ¹⁶ reizend, ¹⁷ Gesicht, ¹⁸ liebte mehr, ¹⁹ Scherz, ²⁰ Frohsinn, ²¹ unglücklicherweise, ²² blieb allein nach, ²³ Verwaltung (Spitze), ²⁴ belastet, ²⁵ Schulden, ²⁶ Gewinn, ²⁷ folgte auf, ²⁸ gewachsen (geeignet), ²⁹ einer so großen Last, ³⁰ Verzagtheit, ³¹ während sie vergebens suchte nach, ³² Mittel und Wege, ³³ auszurichten, ³⁴ war das Ende vom Liede, daß, ꝛc. (endete damit, daß, ³⁵ Treppe vor der Thür, ³⁶ Schürze, ³⁷ vorne übergebeugt, ³⁸ mit müdem Blick, ³⁹ mit leiser Stimme, ⁴⁰ Sorgen, ⁴¹ und wäre ich auch, ⁴² rastlos, ⁴³ Wogen, ⁴⁴ mächtig, ⁴⁵ ausrichten, ⁴⁶ Gnadenreich, ⁴⁷ helfen, ⁴⁸ entachen, ⁴⁹ Unruhe, ⁵⁰ unterbrach, ⁵¹ aufmerksam, ⁵² wie sie sich lehnte, ⁵³ Krücke, ⁵⁴ Walddistel,

⁵⁵ bange, ⁵⁶ rumzig, ⁵⁷ trug, ⁵⁸ nichtsdestoweniger, ⁵⁹ sammelte sich, ⁶⁰ sie ihr dienen könnte, ⁶¹ ich bin's, ⁶² Klage, ⁶³ befreien, ⁶⁴ Leiden, ⁶⁵ Ernst, ⁶⁶ begierig, ⁶⁷ Schüchternheit, ⁶⁸ Zauberstab, ⁶⁹ machen, ⁷⁰ gehorchen, ⁷¹ Befehle, ⁷² gleich, ⁷³ Mantel, ⁷⁴ Zwerge, ⁷⁵ von verschiedener Größe, ⁷⁶ kamen zum Vorschein, ⁷⁷ klein, ⁷⁸ die kräftigsten, ⁷⁹ ersetzen, ⁸⁰ was ihnen abgeht an, ⁸¹ Geschicklichkeit, ⁸² größer (länger), ⁸³ sie verstehen es, ⁸⁴ Noden, ⁸⁵ verrichten, ⁸⁶ Länge (Höhe), ⁸⁷ auf verschiedene Weise, ⁸⁸ besonders, ⁸⁹ im Gebrauch, ⁹⁰ aus welcher Ursache, ⁹¹ gekrönt, ⁹² Fingerhut, ⁹³ wie du bemerkst, ⁹⁴ weniger thätig, ⁹⁵ schätzenswerth, ⁹⁶ leisten, ⁹⁷ was betrifft, ⁹⁸ Gestalt, ⁹⁹ Mangel an, ¹⁰⁰ Nutzen, ¹⁰¹ sie haben Anspruch auf, ¹⁰² Achtung, ¹⁰³ wegen, ¹⁰⁴ daß sie an den Tag legen, ¹⁰⁵ wage ich, ¹⁰⁶ alle zehn, ¹⁰⁷ schlüpften, ¹⁰⁸ Verrichtung, ¹⁰⁹ verschieden, ¹¹⁰ mit Erfolg, ¹¹¹ mit gleicher Leichtigkeit, ¹¹² die rauhesten, ¹¹³ gröbsten, ¹¹⁴ feinsten, ¹¹⁵ waren sie unschlüssig, ¹¹⁶ genügten, ¹¹⁷ stieß aus, ¹¹⁸ Freude, ¹¹⁹ da, ¹²⁰ unbequem, ¹²¹ verbergen, ¹²² was für einen Schatz, ¹²³ wird darauf ankommen, ¹²⁴ Kenntniß, ¹²⁵ regieren, ¹²⁶ entnervt, ¹²⁷ Nutzen, ¹²⁸ leite, ¹²⁹ recht, ¹³⁰ Ruhe, ¹³¹ fürchtest, ¹³² Zauberei, ¹³³ ob, ¹³⁴ eine wirkliche Thatsache, ¹³⁵ geneigt bin, ¹³⁶ überwältigte, ¹³⁷ soviel, ¹³⁸ Rathschläge, ¹³⁹ führte, ¹⁴⁰ in den Stand setzte, ¹⁴¹ abzuzahlen, ¹⁴² zu erübrigen (gewinnen), ¹⁴³ Vermögen, ¹⁴⁴ verheirathet, ¹⁴⁵ zu erziehen, ¹⁴⁶ vermacht hat, ¹⁴⁷ Sorgfalt, ¹⁴⁸ ziehen aus, ¹⁴⁹ Bewegung, ¹⁵⁰ Wohlstand.

Lektion XVII.

Das regelmäßige Zeitwort. Zukünftige Zeit.

Redensarten: *To beg to be remembered to somebody, to send compliments, to be fond of, to be a judge of, what is the use of? to mind.*

Wörter-Verzeichniß.

where, wo.
to dine, zu Mittag essen.
to-morrow, morgen.
at home, zu Hause.
to oblige, verbinden.
if, wenn.
to take dinner, Mittagessen einnehmen.
with, bei.
to finish, beendigen.

game, Spiel.
to hear, hören.
to say, sagen.
aunt, Tante.
is going, geht.
next, künftig.
fall, Herbst.
by the first, am ersten.
month, Monat.
to complete, vollenden.

fortieth, vierzigſt.
generation, Generation.
to die out, ausſterben.
before, ehe.
trace, Spur.
war, Krieg.
to efface, verwiſchen.
pleasure, Vergnügen.
of accompanying, zu begleiten.
home, nach Hauſe.
to be able, im Stande ſein.
way, Weg.
alone, allein.
from school, aus der Schule.
not yet, noch nicht.
presently, gleich.
month, Monat.
passed, vergangen.
swallow, Schwalbe.
to return, zurückkehren.
south, Süden.
to build, bauen.
roof, Dach.
to tell, ſagen.
in, zu Hauſe.
between, zwiſchen.
always, immer.
dreadful, ſchrecklich.
affair, Sache.
as long as, ſo lange als.
to depend on, ankommen auf.
whether, ob.
to fail, fehlſchlagen.
to succeed, gelingen.
nothing, nichts.
to neglect, vernachläſſigen.
to take care, in Acht nehmen.
money, Geld.
is about, iſt im Begriff.
to set, untergehen.

to rise, aufgehen.
am I to do? ſoll ich thun?
a few, ein paar.
that done, wenn das geſchehen.
nap, ein Schläfchen.
mutual, gegenſeitig.
do you wish to be remem-
  bered to him? Wollen Sie
  ihn grüßen laſſen?
best compliments, beſten
  Gruß.
Joe, Joſeph.
sends me word, theilt mir mit.
as soon as, ſobald als.
to move, ziehen.
further, weiter.
give my love, grüßen Sie herz-
  lichſt.
I am fond of, ich bin ein Freund
  von.
talk, Sprechen, Geſchwätz.
to be a judge of, ſich verſtehen
  auf.
painting, Malerei.
what is the use of, was nützt
  es zu.
fellow, Burſche.
advice, Rath.
to mind, ſich kümmern um.
to step, treten.
I beg your pardon, bitte um
  Entſchuldigung.
on purpose, mit Willen.
never mind, ſchadet nichts.
should mind his own busi-
  ness, ſollte ſich um ſeine eigene
  Sachen kümmern.
none of your business, geht
  dich gar nichts an.
no matter, einerlei.

Uebungs-Aufgabe 1.

Where shall we dine to-morrow? I shall dine at home, and you will take dinner with me. When I shall have finished this game, I shall hear what you shall have to say. My aunt is going to South America next fall. How old are you? By the first of next month I shall have completed my fortieth year. This generation will have died out before the traces of this war will have been effaced. We are all going to die. Shall I have the pleasure of accompanying you home? No, thank you; I shall be able to find my way alone. Have the children come home from school? They have not yet; but they will come home presently. Before this month is passed the swallows will have returned from the south. They will build their nests under the roof of our house. I shall be much obliged to you, if you will tell me when Mr. N. will be at home. He will be in between five and six. War will always be a dreadful affair; but as long as there will be men on the earth, we shall have wars. It will depend on yourself whether you fail or succeed. I shall have nothing to do with a man who neglects to take care of his money.

The sun is about to set; it will rise earlier to-morrow than it did to-day. What am I to do now? I think I shall write a few letters, and that done, I will take a nap.

Redensarten.—I shall write a letter to our mutual friend, Mr. Bidwell. Do you wish to be remembered to him? Yes, sir, send him my best compliments, and ask him when he will come to the city? Joe sends me word that he is about to sell his farm. As soon as it shall have been sold, he will move further west; he begs to be kindly remembered to all of you. Please to give my love to all your brothers and sisters, and remember me kindly to your mother. I am not fond of much talk. Most Germans are not only fond of music, but they are also good judges of music. I am no judge of painting. What is the use of giving this fellow any advice? He never minds what you say. You have stepped on my dress. I beg your pardon; I did not do it on purpose. Never mind, it is an old one. Everybody should mind his own business. What have you done with your money? That is none of your business. I shall finish this work, no matter how long time it will take me.

Wörter-Verzeichniß.

Vergnügen, pleasure.
bei uns, at our house.
Europa, Europe.
nächste Woche, next week.
sagen, to say.
hören, to hear.
verlieren, to lose.
schwimmen, swimming.
berühmt, celebrated.
Sängerin, singer.
vergeuden, to squander.
deshalb, for it.
zur Rede stellen, to call to account.
es wird nichts nützen, it will be of no use.
bald, soon.
Ziel unserer Reise, our journey's end.
Versammlung, meeting.
stattfinden, to take place.
einen Gefallen thun, to do a favor.
ausrichten, to tell.
so frei sein, to take the liberty.
kommen zu Jemand, to go and see somebody.

Uebungs-Aufgabe 2.

Wir werden morgen das Vergnügen haben unsere Tante bei uns zu sehen. Wann gehen Sie nach Europa? Ich gehe nächste Woche mit dem Hamburger Dampfer. Was wird dein Vater sagen, wenn er hört, daß du deine Uhr verloren hast? Wirst du morgen Zeit haben, mit mir zum Schwimmen zu gehen? Ich werde keine Zeit haben. Wir werden noch oft das Vergnügen haben diese berühmte Sängerin zu hören. Dein Bruder hat all sein Geld vergeudet; wirst du ihn deshalb zur Rede stellen? Ich werde es nicht; denn es wird nichts nützen. Bald werden wir am Ziel unserer Reise sein. Wo wird die Versammlung stattfinden, zu der du heute Abend gehst? Ich gehe nicht hin, denn ich fühle nicht wohl. Wenn du mir einen Gefallen thun willst, so bitte deinen Vater heute Abend zu mir zu kommen; sage ihm, daß ich nach sechs Uhr zu Hause sein werde. Ich werde es ausrichten. Ich soll Ihnen sagen, daß es ihm nicht möglich sein wird heute Abend zu kommen; aber er wird so frei sein morgen Abend zu Ihnen zu kommen, wenn Sie zu Hause sind.

Lesestück 1.

THE USE OF THE BEAUTIFUL (Der Nutzen des Schönen).

1. Deacon [1] Tilden had the squarest,[2] neatest [3] white house that ever showed its keen [4] angles [5] from the dusky clumps [6] of old lilac [7] bushes. In front of it stood, on each side of the door-way, two thrifty [8] cherry-trees which bore [9] a bushel [10] each every season.[11] Excepting [12] the aforementioned [13] lilac-trees, there was not a flower or shrub [14] round [15] the place. Rose-bushes, the Deacon thought, rotted [16] the house, and the honeysuckle [17] which his wife tried to train [18] over the porch,[19] was torn down [20] when the painters [21] came; and on the whole,[22] the Deacon said, what was the use of [23] putting it up [24] so long as it did not bear anything.[25]

2. By the side of the house was a thrifty, well-kept [26] garden, with plenty [27] of currant-bushes,[28] gooseberry-bushes,[29] and quince-trees; [30] and the beets [31] and carrots [32] and onions [33] were the pride of the deacon's heart; but, as he often proudly said, "every thing was for *use*," there was nothing fancy [34] about it. His wife put in [35] timorously [36] one season [37] for a flower-border [38] —Mrs. Jenkins had given her a petunia, and Mrs. Simpkins had brought her a package of flower-seeds from New York—and so a bed was laid out. But the thrifty [39] Deacon soon found that the weeding [40] of it took time that Mrs. Tilden might give to her dairy,[41] or to making shirts and knitting stockings, and so it really troubled his conscience.[42] The next spring he turned it [43] into his corn-field, and when his wife mildly intimated [44] her disappointment,[45] said placidly,[46] "After

all,⁴⁷ 'twas a thing of no use and took time." And Mrs. Tilden, being a meek⁴⁸ woman, and one of the kind of saints⁴⁹ who always suppose themselves⁵⁰ miserable sinners,⁵¹ especially⁵² confessed⁵³ her sin of being inwardly vexed⁵⁴ about the incident⁵⁵ in her prayer⁵⁶ that night, and prayed that her eyes might be turned off⁵⁷ from beholding vanity,⁵⁸ and that she might be quickened⁵⁹ in the way of minding⁶⁰ her work.

3. The front-parlor of the Deacon's house was the most frigid asylum of neatness⁶¹ that ever discouraged⁶² the eyes and heart of a visitor. The four blank⁶³ walls were guiltless of⁶⁴ any engraving⁶⁵ or painting,⁶⁶ or of any adornment⁶⁷ but⁶⁸ an ordinary wall paper⁶⁹ and a framed⁷⁰ copy of the Declaration of Independence;⁷¹ on each of the three sides stood four chairs; under the looking-glass was a shining mahogany table, with a large Bible and almanac on it, a pair of cold glistening⁷² brass andirons⁷³ illustrated⁷⁴ the fire-place.⁷⁵ The mantel-shelf⁷⁶ above⁷⁷ had a pair of bright brass candlesticks,⁷⁸ with a pair of snuffers⁷⁹ between—and that was all. The Deacon liked it. It was plain and simple, no nonsense about it, everything for *use* and nothing for show⁸⁰—it suited⁸¹ him. His wife sometimes sighed⁸² and looked round, when she was sewing, as if she wanted⁸³ something, and then sung the good old psalm—

> "From vanity turn off my eyes;
> Let no corrupt⁸⁴ design⁸⁵
> Or covetous⁸⁶ desires arise⁸⁷
> Within this heart of mine."

4. The corrupt design to which this estimable matron had been tempted,⁸⁸ had been the purchase⁸⁹ of a pair of Parian⁹⁰ flower-vases, whose beauty had struck⁹¹ to her heart when she went with her butter and eggs to the neighboring city; but recollecting herself⁹² in time, she had resolutely⁹³ shut her eyes to the allurements,⁹⁴ and spent the money *usefully* in buying loaf-sugar.⁹⁵

5. For it is to be remarked [96] that the Deacon was fond of good eating, and prided himself on [97] the bounties of his wife's table.[98] Few women knew better how to set [99] one, and the snowy bread, golden butter, clear preserves [100] and jellies,[101] were themes [102] of admiration at all the tea-tables in the land. The Deacon didn't mind [103] a few cents in a pound more for a nicer ham,[104] and would now and then bring in a treat [105] of oysters from the city when they were dearest. These were *comforts*, he said; one must stretch a point [106] for the comforts of life.

6. The Deacon must not be mistaken [107] for a tyrannical man or a bad husband. When he quietly put his wife's flower-patch [108] into his corn-field, he thought he had done her a service by curing her of an absurd notion [109] for things that took time and made trouble, and were of no use; and she, dear soul, never had breathed a dissent [110] to any course of his loud enough to let him know she had one. He laughed in his sleeve [111] often when he saw her so tranquilly [112] knitting or shirt-making at those times she had been wont [113] to give to her poor little contraband [114] pleasures. As for the flower-vases, they were repented of,[115] and Mrs. Tilden put a handful of spring-anemones into a cracked [116] pitcher [117] and set it on her kitchen-table, till the Deacon tossed [118] them out of the window—"he could not bear to see weeds [119] growing round." [120]

[1] Diaken (Kirchenvorsteher), [2] sauberste, [3] nettlichste, [4] scharf, [5] Ecken, [6] dunkle Gruppen, [7] Syringen, [8] kräftig (blühend), [9] trugen, [10] Buschel (Ver. St. Maaß), [11] Frühjahr (Jahreszeit), [12] ausgenommen, [13] vorerwähnte, [14] Strauch, [15] ringsum, [16] ließen verwittern, [17] Jelängerjelieber (Caprifolium), [18] zu ziehen, [19] Vordach der Thüre, [20] wurde abgerissen, [21] Anstreicher, [22] überhaupt, [23] was nützte es, [24] anzupflanzen, [25] so lange es nichts trug, [26] sorgfältig gepflegt, [27] Menge, [28] Johannisbeerbüsche, [29] Stachelbeerbüsche, [30] Quitten, [31] rothe Beete, [32] gelbe Wurzeln, [33] Zwiebeln, [34] phantastisches, [35] legte ein gutes Wort ein für, [36] schüchtern, [37] Frühjahr (Jahreszeit), [38] Blumenrabatte, [39] fleißig, [40] Gäten, [41] Meierei, [42] Gewissen, [43] warf er es, [44] zu verstehen gab, [45] Enttäuschung, [46] gelassen, [47] am Ende, [48] sanftmüthig, [49] Heilige, [50] die sich immer halten für, [51] arme, elende Sünder, [52] besonders, [53] bekannte, [54] daß sie innerlich beunruhigt sei, [55] Verfall, [56] Gebet, [57] abgewandt werden möchten, [58] Eitelkeit,

⁵⁹ daß sie mit Eifer erfüllt werden möchte, ⁶⁰ zu passen, ⁶¹ der eifigste Zufluchtsort einer Sauberkeit, ⁶² zusammenschnürte (entmuthigten), ⁶³ fahl, ⁶⁴ waren ohne (schuldlos), ⁶⁵ Stablisch, ⁶⁶ Oelgemälde, ⁶⁷ Zierrath, ⁶⁸ ausgenommen, ⁶⁹ gewöhnliche Tapete, ⁷⁰ eingerahmt, ⁷¹ Unabhängigkeits-Erklärung, ⁷² glänzend, ⁷³ messingene Feuerzange, ⁷⁴ zierte, ⁷⁵ Heerd, ⁷⁶ Kamingesims, ⁷⁷ darüber, ⁷⁸ Leuchter, ⁷⁹ Lichtscheere, ⁸⁰ Schein, ⁸¹ behagte, ⁸² seufzte, ⁸³ vermißte, ⁸⁴ verderblich, ⁸⁵ Plan, ⁸⁶ begehrlich, ⁸⁷ entstehen, ⁸⁸ versucht, ⁸⁹ Erwerb, ⁹⁰ von parischem Marmor, ⁹¹ gefesselt hatten, ⁹² sich fassend, ⁹³ muthig, ⁹⁴ Lockungen, ⁹⁵ Hutzucker, ⁹⁶ es muß erwähnt werden, ⁹⁷ setzte seinen Stolz auf, ⁹⁸ die reich besetzte Tafel, ⁹⁹ decken, ¹⁰⁰ eingemachte Früchte, ¹⁰¹ Gelees, ¹⁰² Gegenstände, ¹⁰³ fragte nichts nach, ¹⁰⁴ Schinken, ¹⁰⁵ Tractament (Leckerbissen), ¹⁰⁶ ein Uebriges thun, ¹⁰⁷ man muß nicht irrthümlich halten, ¹⁰⁸ Blumenstück, ¹⁰⁹ Vorliebe, ¹¹⁰ hatte nie eine abweichende Meinung geäußert, ¹¹¹ lachte sich in's Fäustchen, ¹¹² ruhig, ¹¹³ gewohnt gewesen war, ¹¹⁴ verpönt (eingeschmuggelt), ¹¹⁵ darüber hatte sie Buße gethan, ¹¹⁶ halbzerbrochen, ¹¹⁷ Wasserkrug, ¹¹⁸ hinausschmiß, ¹¹⁹ Unkraut, ¹²⁰ umherwachsen.

Lesestück 2.

THE USE OF THE BEAUTIFUL. (Schluß).

1. The poor little woman had a kind of chronic ¹ heart-sickness, like the pining ² of a teething ³ child; but she never knew exactly what it was she wanted.⁴ If she ever was sick, no man could be kinder than the Deacon. He has been known ⁵ to harness ⁶ in all haste, and rush ⁷ to the neighboring town at four o'clock in the morning, that he might bring her some delicacy ⁸ she had a fancy for ⁹—for ¹⁰ that he could see the use of; but he could not sympathize in her craving desire ¹¹ to see Powers' Greek Slave,¹² which was exhibiting ¹³ in a neighboring town. "What did Christian people want of ¹⁴ *stun* (stone) images?" ¹⁵ he wanted to know.¹⁶ He thought the Scriptures ¹⁷ put that thing down.¹⁸ "Eyes have they, but they see not; ears have they, but they hear not; neither speak they through their throat.¹⁹ They that make them are like unto them; so is every one that trusteth in ²⁰ them." There was the Deacon's opinion of the arts; and Mrs. Deacon only sighed and wished she could see it—that was all.

2. But it came to pass ²¹ that the Deacon's eldest son went to live in New York, and from that time

strange changes²² began to appear in the family, that the Deacon didn't like; but as Jethro was a smart,²³ driving²⁴ lad,²⁵ and making money at a great pace,²⁶ he at first said nothing. But on his mother's birthday, down he came and brought a box²⁷ for his mother, which, being unpacked,²⁸ contained²⁹ a Parian statuette³⁰ of Paul and Virginia, simple little group as ever told its story in clay.³¹

3. Everybody was soon standing round it in open-mouthed³² admiration, and poor Mrs. Tilden wiped³³ her eyes more than once as she looked on it. It seemed a vision³⁴ of beauty in the desolate neatness³⁵ of the best room.

"Very pretty, I s'pose," said the Deacon, doubtfully³⁶—for like most fathers of spirited³⁷ twenty-three-olders,³⁸ he began to feel a little in awe³⁹ of his son—"but, dear me,⁴⁰ what a sight⁴¹ of money to give for a thing that, after all,⁴² is of no use!"

"I think," said Jethro, looking at his mother's suffused⁴³ eyes, "it is one of the most *useful* things that has been brought into the house this many a day."⁴⁴

4. "I don't see how you're going to make that out,"⁴⁵ said the Deacon, looking apprehensively⁴⁶ at the young wisdom that had risen⁴⁷ in his household.

"What will you wager⁴⁸ me, father, that I will prove out of your own mouth that this statuette is as useful as your cart⁴⁹ and oxen."

"I know you have a great way⁵⁰ of coming round folks,⁵¹ and twitching them up⁵² before they fairly⁵³ know where they are; but I'll stand⁵⁴ you on this question, anyway."⁵⁵ And the Deacon put his yellow silk bandanna⁵⁶ over his bald⁵⁷ head, and took up his position in the window-seat.

5. "Well now, father, what is the use of your cart and oxen?"

"Why,⁵⁸ I could not work⁵⁹ the farm without them, and you'd all have nothing to eat, drink, or wear."

"Well, and what is the use of your eating, drinking, and wearing?"

"Use? why, we could not keep alive [60] without it."
"And what is the use of our keeping alive?"
"The use of our keeping alive?"
"Yes, to be sure;[61] why do we try and strive [62] and twist [63] and turn [64] to keep alive, and what's the use of living?"
"Living! why, we want to live; we enjoy living.[65] All creatures do. Dogs and cats and every kind of beast. Life is sweet."
"The use of living, then, is that we enjoy it?"
"Yes."

6. "Well, we all enjoy this statuette, so that there is the same value [66] to that that there is in living; and if your oxen and carts, and food and clothes, and all that you call necessary things [67] have no value except to keep in life, and life has no value except enjoyment,[68] then this statuette is a short cut [69] to the great thing for which your farm and everything else is designed.[70] You do not enjoy your cart for what it is, but because of its use to get food and clothes; and food and clothes we value [71] for the enjoyment [72] they give. But a statuette or a picture, or any beautiful thing, gives enjoyment *at once*. We enjoy it the moment we see it for itself,[73] and not for any use we mean to make of it. So that strikes [74] the great end of life [75] quicker than anything else, don't it? Hey, father, haven't I got my case?" [76]

7. "I believe the pigs [77] are getting [78] to the garden," said the Deacon, rushing out [79] of the front-door.

But to his wife he said, before going to bed, "Isn't it amazing [80] the way Jethro can talk? [81] I couldn't do it myself, but I had it in me, though,[82] if I'd had his advantages.[83] Jethro is a chip of the old block." [84]

Mrs. Stowe.

---

[1] chronisch, [2] Dahinsiechen, [3] zahnend, [4] daß ihr fehlte, [5] man wußte von ihm, [6] daß er angespannt hatte, [7] geeilt war, [8] Delicatesse, [9] wonach sie ein besonderes Verlangen hegte, [10] denn, [11] mit ihrem brennenden Verlangen, [12] griechische Sklavin (die Marmorstatue des amerikanischen Bildhauers Powers), [13] die zu sehen war (ausgestellt war), [14] was wollten christliche Leute mit, [15] Bilder,

¹⁶ das möchte er wohl wissen, ¹⁷ die heilige Schrift, ¹⁸ hätte das verboten, ¹⁹ Hals, ²⁰ der sein Vertrauen setzt auf, ²¹ es ereignete sich, ²² merkwürdige Veränderungen, ²³ gescheut, ²⁴ strebsam, ²⁵ Bursche, ²⁶ wie Heu (mit schnellen Schritten), ²⁷ Kästchen, ²⁸ als es ausgepackt wurde, ²⁹ enthielt, ³⁰ Figuren, ³¹ Thon, ³² mit offenem Munde, ³³ wischte sich die Augen, ³⁴ ein Traumgebilde, ³⁵ in der trostlosen Sauberkeit, ³⁶ mit zweifelhafter Miene, ³⁷ geweckt, ³⁸ Kinder von dreiundzwanzig Jahren, ³⁹ Respekt, ⁴⁰ du liebe Zeit, ⁴¹ Haufen, ⁴² am Ende doch, ⁴³ in Thränen schwimmend, ⁴⁴ seit langer Zeit, ⁴⁵ wie du das beweisen willst, ⁴⁶ bedenklich, ⁴⁷ aufgewachsen, ⁴⁸ wetten, ⁴⁹ Arbeitswagen, ⁵⁰ besondere Manier, ⁵¹ die Leute herumzukriegen, ⁵² und sie zu fassen, ⁵³ recht, ⁵⁴ ich will dir Rede und Antwort stehen, ⁵⁵ wie's auch kommen mag, ⁵⁶ Halstuch, ⁵⁷ kahl, ⁵⁸ ei! ⁵⁹ bearbeiten, ⁶⁰ wir könnten nicht am Leben bleiben, ⁶¹ freilich, ⁶² plagen, ⁶³ placken, ⁶⁴ mühen wir uns ab, ⁶⁵ wir haben Freude am Leben, ⁶⁶ Werth, ⁶⁷ nothwendige Bedürfnisse, ⁶⁸ Freude, ⁶⁹ kürzerer Weg, ⁷⁰ bestimmt ist, ⁷¹ schätzen wir, ⁷² Genuß, ⁷³ seiner selbst willen, ⁷⁴ erreicht, ⁷⁵ Lebenszweck, ⁷⁶ habe ich mein Spiel nicht gewonnen? ⁷⁷ Schweine, ⁷⁸ kommen, ⁷⁹ hinausstürzend, ⁸⁰ erstaunlich, ⁸¹ wie Jethro sprechen kann, ⁸² ich hätte es doch in mir gehabt, ⁸³ wenn ich so begünstigt gewesen wäre, ⁸⁴ ein Stück vom alten Stamm (der Apfel fällt nicht weit vom Stamm).

Lektion XVIII.

Das Adverb. Adverbien des Grades und der Weise.

Des Grades: very, much, pretty, almost, even, too, enough, most, very much, very much indeed, greatly, highly.

Der Weise: only, but, pretty well, well, fast, hard.

Redensarten: to settle, to ask, to ask for, to go for, to send for, to start oder depart for, to afford.

Wörter-Verzeichniß.

almost, beinahe.
to get ready, sich fertig machen.
pretty well, ziemlich gut.
highly, höchlich, sehr.
to be regretted, zu bedauern.
to perish, umkommen.
before, ehe.

rescue, Hülfe.
to look like, ähnlich sehen.
so much, so sehr.
to mistake for, (fälschlich) halten für.
to afford, die Mittel haben zu.
enough, genug.

confidence, Zutrauen.
neither have I, ich auch nicht.
greatly obliged, sehr verbun=
　ten.
tolerably, leidlich.
if I am to, wenn ich soll.
fast, schnell.
altogether, durchaus.
puzzled, in Verlegenheit.
highly probable, höchst wahr=
　scheinlich.
separated, getrennt.
greatly, sehr.
to excite, aufregen.
frankly, offen.
to ail, fehlen.
to relieve, helfen.
but ten, nur zehn.
to suspect, argwöhnen.
careless, leichtsinnig.
butcher, Schlachter.
tenderloin-steak, Beefsteak aus
　der Weiche.
displeased, unzufrieden.
foreign, fremd, ausländisch.

to pursue, einschlagen.
to mend, sich bessern.
are apt to commit, begehen
　zuweilen.
blunder, Versehen, Fehler.
to settle, lösen.
difficulty, Knoten.
to settle a bill, eine Rechnung
　bezahlen.
to settle (in a place), sich
　ansiedeln.
it is settled, es ist ausgemacht.
to start for, abreisen nach.
to ask somebody for some-
　thing, Jemand bitten um
　　　　　　　　　　　　etwas.
to lend, leihen.
to ask somebody, Jemand
　fragen, bitten.
to ask for somebody, nach
　Jemand fragen.
to send for, holen lassen.
to go for, holen.
if you have no objection,
　wenn Sie nichts dagegen ha=
　ben.

Uebungs=Aufgabe 1.

It is almost time to get ready for church. How did George do his work? He did it pretty well. It is highly to be regretted that he should perish before we could come to his rescue. You look so much like your brother that I had almost mistaken you for him. I should like to go to California, if I could well afford it; but I find that I have not money enough. Have you any confidence in this man's honesty? Not very much. Neither have I. John sends you his compliments, and he is greatly obliged to you for the basket of apples you sent him last week. How do you do? I am tolerably well, now. If I am to understand what you say, you must not speak so fast. You speak too fast altogether. I am very much puzzled, indeed, what to think of this matter. It is highly probable that it will rain before night. It is hard to be separated from your best friends. If I only knew what it was that so greatly excited her! If you would but frankly tell me what ails you, I might easily find some means of relieving you. There are but ten eggs in this basket; where are the rest? I almost suspect you to have broken them. Yes, it is even so; you are very careless, indeed. Will you go to the butcher's for me? Tell him I want two pounds of tenderloin-steak; but he must give me better meat than he did day before yesterday; tell him that I was greatly displeased with the meat. If you want to learn a foreign language, much, indeed, will depend upon the method you pursue. It is never too late to mend. Even the wisest are apt to commit blunders. Will you help me to settle this difficulty? When do you intend to settle your bill with me? I shall settle them next week. Where do these people intend to settle? They are going to settle in the State of Wisconsin. It is now settled that we shall start for Bremen in July next. I want to ask you for the book I lent you last week. What was the question you asked me? What does the man want? He asks for Mr. Howard. Please, ask your father if you can go with me. What did your mother send for? She sent for some onions and potatoes. John, go for the doctor; your brother is sick. If you have no objection, I should like to borrow your horse and buggy. I have no objection at all. Where do you want to go? I intend to start for the Central Park to-morrow morning. I wish I could afford to keep a horse and carriage; but I cannot now afford it.

Wörter=Verzeichniß.

verbunden, obliged.
Anerbieten, offer.
zu bedauern, to be regretted.

sterben, to die.
Kosten, expenses.
Unternehmen, undertaking.

bestreiten, to defray.
wenn es nicht verlangt wäre, if it were not asking.
zeigen, to show.
machen, to do.
ich freue mich, I am glad.
beendigen, to finish.
Mühe, trouble.
Richtigkeit, correctness.
Ansicht, view.
überzeugen, to convince.
ich wundere mich, I am surprised.
ich fürchte, I am afraid.
faul, lazy.
böse auf, angry with.
zurückerstatten, to pay back.

brauchen, to need.
verdienen, to earn.
die Hälfte, one half.
Chancen, chances.
wie gefiel Ihnen? how were you pleased with?
die gestrige Aufführung, yesterday's performance.
höchst wahrscheinlich, highly probable.
Lebensmittel, victuals.
die diesjährige Ernte, this year's crops.
aller Wahrscheinlichkeit nach, in all probability.
in die Höhe gehen, to go up.

Uebungs-Aufgabe 2.

Ich bin Ihnen sehr verbunden für das Anerbieten, welches Sie mir gemacht haben. Es ist sehr zu bedauern, daß er so jung gestorben ist. Hast du Geld genug, um die Kosten dieses Unternehmens zu bestreiten? Ich habe mehr als genug. Wenn es nicht zu viel verlangt wäre, so würde ich Sie bitten, mir zu zeigen, wie ich dies machen soll. Wie geht es Ihnen heute, mein Freund? Ich danke, es geht mir ziemlich gut; es geht mir viel besser als gestern. Ich freue mich sehr, daß ich meine Arbeit beinahe beendigt habe. Es hat mir ziemlich viel Mühe gekostet, ihn von der Richtigkeit meiner Ansicht zu überzeugen. Ich wundere mich sehr, daß du noch nicht mehr von der englischen Sprache verstehst; du bist doch lange genug in die Schule gegangen; ich fürchte beinahe, du bist sehr faul gewesen. Ich bin recht sehr böse auf ihn, daß er das Geld, das ich ihm geliehen, noch immer nicht zurückerstattet hat. Braucht man in New York viel Geld? Ja, man braucht sehr viel, aber man verdient auch sehr viel und schnell. Wenn ich nur die Hälfte seiner Chancen hätte, ich wäre schon längst viel weiter als er. Wie gefiel Ihnen die gestrige Aufführung des Wallenstein? Sehr gut, wirklich sehr gut. Es ist höchst wahrscheinlich, daß die Lebensmittel theurer werden; sie waren vorigen Winter schon sehr theuer, und die diesjährige Ernte ist so schlecht, daß die Preise aller Wahrscheinlichkeit nach in die Höhe gehen werden.

Lesestück 1.

THE VENTURESOME BOY (Der kleine Wagehals)

1. There was [1] a little boy, by the name of [2] Thomas Ettrick, who lived [3] in the northern [4] part [5] of Ireland. He was a smart [6] active [7] lad, and his parents were very proud [8] and fond of him.[9]

2. Thomas' father was a poor fisherman, and lived in a small cabin,[10] near [11] the sea-shore.[12] He had to get up [13] early [14] every morning, to catch [15] fish, and his wife went out to service [16] in their landlord's [17] family.

3. Thomas was left [18] to take care of himself [19] so much that, when he was twelve years old, he was more bold [20] and fearless [21] than most boys of his age.[22]

4. He earned [23] all he could [24] to help the family by doing errands [25] for the neighbors.[26] He had a warm heart,[27] and was so much attached [28] to Peter, their landlord's son, that he seemed [29] willing [30] to do anything [31] he could to please [32] him.

5. He had heard [33] Peter say, he wished [34] he had a young eagle,[35] and Thomas said he would try [36] to get [37] one for him. He knew [38] where there was [39] a nest of young eagles, about [40] half way up [41] a rocky cliff [42] that stood [43] by the sea-shore; but the rocks were so steep [44] he could not reach [45] them from the water-side.[46]

6. But Thomas was a persevering [47] boy, and finally [48] hit upon [49] a plan by which he hoped [50] to reach the nest and get one of the young eagles. So [51] he got [52] a long rope,[53] and started off,[54] with some other boys, and went to the top [55] of the cliff from the land-side.

7. When he reached the top, Thomas tied [56] the rope

around his waist,⁵⁷ and his companions⁵⁸ let him down⁵⁹ over the rocks. When they had lowered⁶⁰ him a few yards, his courage⁶¹ began to fail;⁶² for, nearly⁶³ two hundred feet below⁶⁴ him, he could see the waves⁶⁵ foaming⁶⁶ and dashing⁶⁷ against the rocks, and he knew, if he fell,⁶⁸ he would be dashed in pieces.⁶⁹

8. But he did not give up the attempt.⁷⁰ He told⁷¹ his companions to let him down slowly,⁷² lest⁷³ he should strike⁷⁴ against the jagged⁷⁵ rocks. When about half way down the cliff, he saw the nest with three young eagles in it,⁷⁶ and he made signs⁷⁷ to his young friends to stop⁷⁸ letting out the rope.⁷⁹

¹ es war einmal, ² Namens, ³ lebte, ⁴ nördlich, ⁵ Theil, ⁶ klug, ⁷ gewandt, ⁸ stolz, ⁹ und hatten ihn sehr lieb, ¹⁰ Hütte, ¹¹ an, ¹² Strand, ¹³ er mußte aufstehen, ¹⁴ früh, ¹⁵ fangen, ¹⁶ auf Tagelohn, ¹⁷ Gutsherr, ¹⁸ blieb sich selbst überlassen, ¹⁹ sehr, ²⁰ verwegen, ²¹ furchtlos, ²² Alter, ²³ verdiente, ²⁴ so viel er nur konnte, ²⁵ indem er Gewerbe ging, ²⁶ Nachbarn, ²⁷ Herz, ²⁸ fühlte sich so hingezogen, ²⁹ schien, ³⁰ bereit, ³¹ alles, was, ³² erfreuen, ³³ gehört, ³⁴ er wünsche, ³⁵ Adler, ³⁶ versuchen, ³⁷ bekommen, ³⁸ wußte, ³⁹ sich befand, ⁴⁰ ungefähr, ⁴¹ halb hinauf, ⁴² Felsklippe, ⁴³ sich erhob, ⁴⁴ steil, ⁴⁵ erreichen, ⁴⁶ Wasserseite, ⁴⁷ beharrlich, ⁴⁸ endlich, ⁴⁹ verfiel auf, ⁵⁰ hoffte, ⁵¹ daher, ⁵² kriegte sich, ⁵³ Strick, ⁵⁴ machte sich auf den Weg, ⁵⁵ Gipfel, ⁵⁶ schlang, ⁵⁷ Leib, ⁵⁸ Kameraden, ⁵⁹ ließen ihn hinab, ⁶⁰ hinuntergelassen, ⁶¹ Muth, ⁶² sinken, ⁶³ beinahe, ⁶⁴ unter, ⁶⁵ Wellen, ⁶⁶ schäumend, ⁶⁷ schlagend, ⁶⁸ wenn er fiele, ⁶⁹ so würde er zerschmettert werden, ⁷⁰ Versuch, ⁷¹ rief zu, ⁷² langsam, ⁷³ damit nicht, ⁷⁴ schlüge, ⁷⁵ zackig, ⁷⁶ darin, ⁷⁷ Zeichen, ⁷⁸ das Tau nicht weiter gehen zu lassen.

Lesestück 2.

THE VENTURESOME BOY. (Schluß.)

1. He swung himself¹ into a little niche² in the rock, close by³ the nest. The young birds made a great outcry;⁴ and he was afraid⁵ the old eagles would hear them, and fly⁶ to their relief.⁷ He caught⁸ one of the young eagles, and then jerked⁹ the rope for¹⁰ the boys to pull him up;¹¹ but no notice was taken of it.¹²

2. He pulled again and again, and called aloud¹³ to his companions to draw¹⁴ him up; but he received¹⁵ no reply.¹⁶ He then gave¹⁷ the rope a hard,¹⁸ sudden¹⁹

jerk,²⁰ which drew it from ²¹ their hands, and it fell on the rocks below him. He was struck with horror ²² at the awful ²³ doom ²⁴ that seemed to await ²⁵ him, and he began to be faint and dizzy.²⁶

3. He could not climb out of the place ²⁷ where he stood, without falling; ²⁸ and no one could hear his cry for help.²⁹ He had but a narrow ³⁰ foothold,³¹ and he feared ³² that when the old eagles returned ³³ to their nest they would sweep him off ³⁴ with their strong wings,³⁵ and hurl ³⁶ him upon the rugged ³⁷ rocks below.

4. He knew his companions would run ³⁸ for help; ³⁹ but as ⁴⁰ it was nearly ⁴¹ two miles to ⁴² the nearest house, it would take them some time to go and return, before any help could reach him. Every minute seemed an hour; for he knew that he could not remain ⁴³ there long unless ⁴⁴ some one ⁴⁵ should soon ⁴⁶ come to his assistance.⁴⁷

5. He knew he had done wrong ⁴⁸ in coming there without the consent ⁴⁹ of his parents; and thought ⁵⁰ that the awful death ⁵¹ that seemed to await him was but a just ⁵² judgment ⁵³ for his misconduct.⁵⁴ He thought, if he could only be saved,⁵⁵ he would never do wrong again.

6. He hid ⁵⁶ his face ⁵⁷ against the rocks, and prayed ⁵⁸ that God would forgive ⁵⁹ him, and deliver ⁶⁰ him from his perilous ⁶¹ position.⁶² Suddenly ⁶³ he felt something seize ⁶⁴ him by the shoulder.⁶⁵ He thought it was the eagle's talons.⁶⁶ But how great was his surprise ⁶⁷ and joy ⁶⁸ when he found it to be his own father's hand!

7. The boys had given the alarm,⁶⁹ and Mr. Ettrick and a few of his neighbors ran to the cliff to rescue ⁷⁰ the venturesome boy. With a strong rope, Mr. Ettrick was let down in the same manner ⁷¹ as Thomas had been, till he reached the eagle's nest.

8. He tied the rope around his son's waist, and the men on the top of the rock drew him up. Then they let down the rope, and Mr. Ettrick was drawn up in

the same way,⁷² bringing two of the young eagles with him.

9. He gave one of the young eagles to Peter, and told him to keep it⁷³ as a memorial⁷⁴ of the dangers⁷⁵ and hardships⁷⁶ to which Thomas had exposed⁷⁷ himself, in order to⁷⁸ obtain⁷⁹ it for him.

10. The other he gave to Thomas and told him to keep it as a memorial of that kind⁸⁰ Providence,⁸¹ who had so mercifully⁸² preserved⁸³ his life, and by whom he had been rescued⁸⁴ from his perilous position.

¹ schwang sich, ² Spalt, ³ ganz dicht an, ⁴ Geschrei, ⁵ fange, ⁶ herbeifliegen, ⁷ Hülfe, ⁸ ergriff, ⁹ zog, ¹⁰ damit, ¹¹ heraufziehen möchten, ¹² es wurde nicht beachtet, ¹³ rief laut, ¹⁴ ziehen, ¹⁵ erhielt, ¹⁶ Antwort, ¹⁷ gab, ¹⁸ stark, ¹⁹ plötzlich, ²⁰ Ruck, ²¹ entzog, ²² er wurde vom Schreck ergriffen, ²³ grauenhaft, ²⁴ Loos, ²⁵ warten, ²⁶ und die Sinne fingen an ihm zu schwinden, ²⁷ Stelle, ²⁸ ohne zu fallen, ²⁹ Hülferuf, ³⁰ engen, ³¹ Anhaltspunkt für die Füße, ³² fürchtete, ³³ zurückkehrten, ³⁴ herunterschlagen, ³⁵ Flügel, ³⁶ schleudern, ³⁷ spitz, ³⁸ eilen, ³⁹ Hülfe, ⁴⁰ da, ⁴¹ beinahe, ⁴² bis nach, ⁴³ bleiben, ⁴⁴ wenn nicht, ⁴⁵ Jemand, ⁴⁶ bald, ⁴⁷ Hülfe, ⁴⁸ Unrecht, ⁴⁹ Erlaubniß, ⁵⁰ dachte, ⁵¹ Tod, ⁵² gerecht, ⁵³ Strafe, ⁵⁴ Ungehorsam, ⁵⁵ gerettet, ⁵⁶ verbarg, ⁵⁷ Gesicht, ⁵⁸ betete, ⁵⁹ vergeben, ⁶⁰ erretten, ⁶¹ gefahrvolle, ⁶² Lage, ⁶³ plötzlich, ⁶⁴ anfassen, ⁶⁵ Schulter, ⁶⁶ Fänge, ⁶⁷ Erstaunen, ⁶⁸ Freude, ⁶⁹ Lärm gemacht, ⁷⁰ befreien, ⁷¹ auf dieselbe Weise, ⁷² auf dieselbe Weise, ⁷³ er solle ihn behalten, ⁷⁴ Andenken, ⁷⁵ Gefahren, ⁷⁶ Angst, ⁷⁷ ausgesetzt, ⁷⁸ um—zu, ⁷⁹ erlangen, ⁸⁰ gütig, ⁸¹ Vorsehung, ⁸² gnädig, ⁸³ bewahrt, ⁸⁴ gerettet worden war.

Lektion XIX.

Das Eigenschaftswort (Adjektiv). Steigerung (Comparation).

Redensarten: to hurry, to be in a hurry, to pay attention, to bear, to wear, to take pains, to succeed, to get rid of, to grow.

Wörter-Verzeichniß.

rich, reich.
as he is, wie er.
also, auch.

poor, arm.
lost, verloren.
parents, Eltern.

always, immer.
happy, glücklich.
cloth, Tuch.
cheap, billig.
handsome, hübsch.
cousin, Cousine.
yet, noch.
old, alt.
new wine, junger Wein.
day, Tag.
short, kurz.
tall, groß (hoch aufgeschossen).
short, klein.
lead, Blei.
heavy, schwer.
iron, Eisen.
metal, Metall.
the more contented, je zufrie=
 dener.
the happier, desto glücklicher.
dresses, kleidet sich.
after the latest fashion, nach
 der neuesten Mode.
late, spät.
nine o'clock, neun Uhr.
weather, Wetter.
bad, schlecht.
to-day, heute.
worse, schlechter.
yesterday, gestern.
boot, Stiefel.
I ever wore, die ich je getragen
 habe.
in town, in der Stadt.

the less, je weniger.
there are, es gibt.
industrious, fleißig.
people, Leute.
attentive, aufmerksam.
most, am meisten.
never, nie.
satisfied, zufrieden.
to possess, besitzen.
to want, wollen, wünschen.
to be in a hurry, in Eile sein.
to finish, beendigen.
to stay, bleiben.
to pay attention, aufmerksam
 sein.
to get along, fertig werden.
to bear, tragen (Last).
to wear, tragen (Kleider).
under-garments, Unterzeug.
we are told, es ist uns geboten.
to bear up, den Kopf oben hal=
 ten.
adverse circumstances, Wi=
 derwärtigkeiten.
to take pains, sich Mühe geben.
in spite of, trotz.
remonstrances, Gegenvorstel=
 lungen.
to calumniate, verläumden.
employer, Arbeitgeber.
to get rid of, los werden.
habit, Gewohnheit.
to grow weary, müde werden.
to listen, zuhören.

Uebungs-Aufgabe 1.

My uncle is rich; he is a very rich man; his brother is not so rich as he is, but his sister is richer. These children are poor; they have lost their parents. A rich man is not always a happy man. Is this cloth as cheap as that? It is cheaper than that, but it is not so good as this is. Mary is a handsome girl; but her cousin is handsomer yet. Old wine is milder than new wine. The days in winter are shorter than in summer. Which is the tallest of these boys? James is the tallest, and Fred is the shortest. Lead is heavier than iron; but gold is the heaviest metal. The more contented a man, the happier will he be. She dresses after the latest fashion. Do not come later than nine o'clock. The weather is very bad to-day, but it was worse yesterday. These are the worst boots I ever wore. Is the butter good? It is better than yours. We have the best milk in town. The less money he has, the happier he is. There are no more industrious people than the Germans. The most attentive boys and girls will learn most. Man is never satisfied; the more he possesses, the more he wants. I am in a great hurry to finish this work. What's your hurry, Emily? I think I cannot stay any longer; my father told me to hurry up. If you want to learn, you must pay attention. How do you get along with your studies? I cannot get along with boys that pay no attention to what I tell them. We bear a burden, but we wear clothes. I always wear light under-garments even in summer. We are told to bear one another's burdens; we sometimes find it difficult to bear up under the weight of adverse circumstances. If you take pains, you will succeed to learn English in less time than you imagine. No gains without pains. In spite of my remonstrances he continued to calumniate his employer. Would you like to get rid of this fellow? To be sure, but I do not know how. Lend him a dollar, and he will no more trouble you. It is a difficult thing to get rid of bad habits. I am growing weary of constantly listening to his lamentations. How is your brother? He is growing worse and worse; I am afraid he is going to die.

Wörter-Verzeichniß.

Ludwig, Lewis.
Karl, Charles.
Fritz, Fred.
jüngste, latest.
Ereigniß, event.
gewichtig, weighty, far-reaching.
Folgen, consequences.
edel, precious.
Silber, silver.
Kupfer, copper.
Metall, metal.
in der ganzen Welt, in all the world.
fruchtbar, fertile.
zusammenhalten, to keep together.
leicht, easy, light.
schwer, heavy.
gefährlich, dangerous.
Trägheit, indolence.
Unmäßigkeit, intemperance.
Ehrlich währt am längsten, honesty is the best policy.
Leute, people.
klug, smart, clever.
aufschieben, to postpone.
schwierig, difficult.
halten für, consider.
Sprachstudium, study of languages.
langweilig, tedious.
die es gibt, in existence.
nächst, nearest.
Fähre, ferry.
kämpfen, to fight.
vorderst, foremost.
Reihen, ranks.
Soldat, soldier.
unangenehm, disagreeable.
Sommerhitze, heat of summer.
Noth, distress.
tugendhaft, virtuous.
Gelegenheit, opportunity.
Glück, fortune.
vernünftig, reasonable.
Sparsamkeit, economy.
verbinden, to unite.

Uebungs-Aufgabe 2.

Ludwig ist fleißig, sein Bruder Karl ist fleißiger, aber Fritz ist am fleißigsten. Die jüngsten Ereignisse in Europa werden von den gewichtigsten Folgen sein. Die trägsten Schüler gehen gewöhnlich am spätesten an die Arbeit. Silber ist edler als Kupfer, aber das Gold ist das edelste Metall. Die englischen Pferde gehören zu den schönsten, nützlichsten, schnellsten und stärksten in der ganzen Welt. Die Vereinigten Staaten von Nordamerika sind das reichste, fruchtbarste Land in der Welt. Es ist hier viel leichter Geld zu verdienen als es zusammenzuhalten. Was ist leichter, ein Pfund Federn oder ein Pfund Gold? Das Eine ist so schwer wie das Andere.

Die gefährlichsten Feinde unsres Lebens sind Trägheit und
Unmäßigkeit. Ehrlich währt am längsten. Die reichsten
Leute sind nicht immer die klügsten. Je länger du diese Ar=
beit aufschiebst, desto schwieriger wird sie dir werden. Die
meisten Menschen halten das Sprachstudium für die schwerste
und langweiligste Arbeit, die es gibt. Können Sie mir den
nächsten Weg nach der Fulton Fähre zeigen? Der General
kämpfte in den vordersten Reihen seiner Soldaten. Nichts
ist mir unangenehmer als die große Sommerhitze. Wenn die
Noth am größten, ist Gottes Hülf' am nächsten. Der tugend=
hafteste Mensch ist auch der Freiste. Du hast in diesem Lande
die größte Gelegenheit dein Glück zu machen, wenn du mit
größtem Fleiß eine vernünftige Sparsamkeit verbindest.

Lesestück.

THE VALLEY OF TEARS. AN ALLEGORY.

Das Thal der Thränen.—Eine Allegorie.

1. I once had a dream—and yet it was not *all* a
dream—in which it seemed to me that I set out[1] upon
a long journey through a dark valley, which was called
the *Valley of Tears*.

2. The valley had this name because those who were
traveling through it met with[2] many sorrowful[3] trials[4]
on their way, and most of them left it in very great
pain and anguish.[5] It was full of all manner of people
—of all ages,[6] and colors, and conditions;[7] yet all
were traveling in the same direction; or rather,[8] although they were taking[9] many different little paths,
these all led[10] to the same common end.

3. I noticed, also, that these people, though differ-
ing so much in complexion,[11] ages, and tempers,[12] were
all alike in one respect:[13] each had a burden on his
back,[14] which he was compelled[15] to carry, through the
toil[16] and heat of the day, until he should arrive at his
journey's end.

4. It would have been very hard for the poor pil-

grims to bear up [17] under the toils of such a journey, had not the lord of the valley, out of compassion for [18] them, provided, [19] among other things, the following means [20] for their relief. [21] In their full view, [22] over the entrance of the valley, he had written, in great letters of gold—" *Bear ye one another's burdens.*" [23]

5. Now I saw, in my vision, [24] that many of the pilgrims hurried on [25] without stopping [26] to read this inscription: some read it, but paid very little attention [27] to it; while a third sort thought it very good advice [28] for other people, but seldom applied it to *themselves.* [29]

6. I saw, indeed, that very many of those who were staggering along [30] wearily [31] under their loads, were of opinion that they had burdens enough of their own, without taking upon themselves those of other people; and so each tried to get along [32] as well as he could, without so much as casting [33] a thought on a poor overloaded neighbor who was toiling [34] by his side.

7. And here I made a singular [35] discovery, [36] which showed to me the great folly [37] of these selfish [38] people; for I observed [39] that things had been so ordered [40] by the lord of the valley, that if any one stretched out his hand to lighten [41] a neighbor's burden, he found that the kind act [42] never failed [43] to lighten his own!

8. As I stood looking upon the passing throng, [44] I noticed a sorrowful [45] widow, bound down [46] with the burden of grief [47] for the loss of an affectionate [48] husband; but I saw that her children stepped forward [49] to aid [50] and comfort [51] her; and their kindness, after a while, so much lightened the burden, that she not only went on her way with cheerfulness, [52] but more than repaid [53] their help by the future assistance which she gave to them.

9. I next [54] saw a poor old man tottering [55] under a burden so heavy, that it seemed every moment as if he must sink under it. I peeped [56] into his pack, and saw it was made up [57] of many sad [58] articles; there were poverty, sickness, debt; [59] and what made by far [60] the

heaviest part, the unkindness⁶¹ of undutiful⁶² children.

10. I was wondering⁶³ how he got along at all,⁶⁴ till my eye fell upon his wife, a kind, meek,⁶⁵ Christian woman, who was doing her utmost⁶⁶ to assist him. I noticed that she quietly went behind him, and gently⁶⁷ putting her hand to the burden, carried much⁶⁸ the larger portion of it. The benefit⁶⁹ seemed to be all the greater,⁷⁰ that she tried to conceal⁷¹ from him the aid which she had rendered.⁷²

11. And she not only sustained⁷³ him by her strength,⁷⁴ but cheered⁷⁵ him by her counsels.⁷⁶ In short, she so supported his fainting⁷⁷ spirit that he was enabled⁷⁸ to "run with patience the race⁷⁹ that was set before him."

12. An infirm⁸⁰ blind woman was creeping forward with a very heavy burden in which were packed sickness and want,⁸¹ with many more of those materials which make up the sum of human⁸² misery.⁸³ She was so weak that she would not have got along at all, had it not been for the kind assistance of another woman almost as poor, and almost as heavily burdened as herself.

13. This friend had, indeed, little or nothing to give; but her voice of kindness and encouragement was a balm⁸⁴ to the soul of the weary one. Then I saw how much good an affectionate look and kind word can do. And I said to myself, "When we know that some human being⁸⁵ cares for us,⁸⁶ how much it lightens the burdens of life!"

---

¹ antrat, ² zu bestehen hatten (begegnete), ³ schwer (traurig), ⁴ Prüfungen, ⁵ Angst, ⁶ Altersstufen, ⁷ Lebenslagen, ⁸ oder richtiger, ⁹ einschlugen, ¹⁰ führten, ¹¹ Hautfarbe, ¹² Temperament, ¹³ Hinsicht, ¹⁴ Rücken, ¹⁵ gezwungen, ¹⁶ Last (Mühsal), ¹⁷ den Kopf oben zu halten, ¹⁸ aus Mitleid mit, ¹⁹ vorgesehen, ²⁰ Mittel, ²¹ Erleichterung, ²² vor den Augen Aller, ²³ Einer trage des Andern Last, ²⁴ Gesicht, ²⁵ weiter eilten, ²⁶ ohne anzuhalten, ²⁷ gaben sehr wenig Acht, ²⁸ Rath, ²⁹ bezog es selten auf sich, ³⁰ dahinwankten, ³¹ mühsam, ³² fortzukommen, ³³ ohne nur zu würdigen (werfen), ³⁴ sich ablagte, ³⁵ eigenthümlich, ³⁶ Entdeckung, ³⁷ Thorheit, ³⁸ selbstsüchtig, ³⁹ beobachtete, ⁴⁰ so angeordnet, ⁴¹ erleichtern, ⁴² That, ⁴³ verfehlte, ⁴⁴ das vorübergehende Gedränge, ⁴⁵ leidtragend, ⁴⁶ nieder-

gebeugt, ⁴⁷ Kummer, ⁴⁸ liebevoll, ⁴⁹ vertraten, ⁵⁰ helfen, ⁵¹ trösten, ⁵² Heiterkeit, ⁵³ wiedervergalt, ⁵⁴ darauf, ⁵⁵ wankend, ⁵⁶ ich that einen verstohlenen Blick, ⁵⁷ bestand aus, ⁵⁸ traurig, ⁵⁹ Schulden, ⁶⁰ bei Weitem, ⁶¹ Lieblosigkeit, ⁶² pflichtvergessen, ⁶³ ich wunderte mich, ⁶⁴ überhaupt, ⁶⁵ sanftmüthig, ⁶⁶ ihr Möglichstes, ⁶⁷ leise, ⁶⁸ bei weitem, ⁶⁹ Wohlthat, ⁷⁰ um so viel größer, ⁷¹ zu verbergen, ⁷² geleistet hatte, ⁷³ hielt aufrecht, ⁷⁴ Kraft, ⁷⁵ heiterte auf, ⁷⁶ Rathschläge, ⁷⁷ ermattet, ⁷⁸ in den Stand gesetzt, ⁷⁹ Lauf, ⁸⁰ schwach, ⁸¹ Mangel, ⁸² menschlich, ⁸³ Elend, ⁸⁴ Balsam, ⁸⁵ Wesen, ⁸⁶ sich um uns kümmert.

Lesestück 3.

THE VALLEY OF TEARS. (Schluß.)

1. But to return [1] to this kind neighbor. She had a little book in her hand, the leaves of which [2] were much worn [3] by use; and when she saw the blind woman ready to faint, [4] she would read to her a few words out of this book such as the following: "Blessed are the poor in spirit, [5] for theirs is the kingdom of heaven." [6] "Blessed are they that mourn, [7] for they shall be comforted." "I will never leave thee, nor forsake [8] thee."

2. These words quickened [9] the pace [10] and sustained the spirits [11] of the blind pilgrim; and the kind neighbor, by thus directing [12] the attention of the poor sufferer [13] to the blessings [14] of a *better* world, did more to enable her to bear the infirmities [15] of *this*, than if she had bestowed [16] upon her any amount [17] of worldly wealth. [18]

3. I saw a pious [19] minister [20] toiling sadly along under the weight of a distressed [21] parish, [22] whose worldly wants [23] sorely troubled [24] him, when a charitable [25] man came forward, and took all the sick and hungry on his *own* shoulders, as *his* part of the load. The two, then, were able to bear the weight of a whole parish; though singly, [26] either of them [27] must have sunk under the attempt. [28] It was always pleasant to see the poor pilgrims sharing [29] one another's burdens; but it troubled me greatly to observe, that of all the laws [30] of the valley, there was not one more frequently broken than the *law of kindness*.

4. I noticed, also, that those pilgrims who were the

most impatient under their burdens, only made them the heavier;³¹ but what surprised³² me most was to learn,³³ that the heaviest of the load which each bore was a certain *inner packet*, which most of the travelers took pains³⁴ to conceal, and which they never complained³⁵ of.

5. In spite of³⁶ all their caution,³⁷ however, I contrived³⁸ to get a peep³⁹ at this *secret*⁴⁰ *packet*. I found that in all it had the same label,⁴¹ and that the word *Sin*⁴² was written on it, and in ink so black that they could not wash it out. But what seemed to me very strange was, that most of them tried not to get rid of⁴³ the *load*, but the *label!* and that those whose secret packet was the largest, most stoutly⁴⁴ denied⁴⁵ that they had any such article!

6. There were some, however, who labored hard⁴⁶ to get rid of the contents⁴⁷ of this inward⁴⁸ packet; and they always found that, as it shrunk⁴⁹ in size, the lighter was the other part of their burden also. Moreover,⁵⁰ I observed that, with such, the traces⁵¹ on the label grew fainter⁵² and fainter, although the odious⁵³ word was never wholly effaced.⁵⁴

7. Then methought I heard a voice, as if it had been the voice of an angel, saying: "Ye unhappy pilgrims, why are ye troubled about the burden which ye are doomed⁵⁵ to bear through this valley of tears? Know ye not, that if ye remove⁵⁶ the secret load of sin which so oppress.s⁵⁷ you, the whole burden will finally⁵⁸ drop off?⁵⁹

8. "Learn, then, and *do* the whole will of the lord of the valley. Let faith⁶⁰ and hope cheer⁶¹ you. The pilgrimage, though it seem long to weary travelers, will soon be ended; and beyond,⁶² there is a land of everlasting rest,⁶³ where ye shall hunger no more, neither thirst any more; where ye shall be led beside living fountains of waters, and all tears shall be wiped away from your eyes."

"Bear ye one another's burdens;
  Bear, ye strong, with weakness,
Youth with age, and age with youth;
  Bear ye, all, in meekness."⁶⁴

Bear ye one another's burdens;
  Joyful hearts with sadness—
Anxious ones with cheerful hope,
  Mourning ones with gladness."⁶⁵

HANNAH MORE.

¹ aber um zurückzukommen, ² dessen Blätter, ³ abgenutzt, ⁴ nahe daran hinzusinken, ⁵ selig sind die armes Geistes sind, ⁶ Himmelreich, ⁷ Leid tragen, ⁸ versäumen, ⁹ beschleunigten (belebten), ¹⁰ Schritt, ¹¹ richteten auf die Lebensgeister, ¹² dadurch, daß sie auf diese Weise richtete, ¹³ Leidende, ¹⁴ Segnungen, ¹⁵ Gebrechlichkeiten, ¹⁶ geschenkt, ¹⁷ Summe, ¹⁸ Reichthum, ¹⁹ fromm, ²⁰ Prediger, ²¹ arm, ²² Pfarrgemeinde, ²³ zeitliche Bedürfnisse, ²⁴ sehr viel Kummer machten, ²⁵ mildthätiger, ²⁶ einzeln, ²⁷ Jeder von Beiden, ²⁸ Versuch, ²⁹ theilend, ³⁰ Gesetze, ³¹ um so viel schwerer, ³² wunderte, ³³ zu erfahren, ³⁴ sich Mühe gaben, ³⁵ beklagten, ³⁶ trotz, ³⁷ Vorsicht, ³⁸ ich brachte es fertig, ³⁹ Blick, ⁴⁰ geheim, ⁴¹ Aufschrift (Etiquette), ⁴² Sünde, ⁴³ loszuwerden, ⁴⁴ am hartnäckigsten, ⁴⁵ leugneten, ⁴⁶ sich viele Mühe gaben, ⁴⁷ Inhalt, ⁴⁸ verbergen, ⁴⁹ zusammenschrumpfte, ⁵⁰ überdies, ⁵¹ Schriftzüge, ⁵² wurden schwächer, ⁵³ häßlich, ⁵⁴ ausgelöscht, ⁵⁵ verurtheilt, ⁵⁶ entfernt, ⁵⁷ drückt, ⁵⁸ am Ende, ⁵⁹ abfallen, ⁶⁰ Glaube, ⁶¹ ermuthigen, ⁶² jenseits, ⁶³ ewige Ruhe, ⁶⁴ Sanftmuth, ⁶⁵ Freudigkeit.

Lektion XX.

Fragende Fürwörter und Adverbien.

Redensarten: to wait for, to wait upon, what is the matter? to take a walk, to take care, afraid of, to part with.

Wörter-Verzeichniß.

do you mean? meinen Sie?
silk, seiden.
they are my mother's, sie gehören meiner Mutter.
whom did you ask? an wen richteten Sie?

question, Frage.
did you give, haben Sie geschenkt?
best, am besten.
the elder, der ältere.
did—kick, hat—geschlagen.
lesson, Lektion.

Fragende Fürwörter und Adverbien.

are we to study, sollen wir lernen?
what day of the month is it? den wievielten haben wir?
pea, Erbse.
brother-in-law, Schwager.
did he enter, kam er herein?
by that, damit.
has done, hat angerichtet.
mischief, Unfug.
patterns, Muster.
to select, auswählen.
whom did he refer to? wen meinte er?
what are you thinking of? woran denken Sie?
is knocking, klopft.
dressmaker, Kleidermacherin.
folly, Thorheit.
to act, handeln.
to observe, bemerken.
velvet cloak, Sammetmantel.
bonnet, Hut.
to wear, tragen.

people, Leute.
to take breakfast, frühstücken.
how do you do? wie befinden Sie sich?
and how do you? und Sie?
top, Kreisel.
to wait for, warten auf.
to take a walk, einen Spaziergang machen.
what is the matter? was giebt's?
serious, ernstlich.
accident, Unfall.
to cross, überschreiten.
to happen, sich ereignen.
what is the matter with you? was fehlt dir?
pale, blaß.
to take care of, in Acht nehmen.
to recover, wiedererlangen.
to wait upon, aufwarten.
to be afraid of, bange sein vor.
to part with, Abschied nehmen von.
to take place, stattfinden.

Uebungs-Aufgabe 1.

Who has seen my umbrella? Which one do you mean? I mean my silk umbrella. Whose apples are these? They are my mother's. Whom did you ask this question? To whom did you give your carriage? Which of these two birds sings best, and which is the older of the two? What did you say? I said nothing. Whom did the horse kick? He kicked a little girl. What lesson are we to study? What day of the month is it to-day? It is the twelfth. What peas are these? In what street does your brother-in-law live? He lives in Rivington Street. By what door did he enter? He entered by the front-door. What do you mean by that? What boy has done this mischief? Here are three different patterns; which of these do you select? Whom did he refer to? What are you thinking of? See who is knocking. Who is there? A lady. What lady? A dressmaker. What a folly to act thus! What kind of cloth do you want? Do you observe that lady? What lady? That lady with the velvet cloak. What style of bonnet is that she wears? Where (oder whence) do these people come from? They come from Europe. Where (oder whither) did he go? He went to the theatre. When shall we take breakfast? At eight. How do you do? I am well, thank you; and how do you? Why do you cry? I have lost my top.

Whom are you waiting for? I am waiting for my cousin who promised to take a walk with me. I am very fond of taking a walk in the Central Park. What is the matter? Why do these people run in the street? A little boy met with a serious accident. In crossing the street he was overrun by one of the horse-cars. Accidents like this often happen. What is the matter with you, this morning? You look pale. You must take care of your health; for it is more easily lost than recovered. With what can I wait upon you? I am afraid of breaking this news to him. What are you afraid of? I am afraid of nothing. When did you part with your friend? When will the exhibition take place? It has taken place.

Wörter-Verzeichniß.

suchen, to look for.
gehören, to belong.
bekommen, to get.
erwarten, to expect.
aufwarten, to wait upon.
freundlich, kind.
bedürfen, to need.
gießen, to pour.
Milchguß, milk-pitcher.

führen, to take.
wunderhübsch, magnificent.
Stoff, stuff, material.
Sammet, velvet.
Nähmaschine, sewing-machine.
Briefpapier, letter-paper, note-paper.
Schreibpapier, writing-paper.

Fragende Fürwörter und Adverbien.

linirt, ruled.
beziehen, to get.
Cigarre, cigar.
direkt, directly.
Rauchtabak, smoking-tobacco.
er bekömmt mir nicht, it does not agree with me.
Bahnzug, train.
abgeben, to start.
präcise, precisely.

Uebungs-Aufgabe 2.

Wer hat meinen Hund gesehen? Was hast du da in deinem Korbe? Wen suchst du? Ich suche meinen Bruder. Wessen Buch ist dies? Es gehört mir. Wem hast du dein Pferd verkauft? Ich habe es meinem Nachbar verkauft. Wie viel hast du dafür bekommen? Zweihundert Dollars. Welchen von deinen Freunden erwartest du heute Abend? Ich erwarte Wilhelm Eggers aus Altona. Wovon sollen wir sprechen? Womit kann ich Ihnen aufwarten? Sie sind sehr freundlich, ich bedarf nichts. Worin soll ich die Milch gießen? Gieße sie in diesen Milchguß. Welches von diesen Mädchen kann englisch sprechen? Keines von allen kann englisch sprechen. Wohin wollen Sie mich führen? Ich will Sie nach dem Park führen. Was für ein wunderhübsches Kleid diese Dame trägt! Aus was für Stoff ist diese Weste gemacht? Sie ist aus Sammet gemacht. Was für ein Instrument ist dieses? Das ist eine Nähmaschine. Mit was für einer Feder schreiben Sie? Ich schreibe immer mit einer Goldfeder. Was für Papier wünschen Sie zu haben? Ich wünsche Briefpapier und Schreibpapier, linirtes und unlinirtes. Woher beziehen Sie Ihre Cigarren? Ich beziehe sie direkt aus der Havannah. Warum rauchen Sie nicht Rauchtabak? Er bekömmt mir nicht. Wer weiß wann der Bahnzug abgeht? Er geht präcise um drei Uhr heute Nachmittag ab.

Lesestück 1.

A WONDERFUL INSTRUMENT. Ein merkwürdiges Werkzeug.

1. A gentleman, just returned from the city, was surrounded[1] by his children, who were eager[2] to hear the news;[3] and still more eager to see the contents[4] of a small portmanteau,[5] which were, one by one,

carefully unfolded [6] and displayed to view.[7] After distributing [8] among them a few presents, the father took his seat again, and the following conversation took place.[9]

2. *Father.* I have brought from the city, for my own use, something far more curious and valuable [10] than any of the little gifts [11] which you have received. It is too good to *present* to any of you, but I will give you a brief [12] description of it, and then, perhaps, allow you to examine [13] it.

3. This small instrument displays [14] the most perfect ingenuity of construction,[15] and the most exquisite [16] beauty of workmanship.[17] From [18] its extreme delicacy [19] it is so easily injured [20] that a sort of light curtain,[21] adorned [22] with a beautiful fringe,[23] is always provided, and so placed as to fall [24] in a moment, on the approach [25] of the slightest [26] danger. Its external [27] appearance is always more or less beautiful, although in this respect there is a great variety in the different sorts.

4. But the internal [28] construction is the same in all, and is, in the highest degree,[29] curious and wonderful. By a slight movement, easily effected [30] by the person to whom it belongs, you can ascertain,[31] with great accuracy,[32] the size,[33] color, shape,[34] weight, and value of any article whatever. A person who has one of these instruments, is saved the trouble [35] of asking a thousand questions, and of making troublesome [36] experiments, and at the same time, by its use, he obtains much more information than he could in any other way.

5. *Edward.* If they are such very useful things, I wonder that everybody that can afford it, does not have one.

6. *Father.* They are not so uncommon as you may suppose. I know several persons who have one or two of them.

7. *Edward.* How large is it, father? Could I hold it in my hand?

8. *Father.* You might; but I should be very sorry to trust⁵⁷ mine with you.
9. *Edward.* You will be obliged to take great care of it, then.
10. *Father.* Indeed, I must. I intend every night to inclose³⁸ it in the small screen³⁹ of which I told you, and it must, besides, sometimes be washed in a certain colorless fluid,⁴⁰ kept for this purpose.⁴¹ But notwithstanding the tenderness⁴² of this instrument, it may be darted⁴³ to a great distance, without the least injury or any danger of losing it.
11. *Henry.* How high can you dart it, father?
12. *Father.* I am almost afraid to tell you, lest⁴⁴ you should think I am jesting.⁴⁵
13. *Edward.* Higher than this house, I suppose!
14. *Father.* Much higher.
15. *Henry.* Then how do you get it again?
16. *Father.* It is easily cast down⁴⁶ by a gentle movement that does it no injury.
17. *Edward.* But who can do this?
18. *Father.* The person whose business it is to take care of it.
19. *Henry.* Well, I cannot understand you at all; but do tell us, father, what it is chiefly⁴⁷ used for.
20. *Father.* Its uses are so various, that I know not which to mention.⁴⁸ It is of great service in deciphering⁴⁹ old manuscripts, and, indeed, has its use in modern prints.⁵⁰ It will assist us greatly in acquiring⁵¹ all kinds of knowledge,⁵² and without it some of the most sublime⁵³ parts of creation⁵⁴ would be matter⁵⁵ of mere conjecture.⁵⁶
21. *Edward.* Well, tell us something more about it.
22. *Father.* It is of a very penetrating⁵⁷ quality, and can often discover secrets⁵⁸ which could be detected⁵⁹ by no other means. It must be confessed,⁶⁰ however, that it is equally liable⁶¹ to reveal⁶² them.
23. *Henry.* What! can it speak, then?
24. *Father.* It is sometimes said to do so; especially if it meets with one of its own species.⁶³

25. *Edward.* Of what color is it?
26. *Father.* They vary in this respect.
27. *Edward.* Of what color is yours?
28. *Father.* I believe it is of a darkish [64] color, but, to confess the truth, I never saw it in my life.
29. *Both. Never saw it in your life?*
30. *Father.* No, nor do I wish to see it; but *I have* seen a representative [65] of it, which is so exact that my curiosity [66] is perfectly satisfied.[67]
31. *Edward.* But why don't you look at the thing itself?
32. *Father.* I should be in danger of losing it, if I did.
33. *Henry.* Then you could buy another.
34. *Father.* Nay, I believe that I could not prevail on [68] anybody to part [69] with such a thing.
35. *Edward.* Then how did you get this one?
36. *Father.* I am so fortunate to have more than one; but how I got them I really cannot recollect.[70]
37. *Edward.* Not recollect? Why, you said you brought them from the city to-night!
38. *Father.* So I did. I should be sorry if I left them behind me.
39. *Henry.* Tell, father, do tell us the name of this wonderful instrument.
40. *Father.* It is called—an *Eye.*

---

[1] umringt, [2] begierig, [3] Neuigkeiten, [4] Inhalt, [5] Reisetasche, [6] auseinandergepackt, [7] zur Schau gestellt, [8] nachdem—vertheilt hatte, [9] fand statt, [10] werthvoll, [11] Geschenk, [12] kurz, [13] untersuchen, [14] zeigt, [15] die sinnreichste Construction, [16] die auserlesenste, [17] in der Ausführung (Arbeit), [18] wegen, [19] Zartheit, [20] verletzt, [21] Vorhang, [22] verziert, [23] Franzen, [24] daß er fällt, [25] beim Herannahen, [26] geringst, [27] äußere, [28] inner, [29] Grad, [30] bewerkstelligt, [31] kann man ermitteln, [32] Genauigkeit, [33] Größe, [34] Form, [35] ist der Mühe überhoben, [36] mühsam, [37] anvertrauen, [38] einschließen, [39] Schirm, Vorhang, [40] Flüssigkeit, [41] Zweck, [42] Zartheit, [43] kann es geschleudert werden, [44] damit nicht, [45] ich scherze, [46] niedergeschlagen, [47] hauptsächlich, [48] erwähnen, [49] im Entziffern, [50] Drucksachen, [51] im Erwerben, [52] Kenntnisse, [53] herrlich, [54] Schöpfung, [55] Gegenstand, [56] Muthmaßung, [57] durchdringend, [58] Geheimnisse, [59] erschlossen, [60] zugegeben, [61] geneigt, [62] offenbaren, [63] Art, [64] schwärzlich, [65] Bild, [66] Neugierde, [67] befriedigt, [68] vermögen über, [69] sich zu trennen, [70] entsinnen.

Lejeſtück 2.

A SILENT PARTNER. (Ein ſtiller Compagnon.)

1. An Italian marquis having invited the gentry[1] of his neighborhood to a grand entertainment,[2] all the delicacies[3] of the season[4] were accordingly provided.[5] Some of the company had already arrived, in order to pay their early respects[6] to his excellency, when the major-domo,[7] in a hurry, entered the room.

2. "My lord," said he, "here is a most wonderful fisherman below,[8] who has brought one of the finest fish, I believe, in Italy; but then he demands[9] such a price for it!"

3. "Regard[10] not his price," cried the marquis, "pay it down directly."

4. "So I would, please your Highness, but he refuses to take money."

5. "Why, what would the fellow have?"

6. "A hundred strokes[11] of the strappado[12] on his bare[13] shoulders, my lord; he says he will not bate[14] a single blow."

7. Here they all run down to have a view[15] of this rarity[16] of a fisherman.

8. "A fine fish!" cried the marquis.

9. "What is your demand, my friend?—you shall be paid on the instant."[17]

10. "Not a penny, my lord; I will not take money. If you would have my fish, you must order[18] me a hundred lashes[19] of the strappado upon my naked back; if not, I shall go and apply[20] elsewhere."

11. "Rather than lose our fish," said his Highness, "let the fellow have his humor.[21] Here," cried he to one of his grooms;[22] "discharge[23] this honest man's demand; but be gentle[24] with thy stripes."

12. The fisherman then stripped,[25] and the groom prepared to put his lord's orders in execution.[26]

13. "Now, my friend," cried the fisherman, "keep

good account,[27] I beseech[28] you, for I am not covetous[29] of a single stroke beyond my due." [30]

14. They all stood suspended with amazement[31] while this operation was carrying on.[32] At length, on the instant[33] that the executioner had given the fiftieth lash, "Hold," cried the fisherman, "I have already received my full share[34] of the price."

15. "Your share!" questioned[35] the marquis, "what can you mean by that?"

16. "Why, my lord, you must know I have a partner in this business. My honor is engaged[36] to let him have half of whatever I should get; and I fancy[37] your Highness will acknowledge[38] by and by, that it would be a thousand pities[39] to defraud[40] him of a single stroke."

17. "And pray, my friend, who is this same partner of yours?"

18. "It is the porter, my lord, who guards[41] the outer gate[42] of your Highness's palace. He refused to admit me[43] but on[44] the condition of promising him the half of what I should get for my fish."

19. "O, ho!" exclaimed the marquis, breaking out into a laugh, "by the blessing[45] of heaven, he shall have his demand doubled to him in full tale." [46]

20. Here the porter was sent for, and stripped to the skin, when two grooms laid on him, until they rendered[47] him fit[48] to be sainted[49] for a second Bartholomew. The marquis then ordered his major-domo to pay the fisherman twenty pounds, and desired him to call yearly for the like sum, in recompense[50] of the friendly office[51] he had rendered him.[52]

---

[1] Abel, [2] Fest, [3] Delikatessen, [4] Jahreszeit, [5] herbeigeschafft, [6] ihre Aufwartung zu machen, [7] Hausmeister (Verwalter), [8] drunten, [9] fordert, [10] kümmere dich, [11] Streiche, [12] Strappado, [13] bloß, [14] nachlassen, [15] sich anzusehen, [16] Rarität, [17] auf der Stelle, [18] geben lassen, [19] Streiche, [20] mich hinwenden, [21] Laune, [22] Bediente, [23] entrichte, [24] gelinde, [25] zog sich nackt aus, [26] Ausführung, [27] Rechnung, [28] bitte, [29] begierig nach, [30] mehr als mir zukommt, [31] stumm vor Verwunderung, [32] Verlauf nahm, [33] Augenblick, [34] Antheil, [35] fragte, [36] verpfändet, [37] ich vermuthe, [38] zugeben, [39] jammerschade, [40] betrügen um,

⁴¹ bewacht, ⁴² Ihrer, ⁴³ mir Zutritt zu geben, ⁴⁴ ausgenommen auf, ⁴⁵ Segnungen, ⁴⁶ Zahl, ⁴⁷ machten, ⁴⁸ tauglich, ⁴⁹ unter die Heiligen aufgenommen zu werden, ⁵⁰ Erlaß, ⁵¹ Dienst, ⁵² den er ihm geleistet hatte.

Lesestück 3.

HOW TO USE THE ALMANAC.
(Wie man den Kalender gebrauchen soll.)

1. About one hundred years since there lived in England a celebrated almanac-maker, named Partridge. One day, while traveling on horseback,[1] he stopped for his dinner at a country inn,[2] and afterwards called for his horse, that he might reach the next town, where he intended to sleep.

2. "If you will take my advice,[3] sir," said the hostler,[4] as he was about to mount[5] his horse, "you will stay where you are for the night, as you will surely be overtaken[6] by a pelting[7] rain."

3. "Nonsense, nonsense," exclaimed the almanac-maker; "there is a sixpence for you, my honest fellow, and good afternoon to you."

4. He proceeded on[8] his journey,[9] and, sure enough,[10] he was well drenched[11] in a heavy shower. Partridge was struck[12] by the man's prediction,[13] and being always intent[14] on the interest of his almanac, he rode back on the instant, and was received by the hostler with a broad grin.[15]

5. "Well, sir, you see I was right after all."[16]

6. "Yes, my lad,[17] you have been so, and here is a crown for you; but I give it to you on condition that you tell me how you knew of this rain."

7. "To be sure, sir," replied the man; "why, the truth is, we have an almanac at our house, called 'Partridge's Almanac,' and the fellow is such a notorious[18] liar, that, whenever he promises us a fine day, we always know that it will be just the contrary.[19] Now, your honor, this day, the 21st of June, is put down in our almanac as 'settled[20] fine weather, no

rain.' I looked at that before I brought your honor's horse out, and so was enabled²¹ to put you on your guard."²²

¹ Zu Pferde, ² Wirthshaus, ³ Rath, ⁴ Stallknecht, ⁵ besteigen, ⁶ überrascht, ⁷ strömend, ⁸ setzte fort, ⁹ Reise, ¹⁰ richtig genug, ¹¹ bis auf die Haut durchnäßt, ¹² überrascht, ¹³ Vorhersagung, ¹⁴ darauf aus, ¹⁵ mit gutmüthigem Greinen, ¹⁶ am Ende doch, ¹⁷ Bursche, ¹⁸ berüchtigt, ¹⁹ das Gegentheil, ²⁰ beständig, ²¹ in den Stand gesetzt, ²² Sie zu warnen, auf Ihrer Hut zu sein.

Lektion XXI.

Der Possessiv-Casus.

Redensarten: to be delighted with, to be about to, to mind, to be struck, to be engaged, to turn out, to enter into, to call upon, to get rid of.

Wörter-Verzeichniß.

have arrived, sind angekommen.
book-store, Buchhandlung.
ought, sollten.
to be respected, respektirt werden.
bonnet, Hut.
to read, lesen.
window, Fenster.
bed-room, Schlafzimmer.
small, klein.
handle, Griff.
ivory, Elfenbein.
dunce, Dummkopf.
at home, zu Hause.
world, Welt.
broad, weit.
field of battle, Schlachtfeld.
hero, Held.
strife, Kampf.
miner, Bergmann.
life, Leben.
hardship, Mühsal.
sailor, Matrose.
rim, Rand.
narrow, schmal.
crown, Kopf.
high, hoch.
you will get, Sie bekommen.

at my hatter's, bei meinem
  Hutmacher.
to take supper, zu Abend
  essen.
amiable, liebenswürdig.
officer, Offizier.
courage, Muth.
to arrest, halten auf.
flight, Flucht.
I want to buy, ich wünsche zu
  kaufen.
cabinet-maker, Tischler.
tool, Werkzeug.
to die, sterben.
miser, Geizhals.
death, Tod.
last, vorig.
magnificent, prächtig.
was taken prisoner, wurde
  gefangen genommen.
military power, Kriegsmacht.
unrivaled, ohne Gleichen.
surnamed, mit dem Zunamen.
to lay, legen.
foundation, Grund.
present, gegenwärtig.
capital, Hauptstadt.
navy, Flotte.
pride, Stolz.

to be about to, im Begriff sein.
I wonder, ich möchte wissen.
what this fellow is about,
  was dieser Bursche vor hat.
to mind, sich kümmern um —,
  folgen, denken an.
to play a trick, einen Streich
  spielen.
a sound thrashing, eine tüch-
  tige Tracht Prügel.
it strikes me, es kommt mir
  vor.
we were struck with, wir waren erstaunt über.
to be engaged to be married,
  verlobt sein.
to turn out, hinauswerfen.
to enter into conversation,
  eine Unterhaltung anfangen.
disengaged, unbeschäftigt.
to call on oder upon, besuchen,
  vorsprechen bei.
to ring the bell, schellen.
to manage, fertig bringen, regieren.
troublesome, lästig.
to be delighted with, entzückt
  sein von.
to congratulate, gratuliren.

Uebungs-Aufgabe 1.

My father's friends have arrived. D. Appleton &
Co.'s bookstore is in Broadway. John's book is old.
An old man's words ought to be respected. Where is
Mary's bonnet? Have you read Charles Dickens's
works? The windows of our bedroom are very small.
The handle of this knife is of ivory. Thomas's brother
is a dunce. These boys' father is not at home. In
this world's broad field of battle, be a hero in the

strife. A miner's life is full of hardship. So is a sailor's and a soldier's. The rim of this hat is too narrow, and the crown too high. You will get a better and cheaper hat at my hatter's. Will you take supper with me at my friend's the captain's. He is one of the most amiable of men. The officer's courage arrested his soldier's flight. I want to buy some cabinet-maker's tools. He died a miser's death. Last Monday's procession was magnificent. The emperor of the French was taken prisoner after the battle of Sedan. Germany's military power is unrivaled. Frederic the Second, surnamed the Great, laid the foundation to Prussia's present greatness. Paris is the capital of France. England's navy is England's pride. We were about to leave for Albany when it began to rain. I wonder what this fellow is about. Everybody should mind his own business. You must mind what I say. George, if you play this trick again, mind me, I shall take a stick and give you a sound thrashing. It strikes me that I have seen you before. We were much struck with the beauty of the scenery. Do you know that Fred is engaged to be married? If you are not quiet, I shall turn you out of the room. When we shall have finished this lesson, we may commence to enter into conversation. I am disengaged after six, and shall be very happy if you will call upon me after that hour. When I called on him this morning, he had left. I rang the bell three times before the door was opened. Did you ring the bell? I did. Ring harder. I managed to get rid of this troublesome visitor. Do you think you can manage a boat in a storm? I am delighted with these flowers. Allow me to congratulate you on your happy arrival to this country.

Wörter-Verzeichniß.

zerrissen, torn.
Schürze, apron.

ganz, quite.
schmutzig, dirty, soiled.

Der Possessiv-Casus.

wessen Schuld ist es? whose fault is it?
kennst du? do you know?
Eltern, parents.
Laden, store.
Ruhe, rest.
Tod, death.
Hader, strife.
Schwager, brother-in-law.
Blatt, leaf.
Arzt, physician.
Wohnung, residence.
Armee, army.
hinlegen, to put.
Kronprinz, crown-prince.
Werk, work.
sich vorbereiten auf, to prepare for.
Winterfeldzug, winter campaign.

Uebungs-Aufgabe 2.

Johannes' Rock ist zerrissen, und Mariens Schürze ist ganz schmutzig. Wessen Schuld ist es, daß wir zu spät gekommen sind? Das ist deines Bruders Schuld. Kennst du dieser Kinder Eltern? Ich kenne nur ihren Vater. In diesem Laden kannst du Herren= und Knabenkleider kaufen. Adams erster Schlaf war seine letzte Ruh. Des Menschen Leben ist kurz, und der Tod macht ein Ende alles Haders. Meines Schwagers Geschäft ist in der untern Stadt. Die Blätter dieses Buches sind alle schmutzig. Dies Messer gehört dem Sohne meines Nachbars. Die Söhne unseres Arztes sind sehr fleißig. Die Wohnung des Präsidenten der Vereinigten Staaten heißt das Weiße Haus. Deutschlands Armeen sind die besten in der Welt. Theodors Vater ist ein Kaufmann; er ist der Bruder meines Vaters. Wo hast du die Bücher deiner Brüder hingelegt? Kaiser Wilhelms ältester Sohn ist der Kronprinz von Preußen; seine Frau ist die Tochter der Königin von England. Haben Sie Shakespeares und Walter Scotts Werke gelesen? Die Soldaten bereiteten sich vor auf einen Winterfeldzug in Frankreich.

Lesestück 1.

OUT OF THE WAY. (Aus dem Wege.)

1. "Old Mr. Worthy,"[1] as he was called,[2] had worked[3] at his trade of watchmaker,[4] until he was

able⁵ to retire⁶ from business on⁷ a very snug⁸ little fortune.⁹ So¹⁰ he bought a pretty little house in the outskirts¹¹ of the town, with a garden full of flowers, and a fountain¹² in the middle¹³ of the garden, and then he enjoyed¹⁴ himself very much.

2. His wife enjoyed herself, too; but never so much as when the neighbors, as they passed by, peeped¹⁵ over the fence,¹⁶ and said, "What a pretty place! What lucky¹⁷ people the watchmaker and his wife are! How they must enjoy themselves!"

3. On such occasions¹⁸ Master Frank, their only¹⁹ son, would be sure to hear²⁰ what the neighbors said; and when they were gone²¹ he would exclaim,²² "Isn't it grand,²³ mother, that everybody should think that?" "It is, my son," his mother would reply;²⁴ but old Mr. Worthy would shake²⁵ his head, and say to his wife, "You are filling²⁶ that boy's head with nonsense."²⁷

4. Now, Frank's mother thought²⁸ her son remarkably²⁹ smart;³⁰ and when she thought his education³¹ was complete, she requested³² Mr. Worthy to dismiss³³ all Frank's teachers, give him a handsome³⁴ sum of money, and let him go off³⁵ to see the world³⁶ and make his fortune.³⁷

5. The old gentleman shook his head at first, and called it all sheer³⁸ folly.³⁹ Moreover,⁴⁰ he declared,⁴¹ that Master Frank was⁴² a mere⁴³ child yet, and would get⁴⁴ into a hundred foolish scrapes⁴⁵ in less⁴⁶ than a week;⁴⁷ but mamma expressed⁴⁸ her opinion so positively,⁴⁹ and repeated⁵⁰ it so often, that at last papa began to entertain⁵¹ it too, and gave his consent⁵² to the plan.

6. When Frank was about⁵³ to leave home, with his pockets full of money, his mother took him privately⁵⁴ aside,⁵⁵ to give him some parting advice.⁵⁶ "Your education," said she, "is now finished.⁵⁷ You can play on the piano, and dance, and sing, and talk before anybody, and make yourself noticed⁵⁸ wherever you go. Now mind⁵⁹ that you *do* make yourself noticed,⁶⁰

or *who* is to find out your merits?⁶¹ Don't be shy⁶²
and downcast⁶³ when you come among strangers.⁶⁴
All you have to think about,⁶⁵ with *your* advantages,⁶⁶
is to put yourself forward,⁶⁷ and make yourself agreeable."⁶⁸

7. But Frank's father, knowing nothing of the lesson⁶⁹ which the vain⁷⁰ mother had just given him,
also took him aside, and spoke to him as follows:⁷¹
"Now, my dear boy, before you go, let me give you
one word of parting advice. We have all made too
much of you,⁷² and praised⁷³ whatever you have done;
and you have been a sort of *idol*⁷⁴ and *wonder*⁷⁵ among
us. But now that you are going⁷⁶ among strangers, you
will find yourself Mr. Nobody;⁷⁷ and you must be contented⁷⁸ to *be* Mr. Nobody at first.

8. "Keep yourself in the background⁷⁹ till people
have found out your merits for themselves, and *never
get in anybody's way*.⁸⁰ Just keep *out* of the way.⁸¹
It's the secret of life⁸² for a young man. Why,⁸³
Frank, how impatient⁸⁴ you are! Now, mark⁸⁵ my
words. All you have to attend to,⁸⁶ with *your* advantages, is to *keep out of the way*."

9. Frank had listened⁸⁷ to his father's advice very
impatiently. As he passed out,⁸⁸ his mother called to
him,⁸⁹ "Remember⁹⁰ what I've said." "Trust me,"⁹¹
was Frank's reply.⁹² The driver⁹³ was calling, so he
walked off to the stage-coach.⁹⁴ He was just in time;⁹⁵
but a sudden⁹⁶ thought struck him,⁹⁷ that it would be
well for the driver and passengers⁹⁸ to know⁹⁹ how
well educated he had been.

10. So, while he stood leisurely¹⁰⁰ pulling on¹⁰¹ his
kid gloves,¹⁰² he began to talk about the country; and
as there were two roads¹⁰³ leading to the next village,
he thought it well to advise the driver which to take.
"Jump in,¹⁰⁴ jump in," called out the driver. "Certainly not till¹⁰⁵ I've made you understand¹⁰⁶ what I
mean," said Master Frank, quite pompously.¹⁰⁷

11. But then, crack went the whip,¹⁰⁸ the horses
made a start¹⁰⁹ forward, and the front-wheel¹¹⁰ passed

over the tip [111] of Master Frank's boot. It might have been worse; but Frank called out, very angrily,[112] about "disgraceful carelessness,"[113] on which the driver cracked his whip again, and shouted,[114] "Gentlemen that won't keep out of the way [115] must expect to have their toes [116] trodden on." Everybody laughed at this, and Frank was obliged [117] to spring hastily inside,[118] or he would have been left behind.

[1] Biedermann, [2] genannt wurde, [3] gearbeitet, [4] Uhrmacherhandwerk, [5] bis er im Stande war, [6] sich zurückzuziehen, [7] mit, [8] hübsch, [9] Vermögen, [10] daher, [11] Umgebungen, [12] Springbrunnen, [13] Mitte, [14] genoß er das Leben, [15] lugten, [16] Einfriedigung, [17] glücklich, [18] bei solchen Gelegenheiten, [19] einziger, [20] hörte gewiß immer, [21] fort, [22] rief er allemal aus, [23] herrlich, [24] antwortete dann stets, [25] schüttelte, [26] du füllst—an, [27] Unsinn, [28] hielt—für, [29] ganz besonders, [30] gescheut, [31] Erziehung, [32] bat, [33] zu entlassen, [34] hübsch, [35] fortgehen, [36] Welt, [37] Glück, [38] schier, [39] Thorheit, [40] überties, [41] erklärte, [42] sei, [43] nur, [44] gerathen, [45] Verlegenheiten, [46] weniger, [47] Woche, [48] drückte aus, [49] bestimmt, [50] wiederholte, [51] zu hegen, [52] Zustimmung, [53] im Begriff, [54] insgeheim, [55] bei Seite, [56] Rath zum Abschied, [57] beendigt, [58] bemerkbar, [59] sorge dafür, [60] daß du dich auch wirklich bemerkbar machst, [61] Vorzüge, [62] schüchtern, [63] verlegen, [64] Fremde, [65] Alles woran du zu denken hast, [66] Vorzüge, [67] ist dich verzudrängen, [68] angenehm, [69] Lektion, [70] eitel, [71] wie folgt, [72] aus dir, [73] gelobt, [74] eine Art Abgott, [75] Wunderkind, [76] wo du im Begriff stehst zu gehen, [77] Herr Niemand, [78] zufrieden, [79] sei zurückhaltend, [80] dränge dich Niemand auf, [81] sei vielmehr zurückhaltend, [82] Geheimniß des Lebens, [83] ei! [84] ungeduldig, [85] gedenke an, [86] Alles worauf du zu achten hast, [87] angehört, [88] als er hinausging, [89] rief—ihm zu, [90] denke daran, [91] keine Sorge! [92] Antwort, [93] Kutscher, [94] Postkutsche, [95] er kam gerade zu rechter Zeit, [96] plötzlich, [97] kam ihm der Gedanke in den Sinn, [98] Passagiere, [99] zu erfahren, [100] gemächlich, [101] anziehend, [102] Glacéehandschuhe, [103] Wege, [104] eingestiegen! [105] ehe, [106] ich Ihnen klar gemacht habe, [107] wichtigthuerisch, [108] die Peitsche knallte, [109] Satz, [110] Vorderrad, [111] Spitze, [112] schrie sehr ungehalten, [113] abscheuliche Nachlässigkeit, [114] laut rief, [115] die nicht aus dem Wege gehen, [116] Zehen, [117] gezwungen, [118] hinein.

Lesestück 2.

OUT OF THE WAY. (Fortsetzung.)

1. After his arrival [1] at the great hotel of the city, he found that there was to be [2] a public [3] dinner there that evening, which everybody might attend [4] who chose [5] to pay for it.[6] So he dressed himself [7] in his neatest suit,[8] and when the time arrived,[9] strode [10] pompously into the large dining-hall,[11] where was a long table, set out [12] with plates,[13] and fast filling [14]

with people, not one of whom [15] he knew.[16] He felt a little confused [17] at first, but recalling [18] his mother's advice, he repeated [19] to himself her parting words, and took courage.[20]

2. He had certainly forgotten [21] the text,[22] "When thou art bidden, go and sit down in the lowest room;" [23] for, passing by [24] the *lower* [25] end of the table, where were several [26] unoccupied [27] places, he walked boldly [28] forward to the *upper* [29] end, where groups [30] of people were already seated,[31] talking [32] and laughing together. Observing [33] an unoccupied seat [34] next [35] to a well-dressed young lady, "Why, this is the very thing," [36] thought he to himself. There was a card [37] it is true,[38] in the plate opposite [39] the vacant [40] seat; but "what of that?" [41] thought he, "first come, first served,[42] I suppose." [43]

3. So, sitting down, and thinking of his mother's advice to "put himself forward," he bowed [44] and smiled [45] to the young lady; but the next instant [46] he was tapped [47] on the shoulder [48] by the waiter,[49] who, pointing [50] to the card in the plate, said in a low voice,[51] "This place is engaged,[52] sir!"

4. "Oh, if that is all," said Frank, speaking quite loud, "here's another to match;" [53] on which [54] he drew [55] one of his own cards from his pocket, and threw [56] it into the plate. "*The place is engaged, sir!*" repeated the waiter, in a louder voice; [57] but Frank showed [58] no disposition [59] to abandon [60] his seat; and as he had already attracted [61] the attention [62] of the whole table,[63] there was a general cry [64] of "Turn him out!" [65]

5. "Turn me out!" [66] shouted Frank, jumping up; [67] but at that moment a voice [68] behind [69] him called out, a hand laying hold of him by the shoulders [70] at the same time, "Young man, I'll trouble you [71] to *get out of my chair;* and OUT OF MY WAY; and to KEEP OUT OF MY WAY!" [72]

6. Frank found himself [73] half way down the room before he knew what was happening; [74] for, after the

gentleman had let go of him,[75] the waiter seized [76] him and hustled [77] him along.[78] There was no longer any room [79] for him at the lower end of the table; but he at length found a seat at a side-table [80] in a corner,[81] at which sat [82] two men in foreign dress [83] not one word of whose language [84] he could understand.

7. His first unlucky adventure [85] had sobered [86] him a little; but presently,[87] with his mother's advice running in his head,[88] he resolved [89] to make another attempt [90] to "put himself forward,"[91] and "make himself agreeable," if possible. So, at the next burst of merriment [92] from the foreign gentlemen, he affected to enter [93] into the joke,[94] threw [95] himself back in his chair, and laughed as loudly as *they* did.

8. The men stared [96] for a second,[97] then frowned;[98] one of them shouted [99] angrily [100] at him, and the other called loudly to the waiter. A moment after, Frank found himself being conveyed [101] by the waiter to the doorway [102] into the hall,[103] with the remark sounding [104] in his ears, "What a foolish [105] young gentleman you must be! Why can't you keep out of people's way!"

9. The waiter advised [106] Frank to go to bed, where he might be out of the way; "but," said Frank, "I understand [107] there's to be dancing [108] here to-night, and I can dance, and—"

10. "Pooh! pooh!"[109] said the waiter; "what's the use of dancing,[110] if you are in everybody's way;[111] and I know you will be." So Frank went to bed, where he lay [112] a long time awake [113] wondering what *could* be the cause [114] of the failure [115] of his attempts[116] to make himself agreeable.

11. The next night he went to a public concert, where he made himself so conspicuous,[117] first applauding,[118] then hissing,[119] and even speaking [120] his opinions to the people around him, that a set [121] of young college students [122] combined together [123] to get rid of him;[124] and so, before the entertainment [125] was half through,[126] Mr. Frank, after a little hard usage,[127] found himself in the street.

12. He had several letters of introduction[123] to people in the city; one to an old partner[129] of his father, who had settled[130] there some years before; another to some people of more consequence.[131] Of course,[132] Mr. Frank went to call upon[133] the latter[134] first, as there seemed a nice chance[135] of making his fortune among such great folks.[136]

13. And, really, the great folks would have been civil[137] enough, if he had not spoiled[138] everything by what he called "making himself agreeable." He was too affectedly[139] polite, too talkative,[140] too instructive[141] by half.[142] He assured the young ladies that he approved very highly[143] of their singing; trilled[144] out a little song of his own,[145] unasked,[146] at his first visit; fondled[147] the pet lap-dog[148] on his knee; congratulated[149] papa on looking wonderfully well for his age; asked mamma if she had tried[150] the last new spectacles;[151] and, in short,[152] gave[153] his opinions, advice, and information so freely,[153] that as soon as he was gone all exclaimed, "What a disagreeable,[154] impertinent fellow!"

¹ Ankunft, ² stattfinden sollte, ³ öffentlich, ⁴ an dem Jeder theilnehmen könnte, ⁵ Lust hatte, ⁶ dafür zu bezahlen, ⁷ er warf sich daher, ⁸ in seinen hübschesten Anzug, ⁹ herbeikam, ¹⁰ spazierte er, ¹¹ Speisesaal, ¹² gedeckt, ¹³ Teller, ¹⁴ sich schnell füllte, ¹⁵ von denen nicht Einen, ¹⁶ kannte, ¹⁷ verwirrt, ¹⁸ sich erinnernd an, ¹⁹ wiederholte, ²⁰ faßte Muth, ²¹ vergessen, ²² Schriftwort, ²³ wenn du geladen wirst, ²⁴ vorübergehend an, ²⁵ untere, ²⁶ mehrere, ²⁷ unbesetzt, ²⁸ keck, ²⁹ obere, ³⁰ Gruppen, ³¹ bereits Platz genommen hatten, ³² schwatzend, ³³ wahrnehmend, ³⁴ Sitz, ³⁵ neben, ³⁶ das ist ja grade recht, ³⁷ Adreßkarte, ³⁸ freilich, ³⁹ gegenüber, ⁴⁰ leer, ⁴¹ was macht das? ⁴² wer erst kommt, mahlt erst, ⁴³ meine ich, ⁴⁴ verbeugte er sich, ⁴⁵ lächelte, ⁴⁶ im nächsten Augenblick, ⁴⁷ wurde ihm geklopft, ⁴⁸ Schulter, ⁴⁹ Kellner, ⁵⁰ zeigend, ⁵¹ leise, ⁵² besetzt, ⁵³ die sich damit messen kann, ⁵⁴ worauf, ⁵⁵ sog, ⁵⁶ warf, ⁵⁷ Ton, ⁵⁸ zeigte, ⁵⁹ Neigung, ⁶⁰ verlassen, ⁶¹ auf sich gezogen hatte, ⁶² Aufmerksamkeit, ⁶³ Tischgesellschaft, ⁶⁴ allgemeines Geschrei, ⁶⁵ Hinaus mit ihm! ⁶⁶ hinaus mit mir, ⁶⁷ aufspringend, ⁶⁸ Stimme, ⁶⁹ hinter, ⁷⁰ eine Hand ihn bei der Schulter packend, ⁷¹ ich muß Sie belästigen, ⁷² und mir aus dem Wege zu bleiben, ⁷³ fand sich, ⁷⁴ wie ihm geschah, ⁷⁵ ihn losgelassen hatte, ⁷⁶ ergriff, ⁷⁷ schob, ⁷⁸ weiter, ⁷⁹ Platz, ⁸⁰ Nebentisch, ⁸¹ Ecke, ⁸² saßen, ⁸³ in ausländischer Tracht, ⁸⁴ Sprache, ⁸⁵ Abenteuer, ⁸⁶ hatte nüchtern gemacht, ⁸⁷ plötzlich, ⁸⁸ da ihm der Rath seiner Mutter durch den Kopf fuhr, ⁸⁹ entschloß er sich, ⁹⁰ noch einen Versuch, ⁹¹ sich vorzudrängen, ⁹² bei dem nächsten Ausbruch von Heiterkeit, ⁹³ stellte er sich als ginge er ein auf, ⁹⁴ Scherz, ⁹⁵ warf, ⁹⁶ starrten an, ⁹⁷ Sekunde,

⁹⁵ runzelten die Stirn, ⁹⁹ schrie an, ¹⁰⁰ zornig, ¹⁰¹ geführt, ¹⁰² durch die offene Thür, ¹⁰³ Vordiele, ¹⁰⁴ klingend, ¹⁰⁵ närrisch, ¹⁰⁶ rieth, ¹⁰⁷ ich höre, ¹⁰⁸ es wird ein Ball stattfinden, ¹⁰⁹ Bah! bah! ¹¹⁰ wozu ist das Tanzen, ¹¹¹ wenn du Jedermann im Wege bist, ¹¹² lag, ¹¹³ wach, ¹¹⁴ Ursache, ¹¹⁵ Mißlingen, ¹¹⁶ Versuche, ¹¹⁷ auffallig, ¹¹⁸ Beifall klatschen, ¹¹⁹ Zischen, ¹²⁰ aussprechend, ¹²¹ Schaar, ¹²² Studenten, ¹²³ sich vereinigte, ¹²⁴ ihn loszuwerden, ¹²⁵ Lustbarkeit, ¹²⁶ halb zu Ende, ¹²⁷ Behandlung, ¹²⁸ mehrere Empfehlungsbriefe, ¹²⁹ Geschäftstheilhaber, ¹³⁰ sich niedergelassen hatte, ¹³¹ von größerem Ansehen, ¹³² natürlich, ¹³³ besuchte, ¹³⁴ Letztere, ¹³⁵ hübsche Gelegenheit, ¹³⁶ Leute, ¹³⁷ höflich, ¹³⁵ verdorben, ¹³⁹ affektirt, ¹⁴⁰ geschwätzig, ¹⁴¹ zu meisternd, ¹⁴² ganz und gar, ¹⁴³ daß er sehr lobenswerth fände, ¹⁴⁴ trällerte, ¹⁴⁵ eins von seinen eignen kleinen Liedern, ¹⁴⁶ unaufgefordert, ¹⁴⁷ streichelte, ¹⁴⁸ Lieblings-Schooßhund, ¹⁴⁹ gratulirte, ¹⁵⁰ versucht, ¹⁵¹ Brille, ¹⁵² kurz, ¹⁵³ war so freigebig mit, ¹⁵⁴ unausstehlich.

Lesestück 3.

OUT OF THE WAY. (Schluß.)

1. Things went on¹ in this way² for some time,³ for he called⁴ very often, as he had too high an opinion of himself to take the hints⁵ that were thrown out⁶ that his visits⁷ were not agreeable. At last, however,⁸ he could find "nobody at home," when he called, as the young ladies managed⁹ to get out of *his* way, as he would not keep out of *theirs*.

2. The unfortunate young man was compelled¹⁰ to take¹¹ the hint at last, and in his despondency¹² he found a good friend in the waiter¹³ at the hotel. "I thought," murmured¹⁴ Frank, in broken, almost sobbing accents,¹⁵ "I thought—the young ladies—would have been delighted—with¹⁶—my song; you see—I've been—so well thought¹⁷—and I can sing—."

3. "Pooh! pooh! nonsense!" interrupted¹⁸ the waiter. "What's the use¹⁹ of singing, if you're not been asked?²⁰ Much better go to bed." Poor Frank, deeply mortified,²¹ now gave himself up to tears,²² and ordered²³ his dinner up stairs,²⁴ for he felt as though he could not be seen²⁵ by any body. The folly²⁶ of his past conduct,²⁷ and of his mother's advice, appeared to him,²⁸ all at once,²⁹ in a new light.³⁰

4. Before the waiter had been gone³¹ five minutes, he returned³² with a letter³³ in his hand. Frank

trembled[31] as he took it. It was an invitation to dinner from his father's old partner. Frank threw[35] the note[36] on the floor[37]—declared[38] he would go nowhere[39]—would see nobody any more![40]

5. The "officious fellow"[41]— as he would have called[42] the waiter at another time[43]—took up the note, and read[44] it. "Why!" said he, "it's from your father's old partner! he wishes you had called;[45] but as you *haven't* called, he asks[46] you to dinner. Now you're wanted,[47] Mr. Frank, and must go."

6. "But I shall only get[48] into *difficulty*[49] again," cried he, despondingly.[50] "Nonsense. You've only to keep out of everybody's way, and all will be right," insisted the waiter, as he left the room.

7. "Only to keep out of everybody's way, and all will be right,"[51] repeated Frank to himself, as he looked at[52] his crestfallen[53] face in the glass.[54] "It's not the rule[55] *mother* gave me for getting on[56] in life!"

8. Frank went, trembling for the consequences,[57] but resolved to take his *father's* advice *this* time. In truth, he felt that he had no courage now to "put himself forward." It was the funniest thing[58] in the world[59] to hear him, as he went along,[60] repeating to himself,[61] "*All you have to do, with your advantages, is to make yourself*—no, no! not to make myself agreeable—*is to —keep out of the way!* That's it!"[62]

9. When Frank arrived at the house, he rang the bell[63] so gently[64] that he had to ring[65] twice[66] before he was heard. When he was ushered into the drawing-room,[67] the old partner came forward to meet him,[68] took him kindly by the hands, and, after one searching look[69] into his downcast[70] face, said:

10. "My dear Mr. Frank, you must put on a bolder face,[71] and ring a louder peal,[72] next time[73] you come to the house of your father's old friend!" Frank answered this warm greeting[74] by a sickly[75] smile;[76] and while he was being introduced[77] to the rest of the family, kept bowing on,[78] thinking of nothing but how he was to keep out of everybody's way.

11. He could scarcely answer their kind greetings [79] with anything more than "Yes" and "No," "Perhaps so," "Do you think so?" and other such little phrases.[80]

12. "How shy [81] he is, poor fellow!" thought the ladies; and then they talked to him all the more.[82] They asked him a thousand questions.[83] They chatted [84] of books, and music, and drawing,[85] and pressed him hard [86] to discover [87] what he knew, what he could do, and what he liked best;[88] and when it came out [89] from his short answers that he had read certain books —and in more than one language; and could sing— just a little;[90] and dance—just a little; and do several other things—just a little, too, they were delighted with him. "Ah! when you know [91] us better," said they, "and are not so shy of us as strangers,[92] we shall find out that you are as clever again [93] as you pretend to be,[94] Mr. Frank!"

13. "I'll tell you what," added [95] the old partner, coming up [96] at this moment, "it's a perfect treat [97] to me, Mr. Frank, to have a young man like you in my house! You're your father all over again [98]—and I can't praise you more.[99] He was the most modest,[100] unobtrusive [101] man in all our town; and yet he knew [102] more of his business than all of us put together.[103]

14. "However, my dear boy—for I really must call you so—it was that very thing [104] that made your father's fortune: I mean, that he was just as unpretending [105] as he was clever. Everybody trusts [106] an *unpretending* man. And *you'll* make *your* fortune, too, in the same manner,[107] before long.[108] Now, boys!" added he, turning [109] to his sons, "you hear what I say, and take the hint!" [110]

15. It is surprising [111] how rapidly [112] Master Frank got along [113] after this, and how many attentions [114] were *thrust* upon him,[115] all because, as everybody said, he was "such an agreeable young man, and as modest as he was well educated." He had been really humbled,[116] and he was greatly changed [117] in character;

Der Possessiv-Casus.

but the more¹¹⁸ he tried to "keep out of the way," the more¹¹⁹ he was brought forward!¹²⁰ What a world of contradictions¹²¹ this is!

16. It was a jovial day¹²² for good old Mr. and Mrs. Worthy, when, two years after¹²³ Master Frank had set out¹²⁴ on his travels,¹²⁵ he returned home a partner in the old partner's business, with one of his smiling¹²⁶ daughters for his bride.¹²⁷

(Mrs. Gatty.)

¹ Es ging fort, ² auf diese Weise, ³ eine Zeitlang, ⁴ sprach vor, ⁵ um die Winke zu verstehen, ⁶ die man fallen ließ, ⁷ Besuche, ⁸ jedoch, ⁹ es so einrichten, ¹⁰ genöthigt, ¹¹ zu verstehen, ¹² Niedergeschlagenheit, ¹³ Kellner, ¹⁴ murmelte, ¹⁵ fast erstickter Stimme, ¹⁶ würden entzückt gewesen sein von, ¹⁷ unterrichtet, ¹⁸ unterbrach, ¹⁹ was nützt, ²⁰ aufgefordert, ²¹ lief getränkt, ²² ließ seinen Thränen freien Lauf, ²³ bestellte, ²⁴ auf sein Zimmer, ²⁵ als ob er sich nicht könnte sehen lassen, ²⁶ Oberkeit, ²⁷ Betragen, ²⁸ erschien ihm, ²⁹ ganz auf einmal, ³⁰ Licht, ³¹ fort war, ³² kam er zurück, ³³ Brief, ³⁴ zitterte, ³⁵ warf, ³⁶ Billet, ³⁷ Fußboden, ³⁸ erklärte, ³⁹ nirgendhin, ⁴⁰ Niemand mehr, ⁴¹ aufdringliche Bursche, ⁴² genannt, ⁴³ zu jeder andern Zeit, ⁴⁴ las, ⁴⁵ vorgesprochen, ⁴⁶ bittet, ⁴⁷ jetzt will man Sie haben, ⁴⁸ gerathen, ⁴⁹ Unannehmlichkeiten, ⁵⁰ niedergeschlagen, ⁵¹ und alles wird gut gehen, ⁵² anblickte, ⁵³ niedergeschlagen, ⁵⁴ Spiegel, ⁵⁵ Regel, ⁵⁶ fortzukommen, ⁵⁷ Folgen, ⁵⁸ Drolligste, ⁵⁹ Welt, ⁶⁰ wie er so dahinging, ⁶¹ für sich wiederholend, ⁶² das ist's, ⁶³ zog er die Schelle, ⁶⁴ leise, ⁶⁵ schellen mußte, ⁶⁶ zweimal, ⁶⁷ als man ihn in's Wohnzimmer zeigte, ⁶⁸ kam ihm entgegen, ⁶⁹ nach einem forschenden Blick, ⁷⁰ niedergeschlagen, ⁷¹ eine herzhaftere Miene annehmen, ⁷² lauter schellen, ⁷³ das nächste Mal, das, ⁷⁴ diesen herzlichen Gruß, ⁷⁵ matt, ⁷⁶ Lächeln, ⁷⁷ während er vorgestellt wurde, ⁷⁸ verbeugte er sich in Einem fort, ⁷⁹ Entgegenkommen, ⁸⁰ derartige kurze Redensarten, ⁸¹ blöde, ⁸² nur um so mehr, ⁸³ Fragen, ⁸⁴ schwatzten vertraulich, ⁸⁵ Zeichen, ⁸⁶ bestürmten ihn, ⁸⁷ auszufinden, ⁸⁸ was er am liebsten hätte, ⁸⁹ hervorging, ⁹⁰ nur ein bischen, ⁹¹ kennen, ⁹² Fremde, ⁹³ noch einmal so gescheut, ⁹⁴ als wofür Sie sich ausgeben, ⁹⁵ setzte—hinzu, ⁹⁶ der dazu kam, ⁹⁷ ein wahres Gaudium, ⁹⁸ auf und nieder, ⁹⁹ ich könnte nichts mehr zu Ihrem Lobe sagen, ¹⁰⁰ bescheidenste, ¹⁰¹ anspruchloseste, ¹⁰² verstand er, ¹⁰³ wir Alle zusammengenommen, ¹⁰⁴ das war es grade was, ¹⁰⁵ anspruchslos, ¹⁰⁶ hat Zutrauen, ¹⁰⁷ Weise, ¹⁰⁸ binnen Kurzem, ¹⁰⁹ sich wendend, ¹¹⁰ beherzigt den Wink, ¹¹¹ erstaunlich, ¹¹² rasch, ¹¹³ fortkam, ¹¹⁴ Aufmerksamkeiten, ¹¹⁵ ihm aufgedrängt, ¹¹⁶ gedemüthigt, ¹¹⁷ hatte sich sehr geändert, ¹¹⁸ je mehr, ¹¹⁹ desto mehr, ¹²⁰ wurde er hervorgezogen, ¹²¹ Widersprüchen, ¹²² Freudentag, ¹²³ nachdem, ¹²⁴ angetreten hatte, ¹²⁵ Reisen, ¹²⁶ hold, ¹²⁷ Braut.

Lektion XXII.

Das Adverb. Bildung des Adverbs vom Adjektiv. Steigerung des Adverbs.

Redensarten: *to owe, to own, to be mistaken, to turn up.*

Wörter-Verzeichniß.

writing, Schrift.
letter, Brief.
well written, gut geschrieben.
a year, das Jahr.
handsome, hübsch.
salary, Gehalt.
musician, Musiker.
were paid, wurden bezahlt.
play, Spiel.
exceedingly, höchst.
annoying, ärgerlich.
to be disturbed, gestört zu werden.
tolerably, ziemlich.
health, Gesundheit.
tolerable, erträglich.
deserve, verdienen.
commendation, Lob.
behavior, Betragen.
highly, höchst.
praiseworthy, lobenswerth.
fast, schnell.
hardly, kaum.
to follow, folgen.
ever, je.
to rise, aufgehen.
never, nie.
to trust, trauen.
slow, langsam.

dunce, Dummkopf.
once for all, ein für allemal.
I could not help it, ich konnte nicht dafür.
it is not worth the while, es ist nicht der Mühe werth.
silly, albern.
business, Arbeit.
war, Krieg.
peace, Frieden.
countryman, Landsmann.
fluent, fließend.
we are drawing nearer, wir kommen näher.
worse, schlechter.
than I anticipated, als ich erwartete.
you will oblige me, Sie werden mich verbinden.
to mail, auf die Post bringen.
disappointed, enttäuscht.
at learning, als er erfuhr.
had left, abgereist war.
giving notice, davon in Kenntniß zu setzen.
to spare, zu entbehren.
does not like, hat keine Lust.
tired of, müde auf.

Das Adverb.

Redensarten.

to owe, schuldig sein.
to own, besitzen.
up-town, in der obern Stadt.
to own, eingestehen.
to suspect, argwöhnen.
cheat, Betrüger.

to be mistaken, sich irren.
he was thought to be, man hielt ihn für. [men.
to turn up, zum Vorschein kom=
to turn up the nose, die Nase rümpfen.

Uebungs=Aufgabe 1.

This writing is very good. Do you not think this letter is well written? Three thousand dollars a year is a handsome salary. The musicians were handsomely paid for their play. It is exceedingly annoying to be disturbed in your work. How do you do? I am tolerably well, thank you. My health is tolerably good. These boys deserve high commendation. Their behavior is highly praiseworthy. Do not walk so fast; I can hardly follow. Did you ever see the sun rise? I never trusted him. He is always very slow. Do you understand me? I would if you did not speak so fast. Why don't you speak more slowly? Do you want any more bread? I have enough. Even a dunce would understand this. I tell you once for all that I could not help it. Now, don't cry. It is not worth the while, it is too silly. I seldom (oder rarely) get up before six o'clock. First business, and then pleasure. Washington was first in war, first in peace, and first in the hearts of his countrymen. He speaks a fluent English; he speaks English fluently, but not very correctly. We are drawing nearer death every day. This work is badly done; it is done even worse than I anticipated. You will oblige me very much, if you will mail this letter for me. He was greatly disappointed at learning that his friend had left without giving him notice. There are but few children that do not feel happy. I have but little time to spare. He has no money; neither have I (oder nor I either—oder I neither). Henry does not like to study French, neither (oder nor) does his cousin. You are tired of this man, and so am I. You can go to the theatre, and so can your brother.

Redensarten: How much do you owe your tailor? I do not owe him anything. He owns three houses in this street, and two more up-town. Do you now own that you were wrong in suspecting this man to be a cheat? I own, I was mistaken. He was thought to be lost, when all at once he turned up in America. You must not turn up your nose at everything. If you want to go bathing, I will join in. Do not by any means trust every man.

Wörter-Verzeichniß.

Handschrift, handwriting.
ich habe unrecht, I am wrong.
diese beiden, these two.
einander, each other.
außerordentlich, exceedingly.
froh, happy; glad.
endlich, at last.
gar nicht, never.
glücklicherweise, fortunately.
böse, schlecht, bad.
gemacht, done.
aufrichtig, frank.
Bekenntniß, confession.
abgelegt, made.
Schuld, guilt.
eingestehen, to confess.
abbrennen, to burn down.
Feuerleute, firemen.
prompt, promptly.
bei der Hand, on the spot.
kämpfen, to battle.
wurde verletzt, was hurt.
deutlich, distinct.

Antwort, answer.
gründlich, thorough.
reinigen, to clean.
Reinigung, cleaning.
Mittel, remedy.
Ungeziefer, vermin.
Unglücksfall, accident.
sich ereignen, to happen.
häufig, frequent.
höflich, polite.
was er mir schuldig ist, what he owes me.
grob, insulting, insolent.
treu, faithful.
mehr werth, worth more.
helfen, to assist.
tüchtig, able.
Advokat, lawyer.
engagiren, to engage.
eine Sache führen, to plead a case.
überzeugt, convinced; persuaded.

vollkommen, perfect.
unschuldig an, innocent of.
Verbrechen, crime.

hübsch, pretty.
gekleidet, dressed.

Uebungs-Aufgabe 2.

Ist dies nicht eine gute Handschrift? Die Handschrift ist sehr gut; der Brief ist sehr gut geschrieben. Ich weiß sehr gut, daß ich unrecht habe. Diese beiden Leute sind sehr glücklich; sie leben sehr glücklich miteinander. Ich bin außerordentlich froh, daß du endlich gekommen bist; besser spät als gar nicht. Glücklicherweise ist es noch nicht zu spät. Wie befindest du dich heute? Ich danke, ich befinde mich ziemlich wohl. Karl ist ein böser Junge; seine Arbeiten sind immer schlecht gemacht. Der Mörder hat endlich ein aufrichtiges Bekenntniß abgelegt. Er hat aufrichtig seine Schuld eingestanden. Gestern brannten zwei Häuser ab. Die Feuerleute waren prompt bei der Hand; sie kämpften kühn mit den Flammen und glücklicherweise wurde Niemand verletzt. Gib mir eine deutliche Antwort. Antworte laut und deutlich. Wir haben unser Haus gründlich gereinigt. Eine gründliche Reinigung ist das beste Mittel gegen Ungeziefer. Unglücksfälle auf Eisenbahnen ereignen sich hier häufiger als in Deutschland. Ich bat aufs Höflichste mir zu bezahlen, was er mir schuldig ist; er hat mir aber sehr grob geantwortet. Ein treuer Freund ist mehr werth als Gold und Silber. Er hat mir treu geholfen bei meiner Arbeit. Er hatte einen tüchtigen Advokaten engagirt. Der Advokat führte seine Sache tüchtig; ich bin überzeugt, er ist vollkommen unschuldig an diesem Verbrechen. Das ist ein hübsches Mädchen. Es ist sehr hübsch gekleidet.

Lesestück 1.

THE LOST CAMEL. (Das verlorene Kameel.)

1. A dervish[1] was journeying[2] alone in the desert,[3] when two merchants[4] suddenly[5] met[6] him. "You have lost a camel," said he to the merchants. "Indeed we have,"[7] they replied. "Was he not blind in

his right⁸ eye,⁹ and lame in his left¹⁰ leg?"¹¹ said the dervish.

2. "He was," replied the merchants. "Had he lost a front tooth?"¹² said the dervish. "He had," rejoined¹³ the merchants. "And was he not loaded¹⁴ with honey¹⁵ on one side, and corn on the other?" "Most certainly¹⁶ he was," they replied; "and as you have seen him so lately,¹⁷ and describe¹⁸ him so well, we suppose¹⁹ you can conduct²⁰ us to him."

3. "My friends," said the dervish, "I have never seen your camel, nor ever heard of him but²¹ from yourselves." "A pretty story,²² truly!"²³ said the merchants; "but where are the jewels²⁴ which formed²⁵ a part²⁶ of his burden?"²⁷ "I have neither seen your camel, nor your jewels," repeated²⁸ the dervish.

4. On this²⁹ they seized³⁰ him, and took³¹ him to the cadi,³² where, on the strictest search,³³ nothing could be found against him; nor could any evidence³⁴ be produced³⁵ to prove him guilty,³⁶ either of falsehood³⁷ or of theft.³⁸ They were then about³⁹ to proceed⁴⁰ against him as a sorcerer,⁴¹ when the dervish, with great calmness,⁴² thus addressed⁴³ the court:⁴⁴

5. "I have been much amused with⁴⁵ your surprise,⁴⁶ and own⁴⁷ that there has been some ground⁴⁸ for you to think that I have been deceiving⁴⁹ you; but I have lived long, and alone; and have found ample room⁵⁰ for observation,⁵¹ even in a desert.

6. "I knew that I had crossed⁵² the track⁵³ of a camel that had strayed⁵⁴ from its owner,⁵⁵ because I saw no mark⁵⁶ of any human footsteps⁵⁷ on the same route:⁵⁸ I knew that the animal was blind of one eye, because it had cropped⁵⁹ the herbage⁶⁰ only on one side of its path;⁶¹ and I perceived⁶² that it was lame in one leg, from the faint⁶³ impression⁶⁴ one foot had made upon the sand.

7. "I also concluded⁶⁵ that the animal had lost one tooth,⁶⁶ because,⁶⁷ wherever⁶⁸ it had grazed,⁶⁹ a small tuft of herbage⁷⁰ was left uninjured,⁷¹ in the centre⁷² of its bite.⁷³ As to that⁷⁴ which formed the burden of

the beast, the busy [75] ants [76] informed [77] me that it was corn on the one side; and the clustering [78] flies, that it was honey on the other."

¹ Derwisch, ² war auf der Reise, ³ Wüste, ⁴ Kaufleute, ⁵ plötzlich, ⁶ entgegenkamen, ⁷ das haben wir in der That, ⁸ recht, ⁹ Auge, ¹⁰ link, ¹¹ Bein, ¹² Vorderzahn, ¹³ erwiderten, ¹⁴ beladen, ¹⁵ Honig, ¹⁶ ganz richtig, ¹⁷ vor Kurzem, ¹⁸ beschreibst, ¹⁹ wir vermuthen, ²⁰ hinführen, ²¹ ausgenommen, ²² eine hübsche Geschichte, ²³ wirklich, ²⁴ Juwelen, ²⁵ bildeten, ²⁶ Theil, ²⁷ Bürde, ²⁸ wiederholte, ²⁹ hierauf, ³⁰ erariffen, ³¹ brachten, ³² Cadi (Richter), ³³ nach der genauesten Untersuchung, ³⁴ Beweis, ³⁵ geliefert werden, ³⁶ ihn zu überführen, ³⁷ Lüge, ³⁸ Diebstahl, ³⁹ im Begriff, ⁴⁰ zu verfahren, ⁴¹ Zauberer, ⁴² Gemüthsruhe, ⁴³ anredete, ⁴⁴ Gerichtshof, ⁴⁵ ich habe mich sehr ergötzt an, ⁴⁶ Verwunderung, ⁴⁷ gebe zu, ⁴⁸ Grund, ⁴⁹ daß ich euch hintergangen habe, ⁵⁰ hinreichend Gelegenheit, ⁵¹ Beobachtung, ⁵² gerathen war, ⁵³ Spur, ⁵⁴ sich verirrt hatte, ⁵⁵ Eigenthümer, ⁵⁶ Spur, ⁵⁷ Fußstapfen, ⁵⁸ Weg, ⁵⁹ abgefressen, ⁶⁰ das Gras, ⁶¹ Pfad, ⁶² bemerkte, ⁶³ leicht, ⁶⁴ Eindruck, ⁶⁵ schloß, ⁶⁶ Zahn, ⁶⁷ weil, ⁶⁸ wo immer, ⁶⁹ gegrast, ⁷⁰ Büschel Gras, ⁷¹ unversehrt, ⁷² Mittelpunkt, ⁷³ Biß, ⁷⁴ was das betrifft, ⁷⁵ emsig, ⁷⁶ Ameisen, ⁷⁷ belehrten, ⁷⁸ haufenweise sitzend.

Lesestück 2.

WHO IS A GENTLEMAN? (Wer ist ein Gentleman?)

1. And do you think you are a gentleman? Why? Is it¹ because you carry² a little dandy³ cane,⁴ smoke cigars, and wear⁵ your hat on one side of your head? Is that the way to be⁶ a gentleman? Read⁷ the following story, and decide⁸ what it is that makes the gentleman.

2. One afternoon,⁹ last spring,¹⁰ there had been a sudden¹¹ gust of wind,¹² and a slight¹³ shower of rain.¹⁴ But the clouds¹⁵ soon passed away.¹⁶ The sun shone out¹⁷ brightly,¹⁸ and the rain-drops¹⁹ sparkled²⁰ like diamonds²¹ upon the trees of Boston Common.²²

3. The Boston boys love the Common; and well they may;²³ for where could they find a more glorious²⁴ play-ground?²⁵ During²⁶ the shower, the boys had²⁷ taken shelter²⁷ under the trees; as soon as it was passed²⁸ they resumed²⁹ their amusements.³⁰

4. On one of the crossings,³¹ or walks, appeared³² a small, plainly-dressed³³ old woman, with a cane in one hand, and a large green umbrella³⁴ in the other.

She was bent [35] with age [36] and infirmity,[37] and walked slowly.[38]

5. The green umbrella was open, and turned up [39] in the most comical [40] manner.[41] The wind had suddenly reversed [42] it, without the consent [43] or knowledge [44] of the old lady, and she now held it in one hand like a huge [45] flower with a long stalk.[46]

6. "Hurrah! hurrah!" cried [47] one of the boys, pointing [48] to the umbrella. "Mammoth cabbages [49] for sale! [50] Mammoth cabbages!"

7. The whole rabble [51] of boys joined [52] in the cry,[53] and ran hooting [54] after [55] the poor old woman. She looked at them with grave wonder,[56] and endeavored [57] to hasten [58] her tottering [59] footsteps.[60]

8. They still pursued [61] her, and at length began [62] pelting [63] with pebbles [64] the up-standing [65] umbrella, some crying "Mammoth cabbages," and others "New-fashioned [66] sun-shades." [67]

9. She turned [68] again, and said, with tears [69] in her eyes, "What have I done, my little lads,[70] that [71] you should thus trouble me?" [71]

10. "It is a shame," [72] said a neatly-dressed,[73] fine-looking [74] boy, who rushed [75] through the crowd [76] to the rescue [77] of the poor old woman.

11. "Madam," said he, "your umbrella was turned [78] by the wind. Will you allow [79] me to close [80] it for you?"

12. "I thank you," she replied. "Then that is [81] what [82] those boys are hooting at! [82] Well, it does look funny," [83] added she,[84] as she looked [85] at the cause [86] of their merriment.[87] The kind-hearted [88] boy endeavored [89] to turn down [90] the umbrella, but it was no easy [91] task; [92] the whalebones [93] seemed [94] obstinately [95] bent on [96] standing upright.[97]

13. The boys now changed [98] the object [99] of their attack,[100] and the pebbles rattled [101] like hail [102] upon the manly [103] fellow who was struggling [104] to relieve [105] the poor woman from [106] her awkward [107] predicament.[108]

14. "You are a mean[109] fellow,[110] to spoil[111] our fun,"[112] said they; "but you can't come it:[113] cabbage leaves[114] will grow upward."

15. He, however,[115] at length succeeded,[116] and, closing the troublesome[117] umbrella, handed[118] it to the old woman with a polite[119] bow.[120]

16. "Thank you, thank you—a thousand thanks, sir," said she, "and I should like to know[121] your name, that I may repay[122] you whenever I can find an opportunity."[123]

17. "By no means,"[124] replied he. "I am happy[125] to have rendered[126] you this trifling[127] service,"[128] and he walked away.

18. "Well," said she, "whoever you are, your father and mother have reason[129] to be proud of you, for you are a gentleman—a perfect[130] gentleman."

19. And so he was a gentleman; and I wish I could tell you his name, that you may see if my prophecy[131] does not prove[132] true.

20. "Manners[133] make the man," you may often have written in very legible[134] characters[135] in your copy-books.[136] They[137] certainly do go very far toward[137] making the gentleman. But a true[138] gentleman must have a good heart also.

---

[1] (Ist es, b. i.) vielleicht, [2] trägt, [3] Stutzer, [4] Spazierstock, [5] trägt, [6] ist man darum, [7] lies, [8] entscheide, [9] eines Nachmittags, [10] im vorigen Frühjahr, [11] plötzlich, [12] Windstoß, [13] leicht, [14] Regenschauer, [15] Wolken, [16] zogen vorüber, [17] strahlte, [18] hell, [19] Regentropfen, [20] glänzten, [21] Diamanten, [22] Gemeindewiese, [23] und sie haben auch Ursache dazu, [24] prächtig, [25] Spielplatz, [26] während, [27] hatten Schutz gesucht, [28] vorüber, [29] nahmen sie wieder auf, [30] Spiele, [31] Uebergänge, [32] erschien, [33] einfach gekleidet, [34] Regenschirm, [35] gebeugt, [36] Alter, [37] Schwäche, [38] langsam, [39] umgeschlagen, [40] fo mich, [41] Weise, [42] umgekehrt, [43] Erlaubniß, [44] Wissen, [45] riesig, [46] Stengel, [47] schrie, [48] zeigend, [49] Riesenkohl, [50] zu verkaufen, [51] Rubel, [52] stimmte ein, [53] das Geschrei, [54] mit neckendem Geschrei, [55] hinter—her, [56] mit großer Verwunderung, [57] versuchte, [58] beschleunigen, [59] wankend, [60] Schritte, [61] verfolgte, [62] fingen an, [63] zu bombardiren, [64] Steine, [65] umgestülpt, [66] neumodisch, [67] Sonnenschirme, [68] wandte sich, [69] Thränen, [70] Burschen, [71] daß ihr mich so belästigt? [72] Schande, [73] nett gekleidet, [74] hübsch, [75] sich hindurchdrängte, [76] Schaar, [77] Befreiung, [78] umgestülpt, [79] erlauben, [80] zuzumachen, [81] das ist es also, [82] worüber jene Jungen einen solchen Standal machen, [83] spaßig, [84] setzte sie hinzu, [85] wahrnahm, [86] Ursache, [87] Heiterkeit, [88] gutherzige, [89] bemühte sich,

⁹⁰ niederzuschlagen, ⁹¹ leicht, ⁹² Aufgabe, ⁹³ Fischbein, ⁹⁴ schien, ⁹⁵ eigensinnig, ⁹⁶ darauf vergessen, ⁹⁷ aufrecht zu stehen, ⁹⁸ wechselten, ⁹⁹ Gegenstand ¹⁰⁰ Angriff, ¹⁰¹ prasselten, ¹⁰² Hagel, ¹⁰³ muthig, ¹⁰⁴ sich abmühte, ¹⁰⁵ zu befreien, ¹⁰⁶ aus, ¹⁰⁷ sonderbar, ¹⁰⁸ Lage, ¹⁰⁹ schlecht, ¹¹⁰ Kerl, ¹¹¹ verderben, ¹¹² Spaß, ¹¹³ du kannst es nicht fertig bringen, ¹¹⁴ Blätter, ¹¹⁵ jedoch, ¹¹⁶ es gelang ihm, ¹¹⁷ widerspenstig, ¹¹⁸ reichte, ¹¹⁹ höflich, ¹²⁰ Verbeugung, ¹²¹ ich möchte auch wissen, ¹²² vergelten, ¹²³ Gelegenheit, ¹²⁴ keine Ursache, ¹²⁵ ich freue mich, ¹²⁶ erzeigt, ¹²⁷ unbedeutend, ¹²⁸ Dienst, ¹²⁹ Ursache, ¹³⁰ ganz, ¹³¹ Aussage, ¹³² erweist, ¹³³ Manieren, ¹³⁴ leserlich, ¹³⁵ Schriftzüge, ¹³⁶ Schreibbücher, ¹³⁷ sie tragen gewiß sehr dazu bei, ¹³⁸ wahr.

Lektion XXIII.

Präpositionen. Conjunktionen.

Präpositionen—*On, upon, of, from, to, with, at, in, into, without, for.*

Conjunktionen—*To, in order to, that, when, if, but, for.*

Redensarten—*To make a motion, to second, to pay one's respects, to happen, in return for, to be engaged, to remember to, to remind.*

Wörter-Verzeichniß.

Thy will be done, dein Wille geschehe.
heaven, Himmel.
to depend upon, ankommen auf.
word of honour, Ehrenwort.
to lock, schließen.
I want you to, ich will, daß du.
to consider, bedenken.
to agree with, übereinstimmen mit.
to get excited, in Hitze gerathen.
single, einzig.
in order to, um zu.
dentist, Zahnarzt.
afterwards, nachher.
but yesterday, erst gestern.
news, Nachricht.
all but, nichts weniger als.
orchard, Obstgarten.
to shake, schütteln.
left, übrig.
the last but one, die nächstletzte.
to resent, wiedervergelten.
incivility, Unhöflichkeit.

Redensarten.
to motion, vorschlagen.
to adjourn, sich vertagen.

Präpositionen. Conjunktionen. 179

motion, Vorschlag.
to second, unterstützen.
in favor of, für (zu Gunsten).
to signify, kundgeben.
contrary, dagegen.
to carry (a motion), anneh=
 men.
to pay one's respects, seine
 Aufwartung machen.
to bid, beißen.
to hold one's tongue, sein
 Maul halten.
without avail, vergeblich.
to mind, gehorchen.

I happened to stand, ich stand
 gerade.
it happens, es passirt.
in return for, zum Dank für.
barrel, Faß.
choice, besonders schön.
engaged, verlobt.
to be married to, sich zu ver=
 heirathen mit.
to engage, dingen.
to dig, graben.
well, Brunnen.
to remind of, erinnern an.

Uebungs=Aufgabe 1.

Dinner is on the table; you forgot to put the butter on the table. "Thy will be done on earth as it is done in heaven." If we wish to live to a good old age, much will depend upon how we take care of our time. I tell you upon my word of honor that I did not leave the room without locking the door. When the clock strikes ten I want you to go to bed. If you consider all the cir-cumstances, you will agree with me that it was very foolish in her to get excited, when Charles broke the pitcher. Of whom do you speak? We are speaking of George who went to America, and from whom we have not yet received a single letter. Can you tell me where these people come from? They come from Hamburg. How far is it from New York to St. Louis? We do not live in order to eat, but we eat in order to live. There is no rose without thorns. When will you be at home? I was at my uncle's this morning. Come, let us go to the dentist's first, we can go to the cap-tain's afterwards. With whom are you going to church to-morrow? I shall go with my father and mother. I was with Henry all day. Will you give this knife to your sister? I gave a poor old woman some bread and meat. I gave some bread and meat to a poor old woman. Will you go with me to the theatre? I guess not, for I was at the theatre but yesterday. The news you have brought me is all but pleasant to me. Who is in my kitchen? Let us go into the orchard and shake some apples from the trees. The dog jumped into the water to fetch a piece of wood that was thrown in. How many bottles of champagne are there left in our cellar? This is the last but one. Will you go for me to the apothecary's, for I am so busy that I cannot go myself. It is very praiseworthy in you that you did not resent his incivility. When your work is done you may go to bed.

Redensarten: I motion to adjourn. A motion is made to adjourn. Is the motion seconded? I second the motion. It is motioned and seconded to adjourn. All who are in favor of this motion will signify by saying, "Aye." Contrary, "No." The motion is carried. When I was in Washington, I paid my respects to the President. Bid these girls hold their tongues. I bid them be silent more than once, but without avail; they won't mind me. I happened to stand in the doorway when the procession passed by. It often happens that I forget the names of my best and most intimate friends. In return for your kind services I send you a barrel of choice apples. Do you know that Emily is engaged? She is engaged to be married to the only son of a rich banker. I have to go out to engage some workmen to dig a well for me. Do you remember all he said? I remember very little. Will you remember me to your sister? I told you to remind me of the meeting to-night.

Wörter-Verzeichniß.

explodiren, to explode.
an Bord, on board.
Chinese, Chinese.
leben von, to live on.

Reis, rice.
stolz auf, proud of.
nach Hause, home.
Vetter von mir, cousin of mine.

Präpositionen. Conjunktionen.

ankommen, to arrive.
Anstrengung, application.
fertig werden mit, to finish.
warten auf, to wait for.
augenblicklich, at present.
beschäftigt, busy.
rufen, to call.
bleiben, to stay.

sich sehnen nach, to long for.
denken an, to think of.
unsicher, uncertain.
böse auf, angry with.
bange vor, afraid of.
erfahren, to ascertain.
Ausflug, trip, excursion.

Uebungs-Aufgabe 2.

Die Quäker haben immer den Hut auf dem Kopfe. Der Dampfer Westfield explodirte mit mehr als zweihundert Menschen an Bord. Die Chinesen leben meist von Reis. Von wem hast du diese Uhr gekauft? Ich habe sie von Ball, Black & Co. gekauft. Er ist sehr stolz auf seine Kinder. Wir kommen so eben aus der Schule und wollen nach Hause gehen. Bist du ein Freund von diesem Manne? Von wem hast du diesen Brief erhalten? Er ist von einem Vetter von mir. Täglich kommen hier Einwanderer an aus allen Theilen von Europa. Willst du mit mir gehen? Ich will mit dir gehen zu deinem Bruder, aber nicht in's Theater. Ohne Anstrengung können wir Nichts lernen. Ich bin ohne Hülfe fertig geworden mit meiner Arbeit. Wo ist Heinrich? Ist er im Garten? Nein, er ist bei seinem Freunde Julius. Für wen sind diese Stiefel? Sie sind für meine Schwester. Wollen Sie auf mich warten? Wenn ich Zeit hätte, so wollte ich auf Sie warten; ich bin aber augenblicklich sehr beschäftigt. Wo warst du, als ich dich rief? Du mußt heute zu Hause bleiben, denn das Wetter ist zu schlecht. Wir sehnen uns nach besseren Zeiten. Es ist weise recht oft an den Tod zu denken; denn nichts ist unsicherer als das Leben, und nichts gewisser als der Tod. Bist du böse auf mich? Ich bin sehr böse auf dich. Warum bist du bange vor ihm? Ich bin nicht bange vor ihm, aber er ist bange vor mir. Ich bin zu Ihnen geschickt, um zu erfahren, ob Sie mit uns einen Ausflug nach Albany machen wollen.

Lesestück 1.

PRINCE HENRY.

1. Henry, Prince of Wales, was the eldest son of Henry IV, King of England. In his youth he was very wild and riotous,[1] and, mingling[2] with low companions, was led[3] by them into base[4] and disgraceful[5] acts.

2. One of his unworthy associates[6] was, upon a certain occasion[7] brought before the chief justice,[8] and being found guilty, was about to be sent to prison. The prince came into court,[9] and insisted[10] that the man should be released;[11] the judge (whose name was Gascoigne), said that he was sworn[12] to do justice, and that he would not break the laws, even in favor of the prince.

3. Upon this Henry became violent,[13] and attempted[14] himself to set the prisoner free. But the chief justice commanded him to stop, and to cease from[15] such riot.[16] This so enraged[17] the prince that he stepped up to the judge, and gave him a blow[18] upon the face.

4. The judge then addressed the prince, "Sir, I pray you to remember that this seat of judgment[19] is not mine, but your father's; to him you owe[20] obedience. If his laws be thus despised[21] by you now, who will obey you when you are sovereign,[22] or administer[23] the laws which you shall make? For this attempt,[24] in your father's name, I commit[25] you to prison, there to be kept till his pleasure[26] be known."

5. Prince Henry was abashed[27] by the rebuke;[28] he stood mute,[29] and looking upon the judge, presently[30] laid down his sword, and having bowed humbly, departed[31] to prison. When the king heard of what had passed, he rejoiced[32] that he had a son who could thus submit[33] to his laws, and that he had a judge who could so fearlessly administer[34] them.

6. When his father died, the prince came to the

throne, under the name of Henry V, and they who knew of his former riotous life, were very anxious[35] to see how he would act as king.

7. Shortly after he was crowned, many of his people came to pay their respects[36] to him. Among the rest came some of his wild companions, confident[37] that now they should be his chief favorites.[38]

8. The king soon showed that he was wiser than he had been. He rebuked them gravely[39] for their misconduct,[40] and forbade them to come within[41] ten miles of his person, till they had proved by their behavior[42] that they had learned better manners; but lest[43] they should be led to evil courses[44] by want,[45] he appointed to them[46] a sufficient allowance[47] to keep them in what was necessary for their living.

9. After these came before him Sir John Gascoigne, fearful[48] what reception[49] he might have. But the king quickly reassured[50] him, thanking him for his former firmness, and bidding[51] him retain[52] the office[53] he discharged[54] so worthily. "Should it happen,"[55] said he, "that hereafter a son of mine should behave as I did, may I have a chief justice as bold[56] and faithful as you to reprove[57] and correct him."

---

[1] ausschweifend, [2] verlehrend, [3] wurde verleitet, [4] gemein, [5] entbehrend, [6] Gefährten, [7] Gelegenheit, [8] Oberrichter, [9] Gerichtshof, [10] bestand darauf, [11] freigelassen, [12] beeidigt, [13] heftig, [14] versuchte, [15] abzustehen von, [16] ungesetzliches Gebahren, [17] setzte in Wuth, [18] Schlag, [19] Richterstuhl, [20] schulden, [21] verachtet, [22] Herrscher, [23] ausführen, [24] Versuch (Anschlag), [25] überantworte ich, [26] Wille, [27] beschämt, [28] Zurechtweisung, [29] stumm, [30] plötzlich, [31] ging fort, [32] freute er sich, [33] unterwerfen, [34] handhaben, [35] begierig (gespannt), [36] ihm ihre Aufwartung zu machen, [37] fest vertrauend, [38] Günstlinge, [39] er schalt sie alles Ernstes, [40] schlechter Lebenswandel, [41] innerhalb, [42] Benehmen, [43] damit nicht, [44] böse Wege, [45] aus Armuth, [46] wies er ihnen an, [47] eine hinreichende Unterstützung, [48] besorgt, [49] Empfang, [50] beruhigte, [51] befehlend, [52] behalten, [53] Amt, [54] verwaltete, [55] sollte es sich zutragen, [56] unerschrocken, [57] tadeln.

Lesestück 2.

DUKE OF ALBA'S BREAKFAST. (Herzog Alba's Frühstück.)

1. In the year 1547, when the Emperor Charles V was passing through Thuringia, the widowed[1] Countess Katharina, of Schwarzburg, a princess of the house of Henneberg, obtained[2] from him a letter of safeguard.[3] This was, in other words, a promise of protection to her subjects[4] from the depredations[5] of the Spanish army in their march through her territory.[6] In return for this,[7] and in consideration[8] of a fair payment,[9] she engaged[10] to have bread, beer, and other provisions sent from Rudolstadt for the use of the emperor's troops.

2. She took precaution,[11] however, to have[12] a bridge, which was close upon the town, hastily pulled down[13] and put up again[14] at a greater distance, in order that[14] the close proximity[15] of the town might not lead her rapacious[16] guests into temptation.[17] Permission was also given to the inhabitants of the villages through which the soldiers passed to take shelter,[18] with their valuables,[19] in the castle of Rudolstadt.

3. In the meantime, the Spanish general, the Duke of Alba, approached[20] the town, accompanied by Heinrich von Braunschweig and his son, and sent a messenger[21] in advance[22] to invite himself to breakfast with the Countess of Schwarzburg. So modest[23] a request,[24] made at the head[25] of an army, could not well be refused.

4. "What the house contains[26] is at your service," was the answer. At the same time the emperor's safeguard was mentioned,[27] and the Spanish general was reminded[28] of the necessity of a scrupulous[29] observance[30] of it. A friendly reception and a well-covered table awaited the duke at the castle. He was obliged[31] to confess[32] that the Thuringian lady kept a good kitchen, and well maintained[33] the laws of hospitality.[34] But scarcely were they seated,[35] when a courier called

the countess from the room, and informed³⁶ her that in some villages on the road the Spanish soldiers had used violence,³⁷ and had driven away the cattle³⁸ of the peasants.³⁹ Katharina was the mother of her people ; what befell the poorest of her subjects, she looked upon in the same light as though it had happened to herself.

5. Greatly displeased,⁴⁰ therefore, with this breach of promise,⁴¹ but preserving⁴² her presence of mind,⁴³ she commanded her whole household to arm⁴⁴ themselves in all haste and silence, and firmly to bolt⁴⁵ the castle gates. She then returned to the hall where the princes were at the table, and complained⁴⁶ to them in the most moving terms⁴⁷ of the outrage⁴⁸ which had been reported to her, and of the manner in which the emperor's promise of protection had been violated.⁴⁹ Her guests laughed, and answered that it was the usage of war,⁵⁰ and that in the march of an army such little incidents⁵¹ were not to be guarded against.⁵²

6. "We will see about that,"⁵³ the countess replied. "My poor subjects," she continued, "must have their own⁵⁴ again, or," raising her voice⁵⁵ in a determined⁵⁶ manner, "princes' blood must flow for oxen's blood!"

7. With this conclusive⁵⁷ declaration she left the apartment, which was in a few moments filled with armed men, who, swords in hand, but with all respect, placed themselves behind the seats of the princes and served⁵⁸ the breakfast. At the entrance of this warlike band,⁵⁹ the Duke of Alba changed color;⁶⁰ in silence and amazement⁶¹ he and his companions looked at each other. Cut off⁶² from the army, surrounded by a multitude⁶³ superior⁶⁴ in number and strength, what remained⁶⁵ to him but⁶⁶ to summon up patience,⁶⁷ and to satisfy the offended⁶⁸ lady upon any terms.⁶⁹

8. Heinrich von Braunschweig, his companion, first regained⁷⁰ his composure,⁷¹ and broke out into a loud fit of laughter. He seized upon⁷² the prudent expedient⁷³ of turning⁷⁴ the whole proceeding⁷⁵ into merriment,⁷⁶ and began an encomium⁷⁷ upon the

motherly care of the countess for her people, and the resolute courage she had shown. He begged her to calm[77] her anxiety,[78] taking it upon himself to persuade the Duke of Alba to all that was just, and, in fact,[79] prevailed upon him[80] to dispatch[81] an order at once to the army, that the plundered cattle should be restored[82] forthwith[83] to their owners. As soon as the countess heard of the restoration,[84] she thanked her guests graciously,[85] and they took their leave of her with much politeness.

9. Doubtless it was this adventure which obtained for the Countess Katharina of Schwarzburg the surname[86] of the Valorous.[87] She is still celebrated[88] for her steadfast[89] activity in promoting[90] the Reformation in her country, in abolishing[91] monasticism,[92] and in improving the education of her people. To many Protestant preachers, who had to undergo[93] persecution[94] on account of their religion, she extended[95] shelter and support.

SCHILLER.

[1] verwittwet, [2] erhielt, [3] Schutzbrief, [4] Unterthanen, [5] gegen die Verheerungen, [6] Gebiet, [7] zum Dank dafür, [8] in Anbetracht, [9] einer hübschen Geldsumme, [10] machte sie sich anheischig, [11] sie traf die Vorsichtsmaßregel, [12] abbrechen zu lassen, [13] wieder aufschlagen zu lassen, [14] damit, [15] die große Nähe, [16] raubsüchtige, [17] Versuchung, [18] Zuflucht zu nehmen, [19] Werthsachen, [20] näherte sich, [21] Bote, [22] voraus, [23] beschieden, [24] Bitte, [25] Spitze, [26] vermag (enthält), [27] wurde erwähnt, [28] erinnert an, [29] gewissenhaft, [30] Beobachtung, [31] er war genöthigt, [32] gestehen, [33] hielt, [34] Gastfreundschaft, [35] kaum hatten sie sich gesetzt, [36] theilte mit, [37] Gewaltthätigkeiten verübt hätten, [38] Vieh, [39] Bauern, [40] sehr ungehalten über, [41] Wortbrüchigkeit, [42] bewahrend, [43] Geistesgegenwart, [44] bewaffnen, [45] zu verriegeln, [46] beklagte sich, [47] in den eindringlichsten Ausdrücken, [48] Schandthat, [49] verletzt, [50] Kriegsbrauch, [51] Vorfälle, [52] sich nicht vermeiden ließen, [53] das wollen wir doch sehen, [54] Eigenthum, [55] ihre Stimme erhebend, [56] entschlossen, [57] bündig, [58] auftrugen, [59] dieser kriegerischen Schaar, [60] wechselte die Farbe, [61] Erstaunen, [62] abgeschnitten, [63] Menge, [64] überlegen an, [65] blieb übrig, [66] als, [67] sich in Geduld zu fassen, [68] beleidigt, [69] auf alle und jede Bedingungen, [70] gewann wieder, [71] Fassung, [72] griff zu, [73] Ausweg, [74] in's Lächerliche zu ziehen, [75] Verfall, [76] Lobrede, [77] zu beschwichtigen, [78] ängstliche Sorge, [79] in der That, [80] vermochte es über ihn, daß, [81] ertheilen, [82] wiedergegeben, [83] auf der Stelle, [84] Zurückerstattung, [85] huldvoll, [86] Beiname, [87] der Unerschrockenen, [88] berühmt, [89] ausdauernd, [90] Förderung, [91] Abschaffung, [92] Klosterwesens, [93] zu leiden, [94] Verfolgung, [95] bot sie.

Lektion XXIV.
Correlative Fürwörter.

He who, she who, that which, who what, those who, those which, all that (which), all who (that).

Redensarten: *To pry into, to pore over, to agree, to abound in, to take pleasure in, to comply with, to incur, to intrude upon, to take by surprise, to find fault with, to catch hold, to shiver with cold, to answer.*

Wörter-Verzeichniß.

taste, Geschmack.
wholesome, gesund.
reward, Belohnung.
furthest, am weitesten.
uppermost, oberste.
shelf, Bücherbord.
to associate, umgeben.
disposition, Gemüthsstimmung.
to keep away, sich fern halten.
style of living, Lebensweise.
means, Mittel.
to believe in, glauben an.
to put on, anziehen.
to differ, sich unterscheiden.
donkey, Esel.
box, Schachtel.

Redensarten.
to pry into, seine Nase in etwas stecken.
to concern one's self, sich kümmern um.
busybody, Klatschschwester.
to pore over, grübeln über.
as far as this is concerned, was dies betrifft.
to agree, übereinstimmen.

to suggest, an's Herz legen, rathen (anregen).
to abound in, Ueberfluß haben an.
paramount to, größer.
to ascertain, in Erfahrung bringen.
to comply with, nachkommen.
as to, was betrifft.
suspicion, Argwohn.
to incur, sich zuziehen.
displeasure, Ungnade, Unzufriedenheit.
to intrude upon one's time, Jemanden stören.
to take by surprise, überraschen.
to find fault with, auszusetzen finden an.
composition, Aufsatz.
to call in, vorsprechen.
to pass by, vorbeikommen.
to be given to, ⎱ ergeben
to be addicted to, ⎰ sein.
to be stung to the quick, in's Mark getroffen werden.

to shiver with, beben vor.
to catch a fever, sich ein Fieber zuziehen.

to answer a purpose, einem Zwecke entsprechen.
to draw to a close, zu Ende gehen.

Uebungs-Aufgabe 1.

He who is contented is rich. Who is contented is rich. That which is pleasant to our taste is not always wholesome. What is pleasant to our taste is not always wholesome. She who has done her work best will receive a reward. Which book do you want? Will you give me the one which is furthest to the right on the uppermost shelf? I do not like to associate with those who are of a sour disposition. Where did you buy these handkerchiefs? Those which I bought are much finer. All (that) I can tell you is, keep away from those whose style of living is above their means. All who believe in Christ as the Son of God are called Christians. What did John read to you? Did you understand all he said? Which coat do you want to put on to-day? I shall put on the one I had on yesterday. Everything I heard of this man is true. Did you tell me everything you know? In what does a horse differ from a donkey? The box into which I put your hat is here.

Redensarten.—A person who always pries into and concerns himself with the affairs of others is called a busybody. I have been poring over this lesson all morning without being able to learn it. As far as this is concerned I fully agree with you. I would suggest to you the necessity of studying English diligently, for although this country abounds in Germans, yet the importance of the English language will always be paramount to the German. Will you ascertain for me how much money it will take me to go to Nebraska? I shall take pleasure in complying with your wishes. As to what I told you about my suspicions of this man, let it remain a secret. I am afraid I have incurred

Correlative Fürwörter. 189

your displeasure. I hope I am not intruding upon your time. It seems that this news has taken you by surprise. I fully agree with you, that it is easier to find fault with a composition, than do it better yourself. Please, call in when you pass by again. Some people are given to lying, and others are addicted to drink. Did you notice, how he was stung to the quick (core) by this insinuation? Will you catch hold of this end of the rope, while I throw it over the house? I am shivering with cold, and that is a sure sign that I caught a fever. If this gun don't answer your purpose, I can get you another. I think it will answer. Our journey is fast drawing to a close.

Wörter-Verzeichniß.

was er will, what he pleases.
der thun will, who wants to do.
was er soll, what he ought to do.
Noth, distress.
verlassen, to forsake.
Zufriedenheit, contentment.
zweifeln, to doubt.
sich verlassen, to rely on.
getrennt, separated.
die Liebsten, the dearest.
was anders, what else.
erwarten, to expect.
betrügen, to deceive, cheat.
vorhersagen, foretell.
eintreffen, to come to pass.
unternehmen, to undertake.
hat er Erfolg gehabt, he has met with success.

grämen, to grieve.
ärgern, to vex.
vor zehn Jahren, ten years ago.
errathen, to guess.
erzählen, to relate, tell.
Angelegenheit, matter.
gemacht, done.
über mich, about me.
beleidigen, to insult.
tödten, to kill.
nicht mögen, are not able to.
Seele, soul.
vielmehr, rather.
Leib, body.
verderben, to destroy.
Hölle, hell.

Uebungs-Aufgabe 2.

Nicht der ist ein freier Mensch, der thun kann, was er will, sondern derjenige ist frei, der immer thun will, was er soll. Derjenige, der seinen Freund in der Noth verlassen kann, ist kein wahrer Freund. Wir erhalten nicht immer, was wir am meisten wünschen. Das, was das Leben glücklich macht, ist die Zufriedenheit. Ich zweifle, ob ich mich auf den verlassen kann, der mir diese Nachricht gebracht hat. Wir sind durch den Ocean von denjenigen getrennt, die uns die Liebsten sind. Was kannst du anders erwarten von dem, der dich schon so oft betrogen hat? Alles, was er mir vorhergesagt hat, ist eingetroffen. In Allem, was er unternommen hat, hat er Erfolg gehabt. Was mich am meisten grämt und ärgert, ist, daß ich nicht schon vor zehn Jahren nach Amerika gegangen bin. Was ist das, was ich hier in der Hand habe? Das kann ich nicht errathen. Weß das Herz voll ist, deß läuft der Mund über. Ich will dir alles erzählen, was ich von dieser Angelegenheit weiß. Diejenigen, die ihre Lektionen gemacht haben, können nach Hause gehen. Du hast mich durch das, was du über mich gesagt hast, sehr beleidigt. Fürchtet euch nicht vor denen, die den Leib tödten, und die Seele nicht mögen tödten. Fürchtet euch aber vielmehr vor dem, der Leib und Seele verderben mag in die Hölle.

Lesestück 1.

THE LITTLE MAN IN BLACK. (Das Männchen in Schwarz.)

1. Soon after my grandfather, Mr. Lemuel Cockloft, had quietly settled himself[1] at the hall, and just about the time that the gossips[2] of the neighborhood, tired of prying into[3] his affairs, were anxious for[4] some new tea-table topic,[5] the busy community[6] of our little village was thrown into[7] a grand turmoil[8] of curiosity and conjecture[9]—a situation very common to little gossiping villages[10]—by the sudden and unaccountable[11] appearance of a mysterious individual.

2. The object of this solicitude[12] was a little black-looking man of a foreign[13] aspect,[14] who took possession of an old building, which, having long had the reputation[15] of being haunted,[16] was in a state of ruinous desolation,[17] and an object of fear to all true believers of ghosts.[18] He usually wore a high sugar-

loaf,[19] hat with a narrow brim,[20] and a little black cloak, which, short as he was, scarcely reached below his knees.

3. He sought[21] no intimacy[22] or acquaintance with any one; appeared to take no interest in the pleasures or the little broils[23] of the village; nor ever talked except sometimes to himself in an outlandish tongue.[24] He commonly carried a large book, covered with sheep-skin,[25] under his arm; appeared always to be lost in meditation;[26] and was often met by the peasantry,[27] sometimes watching[28] the dawning[29] of day; sometimes, at noon,[30] seated under a tree poring[31] over his volume,[32] and sometimes, at evening, gazing[33] with a look of sober[34] tranquillity[35] at the sun as it gradually[36] sunk below the horizon.

4. The good people of the vicinity[37] beheld[38] something prodigiously[39] singular[40] in all this;—a profound[41] mystery seemed to hang[42] about the stranger, which, with all their sagacity,[43] they could not penetrate;[44] and, in the excess[45] of worldly charity,[46] they pronounced[47] it a sure sign "that he was no better than he should be,"—a phrase[48] innocent enough in itself,[49] but which, as applied in common,[50] signifies[51] nearly everything that is bad.

5. The young people thought him a gloomy[52] misanthrope, because he never joined in[53] their sports;[54] the old men thought still more hardly of him, because he followed no trade,[55] nor ever seemed ambitious[56] of earning a farthing; and as to the old gossips, baffled[57] by the inflexible[58] taciturnity[59] of the stranger, they unanimously decreed[60] that a man who could not or would not talk was no better than a dumb beast. The little man in black, careless of[61] their opinions, seemed resolved to maintain[62] the liberty of keeping his own secret; and the consequence was that, in a little while, the whole village was in an uproar;—for, in little communities of this description, the members[63] have always the privilege of being thoroughly[64] versed,[65] and even of meddling, in all the affairs of each other.

6. A confidential [66] conference was held one Sunday morning after sermon,[67] at the door of the village church, and the character of the unknown fully investigated.[68] The school-master gave as his opinion that he was the wandering Jew;[69] the sexton[70] was certain that he must be a Freemason,[71] from his silence; a third maintained, with great obstinacy,[72] that he was a high German doctor, and that the book which he carried about with him contained[73] the secrets of the black-art;[74] but the most prevailing[75] opinion seemed to be that he was a witch,[76]—a race of beings at that time abounding[77] in those parts;[78] and a sagacious[79] old matron from Connecticut proposed to ascertain[80] the fact by sousing[81] him into a kettle of hot water.

7. Suspicion,[82] when once afloat,[83] goes with wind and tide,[84] and soon becomes certainty. Many a stormy night was the little man in black seen, by the flashes of lightning,[85] frisking[86] and curveting[87] in the air upon a broom-stick; and it was always observed that at those times the storm did more mischief[88] than at any other. The old lady in particular,[89] who suggested[90] the humane ordeal[91] of the boiling kettle, lost on one of these occasions a fine brindled[92] cow, which accident was entirely ascribed[93] to the vengeance[94] of the little man in black.

8. If ever a mischievous[95] hireling[96] rode his master's favorite horse to a distant frolic,[97] and the animal was observed to be lame and jaded[98] in the morning, the little man in black was sure to be at the bottom[99] of the affair; nor could a high wind howl through the village at night but[100] the old women shrugged up their shoulders, and observed, "the little man in black was in his *tantrums*."[101] In short, he became the bugbear[102] of every house, and was as effectual[103] in frightening little children into obedience and hysterics[104] as the redoubtable[105] Raw-head-and-bloody-bones himself; nor could a housewife of the village sleep in peace except under the guardianship[106] of a horse-shoe nailed to the door.

9. The object of these direful¹⁰⁷ suspicions remained for some time totally ignorant of the wonderful quandary¹⁰⁸ he had occasioned;¹⁰⁹ but he was soon doomed¹¹⁰ to feel its effects. An individual who is once so unfortunate as to incur¹¹¹ the odium¹¹² of the village, is in a great measure outlawed¹¹³ and proscribed, and becomes a mark¹¹⁴ for injury and insult, particularly if he has not the power or the disposition to recriminate.¹¹⁵

10. The little venomous¹¹⁶ passions which in the great world are dissipated¹¹⁷ and weakened by being widely diffused,¹¹⁸ act¹¹⁹ in the narrow limits¹²⁰ of a country-town with collected vigor,¹²¹ and become rancorous¹²² in proportion as¹²³ they are confined¹²⁴ in their sphere of action.¹²⁵ The little man in black experienced the truth of this. Every mischievous urchin¹²⁶ returning from school had full liberty to break his windows, and this was considered as a most daring¹²⁷ exploit;¹²⁸ for in such awe¹²⁹ did they stand of him, that the most adventurous¹³⁰ schoolboy was never seen to approach his threshold,¹³¹ and at night would prefer¹³² going round by the cross-roads, where a traveler had been murdered by the Indians, rather than pass by the door of his forlorn¹³³ habitation.¹³⁴

11. The only living creature that seemed to have any care or affection¹³⁵ for this deserted¹³⁶ being, was an old turnspit,¹³⁷ the companion of his lowly mansion¹³⁸ and his solitary¹³⁹ wandering, the sharer¹⁴⁰ of his scanty¹⁴¹ meals, and—sorry I am to say it—the sharer of his persecutions. The turnspit, like his master, was peaceable and inoffensive;¹⁴² never known to bark at a horse, to growl¹⁴³ at a traveler, or to quarrel with the dogs of the neighborhood. He followed close at his master's heels¹⁴⁴ when he went out, and when he returned stretched himself in the sunbeams at the door, demeaning¹⁴⁵ himself in all things like a civil¹⁴⁶ and well-disposed¹⁴⁷ turnspit.

12. But notwithstanding his exemplary deportment,¹⁴⁸ he fell likewise under the ill report¹⁴⁹ of the

village, as being the familiar¹⁵⁰ of the little man in black, and the evil spirit that presided¹⁵¹ at his incantations.¹⁵² The old hovel¹⁵³ was considered as the scene of their unhallowed¹⁵⁴ rites,¹⁵⁵ and its harmless tenants¹⁵⁶ regarded with a detestation¹⁵⁷ which their inoffensive conduct never merited. Though pelted¹⁵⁸ and jeered¹⁵⁹ at by the brats¹⁶⁰ of the village, and frequently abused¹⁶¹ by their parents, the little man in black never turned to rebuke¹⁶² them; and his faithful dog, when wantonly¹⁶³ assaulted,¹⁶⁴ looked up wistfully¹⁶⁵ in his master's face, and there learned a lesson of patience and forbearance.¹⁶⁶

13. The movements of this inscrutable¹⁶⁷ being had long been the subject of speculation at Cockloft-Hall, for its inmates¹⁶⁸ were full as much given to wondering as their descendants.¹⁶⁹ The patience with which he bore his persecutions particularly surprised them, for patience is a virtue but little known in the Cockloft family. My grandmother, who, it appears, was rather superstitious,¹⁷⁰ saw in this humility¹⁷¹ nothing but the gloomy sullenness¹⁷² of a wizard,¹⁷³ who restrained¹⁷⁴ himself for the present, in hopes of midnight vengeance; the parson¹⁷⁵ of the village, who was a man of some reading,¹⁷⁶ pronounced it the stubborn¹⁷⁷ insensibility¹⁷⁸ of a Stoic philosopher; my grandfather, who, worthy soul,¹⁷⁹ seldom wandered abroad¹⁸⁰ in search¹⁸¹ of conclusions,¹⁸² took a data¹⁸³ from his own excellent heart, and regarded it as the humble forgiveness of a Christian. But however different were their opinions as to the character of the stranger, they agreed¹⁸⁴ in one particular,¹⁸⁵ namely, in never intruding¹⁸⁶ upon his solitude; and my grandmother, who was at that time nursing¹⁸⁷ my mother, never left the room without wisely putting the large family Bible in the cradle;¹⁸⁸ a sure talisman, in her opinion, against witchcraft¹⁸⁹ and necromancy.¹⁹⁰

---

¹ ſich zur Ruhe geſetzt hatte, ² Klatſchſchweſtern, ³ ihre Naſen zu ſtecken in, ⁴ begierig nach, ⁵ Thema, ⁶ Einwohnerſchaft, ⁷ geriethen in, ⁸ Aufregung (Durchein-

Correlative Fürwörter. 195

anber), ⁹ Muthmaßung, ¹⁰ flatschsüchtig, ¹¹ unbegreiflich, ¹² Unruhe, ¹³ fremd (ausländisch), ¹⁴ Aeußere, ¹⁵ Ruf, ¹⁶ daß es darin spukte, ¹⁷ eines gänzlichen Verfalls, ¹⁸ für alle wahren Anhänger des Geisterglaubens, ¹⁹ zuckerhutförmig, ²⁰ Krempe, ²¹ suchte, ²² Freundschaft, ²³ Streitigkeiten, ²⁴ in einer fremden Sprache, ²⁵ in Schafsleder gebunden, ²⁶ Betrachtung, ²⁷ Bauern, ²⁸ beobachtend, ²⁹ Anbruch, ³⁰ Mittag, ³¹ grübelnd, ³² **Bücherband**, ³³ anschauend, ³⁴ ernst (nüchtern), ³⁵ Ruhe, ³⁶ allmälig, ³⁷ Nachbarschaft, ³⁸ erblickten, ³⁹ wunderbar, ⁴⁰ Merkwürdiges, ⁴¹ rief, ⁴² schweben, ⁴³ Scharfsinn, ⁴⁴ ergründen, ⁴⁵ Uebermaß, ⁴⁶ Güte, ⁴⁷ erklärten sie, ⁴⁸ Redensart, ⁴⁹ an sich, ⁵⁰ wie sie **gewöhnlich angewendet wird**, ⁵¹ bedeutet, ⁵² finster, ⁵³ nahm Theil, ⁵⁴ Vergnügungen, ⁵⁵ Gewerbe, ⁵⁶ ehrgeizig, ⁵⁷ verstört, ⁵⁸ unbeugsam, ⁵⁹ Schweigsamkeit, ⁶⁰ beschlossen, ⁶¹ unbekümmert um, ⁶² zu behaupten, ⁶³ Glieder, ⁶⁴ gründlich, ⁶⁵ vertraut, ⁶⁶ vertraut (geheim), ⁶⁷ Predigt, ⁶⁸ untersucht, ⁶⁹ der ewige Jude, ⁷⁰ Küster, ⁷¹ Freimaurer, ⁷² Halsstarrigkeit, ⁷³ enthielte, ⁷⁴ Schwarzkunst, ⁷⁵ **vorherrschend**, ⁷⁶ Herenmeister, ⁷⁷ reichlich vertreten, ⁷⁸ Gegenden, ⁷⁹ scharfsinnig, ⁸⁰ zu ermitteln, ⁸¹ dadurch, daß sie ihn steckten, ⁸² Argwohn, ⁸³ einmal erregt, ⁸⁴ Fluth, ⁸⁵ Blitzstrahlen, ⁸⁶ tanzend, ⁸⁷ reitend, ⁸⁸ Unheil, ⁸⁹ besonders, ⁹⁰ in Anregung brachte, ⁹¹ Feuerprobe, ⁹² gefleckt, ⁹³ zugeschrieben, ⁹⁴ Rache, ⁹⁵ muthwillig, ⁹⁶ Miethsknecht, ⁹⁷ lustiges Gelage, ⁹⁸ abgejagt, ⁹⁹ war gewiß schuld an der Geschichte, ¹⁰⁰ **daß** nicht, ¹⁰¹ böse Laune, ¹⁰² Schreckgespenst, ¹⁰³ **wirksam**, ¹⁰⁴ krampfhaftes **Weinen**, ¹⁰⁵ schrecklich, ¹⁰⁶ Schutz, ¹⁰⁷ schauderhaft, ¹⁰⁸ Verwirrung, ¹⁰⁹ veranlaßt, ¹¹⁰ verurtheilt, ¹¹¹ zuzuziehen, ¹¹² Abneigung, ¹¹³ vogelfrei (außerhalb des Gesetzes stehend), ¹¹⁴ Zielscheibe, ¹¹⁵ Gegenanklage zu erheben, ¹¹⁶ giftig, ¹¹⁷ verrauchen (sich zerstreuen), ¹¹⁸ **dadurch, daß sie sich weit umher verbreiten**, ¹¹⁹ treten auf, ¹²⁰ Grenzen, ¹²¹ mit concentrirter Kraft, ¹²² bösartig, ¹²³ je nachdem, ¹²⁴ beschränkt, ¹²⁵ Wirkungskreis, ¹²⁶ Knirps, ¹²⁷ kühn, ¹²⁸ Wagstück, ¹²⁹ Furcht, ¹³⁰ waghalsig, ¹³¹ Schwelle, ¹³² vorziehen, ¹³³ öde, ¹³⁴ Behausung, ¹³⁵ Zuneigung, ¹³⁶ verlassen, ¹³⁷ Spießwender (eine Art Hunde, die man zum Wenden des Spießes verwendete, an dem Fleisch geröstet wurde), ¹³⁸ Wohnung, ¹³⁹ einsam, ¹⁴⁰ Mitgenosse, ¹⁴¹ spärlich, ¹⁴² harmlos, ¹⁴³ knurren, ¹⁴⁴ Ferien, ¹⁴⁵ sich aufführend, ¹⁴⁶ höflich, ¹⁴⁷ wohlgesinnt, ¹⁴⁸ Aufführung, ¹⁴⁹ böser Ruf, ¹⁵⁰ **Vertraute**, ¹⁵¹ den Vorsitz führte, ¹⁵² Beschwörungen, ¹⁵³ elende **Hütte**, ¹⁵⁴ **unheilig**, gottlos, ¹⁵⁵ Gebrauche, ¹⁵⁶ Bewohner, ¹⁵⁷ Abscheu, ¹⁵⁸ mit **Steinen** beworfen, ¹⁵⁹ versperrte, ¹⁶⁰ Rangen, ¹⁶¹ verunglimpft, ¹⁶² Vorwürfe **machen**, ¹⁶³ muthwillig, ¹⁶⁴ angegriffen, ¹⁶⁵ forschend, ¹⁶⁶ Nachsicht, ¹⁶⁷ undurchdringlich, ¹⁶⁸ Bewohner, ¹⁶⁹ Nachkommen, ¹⁷⁰ abergläubisch, ¹⁷¹ Demuth, ¹⁷² Verschlossenheit, ¹⁷³ Zauberer, ¹⁷⁴ sich zurückhielt, ¹⁷⁵ Pfarrer, ¹⁷⁶ wohlbeleibt, ¹⁷⁷ eigensinnig, ¹⁷⁸ Gefühllosigkeit, ¹⁷⁹ gute Seele, ¹⁸⁰ weit wanderte, ¹⁸¹ um **zu** suchen nach, ¹⁸² Schlußfolgerungen, ¹⁸³ Folgerung, ¹⁸⁴ stimmte überein, ¹⁸⁵ **in** einem besonderen Punkte, ¹⁸⁶ daß sie ihn **nie** störten in, ¹⁸⁷ die **Brust** gab, ¹⁸⁸ Wiege, ¹⁸⁹ Zauberkünste, ¹⁹⁰ Nekromantie.

Lesestück 3.

THE LITTLE MAN IN BLACK. (Schluß.)

1. One stormy winter night, when a bleak northeast wind moaned¹ about the cottages, and howled around the village steeple,² my grandfather was returning from club, preceded by³ a servant with a lantern. Just as

he arrived opposite[4] the desolate abode[5] of the little man in black, he was arrested[6] by the piteous[7] howling of a dog, which, heard in the pauses of a storm, was exquisitely[8] mournful;[9] and he fancied[10] now and then that he caught[11] the low and broken groans[12] of some one in distress.[13]

2. He stopped for some minutes, hesitating[14] between the benevolence[15] of his heart and a sensation of genuine delicacy,[16] which, in spite of his eccentricity,[17] he fully possessed, and which forbade him to pry into[18] the concerns[19] of his neighbors. Perhaps, too, this hesitation[20] might have been strengthened by a little taint[21] of superstition;[22] for surely, if the unknown had been addicted[23] to witchcraft,[24] this was a most propitious[25] night for his vagaries.[26] At length the old gentleman's philanthropy[27] predominated;[28] he approached the hovel, and pushing open the door—for poverty has no occasion[29] for locks and keys—beheld, by the light of the lantern, a scene[30] that smote his generous heart to the core.[31]

3. On a miserable bed, with pallid[32] and emaciated[33] visage[34] and hollow eyes, in a room destitute[35] of every convenience,[36] without fire to warm or friend to counsel[37] him, lay this helpless mortal,[38] who had been so long the terror[39] and wonder of the village. His dog was crouching[40] on the scanty coverlet,[41] and shivering with[42] cold. My grandfather stepped softly and hesitatingly to the bedside and accosted[43] the forlorn sufferer in his usual accents[44] of kindness. The little man in black seemed recalled[45] by the tones of compassion[46] from the lethargy[47] into which he had fallen; for, though his heart was almost frozen, there was yet one chord[48] that answered to the call of the good old man who bent over him; the tones of sympathy, so novel[49] to his ear, called back his wandering[50] senses, and acted[51] like a restorative[52] to his solitary[53] feelings.

4. He raised his eyes, but they were vacant[54] and haggard.[55] He put forth his hand, but it was cold.

He essayed [56] to speak, but the sound died away [57] in his throat. He pointed to his mouth with an expression of dreadful [58] meaning, [59] and, sad to relate! [60] my grandfather understood that the harmless stranger, deserted [61] by society, [62] was perishing with [63] hunger! With the quick impulse [64] of humanity he dispatched [65] the servant to the hall for refreshment. A little warm nourishment renovated [66] him for a short time, but not long. It was evident [67] his pilgrimage was drawing to a close, [68] and he was about entering that peaceful asylum where "the wicked cease from troubling."

5. His tale [69] of misery was quickly told. Infirmities [70] had stolen upon him, [71] heightened [72] by the rigors [73] of the season: he had taken to his bed without strength to rise and ask for assistance;—"And if I had," said he, in a tone of bitter despondency, [74] "to whom should I have applied? [75] I have no friend that I know of in the world; the villagers avoid [76] me as something loathsome [77] and dangerous; and here, in the midst of Christians, should I have perished, without a fellow-being [78] to soothe [79] the last moments of existence, and close my dying eyes, had not the howlings of my faithful dog excited [80] your attention."

6. He seemed deeply sensible [81] of the kindness of my grandfather; and at one time, as he looked up into his old benefactor's face, a solitary tear was observed to steal adown [82] the parched [83] furrows [84] of his cheek. Poor outcast! [85]—it was the last tear he shed; but I warrant [86] it was not the first by millions! My grandfather watched by him all night. Toward morning he gradually declined, [87] and as the rising sun gleamed through the window, he begged to be raised in his bed that he might look at it for the last time. He contemplated [88] it for a moment with a kind of religious enthusiasm, and his lips moved as if engaged [89] in prayer. [90]

7. The strange conjectures [91] concerning [92] him rushed [93] on my grandfather's mind: "He is an idolator! [94] thought he, "and is worshiping [95] the sun!"

He listened a moment, and blushed [96] at his own uncharitable [97] suspicion: he was only engaged in the pious devotions [98] of a Christian. His simple orison [99] being finished, the little man in black withdrew [100] his eyes from the east, and taking my grandfather's hand in one of his, and making a motion with the other toward the sun,—"I love to contemplate it," said he, "'tis an emblem [101] of the universal benevolence of a true Christian; and it is the most glorious work of Him who is philanthropy itself!"

8. My grandfather blushed still deeper at his ungenerous surmises: [102] he had pitied the stranger at first, but now he revered [103] him. He turned once more to regard [104] him, but his countenance [105] had undergone [106] a change: the holy enthusiasm that had lighted up [107] each feature, [108] had given place to an expression of mysterious [109] import: [110] a gleam [111] of grandeur [112] seemed to steal across [113] his Gothic visage, and he appeared full of some mighty secret which he hesitated to impart. [114] He raised the tattered [115] night-cap that had sunk almost over his eyes, and waving [116] his withered [117] hand with a slow and feeble expression of dignity [118]—"In me," said he, with laconic [119] solemnity, [120]—"in me you behold the last descendant [121] of the renowned [122] LINKUM FIDELIUS!"

9. My grandfather gazed at him with reverence; [123] for though he had never heard of the illustrious [124] personage thus pompously [125] announced, yet there was a certain black-letter [126] dignity in the name that particularly struck his fancy, [127] and commanded [128] his respect. "You have been kind to me," continued the little man in black, after a momentary [129] pause, "and richly will I requite [130] your kindness by making you heir [131] to my treasures! [132] In yonder large deal box [133] are the volumes [134] of my illustrious ancestor, [135] of which I alone am the fortunate possessor. Inherit them, [136] ponder [137] over them, and be wise!"

10. He grew faint [138] with the exertion [139] he had made, and sunk back almost breathless on his pillow. [140]

His hand, which, inspired [111] with the importance of his subject,[112] he had raised to my grandfather's arm, slipped from his hold,[113] and fell over the side of the bed, and his faithful dog licked it, as if anxious to soothe the last moments of his dying master, and testify[114] his gratitude to the hand that had so often cherished[115] him. The untaught[116] caresses[117] of the faithful animal were not lost upon his dying master: he raised his languid[118] eyes, turned them on the dog, then on my grandfather, and having given this silent recommendation—closed them forever.

11. The remains[119] of the little man in black, notwithstanding the objections of many pious people, were decently[120] interred[121] in the churchyard of the village; and his spirit, harmless as the body it once animated,[122] has never been known to molest a living being. My grandfather complied,[123] as far as possible, with his last request: he conveyed[124] the volumes of Linkum Fidelius to his library;[125] he pondered over them frequently; but whether he grew wiser, the tradition doth not mention. This much is certain, that his kindness to the poor descendant of Fidelius was amply[126] rewarded by the approbation[127] of his own heart, and the devoted[128] attachment[129] of the old turnspit, who transferred[130] his affection from his deceased master to his benefactor, and became his constant attendant.[131] And thus was the Cockloft library first enriched by the invaluable[132] folios of the sage[133] *Linkum Fidelius.*

WASHINGTON IRVING.

---

¹ stöhnte, ² Kirchthurm, ³ voraus, ⁴ gegenüber, ⁵ Bebauung, ⁶ aufgehalten, ⁷ kläglich, ⁸ äußerst, ⁹ traurig, ¹⁰ er meinte, ¹¹ vernahm, ¹² Seufzer, ¹³ Noth, ¹⁴ schwankend, ¹⁵ Wohlwollen, ¹⁶ echtes Zartgefühl, ¹⁷ excentrisches Wesen, ¹⁸ sich zu mischen in, ¹⁹ Angelegenheiten, ²⁰ Zaudern, ²¹ Anflug, ²² Aberglauben, ²³ sich abgegeben hätte, ²⁴ Zauberkünste, ²⁵ günstig, ²⁶ wildes Treiben, ²⁷ menschenfreundlicher Sinn, ²⁸ gewann die Oberhand, ²⁹ Gebrauch, ³⁰ Anblick, ³¹ der sein edles Herz bis ins Innerste erschütterte, ³² bleich, ³³ abgemagert, ³⁴ Gesicht, ³⁵ entblößt von, ³⁶ Bequemlichkeit, ³⁷ trösten, ³⁸ Sterbliche, ³⁹ Schrecken, ⁴⁰ kauerte zusammen, ⁴¹ Bettdecke, ⁴² bebend vor, ⁴³ redete an, ⁴⁴ Ton, ⁴⁵ zu sich zu kommen, ⁴⁶ Mitleid, ⁴⁷ Geistesstumpfheit, ⁴⁸ Saite,

⁴⁹ fremd (neu), ⁵⁰ zerstreut, ⁵¹ wirkten, ⁵² Belebungsmittel, ⁵³ Gefühl der Verlassenheit, ⁵⁴ stier, ⁵⁵ eingefallen, ⁵⁶ versuchte, ⁵⁷ erstarb, ⁵⁸ schrecklich, ⁵⁹ Bedeutung, ⁶⁰ erzählen, ⁶¹ verlassen, ⁶² von der menschlichen Gesellschaft, ⁶³ umkam vor, ⁶⁴ Antrieb, ⁶⁵ schickte er ab, ⁶⁶ belebte ihn wieder, ⁶⁷ augenscheinlich, ⁶⁸ näherte sich dem Ende, ⁶⁹ Geschichte, ⁷⁰ Krankheiten, ⁷¹ hatten sich bei ihm eingeschlichen, ⁷² erhöht, ⁷³ Strenge, ⁷⁴ Verzweiflung, ⁷⁵ an wen hatte ich mich wenden sollen, ⁷⁶ meiden, ⁷⁷ Ekelhaftes, ⁷⁸ Mitgeschöpf, ⁷⁹ lindern, ⁸⁰ erregt, ⁸¹ durchdrungen von, ⁸² niederschleichen, ⁸³ welk, ⁸⁴ Runzel, ⁸⁵ Verstoßener, ⁸⁶ ich bin gut dafür (ich wette), ⁸⁷ nahmen seine Kräfte allmälig ab, ⁸⁸ betrachtete, ⁸⁹ beschäftigt, ⁹⁰ Gebet, ⁹¹ Muthmaßungen, ⁹² betreffs seiner, ⁹³ drängten sich, ⁹⁴ Götzendiener, ⁹⁵ betet an, ⁹⁶ erröthete, ⁹⁷ liebloS, ⁹⁸ Andachtsübungen, ⁹⁹ Gebet, ¹⁰⁰ wendete ab, ¹⁰¹ Sinnbild, ¹⁰² Vermuthungen, ¹⁰³ verehrte, ¹⁰⁴ anblicken, ¹⁰⁵ Antlitz, ¹⁰⁶ hatte erfahren, ¹⁰⁷ verklärt hatte, ¹⁰⁸ Gesichtszug, ¹⁰⁹ geheimnißvoll, ¹¹⁰ Bedeutung, ¹¹¹ Schimmer; Glanz, ¹¹² Erhabenheit, ¹¹³ schien sich unvermerkt zu legen, ¹¹⁴ mitzutheilen, ¹¹⁵ zerlumpt, ¹¹⁶ schwenkend, ¹¹⁷ welk, ¹¹⁸ Würde, ¹¹⁹ lakonisch (kurz), ¹²⁰ Feierlichkeit, ¹²¹ Sprößling, ¹²² berühmt, ¹²³ Ehrfurcht, ¹²⁴ berühmt, ¹²⁵ hochtrabend, ¹²⁶ vergilbt (d. i. geschrieben in altenglischer oder gothischer Schrift), ¹²⁷ wunderbar vorkam, ¹²⁸ abnöthigte, ¹²⁹ kurz, momentan, ¹³⁰ vergelten, ¹³¹ Erbe, ¹³² Schätze, ¹³³ Kasten von Föhrenholz, ¹³⁴ Bände, ¹³⁵ Verfahr, ¹³⁶ nimm sie als dein Erbe, ¹³⁷ denke nach, ¹³⁸ schwach, ohnmächtig, ¹³⁹ Anstrengung, ¹⁴⁰ Kopfkissen, ¹⁴¹ erfüllt, ¹⁴² Gegenstand, ¹⁴³ ließ ihren Halt fahren, ¹⁴⁴ bezeugen, ¹⁴⁵ gepflegt, ¹⁴⁶ nicht angelernt, ¹⁴⁷ Liebkosungen, ¹⁴⁸ matt, ¹⁴⁹ Ueberreste, ¹⁵⁰ anständig, ¹⁵¹ beerdigt, ¹⁵² beseelte, ¹⁵³ kam nach, ¹⁵⁴ brachte, ¹⁵⁵ Bibliothek, ¹⁵⁶ reichlich, ¹⁵⁷ Billigung, ¹⁵⁸ hingebend, ¹⁵⁹ Zuneigung, ¹⁶⁰ übertrug, ¹⁶¹ Begleiter, ¹⁶² unschätzbar, ¹⁶³ des Weisen.

Lektion XXV.

Unregelmäßige Zeitwörter. Conjunktionen.

Infinitiv	Imperfect	Particip
to arise (rise)	arose	arisen.
to bite	bit,	bitten.
to break	broke	broken.
to bring	brought	brought.
to build	built	built.
to burn	burnt / burned	burnt. / burned.
to buy	bought	bought.
to catch	caught	caught.
to choose	chose	chosen.
to come	came	come.
to cost	cost	cost.

Unregelmäßige Zeitwörter.   Conjunktionen.

Infinitiv	Imperfect	Particip
to cut	cut	cut.
to do	did	done.
to drink	drank	drunk.
to dwell	{ dwelt { dwelled	dwelt. dwelled.
to eat	ate	eaten.
to fall	fell	fallen.
to fight	fought	fought.
to find	found	found.
to forget	forgot	forgotten.
to forsake	forsook	forsaken.
to get	got	got.
to give	gave	given.
to go	went	gone.

Conjunktionen—*while, till, until, since, because.*

Redensarten.—*to be sorry for, to watch for, to grow to be, to lie, to lay without* (mit dem Particip), *to commit to memory, to sit down, to be seated, to take a seat, to amount to, ought.*

Wörter-Verzeichniß.

to arise, aufstehen.
kittens, Kätzchen.
tumbler, Trinkglas.
grocer, Krämer.
conflagration, Feuersbrunst.
block of houses, Häusergeviert.
dry-goods, Manufakturwaaren.
to catch cold, sich eine Erkältung zuziehen.
to choose, belieben, wählen.
chosen, auserwählt.
to come to see, besuchen.
member, Mitglied.
meeting, Versammlung.

in time, zu rechter Zeit.
pine-apple, Ananas.
to cut, schneiden.
it agrees with you, du kannst vertragen.
tipsy, betrunken.
to dwell, wohnen.
report, Knall.
peas, Erbsen.
to suffer from, leiden an.
headache, Kopfweh.
lately, vor Kurzem.
since, da.
smart, klug.

flock, Schaar.
sparrow, Sperling.
go get, hole.
careful, vorsichtig.
previous, früher.
engagement, Engagement.
to be sorry, leid thun.
to render assistance, Hülfe leisten.
to watch for, lauern auf, warten auf.
opportunity, Gelegenheit.
to grow old, alt werden.
to grow out of, werden aus.
company, Gesellschaft.
to bid good bye, Lebewohl sagen.
to linger, zögern.

she lingered, sie lag lange krank.
consumption, Schwindsucht.
a lingering disease, eine schleppende Krankheit.
to detect, entdecken.
mistake, Fehler.
to commit to memory, auswendig lernen.
disconnected, zusammenhangslos, abgerissen.
to be seated, sich setzen.
to take a seat, Platz nehmen.
to sit down, sich niedersetzen.
business transactions, Geschäfte.
countless, zahllos.
blessing, Segnung.

Uebungs-Aufgabe 1.

When do you arise in the morning? I generally rise at six; yesterday I rose at seven. Has (is) your father risen? He is not yet risen. Your dog bit all my kittens. Don't break the tumbler; you only broke one yesterday. Bring me a few oranges. What has the grocer brought? He brought me some tea and coffee an hour ago. Can you tell me who built the Strasburg Cathedral? The builder's name is Erwin. There was a great conflagration in Forty-sixth Street. A whole block of houses burnt down. I want to buy ten yards of silk and fifty yards of muslin. Last year I bought all my dry goods of Stewart's, but I now buy them of Lord & Taylor's. Where did you catch your cold? I caught it at a picnic in Jones' Wood. Take anything you choose. Many are called but few are chosen. I bought some stockings and chose the finest for you. When will you come to see me? All the members have come, and we can open the meeting. I came just in time to see the parade. How much do these pine-apples cost apiece? They cost ten cents apiece; yesterday they cost fifteen. He has cut a hole in his new coat. Shall I cut some bread? No, thank you; I cut some already. What are you doing? I do what I did yesterday. My work is done. I have done my work. You must not drink more than agrees with you. A person who has drunk too much is tipsy. Who dwells in this house? I dwelt three years in this house. I have been dwelling (dwelt) three years in this house. While I was eating my dinner, I heard the report of a pistol. I ate some fine peas an hour and a half ago. You will have to wait till I have eaten my supper. I never suffered from headache until lately. Since you seem to be so smart, tell me who fought the battle of Leipsic. I shot at a flock of sparrows and three of them fell to the ground. Where did you find my keys? I found them on the stairs. You must not forget what I told you about reading books in a foreign language. Never fear! I never forgot what was told me. I have forgotten most of my French. Go get me a bottle of wine. He gave me some good advice. You should be more careful with what has been given you. Where has your cousin gone? He has gone to Europe; he went to Europe last week. All my hopes are gone. I cannot go with you to the concert because of a previous engagement. I shall not go to Europe because I have no money.

Redensarten.—I am very sorry that I am unable to render you any assistance. Charles, are you sorry for what you have done? The cat is watching for the rat to come out of his hole. You must watch for another opportunity. He is grown very old. She has grown to be very handsome. What do you think will grow out of this? I am growing tired of his company. I must bid you good-bye, for if I linger any longer I shall be too late for the train. She lingered long before she died. Consumption is a lingering disease. Be busy at your work. Tell me once again (once more) which way I must go. A person who lies is a liar. Where did you lay my segars? I laid them on your desk. The spade has lain in the rain all night. It lay there this morning. You must not do that again without asking me. I examined his bill without being able to detect a single mistake. You must never commit to memory disconnected words. Will you commit this piece to memory (learn this piece by heart)? Please be seated, and we will talk this matter over. That's right, I will take a seat near the fire. Won't you sit down, too? Thank you, I have been sitting all day. What does all this talk amount to? You ought to have been more careful in your business-transactions with this man. We ought to be very thankful for countless blessings.

Wörter-Verzeichniß.

um sieben, at seven.
mich in's Bein, my leg.
Kruste, crust.
Trinkglas, tumbler.
daraus, out of it.
wollte, was about.
Eier, eggs.
abbrennen, to burn down.
einen Gefallen thun, to do a favor.
Ausgabe, edition.
Wörterbuch, dictionary.
Anzug, suit of clothes.
Frühjahr, spring.
sich erkälten, to catch cold.
leicht, easily.
sich losreißen, to cut loose.
Band, ribbon.
fort, gone.

abschneiden, to cut off.
bedienen Sie sich, help yourself.
darin, in it.
Heldenmuth, heroic courage.
und ob auch, and though.
weichen, to give way.
fortfahren, to continue.
bis, until.
Sieg, victory.
erringen, to gain.
meinen, to think.
tüchtig, hard.
verlassen, forsaken.
sterben, to die.
Elend, misery.
Schüler von mir, pupil of mine.
Erlaubniß, permission.
pflücken, to pick.

Unregelmäßige Zeitwörter. Conjunktionen.

Uebungs-Aufgabe 2.

Ich stand heute Morgen sehr spät auf; die Sonne war schon aufgegangen. Im Winter stehe ich um sieben Uhr auf und im Sommer um sechs. Ich werde Ihren Hund erschießen; er hat mich in's Bein gebissen. Alte Leute können die Kruste vom Brod nicht mehr beißen. Wer hat mein Trinkglas zerbrochen? hast du es zerbrochen, Fritz? Ich nicht; Wilhelm zerbrach es, als er daraus trinken wollte. Was brachte die Frau dir heute Morgen? Sie brachte mir einen Korb Eier. Wenn Sie heute Abend kommen, so bringen Sie Ihren Freund August mit. Das neue Haus, das wir gestern sahen, brannte die vorige Nacht ab; es war aus braunem Sandstein gebaut und kostete sehr viel Geld. Wenn du mir einen Gefallen thun willst, so kaufe mir eine neue Ausgabe von Webster's Wörterbuch. Wo hast du deinen neuen Anzug gekauft? Ich habe ihn da gekauft, wo du den deinigen vorige Woche kauftest. Im Frühjahr kann man sich leicht erkälten. Früher erkältete ich mich oft, doch jetzt erkälte ich mich nur selten. Geh und greif mir das Pferd; es hat sich losgerissen. Welches von diesen Bändern würdest du wählen? Ich habe schon gewählt. Komm mit mir, wir wollen in's Theater gehen. Als mein Bruder kam, war ich schon fort. Wollen Sie mir ein Stück Brod abschneiden? Ich habe Brod und Fleisch geschnitten. Bedienen Sie Sich. Wer hat mein Glas Wein getrunken? Hast du es gethan, Georg? Nein, ich nicht. Wer hat es denn gethan? Ich weiß es nicht. Wie viele Familien wohnen in diesem Hause? Früher wohnte nur eine Familie darin; jetzt wohnen drei darin. Willst du mit mir essen? Ich danke, ich habe schon gegessen; ich aß vor einer halben Stunde. Die deutschen Soldaten fochten mit Heldenmuth, und ob auch Tausende fielen, so wichen sie doch keinen Fußbreit, sondern fuhren fort zu kämpfen, bis sie den Sieg errungen hatten. Manche Leute meinen, wenn sie hierherkommen, sie könnten das Geld auf der Straße finden. Sie haben aber Alle bald gefunden, daß man hier tüchtig arbeiten muß, wenn man Geld haben will. Vergiß nicht was ich dir gesagt habe. Ich habe die Nummer der Straße vergessen, wo er wohnt. Von allen seinen Freunden verlassen, starb er im Elend. Wo haft du dies schöne neue Buch her? Ich habe es von einem frühern Schüler von mir. Gib mir ein Glas Wasser; ich bin sehr durstig; ich habe heute Morgen noch nichts getrunken. Ich gab dir Erlaubniß in den Garten zu gehen, ich habe dir aber keine Erlaubniß gegeben, Kirschen zu pflücken.

Lesestück 1.

A CHILD'S DREAM OF A STAR.

(Der Traum eines Kindes von einem Stern.)

1. There was once a child, and he strolled about[1] a good deal,[2] and thought of a number of things.[3] He had a sister, who was a child too, and his constant[4] companion. These two used[5] to wonder[6] all day long; they wondered at the depth of the bright water; they wondered at the goodness and the power[7] of God, who made the lovely world.

2. They used to say to one another, sometimes: "Supposing[8] all the children upon earth were to die,[9] would the flowers, and the water, and the sky,[10] be sorry?"[11] They believed they would be sorry. For, said they, the buds[12] are the children of the flowers, and the little playful streams,[13] that gambol[14] down the hill-sides, are the children of the water; and the smallest bright specks[15] playing at hide-and-seek[16] in the sky all night, must surely be the children of the stars; and they would all be grieved[17] to see their playmates,[18] the children of men, no more.

3. There was one clear, shining star, that used to come out in the sky before the rest, near the church-spire,[19] above the graves. It was larger and more beautiful, they thought, than all the others, and every night they watched for it, standing hand in hand at a window. Whoever saw it first, cried out, "I see the star!" And often they cried out both together, knowing so well when it would arise,[20] and where. So they

grew to be[21] such friends with it that, before lying down in their beds, they always looked out once again, to bid[22] it good night; and when they were turning round to sleep, they used to say, "God bless[23] the star!"

4. But while[24] she was still very young,—oh, very, very young,—the sister drooped,[25] and came to be so weak that she could no longer stand in the window at night; and then the child looked sadly[26] out by himself, and, when he saw the star, turned round and said to the patient, pale face on the bed, "I see the star!" and then a smile[27] would come upon the face, and a little weak voice[28] used to say, "God bless my brother and the star!"

5. And so the time came—all too soon[29]—when the child looked out alone, and when there was no face on the bed; and when there was a little grave among the graves, not there before; and when the star made long rays[30] down towards him, as he saw it through his tears.

6. Now, these rays were so bright, and they seemed to make such a shining way from earth to heaven, that when the child went to his solitary[31] bed, he dreamed about the star; and he dreamed that, lying where he was, he saw a train[32] of people taken up that sparkling[33] road by angels. And the star, opening, showed him a great world of light, where many more such angels waited to receive them.

7. All these angels, who were waiting, turned their beaming[34] eyes upon the people who were carried up into the star; and some came out from the long rows[35] in which they stood, and fell upon the people's necks, and kissed them tenderly,[36] and went away with them down avenues[37] of light, and were so happy in their company, that, lying in his bed, he wept for joy.

8. But there were many angels who did not go with them, and among them one he knew. The patient face that once had lain upon the bed was glorified[38] and

radiant;⁵⁹ but his heart found out his sister among all the host.⁴⁰

9. His sister's angel lingered⁴¹ near the entrance⁴² of the star, and said to the leader⁴³ among those who had brought the people thither,⁴⁴ "Is my brother come?"

10. And he said, "No."

11. She was turning hopefully away, when the child stretched out his arms, and cried, "O sister, I am here! Take me." And then she turned her beaming⁴⁵ eyes upon him, and it was night; and the star was shining into the room, making long rays down towards him as he saw it through his tears.

12. From that hour forth,⁴⁶ the child looked out upon the star as on the home⁴⁷ he was to go to, when his time should come; and he thought that he did not belong to the earth alone, but to the star too, because⁴⁸ of his sister's angel gone before.

13. There was a babe born to be a brother to the child; and while he was so little that he never yet had spoken a word, he stretched his tiny⁴⁹ form out on his bed, and died.

14. Again the child dreamed of the opened star, and of the company of angels, and the train of people, and the rows of angels, with their beaming eyes all turned upon those people's faces.

15. Said his sister's angel to the leader, "Is my brother come?"

16. And he said, "Not that one, but another."

17. As the child beheld⁵⁰ his brother's angel in her arms, he cried, "O sister, I am here! Take me!" And she turned and smiled upon him, and the star was shining.

18. He grew to be a young man, and was busy⁵¹ at his books, when an old servant came to him, and said, "Thy mother is no more. I bring her blessing⁵² on her darling⁵³ son."

19. Again at night he saw the star, and all that

former company. Said his sister's angel to the leader, "Is my brother come?"

20. And he said, "Thy mother!"

21. A mighty cry of joy⁵¹ went forth⁵⁵ through all the star, because the mother was reunited⁵⁶ to her two children. And he stretched out his arms, and cried, "O mother, sister, and brother, I am here! Take me!" And they answered him, "Not yet." And the star was shining.

22. He grew to be a man, whose hair was turning gray, and he was sitting in his chair by the fire-side, heavy with grief,⁵⁷ and with his face bedewed⁵⁸ with tears, when the star opened once again.

23. Said his sister's angel to the leader, "Is my brother come?"

24. And he said, "Nay, but his maiden⁵⁹ daughter."

25. And the man who had been the child saw his daughter, nearly⁶⁰ lost to him, a celestial⁶¹ creature among those three, and he said, "My daughter's head is on my sister's bosom,⁶² and her arm is round my mother's neck, and at her feet there is the baby of old time, and I can bear the parting⁶³ from her, God be praised!" And the star was shining.

26. Thus the child came to be an old man, and his once smooth⁶⁴ face was wrinkled,⁶⁵ and his steps were slow and feeble, and his back was bent.⁶⁶ And one night, as he lay upon his bed, his children standing round, he cried, as he had cried so long ago, "I see the star!"

27. They whispered⁶⁷ one another, "He is dying."

28. And he said, "I am. My age is falling from me like a garment,⁶⁸ and I move towards the star as a child. And oh, my Father, now I thank thee that it has so often opened to receive those dear ones who await me!"

29. And the star was shining; and it shines upon his grave.

---

¹ ſtreifte umher, ² ſehr viel, ³ an eine Menge Dinge, ⁴ beſtändig, ⁵ pflegten, ⁶ ſich zu wundern, ⁷ Nacht, ⁸ geſetzt den Fall, ⁹ müßten ſterben, ¹⁰ Himmel,

¹¹ leid thun, ¹² Knospen, ¹³ munter (spielend), ¹⁴ hinunterhüpfen, ¹⁵ Pünktchen, ¹⁶ die Verstecken spielen, ¹⁷ betrübt, ¹⁸ Spielkameraden, ¹⁹ Thurm, ²⁰ aufgeben, ²¹ wurden, ²² zu bieten, ²³ sagne, ²⁴ während, ²⁵ siechte hin, ²⁶ traurig, ²⁷ Lächeln, ²⁸ Stimme, ²⁹ viel zu früh, ³⁰ Strahlen, ³¹ einsam, ³² Zug, ³³ funkelnd, ³⁴ strahlend, ³⁵ Reiben, ³⁶ zärtlich, ³⁷ breite Straßen, ³⁸ verklärt, ³⁹ strahlend, ⁴⁰ Schaar, ⁴¹ stand zögernd, ⁴² Eingang, ⁴³ Führer, ⁴⁴ dahin, ⁴⁵ strahlend, ⁴⁶ an, ⁴⁷ Heimath, ⁴⁸ weil, ⁴⁹ zart, ⁵⁰ erblickte, ⁵¹ fleißig, ⁵² Segen, ⁵³ Liebling, ⁵⁴ Freudenruf, ⁵⁵ erscholl, ⁵⁶ wiedervereinigt, ⁵⁷ Kummer, ⁵⁸ benetzt (bethaut), ⁵⁹ jungfräulich, ⁶⁰ vor Kurzem, ⁶¹ himmlisch, ⁶² Busen, ⁶³ Trennung, ⁶⁴ glatt, ⁶⁵ runzelig, ⁶⁶ gekrümmt, ⁶⁷ flüsterten, ⁶⁸ Gewand.

Lesestück 2.

THE FORGIVEN DEBT. (Die erlassene Schuld.)

1. About the beginning of the present[1] century,[2] a Boston merchant, who had been extensively engaged in commerce,[3] died at a good old age, without leaving any will.[4] He had been for many years largely interested[5] in the fishing business, and his name was familiar[6] to all the hardy[7] fishermen of Cape Cod. His eldest son administered upon[8] the estate.[9]

2. Among his papers a package of considerable size[10] was found after his death, carefully tied up,[11] and labelled[12] as follows: "Notes, due bills,[13] and accounts[14] against sundry[15] persons down along shore.[16] Some of these may be got[17] by a suit[18] or severe dunning.[19] But the people are poor; most of them have had fisherman's luck. My children will do as they think best.[20] Perhaps they will think with me that it is best to burn this package entire."[21]

3. "About a month," said my informant,[22] "after our father died, the sons met together, and after some general[23] remarks, our eldest brother, the administrator, produced[24] this package, of whose existence we were already apprised,[25] read the superscription,[26] and asked what course should be taken[27] in regard[28] to it. Another brother, a few years younger than the eldest, a man of strong, impulsive[29] temperament, unable at the moment to express his feeling by words, while he brushed[30] the tears from his eyes with one hand, by a spasmodic[31] jerk[32] of the other towards the fire-place,

indicated[33] his desire to have the papers put into the flames.

4. "It was suggested[34] by another of our number that it might be well first to make a list of the debtors'[35] names, and of the dates and accounts, that we might be enabled,[36] as the intended[37] discharge[38] was for all, to inform such as might offer payment, that their debts were forgiven. On the following day we again assembled; the list had been prepared, and all the notes, due bills, and accounts, whose amount,[39] including[40] interest,[41] exceeded[42] thirty-two thousand dollars, were committed[43] to the flames.

5. "It was in the month of June, about four months after our father's death, that, as I was sitting in my eldest brother's counting-room,[44] waiting for an opportunity[45] to speak to him, there came in a hard-favored,[46] little old man, who looked as if time and rough[47] weather had been to the windward[48] of him for seventy years. He asked if my brother was not the executor.[49] He replied that he was administrator, as our father died intestate.[50] 'Well,' said the stranger, 'I have come up from the Cape to pay a debt I owed[51] the old gentleman.' My brother," continued my informant, "requested him to be seated,[52] being at the moment engaged.[53]

6. "The old man sat down, and putting on his glasses,[54] drew out a very ancient[55] leather wallet.[56] When he had done this and sat, with quite a parcel[57] of notes, waiting his turn,[58] slowly twirling[59] his thumbs,[60] with his old, gray, meditative[61] eyes upon the floor, he sighed;[62] and I well knew the money, as the phrase runs,[63] came hard, and I secretly wished the old man's name might be found upon the forgiven list. My brother was soon at leisure,[64] and asked him his name and other common questions. The original debt was four hundred and forty dollars; it had stood a long time, and with the interest amounted to[65] a sum between seven and eight hundred dollars.

7. "My brother went to his table, and after examin-

ing the forgiven list attentively,[66] a sudden[67] smile lighted up[68] his countenance,[69] and told me the truth at a glance[70]—the old man's name was there. My brother quietly took a chair by his side, and a conversation ensued[71] between them which I shall never forget. 'Your note is outlawed,'[72] said my brother; 'it was dated[73] twelve years ago, payable in two years; there is no witness,[74] and no interest has ever been paid; you are not bound[75] to pay this note; we cannot recover[76] the amount.'

8. "'Sir,' said the old man, 'I wish to pay it. It is the only heavy debt I have in the world. I should like to pay it;' and he laid the bank-notes before my brother and requested him to count them over. 'I cannot take this money,' said my brother.

9. "The old man became alarmed.[77] 'I have cast[78] simple interest for twelve years and a little over,' said the old man. 'I will pay you compound interest,[79] if you say so. That debt ought to have been paid[80] long ago; but your father, sir, was very indulgent;[81] he knew that I had been unfortunate, and told me not to worry[82] about it.'

10. "My brother then set the matter plainly before him, and taking the bills, returned them to the old man, telling him that, although our father left no formal will, he had recommended his children to destroy[83] certain notes, due bills, and other evidences of debt,[84] and release[85] those who might be legally[86] bound to pay them. For a moment the worthy old man seemed to be stupefied.[87] After he had collected himself,[88] and wiped a few tears from his eyes, he stated,[89] that from the time of our father's death he had raked[90] and scraped,[91] and pinched[92] and spared, to get the money together for the payment of this debt.

11. "'About ten days ago,' said he, 'I had made up the sum within[93] twenty dollars. My wife knew how much the payment of this debt lay upon my spirits,[94] and advised me to sell a cow, and make up the difference, and get the heavy burden[95] off my spirits. I did

so—and now what will my wife say? I must get home to the Cape, and tell her this good news. She'll probably say over⁹⁶ the very words she said when she put her hands on my shoulder as we parted: "I have never seen the righteous man forsaken, nor his seed begging bread."'⁹⁷ After a hearty shake of the hand,⁹⁸ and a blessing upon our father's memory,⁹⁹ he went upon his way rejoicing.

12. "After a short silence, seizing his pencil, and making a computation,¹⁰⁰—'There,' exclaimed¹⁰¹ my brother, 'your part of the amount would be so much: contrive¹⁰² a plan to convey¹⁰³ to me your share of the pleasure derived¹⁰⁴ from this operation,¹⁰⁵ and the money is at your service.'"

L. M. SARGENT.

---

¹ gegenwärtig, ² Jahrhundert, ³ der ausgedehnte Handelsbeziehungen gehabt hatte, ⁴ letzter Wille, Testament, ⁵ interessirt, ⁶ wohlbekannt, ⁷ kräftig, abgehärtet, ⁸ verwaltete, ⁹ Hinterlassenschaft, ¹⁰ Umfang, ¹¹ zusammengebunden, ¹² mit der Aufschrift versehen, ¹³ fällige Rechnungen, ¹⁴ Conto, ¹⁵ verschiedene, ¹⁶ Küste, ¹⁷ mögen eingetrieben werden, ¹⁸ Prozeß, ¹⁹ dringendes Mahnen, ²⁰ für's Beste halten, ²¹ ganz, ²² Gewährsmann, ²³ allgemein, ²⁴ brachte zum Vorschein, ²⁵ in Kenntniß gesetzt, ²⁶ Aufschrift, ²⁷ welcher Weg eingeschlagen werden sollte, ²⁸ mit Bezug, ²⁹ aufbrausend, ³⁰ abwischte, ³¹ unwillkürlich, ³² Handbewegung, ³³ gab zu erkennen, ³⁴ vorgeschlagen, ³⁵ Schuldner, ³⁶ in den Stand gesetzt, ³⁷ beabsichtigt, ³⁸ Erlassima, ³⁹ Betrag, ⁴⁰ mit Einschluß, ⁴¹ pissen, ⁴² überstieg, ⁴³ übergeben, ⁴⁴ Comptoir, ⁴⁵ Gelegenheit, ⁴⁶ vom Schicksal wenig begünstigt, ⁴⁷ rauh, ⁴⁸ auf der Wetterseite, ⁴⁹ Testamentsvollstrecker, ⁵⁰ ohne Testament, ⁵¹ die ich schuldig war, ⁵² sich zu setzen, ⁵³ beschäftigt, ⁵⁴ Brille, ⁵⁵ altmodisch, ⁵⁶ Geldbeutel, ⁵⁷ mit einem ansehnlichen Packen, ⁵⁸ bis die Reihe an ihn kam, ⁵⁹ umdrehend (reibend), ⁶⁰ Daumen, ⁶¹ nachdenklich, ⁶² seufzte, ⁶³ wie man zu sagen pflegt, ⁶⁴ Muße, ⁶⁵ belief sich auf, ⁶⁶ aufmerksam, ⁶⁷ plötzlich, ⁶⁸ flog wie ein Blitzstrahl über, ⁶⁹ Antlitz, ⁷⁰ auf einen Blick, ⁷¹ folgte, ⁷² verjährt, ⁷³ datirt, ⁷⁴ Zeuge, ⁷⁵ gewonnen, ⁷⁶ eintreiben, ⁷⁷ beunruhigt, ⁷⁸ dazugerechnet (dazugeworfen), ⁷⁹ Zins auf Zins, ⁸⁰ hätte abgetragen werden sollen, ⁸¹ nachsichtig, ⁸² ich solle mir keine graue Haare deswegen wachsen lassen, ⁸³ zu zerstören, ⁸⁴ Schuldbeweise, ⁸⁵ freizumachen, ⁸⁶ nach dem Gesetz, ⁸⁷ versteinert, ⁸⁸ sich gesammelt hatte, ⁸⁹ erzählte er, ⁹⁰ zusammengescharrt, ⁹¹ gekratzt, ⁹² gewackt, ⁹³ bis auf, ⁹⁴ mich drückte (auf meinem Geiste lastete), ⁹⁵ Last, ⁹⁶ wiederholen, ⁹⁷ ich habe nie den Gerechten verlassen, noch seinen Samen nach Brod gehen sehen, ⁹⁸ nach einem herzlichen Handedruck, ⁹⁹ Andenken, ¹⁰⁰ Ueberschlag, ¹⁰¹ rief aus, ¹⁰² sinne aus, ¹⁰³ zu übertragen, ¹⁰⁴ erwachsen, ¹⁰⁵ Verfahren.

Lektion XXVI.

Unregelmäßige Zeitwörter. Präpositionen.

Infinitiv Präsens.	Imperfekt.	Particip der Vergangenheit.
to hear	heard	heard.
to hide	hid	hidden.
to hold	held	held.
to hurt	hurt	hurt.
to keep	kept	kept.
to kneel	knelt / kneeled	knelt. / kneeled.
to know	knew	known.
to lead	led	led.
to leave	left	left.
to lend	lent	lent.
to lose	lost	lost.
to make	made	made.
to mean	meant	meant.
to meet	met	met.
to pay	paid	paid.
to put	put	put.
to read	read	read.
to ride	rode	ridden.
to run	ran	run.

Präpositionen—About, by, during, after, against, among (amongst), towards, between, betwixt, through, before, behind, below, beneath, within.

Redensarten—Whose turn is it? to part with, to be on the rack, it strikes me, to let alone, to take aim, to find fault with, fond of, to play at cards, to pretend to, to bear malice against, in time, to make haste, to be in a hurry.

Unregelmäßige Zeitwörter. Präpositionen.

Wörter-Verzeichniß.

during, während.
kitten, Kätzchen.
to hide, sich verstecken.
hold your tongue, halt's Maul!
stable, Stall.
farming, Ackerbau.
to owe, schuldig sein.
within, innerhalb.
adventure, Abenteuer.
to spare, entbehren.
equally, ebenso.
to order, bestellen.
towards, gegen.
he surely meant no harm by it, er hatte es gewiß nicht so böse gemeint damit.
considerate, rücksichtsvoll.
in future, in Zukunft.

Redensarten.

whose turn is it? an wem ist die Reihe?
to part with, Abschied nehmen von.
to shake hands with a person, sich die Hände schütteln.
to be on the rack for, sehr gespannt sein auf.
theatre of war, Kriegsschauplatz.

it strikes me, es will mir scheinen.
to let alone, in Frieden lassen.
are not you struck with? sind Sie nicht frappirt von?
to take aim, sein Ziel nehmen; zielen.
mark, Ziel.
to find fault with, auszusetzen finden an; mäkeln.
to play at cards, Karten spielen.
to prefer to, vorziehen.
a precious fellow, ein schöner Bursche.
stories, Windbeuteleien.
to pretend to, sich anmaßen.
mastery, Meisterschaft.
to make up one's mind, entschlossen sein.
distant, fern.
to abuse, schmähen, verunglimpfen.
to deal with, handeln gegen.
to bear malice, feindlich gesinnt sein.
to bear a grudge to a person, Jemandem grollen.
to make haste, eilen.
to be in a hurry, Eile haben.

Uebungs-Aufgabe 1.

During the month of May the Steamship Company lost two of their best ships. During her last moments I held her head in my arms. I have lost all my friends; it is a sad thing to lose a mother. The kitten hid in the corner behind the stove. What have you hidden in your pocket? I have nothing hidden. Hold your tongue! I cannot hear what he says. I was hurt by a stone which a boy threw through the window. With what did he hurt you? He hurt me with a knife. They keep a store below Twentieth Street. Where have you kept your horses? I kept them among some others in my stable all winter. She knelt down before a crucifix and prayed. What do you know about farming? I do not know more about it than you do. He very well knew that I had paid him what I owed him. If I had known that you were going to spend all your money within such a short time, I should certainly not have lent you a single dollar. A person that spends his money so fast and foolishly, is called a spendthrift. I have been much amused by what I read about the adventures of a traveler who traveled through the forests of Brazil. I should like to borrow this book from you, if you can spare it. I cannot lend you this one before next week, but I will lend you another equally interesting. When will you make the bedstead for me that I ordered about two months ago? It will be done towards the end of next week. You must not be offended, for he surely meant no harm by it. He promised to pay between to-day and day after to-morrow. I shall go out riding in the Park. I rode out in a carriage. Quick! run after that boy, and tell him to come back. I have no ill feelings against him, but I want him to be more considerate towards his friends in future.

Nebensarten: Whose turn is it to read? I believe it is mine. It will be your turn next. I shall tell you when your turn comes. When people part with their friends, they shake hands with them. Come, let us shake hands and be friends! I am on the rack for the next news from the theatre of war. It strikes me that you would have done better, if you had let this fellow alone. Are not you struck with the peculiar beauty of this landscape? Make sure always to take your aim high. If you want to hit the mark, you must take better aim. I did not find fault with your work at all, I only found fault with the time it took you to finish it. It is easier to find fault with a person's work than to do it better yourself. The Germans are very fond of playing at cards. I prefer a game of billiards to a game at cards. You are a precious fellow, indeed! to tell me such stories. I do not yet pretend to a mastery of the English language, but I have made up my mind to master it at no very distant time; and you know, where there is a will, there is a way. It is a shame, indeed, thus to abuse a man who has always dealt honestly with him. I shall not bear any malice against him, for what he has done, but I cannot help bearing him a little grudge for it. If you wish to be in time for the boat, you must make haste. I am in a great hurry to finish this letter.

Wörter-Verzeichniß.

Geräusch, noise.
man solle nicht, you ought not.
aufschieben, to put off to.
Versteden, hide and go seek.
Mantel, cloak.
Garn, yarn.
abwickeln, to unwind.
sich weh thun, to hurt one's self.
schlimm, bad.
geschwind, quickly.
mit nichten, by no means.
sich beruhigen, keep quiet.
es hat nichts zu sagen, it's of no consequence.
Bedeutung, consequence.
Geheimniß, secret.
Haushalten, to keep house.
ausgezeichnet, excellent.
Haushälterin, housekeeper.

Sterbebette, death-bed.
bitten um, to ask for.
Segen, blessing.
wiederkommen, to return.
gewiß, certain.
fortgeben, to leave.
wegbleiben, to stay away.
geben nach, to leave for.
vor, previous to.
Abreise, departure.
in's dichteste Feuer, into the thickest of the fight.
irreführen, to leave for.
reisen nach, to leave for.
kriegen, to get.
suchen, to try.
Borgen stumpft der Wirthschaft Spitze ab, borrowing blunts the edge of husbandry.

Borgen macht Sorgen, to borrow makes sorrow.
sich beeilen, make haste.
zu rechter Zeit, in time.
zu verlieren, to be lost.
Pult, desk.
bestellen, to order.
bedeuten, to mean.
auf deutsch, in German.
beabsichtigen, to mean.
nöthig haben, to need.
übermorgen, day after tomorrow.
zusammentreffen mit, to meet.
hast du etwas an ihn zu bestellen? have you any message to send to him?
Rechnung, bill.
Fußteppich, carpet.
bekommen, to get.
Reiten, riding on horseback.
Fußteppich, carpet.
ich gehe lieber zu Fuß, I prefer going on foot.

Uebungs-Aufgabe 2.

Was hörst du? Ich höre ein Geräusch. Hast du nicht etwas gehört? Nein, ich habe nichts gehört. Du? Nein, ich auch nicht. Ich habe meinen Vater oft sagen hören, man solle nicht auf morgen aufschieben, was man heute thun kann. Hast du die Katze nach der Maus laufen sehen? Die Maus hat sich unter's Bett versteckt. Die Kinder spielen Verstecken. Was hast du versteckt unter deinem Mantel? Ich habe nichts darunter versteckt. Willst du dies Garn für mich halten, daß ich es abwickle. Er hat sein Versprechen nicht gehalten. Ich habe mir wehgethan. Ist es schlimm? Soll ich geschwind nach dem Doktor laufen? Mit nichten; beruhigen Sie sich; es hat nichts zu sagen; es ist von keiner Bedeutung. Kannst du ein Geheimniß für dich behalten? Ja; ich auch. Wie lange haben Sie Haus gehalten? Ich habe zehn Jahre Haus gehalten. Meine Frau ist eine ausgezeichnete Haushälterin. Er kniete an dem Sterbebette seiner Mutter und bat um ihren Segen. Weißt du, wann dein Vater wiederkommt? Ich weiß es nicht gewiß; er sagte mir, als er fortging, er würde nicht lange wegbleiben. Ich kenne diesen Mann schon über fünfzehn Jahre. Wußte er, daß du nach Amerika gehen würdest? Er wußte es nur ein Paar Tage vor meiner Abreise. Der General führte seine Truppen in's dichteste Feuer. Du hast mich irregeführt. Die „Silesia" ging heute nach Hamburg. Wir werden mit dem nächsten Dampfer nach Bremen reisen. Kannst du mir zehn Thaler leihen? Ich kann dir wohl so viel leihen, aber ich kriege ja doch mein Geld nicht wieder von dir; darum mußt du anderswo suchen Geld zu borgen. „Das Borgen," sagt Shakespeare in seinem „Hamlet," „stumpft der Wirthschaft Spitze ab;" und die Deutschen sagen, „Borgen macht Sorgen." Beeile dich! wenn du zu rechter Zeit kommen willst, dann mußt du laufen; es ist keine Zeit zu verlieren. Was hast du verloren? Ich habe meinen Schlüssel verloren. Hast du ihn versteckt? Ich habe ihn gefunden und in dein Pult gelegt. Hat der Tischler die Stühle gemacht, die ich bestellt habe? Er hat sie noch nicht gemacht. Was bedeutet das Wort comfortable auf Deutsch? Ich beabsichtige diesen Winter so viel Englisch zu lernen, daß ich keinen Lehrer mehr nöthig habe. Uebermorgen werde ich mit deinem Vetter zusammentreffen; hast du etwas an ihn zu bestellen? Wenn du mir einen Gefallen thun willst, dann bezahle diese Rechnung für mich. Wie viel haben Sie für diesen Fußteppich bezahlt? Ich habe ihn sehr billig bekommen; ich habe einen Dollar und dreißig Cents die Yard bezahlt. Stecke dies Geld in die Tasche. Als ich heute Morgen ausfuhr, hatte ich vergessen Geld zu mir zu stecken. Sind Sie ein Freund vom Reiten? Ich gehe lieber zu Fuß.

Lesestück 1.

AN INDIAN STRATAGEM. (Eine indianische Kriegslist.)

1. During the war[1] of the American revolution, a regiment of foot soldiers was stationed upon the confines[2] of a boundless[3] savanna, in the southern[4] part of the Union. Its particular office[5] was to guard[6] every avenue of approach[7] to the main army.[8] The sentinels,[9] whose posts penetrated[10] into the woods, were supplied[11] from the ranks;[12] but they were perpetually[13] surprised[14] upon their posts by the Indians, and borne off[15] their stations,[16] without communicating any alarm,[17] or being heard of afterwards.[18]

2. One morning, the sentinels having been stationed as usual over night, the guard[19] went at sunrise to re-

lieve²⁰ a post which extended²¹ a considerable²² distance into the wood. The sentinel was gone. The surprise²³ was great; but the circumstance had occurred²⁴ before. They left another man, and departed,²⁵ wishing him better luck. "You need not be afraid,"²⁶ said the man, with warmth; "I shall not desert."²⁷

3. The sentinels were replaced²⁸ every four hours, and at the appointed²⁹ time the guard again marched to relieve the post. To their inexpressible³⁰ astonishment the man was gone. They searched³¹ round the spot, but no traces³² of him could be found. It was now more necessary than ever that the station should not remain³³ unoccupied;³⁴ they left another man, and returned to the guard-house.

4. The superstition³⁵ of the soldiers was awakened,³⁶ and terror³⁷ ran through the regiment. The colonel, being apprised³⁸ of the occurrence,³⁹ signified⁴⁰ his intention to accompany⁴¹ the guard when they relieved the sentinel they had left. At the appointed time they all marched together; and again, to their unutterable⁴² wonder, they found the post vacant,⁴³ and the man gone.

5. Under these circumstances the colonel hesitated⁴⁴ whether he should station a whole company on the spot, or whether he should again submit⁴⁵ the post to a single sentinel. The cause⁴⁶ of these repeated⁴⁷ disappearances⁴⁸ of men, whose courage and honesty were never suspected,⁴⁹ must be discovered; and it seemed not likely⁵⁰ that this discovery could be obtained by persisting⁵¹ in the old method.

6. Three brave men were now lost to the regiment, and to assign⁵² the post to a fourth seemed nothing less than giving him up to destruction.⁵³ The poor fellow whose turn it was⁵⁴ to take the station, though a man in other respects⁵⁵ of incomparable⁵⁶ resolution, trembled from head to foot.

7. "I must do my duty," said he to the officer; "I know that; but I should like to lose my life with more credit."⁵⁷ "I will leave no man," said the colonel,

"against his will." A man immediately stepped from the ranks, and desired to take the post. Every mouth commended⁵⁸ his resolution.

"I will not be taken alive,"⁵⁹ said he, "and you shall hear of me at the least alarm. At all events,⁶⁰ I will fire my piece⁶¹ if I hear the least noise. If a crow chatters⁶² or a leaf falls, you shall hear my musket. You may be alarmed when nothing is the matter;⁶³ but you must take the chance⁶⁴ as the condition of the discovery."

9. The colonel applauded his courage, and told him he would do right to fire upon the least noise that he could not satisfactorily⁶⁵ explain.⁶⁶ His comrades shook⁶⁷ hands with him, and left him with a melancholy foreboding.⁶⁸ The company marched back, and waited the event⁶⁹ in the guard-house.

10. An hour had now elapsed,⁷⁰ and every ear was upon the rack⁷¹ for the discharge⁷² of the musket, when, upon a sudden, the report⁷³ was heard. The guard immediately marched, accompanied, as before, by the colonel and some of the most experienced officers of the regiment.

11. As they approached the post, they saw the man advancing toward them, dragging⁷⁴ another man on the ground by the hair of his head. When they came up to him, it appeared to be an Indian whom he had shot. An explanation⁷⁵ was immediately required.

12. "I told you, colonel," said the man, "that I should fire if I heard the least noise.⁷⁶ That resolution I took has saved⁷⁷ my life. I had not been long at my post when I heard a rustling⁷⁸ at some short distance; I looked, and saw a wild hog,⁷⁹ such as are common⁸⁰ in the woods, crawling⁸¹ along the ground, and seemingly⁸² looking for nuts under the trees, among the leaves.

13. "As these animals are so very common, I ceased⁸³ to consider it seriously,⁸⁴ but kept my eyes fixed upon it, and marked its progress⁸⁵ among the trees; still there was no need⁸⁶ to give the alarm. It

struck me,⁸⁷ however, as somewhat singular to see this animal making,⁸⁸ by a circuitous passage,⁸⁹ for ⁸⁸ a thick grove⁹⁰ immediately behind my post. I therefore kept my eye more constantly fixed upon⁹¹ it, and, as it was now within ⁹² a few yards of the coppice,⁹³ I hesitated whether I should fire.

14. "My comrades, thought I, will laugh at me for alarming them by shooting a pig. I had almost resolved to let it alone,⁹⁴ when, just as it approached the thicket,⁹⁵ I thought I observed it give an unusual ⁹⁶ spring. I no longer hesitated: I took my aim,⁹⁷ discharged ⁹⁸ my piece, and the animal was immediately stretched before me, with a groan ⁹⁹ which I thought to be that of a human creature.

15. "I went up to it, and judge¹⁰⁰ my astonishment when I found that I had killed an Indian. He had enveloped ¹⁰¹ himself with the skin ¹⁰² of one of these wild hogs so artfully¹⁰³ and completely, his hands and his feet were so entirely concealed ¹⁰⁴ in it, and his gait ¹⁰⁵ and appearance were so exactly correspondent¹⁰⁶ to that of the animals, that imperfectly as¹⁰⁷ they were always seen through the trees and bushes, the disguise ¹⁰⁸ could not be detected ¹⁰⁹ at a distance, and scarcely discovered upon the nearest inspection. He was armed with a dagger¹¹⁰ and tomahawk."

16. The cause of the disappearance of the other sentinels was now apparent.¹¹¹ The Indians, sheltered ¹¹² in this disguise, secreted ¹¹³ themselves in the coppice, watched ¹¹⁴ the moment when they could throw it off, burst upon ¹¹⁵ the sentinels without previous ¹¹⁶ alarm, and, too quick to give them an opportunity to discharge their pieces, either stabbed ¹¹⁷ or scalped ¹¹⁸ them. They then bore their bodies away, and concealed them at some distance in the leaves.

---

¹ Krieg, ² Gränzen, ³ unabsehbar, ⁴ südlich, ⁵ besondere Aufgabe, ⁶ zu bewachen, ⁷ Zugang, ⁸ Haupt-Armee, ⁹ Schildwachen, ¹⁰ vorgeschoben waren, ¹¹ ersetzt, ¹² Linie, ¹³ beständig, ¹⁴ überrumpelt, ¹⁵ weggekapert, ¹⁶ Posten, ¹⁷ ohne Lärm zu schlagen, ¹⁸ oder daß man später von ihnen hörte, ¹⁹ Wache, ²⁰ abzulösen, ²¹ vorgeschoben war, ²² beträchtlich, ²³ Ueberraschung, ²⁴ hatte sich

zugetragen, ²⁵ gingen fort, ²⁶ ihr braucht nicht bange zu sein, ²⁷ desertiren, ²⁸ wiederbesetzt, ²⁹ festgesetzt, ³⁰ unbeschreiblich, ³¹ durchsuchten, ³² Spuren, ³³ bleiben, ³⁴ unbesetzt, ³⁵ Aberglaube, ³⁶ war erregt, ³⁷ Schrecken, ³⁸ in Kenntniß gesetzt, ³⁹ Vorfall, ⁴⁰ bezeigte, ⁴¹ begleiten, ⁴² unaussprechlich, ⁴³ unbesetzt, ⁴⁴ ward unschlüssig, ⁴⁵ übergeben, ⁴⁶ Ursache, ⁴⁷ wiederholt, ⁴⁸ Verschwinden, ⁴⁹ in Verdacht gezogen, ⁵⁰ wahrscheinlich, ⁵¹ dadurch, daß man beharrte bei, ⁵² anzuweisen, ⁵³ Verderben, ⁵⁴ an dem die Reihe war, ⁵⁵ in jeder andern Hinsicht, ⁵⁶ unvergleichlich, ⁵⁷ Ehre, ⁵⁸ lobte, ⁵⁹ lebendig, ⁶⁰ auf jeden Fall, ⁶¹ Flinte, ⁶² frage, ⁶³ wenn nichts los ist, ⁶⁴ Zufall, ⁶⁵ hinreichend, ⁶⁶ erklären, ⁶⁷ schüttelten, ⁶⁸ Verahmung, ⁶⁹ Ereigniß, ⁷⁰ verflossen, ⁷¹ jedes Ohr war gespitzt, ⁷² Abfeuern, ⁷³ Knall, ⁷⁴ schleifend, ⁷⁵ Erklärung, ⁷⁶ das geringste Geräusch, ⁷⁷ rettete, ⁷⁸ Rascheln, ⁷⁹ Schwein, ⁸⁰ gewöhnlich, ⁸¹ friechend, ⁸² wie es schien, ⁸³ horte ich auf, ⁸⁴ es für gefährlich zu betrachten, ⁸⁵ Weitergehen, ⁸⁶ Noth, ⁸⁷ es fiel mir auf, ⁸⁸ seinen Weg einschlagen, ⁸⁹ auf einem Umwege, ⁹⁰ dichtes Gebüsch, ⁹¹ darauf gerichtet, ⁹² bis auf, ⁹³ Gebüsch, ⁹⁴ es in Frieden zu lassen, ⁹⁵ Dickicht, ⁹⁶ sonderbar, ⁹⁷ zielte, ⁹⁸ feuerte, ⁹⁹ Gestöhn, ¹⁰⁰ stellt euch vor, ¹⁰¹ eingewickelt, ¹⁰² Haut, ¹⁰³ künstlich, ¹⁰⁴ verbergen, ¹⁰⁵ Gang, ¹⁰⁶ entsprechend, ¹⁰⁷ so unvollkommen auch, ¹⁰⁸ Vermummung, ¹⁰⁹ entdeckt, ¹¹⁰ Dolch, ¹¹¹ offenbar, ¹¹² geschützt, ¹¹³ versteckten, ¹¹⁴ lauerten auf, ¹¹⁵ stürzten sich auf, ¹¹⁶ vorhergehend, ¹¹⁷ erdolchten, ¹¹⁸ scalpirten.

Lesestück 2.

AFTER MARRIAGE. (Nach der Hochzeit.)

Lady Teazle and Sir Peter.

Sir Peter. Lady Teazle, Lady Teazle, I'll not bear[1] it!

Lady Teazle. Sir Peter, Sir Peter, you may bear it or not, as you please; but I ought to have my own way in every thing; and what's more, I will, too. What! though I was educated[2] in the country, I know very well that women of fashion in London are accountable[3] to nobody after they are married.[4]

Sir P. Very well, ma'am, very well—so a husband[5] is to have[6] no influence, no authority?

Lady T. Authority! No, to be sure:—if you wanted authority over me, you should have adopted[7] me, and not married me; I am sure you were old enough.

Sir P. Old enough!—ah—there it is. Well, well, Lady Teazle, though my life may be made unhappy[8] by your temper,[9] I'll not be ruined by your extravagance.[10]

Lady T. My extravagance! I'm sure I'm not more extravagant than a woman ought to be.

Sir P. No, no, madam, you shall throw away no more sums on such unmeaning [11] luxury. Indeed! to spend as much to furnish [12] your dressing-room [13] with flowers in winter as would suffice [14] to turn [15] the Pantheon into a green-house! [16]

Lady T. Why, Sir Peter! am I to blame,[17] because flowers are dear in cold weather? You should find fault with [18] the climate and not with me. For my part,[19] I'm sure, I wish it were spring all the year round, and that roses grew under our feet!

Sir P. Zounds![20] madam—if you had been born to this,[21] I shouldn't wonder at your talking thus; but you forget what your situation was when I married you.

Lady T. No, no, I don't; 'twas a very disagreeable[22] one, or I should never have married you.

Sir P. Yes, yes, madam, you were then in somewhat a humbler style[23]—the daughter of a plain county squire.[24] Recollect,[25] Lady Teazle, when I saw you first sitting at your tambour,[26] in a pretty figured [27] linen gown,[28] with a bunch of keys[29] at your side, your hair combed smooth over a roll, and your apartment hung round [30] with fruits in worsted[31] of your own working.

Lady T. Oh yes! I remember it very well, and a curious life I led,—my daily occupation to inspect the dairy,[32] superintend[33] the poultry,[34] make extracts from the family receipt-book, and comb my aunt Deborah's lap-dog.[35]

Sir P. Yes, yes, ma'am; 'twas so, indeed.

Lady T. And then, you know, my evening amusements;—to draw [36] patterns [37] for ruffles,[38] which I had not materials to make up; to play Pope Joan [39] with the curate; [40] to read a novel [41] to my aunt; or to be stuck down [42] to an old spinet [43] to strum my father to sleep after a fox-chase.[44]

Sir P. I am glad you have so good a memory.[45]

Yes, madam, these were the recreations [46] I took you from; but now you must have your coach—*vis-à-vis*—and three powdered [47] footmen [48] before your chair; and, in the summer, a pair of white cats to draw you to Kensington Gardens. No recollection, I suppose, when you were content [49] to ride double, [50] behind the butler, [51] on a docked [52] coach-horse.

Lady T. No—I never did that; I deny [53] the butler and the coach-horse.

Sir P. This, madam, was your situation; and what have I done for you? I have made you a woman of fashion, of fortune, [54] of rank; in short, I have made you my wife.

Lady T. Well, then; and there is but one thing more you can make me, to add to the obligation, [55] and that is—

Sir P. My widow, I suppose?

Lady T. Hem! hem!

Sir P. I thank you, madam; but don't flatter yourself; [56] for though your ill conduct [57] may disturb my peace of mind, it shall never break my heart, I promise you: however, [58] I am equally obliged to you for the hint. [59]

Lady T. Then why will you endeavor [60] to make yourself so disagreeable to me, and thwart me [61] in every little elegant expense? [62]

Sir P. Indeed, madam! had you any of these little elegant expenses when you married me?

Lady T. Why, Sir Peter! would you have me be out of the fashion?

Sir P. The fashion, indeed! What had you to do with the fashion before you married me?

Lady T. For my part, I should think you would like to have your wife thought a woman of taste. [63]

Sir P. Ay; there again—taste. Zounds! madam, you had no taste when you married me!

Lady T. That's very true, indeed, Sir Peter; and after having married you, I should never pretend to [64] taste again, I allow. [65] But now, Sir Peter, since we have finished our daily jangle," I presume⁶⁷ I may go to my engagement at Lady Sneerwell's.

Sir P. Ay, there's another precious circumstance⁶⁸ —a charming set⁶⁹ of acquaintance you have made there.

Lady T. Nay, Sir Peter, they are all people of rank and fortune, and remarkably tenacious of⁷⁰ reputation.⁷¹

Sir P. Yes, they are tenacious of reputation with a vengeance;⁷² for they don't choose anybody should have⁷³ a character but themselves! Such a crew!⁷⁴ Ah! many a wretch⁷⁵ has rid on a hurdle⁷⁶ who has done less mischief⁷⁷ than these utterers⁷⁸ of forged tales,⁷⁹ coiners of scandal,⁸⁰ and clippers of reputation.⁸¹

Lady T. What! would you restrain⁸² the freedom of speech?⁸³

Sir P. Ah! they have made you just as bad as any one of the society.

Lady T. Why, I believe I do bear a part with a a tolerable grace.⁸⁴

Sir P. Grace, indeed!

Lady T. But I vow⁸⁵ I bear no malice⁸⁶ against the people I abuse.⁸⁷ When I say an ill-natured thing,⁸⁸ it's out of pure good humor;⁸⁹ and I take it for granted⁹⁰ they deal exactly in the same manner with me. But, Sir Peter, you know you promised to come to Lady Sneerwell's too.

Sir P. Well, well; I'll call in just to look after my own character.

Lady T. Then, indeed, you must make haste⁹¹ after me, or you'll be too late. So, good-bye to you. [*Exit Lady Teagle.*]

Sir P. So—I have gained much by my intended expostulation;⁹² yet, with what a charming air⁹³ she contradicts every thing I say, and how pleasing she shows her contempt⁹⁴ for my authority! Well, though I can't make her love me, there is great satisfaction in quarreling with her; and I think she never appears to such advantage⁹⁵ as when she is doing everything in her power to plague me. [*Exit.*]

SHERIDAN.

¹ dulden, ² aufgezogen, ³ verantwortlich, ⁴ verheirathet, ⁵ Ehemann, ⁶ soll haben, ⁷ adoptirt, ⁸ obschon mir das Leben verleidet werden kann, ⁹ hitziges Temperament, ¹⁰ Verschwendung, ¹¹ nichtssagend, ¹² zu versehen, ¹³ Ankleidezimmer, ¹⁴ hinreichen würde, ¹⁵ verwandeln, ¹⁶ Gewächshaus, ¹⁷ tadeln, ¹⁸ beschuldigen, ¹⁹ was mich betrifft, ²⁰ Donnerwetter! ²¹ wenn Ihr dabei geboren und aufgewachsen wäret, ²² unangenehm, ²³ in einer etwas bescheideneren Lebensweise, ²⁴ Landedelmann, ²⁵ erinnert Euch, ²⁶ Stickrahmen, ²⁷ geblümt, ²⁸ Hauskleid, ²⁹ Schlüsselbund, ³⁰ rings behängt, ³¹ Stickerei, ³² Milchkammer, ³³ die Aufsicht zu führen über, ³⁴ Geflügel, ³⁵ Schooshündchen, ³⁶ zeichnen, ³⁷ Muster, ³⁸ Hemdkrausen, ³⁹ Papst Johanna (ein Kartenspiel), ⁴⁰ Pfarrer, ⁴¹ Roman, ⁴² festgebannt, ⁴³ Guitarre, ⁴⁴ Fuchsjagd, ⁴⁵ Gedächtniß, ⁴⁶ Erholungen, ⁴⁷ gepudert, ⁴⁸ Diener, ⁴⁹ zufrieden, ⁵⁰ selbander, ⁵¹ Wirthschafter (Verwalter), ⁵² mit Stumpfschwanz, ⁵³ leugne, ⁵⁴ Vermögen, ⁵⁵ um meine Verbindlichkeit zu vergrößern, ⁵⁶ schmeichelt Euch nicht, ⁵⁷ Euer übles Benehmen, ⁵⁸ übrigens, ⁵⁹ Wink, ⁶⁰ bemühen, ⁶¹ mir in die Queere kommen, ⁶² Ausgabe für Luxusgegenstände, ⁶³ von gutem Geschmack, ⁶⁴ würde ich mir niemals anmaßen, ⁶⁵ das gebe ich zu, ⁶⁶ Streit, ⁶⁷ so vermuthe ich, ⁶⁸ das ist noch ein prächtiger Umstand! ⁶⁹ eine schöne Sippschaft, ⁷⁰ und halten außerordentlich auf, ⁷¹ guter Namen, ⁷² fürwahr, ⁷³ sie wollen, daß Niemand haben soll, ⁷⁴ Sippschaft, ⁷⁵ elender Lump, ⁷⁶ Armesünderkarren, ⁷⁷ Unheil, ⁷⁸ Verbreiter, ⁷⁹ von lügenhaften Geschichten, ⁸⁰ Skandalmacher, ⁸¹ Verläumder, ⁸² beschränken, ⁸³ Redeschreiben, ⁸⁴ mit ziemlicher Grazie, ⁸⁵ ich versichere, ⁸⁶ ich trage nichts nach, ⁸⁷ verunglimpfe, ⁸⁸ etwas Böses, ⁸⁹ Laune, ⁹⁰ ausgemacht, ⁹¹ müßt Ihr eilen, ⁹² Gegenvorstellungen, ⁹³ mit welch einer reizenden Stimme, ⁹⁴ Verachtung, ⁹⁵ sie zeigt sich nie so sehr zu ihrem Vortheil.

Lektion XXVII.

Unregelmäßige Zeitwörter. Conjunktionen. Redensarten.

Infinitiv.	Imperfect.	Particip.
to say	said	said.
to see	saw	seen.
to sell	sold	sold.
to send	sent	sent.
to shake	shook	shaken.
to show	showed	shown.

Infinitiv.	Imperfect.	Particip.
to shine	shone	shone.
to shoot	shot	shot.
to shut	shut	shut.
to sing	sang	sung.
to sink	sank	sunk.
to sit	sat	sat.
to sleep	slept	slept.
to speak	spoke	spoken.
to spend	spent	spent.
to spring	sprang	sprung.
to stand	stood	stood.
to steal	stole	stolen.

Conjunktionen (Bindewörter)—As, lest, when, though, either—or, neither—nor, yet.

Redensarten—To take pains, to die away, worth while, to encounter, to meet with, conscience, conscientious, conscientiousness, consciousness, conscious, imminent, eminent, in spite of, angry, anxious, to cherish, that will do, what day of the month?

Wörter-Verzeichniß.

wonderful, merkwürdig.
the like of this, dergleichen.
see to it, sieh dich vor.
to spoil, verderben.
real estate, Grundeigenthum.
bed-room furniture, Schlaf-
 stubenmöbel.
to show proof, Beweis führen.
crime, Verbrechen.
to shake, schütteln, zittern.
fist, Faust.

disappointed, getäuscht.
rabbit, Hase.
partridge, Rebhuhn.
either—or, entweder—oder.
to enter, eintreten.
to spend, zubringen.
to spring a leak, einen Leck
 bekommen.
departure, Abfahrt.
lest, damit nicht.
detected, entdeckt.

Redensarten.

to take pains, sich Mühe geben.
in spite of, trotz.
tremendous, ungeheuer.
pronunciation, Aussprache.
foreigner, Ausländer.
to overcome, überwinden.
to meet with, erleiden.
serious, ernstlich.
accident, Unfall.
to be capsized, umschlagen.
squall, Windstoß.
one of the hands, einer von der Mannschaft.
to be drowned, ertrinken.
worth while, der Mühe werth.
to apply for, sich bemühen um.
appointment, Ernennung.
Arctic expedition, Polarexpedition.
to encounter, aufstoßen.
obstacle, Hinderniß.
attempt, Versuch.
conscience, Gewissen.
conscientious, gewissenhaft.
conscientiousness, Gewissenhaftigkeit.
angry at, böse auf.
conscious, bewußt.
of having promised you, daß ich Ihnen versprochen habe.
consciousness, Bewußtsein.
duty, Pflicht.
gratifying, wohlthuend.
eminent, groß.
naturalist, Naturforscher.
imminent, drohend.
to forfeit, verscherzen.
anxious, begierig.
to cherish, hegen.
towards, gegen.
that will do, das ist genug.
will this paper do? ist dies Papier recht?
what day of the month? der wievielte?

Uebungs-Aufgabe 1.

I do not understand what you say; please say it again. I said that you should always speak the truth. I have seen many wonderful things, but I never saw the like of this. See to it that you do not spoil my umbrella. When I sold my house in Fourteenth Street, real estate was not as high yet as it is now. What have you sold to-day? I have sold more than yesterday; for yesterday I sold but one set of bed-room furniture, for three sets that I sold this morning. Whom did you send to the doctor? I sent my boy. Though he could not show proof of his innocence, yet everybody believed him to be innocent of this crime. He shook his fist at me, when he found himself disappointed. Please, send for a doctor, as I am shaking with a fever. The earth fairly shook with the roar of cannon. The sun is shining. We were out shooting last week. We shot five rabbits and about a dozen partridges. Please shut the door. I have shut it. Either sing a song or play a piece on the piano. She sang to us one of Mendelssohn's songs. When I have sung this song, I want you to sing one, too. Won't you sit by me? Thank you, I have been sitting all day. I sat by his side when his brother entered the room. Good night, sleep well. I slept but four hours last night. Arise; you have slept more than eight hours. Where did you spend last night? I spent it at a concert in Steinway Hall. I have spent many an hour in his company. The ship sprang a leak the third day after its departure. He stood beside me. Will you stand here until I have finished my business. He told us to stand still, lest we should be detected. Thou shalt not steal. This money is stolen.

Redensarten: This work is badly done; in future you must take more pains. I took great pains to learn English, and in spite of the tremendous difficulties of its pronunciation for a foreigner, I may now say that I have overcome most of them. In sailing down the river in an open boat, they met with a serious accident; their boat was capsized in a squall, and one of the hands on board was drowned. Do you think it worth my while to apply for this position? I do not think it worth your while, as all the appointments were made yesterday. What day of the month is the Arctic expedition under Captain Hall to start? They have started already, and you may be sure they will encounter great obstacles in their attempt at reaching the Arctic Ocean. A man of conscience will always act conscientiously. The money that was given him he spent with the utmost conscientiousness. I am very angry at you for disappointing me thus. I am sorry that I have disappointed you, but I am not conscious of having promised you that I would come. The consciousness of having done your whole duty is a gratifying feeling. Alexander von Humboldt was a very eminent naturalist. You are in imminent danger of forfeiting his affection. I am very anxious to see your cousin. Are you angry with me yet? No, not at all; I cherish none but the friendliest feelings towards you. Please to pour out a cup of coffee for me. That will do. Will this paper do? I guess it will. What day of the month is it to-day? It is the twenty-fifth.

Wörter-Verzeichniß.

dafür, for it.
sein Leben machen, to get a living.
vor allen Dingen, above all.
noch einmal, once more.
damit ich kann, that I may.
recht machen, to do right.
auf den ersten Blick, at the first glance.
eben im Begriff, just about.
Hammelfleisch, mutton.
bestellen, to order.
rütteln, schütteln, to shake.

Postamt, post-office.
auf der Jagd, hunting.
freundlich, bright.
kein Lüftchen regte sich, not a breath of air was stirring.
vom Blatte, at first sight.
scheitern, to be wrecked.
Faden, fathom.
ich stehe lieber, I prefer standing.
Dieb; Einbrecher, burglar.
Banknoten, bank-bills.
sich beschädigen, to get hurt.

Uebungs-Aufgabe 2.

Was sagst du zu meinem neuen Wagen? Ich sage, er ist sehr hübsch; du hast aber zu viel dafür bezahlt. Sage mir, was ich thun muß, um hier mein Leben zu machen. Das will ich dir sagen. Du mußt vor allen Dingen englisch lernen. Sage dies noch einmal, aber sprich etwas lauter, damit ich es verstehen kann. Wollen Sie sehen, ob ich dies recht gemacht habe? Ich sehe auf den ersten Blick, daß es verkehrt ist. Als ich deinen Bruder zum letzten Mal sah, war er eben im Begriff nach dem Westen zu gehen. Wie theuer verkaufen Sie diesen Tisch? Dieser Tisch ist verkauft; aber ich verkaufe Ihnen einen andern eben so guten für $30. Hast du deine beiden Pferde verkauft? Ich habe weder das Eine noch das Andere verkauft. Was soll ich Ihnen schicken? Schicken Sie mir zwei Pfund Butter und ein Pfund guten Käse. Hat der Fleischer schon das Hammelfleisch geschickt, das ich diesen Morgen bei ihm bestellte? Er hat es noch nicht geschickt. Rüttle nicht an dem Tisch; ich kann nicht schreiben. Hast du alle Aepfel von diesem Baume abgeschüttelt? Wollen Sie mir zeigen, wo das Postamt ist? Hast du meinen Brief deinem Vater gezeigt? Ich habe ihn ihm noch nicht gezeigt, aber sobald er nach Hause gekommen ist, will ich ihm denselben zeigen. Wir waren gestern auf der Jagd. Die Sonne schien so freundlich und kein Lüftchen regte sich. Wir schossen fünf Hasen und etwa ein Dutzend Rebhühner. Hast du die Thür zugemacht? wenn nicht, so mache sie gleich zu. Sie ist zu. Können Sie singen? Gewiß. Dann singen Sie mir, ich bitte, dieses Lied vor. Ich muß Sie bitten mich zu entschuldigen, ich kann nicht vom Blatte singen. Das Schiff scheiterte an der Küste von Florida und sank unter in zehn Faden Wasser. Setzen Sie sich gefälligst. Ich danke, ich stehe lieber; ich habe den ganzen Tag gesessen. Wo hast du heute den ganzen Tag zugebracht? Ich brachte ihn auf dem Lande zu mit einigen meiner Freunde. Wie viele Sprachen können Sie sprechen? Ich spreche deutsch, französisch und englisch; früher sprach ich auch dänisch; ich habe diese Sprache aber fast vergessen. Vorige Nacht sprang ein Dieb bei mir zum Fenster hinein und stahl mir meine goldene Uhr und fünfzig Thaler in Banknoten. Stehe nicht zu nahe bei der Maschine, damit du dich nicht beschädigst.

Lesestück 1.

A STORM AT SEA. (Ein Seesturm.)

1. This day I was gratified[1] with what I had often desired to witness[2]—the condition of the sea in a tempest.[3] I had contemplated[4] the ocean in all its other phases,[5] and they are almost innumerable. At one time it is seen reposing[6] in perfect stillness under the

blue sky and bright sun.. At another, slightly ruffled;[7] and then its motion causes[8] his rays[9] to tremble[10] and dance in broken fragments of silvery or golden light,— and the sight[11] is dazzled[12] by following[13] the track[14] from whence his beams[15] are reflected, — while all besides[16] seems to frown[17] in the darkness of its ripple.[18]

2. Again it may be seen somewhat more agitated[19] and of a darker hue,[20] under a clouded sky[21] and a stronger and increasing wind. Then you see an occasional[22] wave, rising a little above the rest, and crowning[23] its summit[24] with that crest of white,[25] breaking from its top[26] and tumbling over[27] like liquid[28] alabaster. I had seen the ocean, too, by moonlight, and as much of it as may be seen in the darkness, when the moon and stars are veiled.[29] But until to-day I had never seen it in correspondence with the *Tempest.*

3. After a breeze[30] of some sixty hours from the north and north-west, the wind died away[31] about four o'clock yesterday afternoon. The calm[32] continued till about nine in the evening. The mercury[33] in the barometer fell, in the meantime, at an extraordinary rate;[34] and the captain predicted[35] that we should encounter[36] a "gale"[37] from the south-east. The "gale" came on, at about eleven o'clock; not violent[38] at first, but increasing every moment. I awoke with a confused recollection of a good deal of rolling and thumping[39] through the night, which was occasioned[40] by the dashing[41] of the waves against the ship.

4. Hurrying on my clothes,[42] I found such of the passengers as could stand, at the doors of the hurricane-house,[43] "holding on," and looking out in the utmost consternation.[44] It was still quite dark. Four of the sails were already in ribbons;[45] the winds whistling through the cordage;[46] the rain dashing furiously[47] and in torrents;[48] the noise and spray[49] scarcely less than I found them under the great sheet[50] at Niagara. And in the midst of all this, the captain, with his speaking trumpet, the officers, and the sailors,

screaming[51] to each other in efforts[52] to be heard—this, all this, in the darkness which precedes[53] the dawning[54] of day, and with the fury of the hurricane, combined[55] to form as much of the *terribly* sublime[56] as I ever wish to witness concentrated in one scene.[57]

5. The passengers, though silent, were filled with apprehension.[58] What the extent[59] of danger, and how all this would terminate,[60] were questions which rose in my own mind,[61] although I was unconscious[62] of fear or trepidation.[63] But to such questions there are no answers; for this knowledge[64] resides[65] only with him who " guides[66] the storm, and directs[67] the whirlwind." We had encountered, however, as yet, only the commencement[68] of a gale, whose terrors[69] had been heightened[70] by its suddenness,[71] by the darkness, and by the confusion. It continued to blow furiously for twenty-four hours; so that during the whole day I enjoyed[72] a view,[73] which, apart from[74] its dangers, would be worth a voyage across the Atlantic.

6. The ship was driven madly[75] through the raging[76] waters, and when it was impossible to walk the decks without imminent[77] risk of being lifted up and carried away by the winds, the poor sailors were kept aloft,[78] tossing[79] and swinging about the yards[80] and in the tops,[81] clinging[82] by their bodies, feet, and arms, with mysterious[83] tenacity,[84] to the spars, while their hands were employed in taking in[85] and securing[86] sail.

[1] erfreut, [2] zu sehen, [3] Sturm, [4] betrachtet, [5] Gestaltungen (Phasen), [6] ruhend, [7] leicht gekräuselt, [8] macht; läßt, [9] Strahlen, [10] zittern, [11] das Auge, [12] wird geblendet, [13] wenn es folgt, [14] Spur, [15] Strahlen, [16] während Alles außerhalb, [17] zu grellen scheint, [18] in dem dunklen Gekräusel, [19] bewegt, [20] Farbe, [21] bei umwölktem Himmel, [22] gelegentlich, [23] säumend, [24] Spitze, [25] mit einem weißen Kamme, [26] Gipfel, [27] überstürzend, [28] flüssig, [29] bedeckt, [30] Brise, [31] legte sich, [32] Windstille, [33] Quecksilber, [34] mit außerordentlicher Schnelle, [35] prophezeite, [36] daß wir bestehen würden, [37] Sturm, [38] heftig, [39] Stampfen, [40] verursacht, [41] Schlagen, [42] mich schnell in die Kleider werfend, [43] Orkanbaus, [44] größter Angstverwirrung, [45] Fetzen, [46] Takelage, [47] goß wie rasend herab, [48] in Strömen, [49] Staubregen, [50] Wasserfall, [51] schreiend, [52] Anstrengung, [53] vorausgeht, [54] Tagesanbruch, [55] kam zusammen, [56] von dem Schrecklich-Erhabenen, [57] Anblick, [58] mit Angst erfüllt, [59] Größe, [60] enden, [61] Geist, [62] frei (unbewußt), [63] Zittern, [64] Wissen, [65] befindet sich, [66] lenkt,

⁶⁷ regiert, ⁶⁸ Anfang, ⁶⁹ Schrecken, ⁷⁰ erhöht worden waren, ⁷¹ Plötzlichkeit, ⁷² genest, ⁷³ Anblick, ⁷⁴ abgesehen von, ⁷⁵ wilde, ⁷⁶ tobend, ⁷⁷ drohend, ⁷⁸ oben in den Masten, ⁷⁹ hin und her geschleudert, ⁸⁰ Raen, ⁸¹ Mastspitze, ⁸² sich festhaltend, ⁸³ räthselhaft, ⁸⁴ Zähigkeit, ⁸⁵ Reffen, ⁸⁶ Festmachen.

Lesestück 2.

A STORM AT SEA. (Schluß.)

1. On deck, the officers and men made themselves safe[1] by ropes;[2] but how the gallant[3] fellows aloft kept from being blown out of the rigging,[4] was equally a matter[5] of wonder[6] and admiration.[7] However, about seven o'clock they had taken in what canvass[8] had not blown away, except the sails by means of which[9] the vessel[10] is kept steady.[11] At nine o'clock the hurricane had acquired[12] its full force. There was no more work to be done. The ship lay to,[13] and those who had her in charge[14] only remained on deck to be prepared for whatever of disaster[15] might occur.[16] The breakfast-hour came and passed, unheeded[17] by most of the passengers.

2. By this time the sea was rolling up its hurricane waves; and that I might not lose the grandeur[18] of such a view, I fortified[19] myself against the rain and spray, and in spite of[20] the fierceness[21] of the gale, planted myself in a position[22] favorable for a survey[23] of all round me, and in safety,[24] so long as the ship's strong ribs might hold together. I had often seen paintings of a storm at sea, but here was the original. These imitations[25] are oftentimes graphic[26] and faithful, as far as they go; but they are necessarily[27] deficient[28] in accompaniments[29] which paintings cannot supply,[30] and are therefore feeble and ineffective.[31]

3. You have, upon canvas,[32] the ship and the sea, but, as they come from the hands of the artist, so they remain. The universal *motion*[33] of both is thus arrested[34] and made stationary.[35] There is no subject in which the pencil of the painter acknowledges[36] more its indebtedness[37] to the imagination[38] than in its attempts[39] to delineate[40] the sea storm.

4. It was not the least remarkable, and by far the most comfortable circumstance [41] in this combination [42] of all that is grand and terrible, that, furious as were the winds, towering [43] and threatening [44] as were the billows, [45] our glorious bark preserved [46] her equilibrium [47] against the fury of the one, and the buoyancy [48] in despite of the alternate precipice and avalanche of the other. [49] True it is, she was made to whistle through her cordage, [50] to creak [51] and moan [52] through all her timbers, [53] even to her masts. True it is, she was made to plunge [54] and rear, [55] to tremble and reel and stagger. [56] Still, she continued to scale [57] the watery mountain, [58] and ride on its very summit, until, as it rolled onward from beneath [59] her, she descended [60] gently on her pathway, [61] ready to triumph again and again over each succeeding wave.

5. At such a moment it was a matter [62] of profound deliberation [62] which most to admire, the majesty of God in the winds and waves, or his goodness and wisdom in enabling [63] his creatures to contend [64] with and overcome [65] the elements even in the fierceness of their anger. [66] To cast one's eye abroad [67] on the scene that surrounded me at this moment, and to think man should have said to himself, "I will build myself an ark [68] in the midst of you, and ye shall not prevent [69] my passage; nay, ye indomitable [70] waves shall bear me up, and ye winds shall waft [71] me onward!" And yet there we were in the fulness [72] of this fearful experiment!

6. I had never believed it possible for a vessel to encounter such a hurricane without being dashed or torn to pieces, at least in all her masts and rigging; for I am persuaded [73] that had the same tempest passed as furiously over your town, during the same length of time, it would have left scarcely a house standing. The yielding [74] character of the element in which the vessel is launched [75] is the great secret of safety on such occasions. Hence, when gales occur upon the wide ocean, there is little danger; but when they drive

you upon breakers,[76] on a lee shore,[77] where the keel comes in contact[78] with "the too solid earth," then it is impossible to escape shipwreck.

7. I never experienced a sensation[79] of fear on the ocean; but this tempest has increased my confidence tenfold, not only in the sea but in the ship. It no longer surprises me that few vessels are lost at sea, for they and their element are made for each other. And the practical conclusion[80] from this experience of a gale is encouraging for all my future navigation. I shall have confidence in my ship now, as I have ever had in the sea. Ever since my eyes first rested on the ocean, I have cherished[81] an instinctive[82] affection for it, as if it were something capable[83] of sympathy and benevolence. When calm, it is to me a slumbering infant. How tranquilly[84] it sleeps!

[1] banden sich fest, [2] Taue, [3] wacker, [4] Takelage, [5] ebenso sehr eine Sache, [6] Verwunderung, [7] Bewunderung, [8] Segel, [9] vermittelst deren, [10] Schiff, [11] fest im Cours gehalten wird, [12] erlangt, [13] legte bei, [14] Aufsicht, [15] Unglück, [16] sich ereignen möchte, [17] unbeachtet, [18] Großartigkeit, [19] waffnete ich mich, [20] troß, [21] Wuth, [22] postirte mich in eine Position, [23] Ueberblick, [24] geschüßt, [25] Nachbildungen, [26] sprechend ähnlich (treffend), [27] nothwendigerweise, [28] mangelhaft, [29] im Zubehör, [30] liefern, [31] ohne Wirkung, [32] Leinwand, [33] die ganze Bewegung, [34] festgebannt, [35] fixirt, [36] anerkennt, [37] Verrflichtung, [38] Phantasie, [39] versuchen, [40] abzubilden, [41] der tröstlichste Umstand, [42] zusammentreffen, [43] sich thürmend, [44] drohend, [45] Wogen, [46] bewahrte, [47] Gleichgewicht, [48] Seetüchtigkeit, [49] troß der Abgründe und dem lawinenartigen Niederstürzen der andern, [50] Taue, [51] krachen, [52] stöhnen, [53] Rippen, [54] kopfüber hinabstürzen, [55] sich bäumen, [56] taumeln, [57] zu erklimmen, [58] Wasserberg, [59] unter, [60] glitt sanft hinab, [61] Pfad, [62] höchst fraglich, [63] darin, daß er in den Stand setzt, [64] kämpfen, [65] besiegen, [66] Wuth, [67] seine Augen schweifen zu lassen über, [68] Arche, [69] hindern, [70] unbezwinglich, [71] tragen, [72] mitten in, [73] überzeugt, [74] nachgebend, [75] dahinsegelt, [76] Brandung, [77] an der Leeseite, [78] Berührung, [79] Gefühl, [80] Schlußfolgerung, [81] gehegt, [82] instinktartig, [83] fähig, [84] ruhig.

Lektion XXVIII.

Unregelmäßige Zeitwörter. Präpositionen. Conjunktionen. Redensarten.

Präsens.	Imperfekt.	Perf. Part.
to stick	stuck	stuck.
to sting	stung	stung.
to strike	struck	struck, stricken.
to strive	strove	striven.
to swear	swore	sworn.
to sweep	swept	swept.
to swim	swam	swum.
to take	took	taken.
to teach	taught	taught.
to tear	tore	torn.
to tell	told	told.
to think	thought	thought.
to throw	threw	thrown.
to tread	trod	trodden.
to wear	wore	worn.
to weep	wept	wept.
to win	won	won
to wind	wound	wound
to work	{ wrought / worked	wrought. / worked.
to wring	wrung	wrung.
to write	wrote	written.

Präpositionen—Above, across, along, amid, around, below, beneath, beside, beyond, but, down, except, out of, over, past, save, since, under, underneath, up.

Conjunktionen—Though, although, before, as soon as, however, whereas.

Redensarten—*In behalf of, both—and, to prefer to, to fall to the share, to award, to reward, as to, to concur with somebody in something, to dispose of, on my part, very* (als Adjektiv), *to attribute, to contribute, to tender, to adjourn.*

Wörter-Verzeichniß.

to strive, sich bemühen, kämpfen.
to wade, waten.
swamp, Sumpf.
to stick fast, stecken bleiben.
to sting, stechen.
to obtain, erlangen.
livelihood, Lebensunterhalt.
to excel, übertreffen.
temptation, Versuchung.
to wring, wringen.
feat, That, Kunststück.
boldness, Kühnheit.
drawer, Schublade.
to tear, zerreißen.
in entering, beim Hereinsteigen.
to come and see, besuchen.
beneath me, unter meiner Würde.
to chop, hacken.
prospect, Aussicht.
ill-humor, üble Laune.
to tread, treten.
toe, Zehe.
to guess, rathen.
coffin, Sarg.
darling, Liebling.
at first sight, auf den ersten Blick.
yarn, Garn.
as a general thing, für gewöhnlich.
wrought iron, Schmiedeeisen.
cast iron, Gußeisen.

Redensarten.
in behalf of, zu Gunsten.
both—and, sowohl—als auch.
to plead, plaidiren.
to prefer, vorziehen.
to concur with, übereinstimmen mit.
it has fallen to my share, es ist mir die Aufgabe zu Theil geworden.
to award, ertheilen, geben.
fitting, passend.
reward, Belohnung.
perseverance, Ausdauer.
as to, in Hinsicht auf.
to dispose of, verfügen über.
library, Bibliothek.
the very height of folly, die Quintessenz von Narrheit.
the very day, am nämlichen Tage.
exceedingly, außerordentlich.
to attribute, zuschreiben.
courtesy, Höflichkeit.
to contribute, beisteuern.
erection, Bau.
on my part, von meiner Seite.
to tender resignation, seine Resignation einreichen.
heartfelt, herzlich.
favors, Gunstbezeugungen.
bestowed, erwiesen.
to adjourn, sich vertagen.

Uebungs-Aufgabe 1.

I was striving to wade through the swamp; but before I was half way through it I stuck fast. Will you stick a pin in my collar? I have stuck one in already. Bees and musquitoes and some other insects sting; I was stung by musquitoes last night. When the clock strikes nine I want you to go to bed. The clock has struck. I am striving hard to obtain a livelihood. All my scholars have striven to excel each other. I often strove against this temptation. I could swear to it that this is the very man who struck the woman, although I have seen him but once. He has sworn to tell the truth. As soon as you have swept the room I want you to wring out the wash; the room has not been swept since last week. Byron swum across the Hellespont, a feat which was accomplished before him by Leander, who finally, however, paid his boldness with his life. How much money did you take out of the drawer? I took no money from the drawer. I have taken medicine. Most people will teach as they have been taught, although they may have been taught quite wrong. Don't tear your dress. You only tore one yesterday. My new coat is torn; I tore it in entering the stage. I told you to come and see me at any time past two o'clock. Please to tell us another story. Do you chop your wood yourself? Yes, sir; I certainly do not think it beneath me to chop my own wood? What do you think of the prospects of peace? He thought he would obtain employment as soon as he came here; but in this he was greatly disappointed. Throw off your ill-humor. Jack has thrown away his new ball; he threw it out of the window across the street. Do not tread upon my toes. This path has been trodden so often that it is quite hard. How much did you pay for your new set of clothes which you wore yesterday? Well, guess. You did not pay more than fifty dollars, did you? You are nearly right; it cost fifty dollars less two. How long have you worn this coat? I have worn it one winter; I never wear a coat longer than a year. What are you weeping for? I am weeping over my misfortune. She stood beside the open coffin and wept over the loss of her darling child. How much have you won? I did neither win nor lose anything. She won my heart at first sight. Please, wind up this yarn for me. When you have wound up the yarn you must write a letter. How many hours do you work a day? As a general thing I work eight hours every day, but to-day I have worked ten hours. Do you know what wrought iron is? Wrought iron is much more expensive than cast iron.

Redensarten.—I wish to say a word in behalf of a very unfortunate man who lost both his sons and property during the late war. The advocate pleaded for more than an hour in behalf of the prisoner. I prefer riding on horseback to riding in a carriage. I fully concur with you in preferring a sea-voyage to traveling by railroad. It has fallen to my share to award this handsome medal to you as a fitting reward for your diligence and perseverance. There can be no doubt as to the duty of children to obey their parents. These opinions were concurred in by the majority of those present. I have disposed of all my property but my library. This seems to me the very height of folly. I started the very day my brother died. It is sometimes exceedingly difficult to attribute a natural phenomenon to its proper causes. This want of courtesy must be attributed to his ignorance. I have come to learn if you will contribute something towards the erection of a new school-house which we intend to build in our district. If I do not contribute more than a hundred dollars, you must not attribute it to any want of interest on my part. I hereby tender my resignation as Secretary of your Board. In tendering you my heartfelt thanks for the many favors bestowed upon me, I have the honor to be yours, &c. (and so forth). I make a motion to adjourn. A motion of adjournment has been made and seconded. All in favor of this motion will signify by saying aye! contrary, no! The motion is carried.

Wörter-Verzeichniß.

Stecknadel, pin.
Kragen, collar.
brauchen, to want.
sieh' dich vor, take care.
empfindlich, sensitive.
au! ow!
sich einbilden, to imagine.
soeben, just now.
Blitz, lightning.
neben, beside.
Boden, ground.
sich bemühen, to take pains; to try hard.
Zorn, temper.
besiegen, to conquer.
Bürger, citizen.
Treue schwören, to swear the oath of allegiance.
Regierung, government.
Vaterland, country.

bis auf, but.
Dichter, poet.
noch einer, another.
sich in Acht nehmen vor, to be on one's guard against; to beware of.
trauen, to trust.
Umstände, condition.
lehren, to teach.
unterrichten, to instruct.
Zeug, clothes.
bestrafen, to punish.
am weitesten, farthest.
Hühneraugen, corns.
sterben, to die.
Schande, disgrace.
Wette, bet.
Wäsche, wash.
auswringen, to wring.
Wäschewringer, clothes-wringer.

Uebungs-Aufgabe 2.

Willst du mir eine Nadel in meinen Kragen stecken? Ich habe schon eine hineingesteckt, aber ich brauche noch eine mehr. Sieh' dich aber vor und stich mich nur nicht; ich bin sehr em= pfindlich. Au! du hast mich schon gestochen! Ich habe dich nicht gestochen; du bildest dir das blos ein. Was schlug die Uhr soeben? Die Uhr hat soeben neun geschlagen. Der Blitz schlug neben unserm Hause in den Boden. Du mußt dich bemühen deinen Zorn zu besiegen. Ich habe mir oft Mühe gegeben, aber immer umsonst. Wenn du hier Bürger werden willst, dann mußt du der Regierung deines neuen Va= terlandes Treue schwören. Hat das Dienstmädchen die Zim=

mer schon gekehrt? Sie hat alle gekehrt bis auf das Empfangszimmer. Der englische Dichter Byron schwamm über den Hellespont hinüber. Nehmen Sie noch eine Cigarre aus der Kiste. Ich danke, ich habe schon eine genommen. Nehmen Sie sich in Acht vor diesem Menschen; trauen Sie ihm unter keinen Umständen. Wer hat dich schwimmen gelehrt? Niemand hat mich darin unterrichtet; ich habe das von mir selber gelernt. Du hast schon wieder deinen Rock zerrissen; ich sagte dir doch heute Morgen, du solltest dich in Acht nehmen, dein Zeug nicht zu zerreißen; ich denke ich muß dich jetzt bestrafen. Was haben Sie gedacht, als Sie hörten, ich hätte meine Farm verkauft? Ich dachte, Sie hätten sehr klug daran gethan. Lasset uns sehen, wer von uns am weitesten werfen kann. Ich habe am weitesten geworfen. Als ich heute Morgen in dem Omnibus war, trat mir Jemand auf meine Hühneraugen. Ich habe diesen Ueberrock jetzt lange genug getragen; ich werde ihn nicht länger tragen. Nie habe ich mehr geweint, als da meine Mutter starb. Es ist keine Schande für einen Mann, zu weinen. Wer von euch beiden hat die Wette gewonnen? Heinrich hat sie gewonnen; er gewinnt immer. Wie lange hast du heute gearbeitet? Ich habe sechs Stunden gearbeitet; für gewöhnlich arbeite ich acht Stunden. Hast du die Wäsche ausgewrungen? Ich habe sie auf dem Wäschewringer ausgewrungen. Sobald als ich wieder gesund bin, werde ich dir einen langen Brief schreiben.

Lesestück 1.

THE UNITED STATES OF AMERICA.

(Die Vereinigten Staaten von Amerika.)

The **United States of America** constitute[1] an essential[2] portion[3] of a great political system, embracing[4] all the civilized nations of the earth. At a period when the force of moral opinion is rapidly increasing,[5] they have the precedence[6] in the practice and in the defence[7] of the equal rights of man. The sovereignty of the people[8] is here a conceded[9] axiom,[10] and the laws, established upon that basis, are cherished[11] with faithful patriotism. While the nations of Europe aspire [12] after change, our Constitution engages [13] the fond [14] admiration of the people, by which it has been established. Prosperity [15] follows the execution of even [16] justice; invention is quickened by the freedom of competition; [17] and labor rewarded with sure and unexampled returns. Domestic [18] peace is maintained [19] without the aid of a military establishment; public sentiment [20] permits the existence of but few standing troops, and those only along the seaboard and on the frontiers. [21] A gallant [22] navy [23] protects our commerce, which spreads its banners on every sea, and extends [24] its enterprise to every clime. Our diplomatic relations [25] connect us on terms of equality and honest friendship with the chief [26] powers of the world; while we avoid entangling [27] participation in [28] their intrigues, their passions, [29] and their wars. Our national resources [30] are developed [31] by an earnest culture of the arts of peace. Every man may enjoy the fruits of his industry; every mind is free to publish [32] its convictions. [33] Our government, by its organization, is necessarily identified with the interests of the people, and relies [34] exclusively on their attachment [35] for its durability and support. Even the enemies of the state, if there are any among us, have liberty to express their opinions undisturbed; and are safely tolerated, [36] where reason [37] is left free to combat [38] their errors. [39] Nor is the Constitution a dead letter, unalterably [40] fixed; it has the capacity for improvement; adopting whatever changes time and the public will may require, and safe from [41] decay, [42] as long as that will retains [43] its energy. [44] New States are forming in the wilderness; canals, intersecting [45] our plains and crossing our highlands, open numerous channels to internal [46] commerce; manufactures prosper [47] along our watercourses; [48] the use of steam on our rivers and railroads annihilates [49] distance by the acceleration [50] of speed. Our wealth and population, already giving us a place in the first rank of nations, are so rapidly cumulative, [51] that the former is increased fourfold, and the latter is doubled in every period of twenty-two or twenty-three years. There is no national debt; the community is opulent;[52] the government economical, and the public treasury[53] full. Religion, neither persecuted[54] nor paid by the State, is sustained[55] by the regard[56] for public morals and the convictions of an enlightened faith.[57] Intelligence is diffused[58] with unparalleled[59] universality;[60] a free press teems[61] with the choicest[62] productions of all nations and ages. There are more daily journals in the United States than in the world beside. A public document of general interest is, within a month, reproduced[63] in at least a million of copies, and is brought within the reach of every freeman in the country. An immense concourse[64] of emigrants of the most various lineage,[65] is perpetually[66] crowding[67] to our shores; and the principles of liberty, uniting all interests by the operation of equal laws, blend[68] the discordant[69] elements into harmonious union. Other governments are convulsed by the innovations[70] and reforms of neighboring states; our Constitution, fixed in the affections of the people, from whose choice[71] it has sprung, neutralizes the influence of foreign principles, and fearlessly opens an asylum to the virtuous,[72] the unfortunate, and the oppressed[73] of every nation.

And yet it is but little more than two centuries,[74] since the oldest of our States received its first permanent[75] colony. Before that time the whole territory was an unproductive[76] waste. Throughout its wide extent[77] the arts had not erected a monument. Its only inhabitants were a few scattered[78] tribes[79] of feeble barbarians, destitute[80] of commerce and of political connection. The axe and the ploughshare were unknown. The soil,[81] which had been gathering fertility[82] from the repose[83] of centuries, was lavishing[84] its strength in magnificent but useless vegetation. In the view of civilization, the immense domain was but a solitude.[85] . . . .

BANCROFT.

¹ bilden, ² wesentlich, ³ Bestandtheil, ⁴ umfassend, ⁵ rasch in der Zunahme begriffen ist, ⁶ Vorsprung, ⁷ Wahrung, ⁸ Volkssouveränität, ⁹ anerkannt, ¹⁰ Grundsatz, ¹¹ gepflegt, ¹² trachten, ¹³ besitzt, ¹⁴ innig, ¹⁵ Wohlstand, ¹⁶ unpartheiisch, ¹⁷ Mitbewerbung, ¹⁸ nach innen, ¹⁹ aufrechterhalten, ²⁰ Meinung, ²¹ Gränze, ²² tapfer, ²³ Flotte, ²⁴ ausbreitete, ²⁵ Beziehungen, ²⁶ Haupt, ²⁷ vermeiden, ²⁸ uns zu verwickeln in, ²⁹ Leidenschaften, ³⁰ Hülfsquellen, ³¹ erweitern sich, ³² laut werden zu lassen, ³³ Ueberzeugungen, ³⁴ verläßt sich, ³⁵ Zuneigung, ³⁶ geduldet, ³⁷ Vernunft, ³⁸ bekämpfen, ³⁹ Irrthümer, ⁴⁰ unabänderlich, ⁴¹ sicher vor, ⁴² Verfall, ⁴³ behält, ⁴⁴ Lebenskraft, ⁴⁵ durchschneidend, ⁴⁶ einheimisch, ⁴⁷ blühen, ⁴⁸ Wasserstraßen, ⁴⁹ hebt auf, ⁵⁰ Vergrößerung, ⁵¹ sind so rasch im Zunehmen, ⁵² reich, ⁵³ Schatz, ⁵⁴ verfolgt, ⁵⁵ gestützt, ⁵⁶ Rücksicht, ⁵⁷ eines erleuchteten Glaubens, ⁵⁸ verbreitet, ⁵⁹ unvergleichlich, ⁶⁰ Allgemeinheit, ⁶¹ strömt über, ⁶² auserlesen, ⁶³ vervielfältigt, ⁶⁴ Zufluß, ⁶⁵ Herkunft, ⁶⁶ beständig, ⁶⁷ ergießt sich, ⁶⁸ verbinden, ⁶⁹ widerstreitend, ⁷⁰ Neuerungen, ⁷¹ Wahl, ⁷² tugendhaft, ⁷³ unterdrückt, ⁷⁴ Jahrhunderte, ⁷⁵ dauernd, ⁷⁶ unfruchtbar, ⁷⁷ Gebiet, ⁷⁸ zerstreut, ⁷⁹ Stämme, ⁸⁰ ohne, ⁸¹ Boden, ⁸² Fruchtbarkeit, ⁸³ Ruhe, ⁸⁴ verschwendete, ⁸⁵ Wüste.

Lesestück 2.

NEW YORK IN THE DUTCH TIMES.

(Neu-York zur Zeit der Holländer.)

1. In those happy days, a well-regulated family always rose with the dawn, dined at eleven, and went to bed at sun-down. Dinner was invariably[1] a private meal,[2] and the fat old burghers showed incontestable[3] symptoms of disapprobation[4] and uneasiness[5] at being surprised by a visit from a neighbor on such occasions.[6] But though our worthy ancestors[7] were thus singularly[8] averse[9] to giving dinners, yet they kept up the social bands[10] of intimacy by occasional[11] banquetings, called tea-parties.

2. These fashionable parties were generally confined[12] to the higher classes or noblesse; that is to say, such as kept their own cows, and drove their own wagons. The company commonly assembled[13] at three o'clock, and went away about six, unless it was in winter time, when the fashionable hours were a little earlier, that the ladies might get home before dark. The tea-table was crowned[14] with a huge[15] earthen[16] dish, well stored[17] with slices of fat pork, fried brown, cut up into morsels,[18] and swimming in gravy.[19]

3. The company being seated around the genial[20] board, and each furnished with a fork, evinced[21] their dexterity[22] in launching[23] at the fattest pieces in this mighty dish—in much the same manner as sailors harpoon porpoises[24] at sea, or our Indians spear[25] salmon[26] in the lakes. Sometimes the table was graced[27] with immense apple-pies,[28] or saucers full of preserved[29] peaches and pears; but it was always sure to boast[30] an enormous dish of balls,[31] of sweetened dough,[32] fried in hog's fat, and doughnuts, olykoeks—a delicious kind of cake, at present scarce known in this city, excepting in genuine[33] Dutch families.

4. The tea was served out[34] of a majestic delf teapot, ornamented[35] with paintings of fat little Dutch shepherds and shepherdesses tending[36] pigs—with boats sailing in the air, and houses built in the clouds, and sundry[37] other ingenious[38] Dutch fantasies.[39] The beaux[40] distinguished themselves by their adroitness[41] in replenishing[42] this pot from a huge copper teakettle, which would have made the pigmy[43] macaronies[44] of these degenerate[45] days sweat merely to look at it. To sweeten the beverage,[46] a lump of sugar was laid beside each cup—and the company alternately[47] nibbled and sipped[48] with great decorum,[49] until an improvement was made by a shrewd[50] economic old lady, which was to suspend a large lump directly over the tea-table by a string from the ceiling,[51] so that it could be swung from mouth to mouth—an ingenious expedient[52] which is still kept up by some families in Albany; but which prevails without exception in Communipaw, Bergen, Flatbush, and all our uncontaminated[53] Dutch villages.

5. At these primitive[54] tea-parties the utmost propriety[55] and dignity[56] of deportment[57] prevailed. No flirting[58] or coquetting—no gambling of old ladies, nor hoyden chattering and romping[59] of young ones—no self-satisfied[60] struttings[61] of wealthy gentlemen, with their brains in their pockets—nor amusing conceits[62] and monkey divertissements[63] of smart young gentle-

men with no brains at all. On the contrary, the young ladies seated themselves demurely[61] in their rush-bottomed chairs, and knit their own woolen stockings; nor ever opened their lips, excepting to say *Ja, Mynheer*, or *Ja, Jufvrouw*, to any question that was asked them; behaving in all things like decent, well-educated damsels.[65]

6. As to the gentlemen, each of them tranquilly[66] smoked his pipe, and seemed lost in contemplation[67] of the blue and white tiles[68] with which the fire-places were decorated; wherein sundry passages of Scripture were piously portrayed—Tobit and his dog figured to great advantage; Haman swung conspicuously[69] on his gibbet,[70] and Jonah appeared most manfully bouncing out[71] of the whale,[72] like Harlequin through a barrel of fire.

7. The parties broke up without noise and without confusion. They were carried home by their own carriages, that is to say, by the vehicles[73] Nature had provided them, excepting such of the wealthy as could afford to keep a wagon. The gentlemen gallantly attended their fair ones to their respective abodes,[74] and took leave of them with a hearty smack[75] at the door; which as it was an established[76] piece of etiquette, done in perfect simplicity and honesty of heart, occasioned[77] no scandal at that time, nor should it at the present: if our great-grandfathers approved of[78] the custom, it would argue[79] a great want of reverence in their descendants[80] to say a word against it.

WASHINGTON IRVING.

[1] ohne Ausnahme, [2] Mahlzeit, [3] unleugbar, [4] Mißbilligung, [5] Unruhe, [6] Gelegenheiten, [7] Vorfahren, [8] sonderbar, [9] abgeneigt, [10] die geselligen Bande, [11] gelegentlich, [12] beschränkten sich, [13] versammelte sich, [14] geziert, [15] ungeheuer, [16] irden, [17] beladen, [18] Stückchen, [19] Sauce, [20] traulich, [21] bewies, [22] Geschicklichkeit, [23] im Gabeln nach, [24] Schweinefische, [25] aufspießen, [26] Lachs, [27] geziert, [28] Apfelkuchen, [29] eingemacht, [30] rühmen, [31] Klöße, [32] Teig, [33] echt, [34] servirt, [35] verziert, [36] hütend, [37] verschiedene, [38] sinnreiche, [39] Phantasiegebilde, [40] Conrmacher (Liebhaber), [41] Gewandtheit, [42] mit der sie wieder füllten, [43] winzig, [44] Gecken, [45] entartet, [46] Getränk, [47] abwechselnd, [48] schlürfte, [49] Ehrbarkeit, [50] schlau, [51] Zimmerdecke, [52] Auskunftsmittel, [53] unverdorben, [54] altertümlich, [55] Schicklichkeit, [56] Würde, [57] Anstand, [58] Flaniren, [59] Lärmen, [60] selbstgefällig,

⁶¹ Großthuerei, ⁶² Wichtigthuerei, ⁶³ Unterhaltungen, ⁶⁴ gravitätisch, ⁶⁵ Jungfern, ⁶⁶ gemüthlich, ⁶⁷ Betrachtung, ⁶⁸ Fliesen, ⁶⁹ deutlich, ⁷⁰ Galgen, ⁷¹ herausbringend, ⁷² Wallfisch, ⁷³ Fuhrwerk, ⁷⁴ Wohnungen, ⁷⁵ Schmaß, ⁷⁶ althergebracht, ⁷⁷ richtete an, ⁷⁸ guthießen, ⁷⁹ zeugen von, ⁸⁰ Nachkommen.

Lektion XXIX.

Reflexive Zeitwörter. Vergleichende Wörter und Sätze. Redensarten.

Wörter-Verzeichniß.

to trouble one's self about, sich graue Haare wachsen lassen um; sich Sorge machen.
to enjoy one's self, sich ergötzen an.
doll, Puppe.
to be in the habit of, pflegen zu.
to avail one's self, benutzen.
opportunity, Gelegenheit.
to offer, sich darbieten.
captivity, Gefangenschaft.
apt, geneigt.
to behave, sich benehmen.
trustworthy, zuverlässig.
to dress, ankleiden.
he knew her to be, er wüßte, sie sei.
quarrelsome, streitsüchtig.
to apply one's self, Fleiß anwenden.
to succeed, gelingen.
forced, gezwungen.
to discontinue, abbrechen; aufgeben.
for want of, aus Mangel an.
to shave, sich rasiren.
as often as, nicht weniger als.
not near so, lange nicht so.
preceding, vorhergehend.
by far, bei weitem.
as far as is concerned, so weit es betrifft.
by no means, durchaus nicht.

Redensarten.

nothing but, nichts als.
none but, Niemand als.
to keep silent, stillschweigen.
to enter (a room), hineintreten in.
to enter (a conversation), eine Unterhaltung anknüpfen.
to be greatly indebted to somebody, Jemandem zu großem Dank verpflichtet sein.
to be desirous of, wünschen zu.
to prove, beweisen.
to suffer from, leiden an.
indeed? so? wirklich?
to invest, anlegen (als Gelt).
I believe so, ich glaube es.
foolish, thöricht.

to succeed, Erfolg haben.
bashful, blöde.
to deem, halten für.
unless, es sei denn.
to improve, bessern (Gebrauch) machen von.
heretofore, bisher.
to pass away, verfließen.
Ned, Eduard.
to manage something, etwas zu Wege bringen.
to lay claim to, } Anspruch ma=
to claim, } chen auf.
to cash, baar auszahlen.

Uebungs=Aufgabe 1.

Do not trouble yourself about the money that I lent you. I always trouble myself about many things. Did you amuse yourself at the opera last night? She greatly enjoyed herself with her new doll. Americans are in the habit of saying: Help yourself; and indeed, if we don't help ourselves, nobody will help us. He availed himself of the first opportunity that offered, to escape from his captivity. We are apt to consider ourselves better and wiser than our forefathers. How did the soldiers behave in their first fight? They did not behave themselves as nobly as their commander expected. I myself lost as much by this operation as you. Did you see it yourself? I did not see it myself, but I have it from a person who is as trustworthy as he is intelligent. Will you dress this little girl? No, madam; let her dress herself. These two boys are very fond of each other's company. Gentlemen, you may judge yourselves what such a service is worth. He assured me himself that he knew her to be as quarrelsome a woman as her sister is. As soon as I arrived in America I availed myself of the first opportunity to learn English. The more you apply yourself, the sooner you will succeed in mastering this language. He found himself forced to discontinue his studies for want of time. Do you shave yourself? I always shave myself. I shave myself as often as three times a week. This is as fine and as strong a horse as you would wish to have yourself. Don't you think yourself that this is too easy a task? It is not near so difficult as the preceding. It is by far more important for us in this country to know English than German. As far as pronunciation is concerned, English is by no means so easy as German.

Redensarten: I have nothing but trouble with you. I shall be very happy to see you at my house to-night; we shall have some good music, and none but good friends have been invited. It is sometimes more difficult to keep silent than to speak. He entered the room without knocking. Will you enter into a conversation with me? We are greatly indebted to you for the advice you gave us, and we are greatly desirous of proving our gratitude by presenting to you this gold watch-chain. Did you ever suffer from toothache? I never suffered from toothache. Indeed? That is more than I can say. Did he invest all his money in this enterprise? I believe so. I think it very foolish to invest all your money in one enterprise. I think so too. If you want to succeed in America, you must not be bashful. He always succeeds in everything he undertakes. I deem it my duty to warn you that, unless you improve your opportunities better than you have done heretofore, you will never succeed. Winter has passed away without bringing us any news from our friend Ned. Do you think he will manage to come and see us to-night? I hope so, indeed. I do not lay claim to a thorough knowledge of the English language, but I claim to know more about it than you do. I presented to him a note for one thousand five hundred dollars, and he cashed it at once. Indeed! I should not have thought it possible.

Wörter-Verzeichniß.

geredt, spread.
sich setzen, to take a seat.
blöde, bashful.
sich bedienen, to help one's self.

das Nöthigen, coaxing.
aufwarten mit, to help to.
Rindsbraten, roast-beef.
Blumenkohl, cauliflower.

satt sein, to have enough.
sich schämen, to be ashamed of one's self.
sich aufführen, to behave one's self.
sich amüsiren, to amuse one's self.
Gebrauch machen von, to avail one's self of.
Güte, kindness.
sich betrachten als, to consider one's self.
Betragen, conduct.
verscherzen, to forfeit.
sich anziehen, to dress one's self.
bis Ende, by the end.
anwenden, to apply one's self.
Aufmerksamkeit, attention.
zuwenden, to direct.
bekritteln, to find fault with.
sich machen zum Narren, to make a fool of one's self.

Uebungs-Aufgabe 2.

Der Tisch ist gedeckt. Bitte, setzen Sie sich. Seien Sie nicht blöde; bedienen Sie sich, das Nöthigen ist bei uns keine Mode. Darf ich Ihnen mit einem Stückchen Rindsbraten aufwarten? nehmen Sie sich etwas Blumenkohl. Sind Sie schon satt? Sie müssen noch ein Stückchen von diesem Kuchen essen; meine Frau hat ihn selbst gemacht. Ist er nicht so gut, als hätte ihn der beste Bäcker gebacken? Er ist viel besser. Schäme dich, Karl, deine Schwester zu schlagen; wenn du dich nicht besser aufführst, muß ich dich bestrafen. Haben Sie sich gestern gut amüsirt auf dem Picnic? Ich habe mich nicht so gut amüsirt, als ich erwartete. Ich werde von Ihrer Güte nicht eher Gebrauch machen, als bis es nothwendig sein wird. Ich werde mich immer als Ihren Freund betrachten, so lange Sie nicht selbst durch Ihr Betragen meine Freundschaft verscherzen. Willst du dich jetzt so schnell als möglich anziehen? Ich werde mich so schnell ich nur kann anziehen. Wenn Sie diese Arbeit bis Ende der Woche fertig haben wollen, so müssen Sie großen Fleiß anwenden. Haben Sie diese Arbeit selbst gemacht, oder hat Ihnen Jemand dabei geholfen? Ich habe sie selbst gemacht. Sobald ich nicht mehr so viel zu thun haben werde wie jetzt, werde ich wieder meine Aufmerksamkeit dem Englischen zuwenden. Es ist leichter eine Arbeit zu bekritteln, als sie selbst besser zu machen. Mache dich doch nicht zum Narren. Du bist selbst ein Narr.

Reflexive Zeitwörter.

Lesestück 1.

A GOOD INVESTMENT. (Eine gute Kapitalanlage.)

1. "Can you lend me two thousand dollars to establish¹ myself in a small retail business?"² inquired a young man, not yet out of his teens,³ of a middle-aged⁴ gentleman, who was poring over⁵ his ledger⁶ in the counting-room⁷ of one of the largest establishments in Boston. The person addressed⁸ turned towards the speaker, and regarding⁹ him for a moment with a look of surprise,¹⁰ inquired,¹¹ "What security¹² can you give me, Mr. Strosser?"

2. "Nothing but my note,"¹³ replied the young man, promptly.¹⁴

3. "Which, I fear, would be below par¹⁵ in the market," replied the merchant, smiling.

4. "Perhaps, sir," said the young man; "but, Mr. Barton, remember that the boy is not the man; the time may come when Hiram Strosser's note will be as readily¹⁶ accepted¹⁷ as that of any other man."

4. "True, very true," replied Mr. Barton, mildly; "but you know business-men seldom lend money without adequate¹⁸ security; otherwise¹⁹ they might soon be reduced to penury."²⁰

6. At this remark the young man's countenance²¹ became very pale,²² and, having kept silent²³ for several moments, he inquired, in a voice whose tones indicated²⁴ his deep disappointment,²⁵ "Then you cannot accommodate²⁶ me—can you?"

7. "Call upon me to-morrow, and I will give you a reply," said Mr. Barton; and the young man retired.²⁷

8. Mr. Barton resumed²⁸ his labors at the desk,²⁹ but his mind³⁰ was so much upon³¹ the boy and his singular³² errand,³³ that he could not pursue³⁴ his task³⁵ with any correctness; and, after having made several sad³⁶ blunders,³⁷ he closed the ledger, and took his hat, and went out upon the street. Arriving opposite³⁸

the store of a wealthy merchant upon Milk Street, he entered the door.

9. "Good morning, Mr. Hawley," said he, approaching⁵⁵ the proprietor⁴⁰ of the establishment, who was seated at his desk, counting over the profits of the week.

10. "Good morning," replied the merchant, blandly.⁴¹ "Happy to see you. Have a seat? Any news? How's trade?" ⁴²

11. Without noticing⁴³ these interrogations,⁴⁴ Mr. Barton said, "Young Strosser is desirous⁴⁵ of establishing himself in a small retail business in Washington Street, and called this morning to secure⁴⁶ of me a loan⁴⁷ of two thousand dollars for that purpose."

12. "Indeed!" exclaimed Mr. Hawley, evidently⁴⁸ surprised at this announcement; "but you do not think of lending that sum—do you?"

13. "I do not know," replied Mr. Barton. "Mr. Strosser is a young man of business talent and strict integrity,⁴⁹ and will be likely to succeed⁵⁰ in whatever⁵¹ he undertakes."

14. "Perhaps so," replied Mr. Hawley, doubtfully; "but I am heartily tired of helping to establish these young aspirants for commercial honors."

15. "Have you ever suffered⁵² from such a course?"⁵³ inquired Mr. Barton, at the same time casting⁵⁴ a roguish glance⁵⁵ at Mr. Hawley.

16. "No," replied the latter, "for I never felt inclined⁵⁶ to make an investment of that kind."

17. "Then here is a fine opportunity to do so. It may prove better than stock⁵⁷ in the bank. As for myself, I have concluded that, if you will advance⁵⁸ him one thousand dollars, I will contribute an equal sum."

18. "Not a single farthing⁵⁹ would I advance for such a purpose; and if you make an investment of that kind, I shall consider you very foolish."

19. Mr. Barton was silent for several minutes, and then arose to depart.⁶⁰ "If you do not feel disposed⁶¹

to share[62] with **me in** this enterprise, I shall advance the whole sum myself." Saying which, he left the store.

[1] einzurichten (etabliren), [2] Detailgeschäft, [3] aus seinen Zehner Jahren (d. h. aus den Jahren von dreizehn bis neunzehn), [4] in mittleren Jahren, [5] der fleißig saß über, [6] Hauptbuch, [7] Comptoir, [8] angeredet, [9] betrachtend, [10] mit erstaunten Blicken, [11] fragte, [12] Sicherheit; Caution, [13] Schuldschein; Wechsel, [14] rasch, [15] unter pari, [16] bereitwillig, [17] acceptirt, [18] entsprechend, genügend, [19] sonst, [20] möchten sie bald an den Bettelstab gerathen, [21] Gesicht, [22] blaß, [23] als er geschwiegen, [24] verriethen, [25] bittere Täuschung, [26] helfen, [27] entfernte sich, [28] nahm wieder auf, [29] Pult, [30] seine Gedanken, [31] so sehr beschäftigt mit, [32] eigenthümlich, [33] Anliegen, [34] verfolgen, [35] Aufgabe, [36] arg, [37] Schnitzer, [38] gegenüber, [39] sich nahernd, [40] Eigenthümer, [41] freundlich, [42] wie geben die Geschäfte, [43] zu achten auf, [44] Fragen, [45] wünscht, [46] sich zu sichern, [47] Anleihe, [48] offenbar, [49] Unbescholtenheit, [50] wird wahrscheinlich Erfolg haben, [51] in Allem was, [52] haben Sie je Nachtheil gehabt, [53] Verfahren, [54] werfend, [55] einen schlauen Seitenblick, [56] bewogen, [57] Grundkapital, [58] vorstrecken, [59] Heller, [60] gehen, [61] geneigt, [62] theilnehmen an.

Lesestück 2.

A GOOD INVESTMENT. (Schluß.)

1. Ten years have passed **away**[1] since the occurrence[2] of the conversation **recorded**[3] in the preceding[4] dialogue, and Mr. Barton, **pale and** agitated,[5] is standing at the same desk at which he stood when first introduced[6] to **the reader's attention.** As page[7] after **page of his** ponderous[8] ledger was examined, his despair[9] became deeper and keeper, till at last he exclaimed, "I am ruined—utterly[10] ruined!"

2. "How so?" inquired Hiram Strosser, who entered the **counting-room in season**[11] to hear Mr. Barton's remark.

3. "The last European steamer brought news of the failure[12] of the house of Perlet, Jackson & Co., London, who are indebted[13] to me in the sum of nearly two hundred thousand dollars. News of the failure has become general,[14] and my creditors, panic-stricken,[15] are pressing[16] for payment of their demands.[17] The banks refuse me credit, and I have not the means to meet my liabilities.[18] If I could pass[19] this crisis, per-

haps I could rally [20] again; but it is impossible: my creditors are importunate,[21] and I cannot much longer keep above the tide,"[22] replied Mr. Barton.

4. "What is the extent[23] of your liabilities?" inquired Strosser.

"Seventy-five thousand dollars," replied Mr. Barton.

"Would that sum be sufficient to relieve[24] you?"

"It would."

5. "Then, sir, you shall have it," said Strosser, as he stepped up to the desk, and drew a check[25] for twenty thousand dollars. "Take this, and when you need more, do not hesitate[26] to call upon me. Remember that it was from you I received money to establish myself in business."

6. "But that debt was canceled[27] several years ago," replied Mr. Barton, as a ray[28] of hope shot[29] across his troubled mind.[30]

7. "True," replied Strosser, "but the debt of *gratitude*[31] that I owe[32] has never been canceled; and now that the scale is turned,[33] I deem[34] it my duty to come up to the rescue."[35]

8. At this singular turn[36] in the tide of fortune, Mr. Barton fairly[37] wept for joy.

Every claim[38] against him was paid as soon as presented, and in less than a month he had passed the crisis, and stood perfectly safe and secure; his credit improved,[39] and his business increased,[40] while several others sank under the blow,[41] and could not rally, among whom was Mr. Hawley, alluded to[42] at the commencement of this article.

9. "How did you manage[43] to keep above the tide?" inquired Mr. Hawley of Mr. Barton, one morning, several months after the events[44] last recorded, as he met the latter upon the street, on his way to his place of business.

10. "Very easily, indeed! I can assure you," replied Mr. Barton.

"Well, do tell me how," continued Mr. Hawley; "I

lay claim to[15] a good degree[16] of shrewdness,[17] but the strongest exercise[18] of my wits[19] did not save me; and yet you, whose liabilities were twice as heavy as my own, have stood the shock,[50] and have come off[51] even bettered[52] by the storm."

11. "The truth is," replied Mr. Barton, "I cashed[53] my paper as soon as it was sent in."

"I suppose so," said Mr. Hawley, regarding[54] Mr. Barton with a look of surprise; "but how did you obtain the funds?[55] As for me, I could not obtain a dollar's credit: the banks refused to take my paper, and even my friends deserted me."

12. "A little investment that I made some ten years ago," replied Mr. Barton, smiling,[56] "has recently[57] proved exceedingly[58] profitable."

"Investment!" echoed[59] Mr. Hawley, "what investment?"

13. "Why, do you not remember how I established young Strosser in business some ten years ago?"

"O, yes, yes," replied Mr. Hawley, as a ray of suspicion[60] lighted up[61] his countenance; "but what of that?"[62]

14. "He is now one of the largest dry goods dealers[63] in the city; and when this calamity[64] came on, he came forward, and very generously advanced me seventy-five thousand dollars. You know I told you, on the morning I called to offer you an equal share to the stock, that it might prove better than an investment in the bank."

15. During this announcement,[65] Mr. Hawley's eyes were bent[66] upon the ground, and, drawing a deep sigh,[67] he moved on, dejected[68] and sad, while Mr. Barton returned to his place of business, with his mind cheered[69] and animated[70] by thoughts of his singular investment.

FREEMAN HUNT.

---

[1] find vergangen, [2] stattfinden, [3] berichtet, [4] vorhergehend, [5] erregt, [6] vorgestellt, [7] Seite, [8] gewichtig, [9] Verzweiflung, [10] ganz und gar, [11] zeitig genug,

¹² Bankerott, ¹³ die mir schulden, ¹⁴ allgemein bekannt, ¹⁵ vom Schrecken gelähmt, ¹⁶ drängen auf, ¹⁷ Forderungen, ¹⁸ meinen Verbindlichkeiten zu genügen, ¹⁹ überstehen, ²⁰ erholen (aufrappeln), ²¹ drängen, ²² mich oben halten, ²³ Umfang, ²⁴ helfen, ²⁵ einen Wechsel zog, ²⁶ zögen Sie nicht, ²⁷ gestrichen, ²⁸ Strahl, ²⁹ fuhr, ³⁰ durch seine bekümmerte Seele, ³¹ Dankbarkeit, ³² die ich schuldig bin, ³³ wo sich das Blatt gewendet hat, ³⁴ halte ich es für, ³⁵ zur Hülfe zu kommen, ³⁶ bei dieser eignen Wendung, ³⁷ wirklich, ³⁸ Schuldforderung, ³⁹ besserte sich, ⁴⁰ erweiterte sich, ⁴¹ Schlag, ⁴² erwähnt, ⁴³ brachten Sie es fertig, ⁴⁴ Vorfalle, ⁴⁵ ich mache Anspruch auf, ⁴⁶ Grab, ⁴⁷ Pfiffigkeit, ⁴⁸ Aufbieten, ⁴⁹ meines Witzes, ⁵⁰ haben den Stoß ausgehalten, ⁵¹ davongekommen, ⁵² besser gestellt, ⁵³ zahlte baar aus, ⁵⁴ betrachtend, ⁵⁵ Geldmittel, ⁵⁶ lächelnd, ⁵⁷ kürzlich, ⁵⁸ außerordentlich, ⁵⁹ wiederholte, ⁶⁰ Argwohn, ⁶¹ über sein Gesicht fuhr, ⁶² was hat das hiermit zu thun? ⁶³ Manufakturwaarenhändler, ⁶⁴ Unglück, ⁶⁵ Mittheilung, ⁶⁶ gesenkt, ⁶⁷ einen tiefen Seufzer holend, ⁶⁸ niedergeschlagen, ⁶⁹ erheitert, ⁷⁰ voll von.

Lektion XXX.

Das Passivum (Passive Voice). Redensarten.

Wörter-Verzeichniß.

enemy, Feind.
orchard, Obstgarten.
struck, getroffen.
lightning, Blitz.
thunder-storm, Gewitter.
Franco-German, französisch-deutsch.
goods, Waaren.
at cost, zum Kostenpreis.
passenger-train, Passagierzug.
met with, stieß zu.
serious, ernstlich.
unusual, ungewöhnlich.
attendance, Besuch.
dignitary, Würdenträger.
stay, Aufenthalt.
crop, Ernte.

treaty, Vertrag.
to demand, fordern.
illegal, ungesetzlich.
to excite, erregen.
report, Gerücht.
to stipulate, feststellen.
to evacuate, räumen.
to restore, wiederherstellen.
to assault, angreifen.
ruffian, } Raufbold.
rough,
to float, schwimmen, treiben.
what is to be done, was ist zu thun.
negotiation, Unterhandlung.
pending, in der Schwebe.
amicable, freundschaftlich.

Das Passivum.

overbearing, hochfahrend.
to tolerate, ertragen.
to embark in, sich einlassen auf.
evil doings, Uebelthaten.
to connive at, durch die Finger sehen; ein Auge zudrücken.
  Redensarten.
originally, ursprünglich.
propitious, günstig.
to control, beherrschen.
you are to, du mußt, sollst.
decision, Entscheidung.
delivery, Ablieferung.
by no means, auf keinen Fall.
on the contrary, im Gegentheil.
by all means, auf alle Fälle.

to avoid, vermeiden.
to feed on, leben von.
carnivorous, fleischfressend.
herbs, Kräuter.
to fall in love with, sich verlieben in.
at first sight, auf den ersten Blick.
to be pleased with, sich freuen über.
zeal, Eifer.
perseverance, Ausdauer.
to mind one's own business, sich um seine eigenen Angelegenheiten kümmern.
to meddle with, sich mischen in.
to look like, aussehen wie.

Uebungs-Aufgabe 1.

Parents love their children; children are loved by their parents. The teacher praises the diligent scholar. The diligent scholar is praised by his teacher. Our enemies hate us. We are hated by our enemies. Mr. N. instructs me in English. I am instructed in English by Mr. N. I planted an apple-tree in my orchard. This apple-tree was planted by me last spring. Our house was struck by lightning during the last thunderstorm. He persuaded me to go with him out West. I was persuaded to go with him out West. In the late Franco-German war the French were beaten in nearly every battle. I have often been asked: which of the two languages is the easier, the German or the English? The goods have all been sold at cost. A passenger-train on the Nashville railroad met with a serious accident, by which fifteen persons were killed, and thirty wounded. There has been an unusual attendance of cardinals and other high dignitaries of the Church at court during the king's stay in Rome. It is feared that the crops will be very poor this year.

A commission will be appointed to examine into the working of the commercial treaties. Satisfaction has been demanded by France for the illegal arrest of a French citizen in Cairo. Great interest had been excited by the report that Mr. Clay was to speak last night. By the treaty of peace made at Frankfort, it was stipulated that the forts around Paris should be evacuated as soon as the Germans were satisfied that order had been restored. A man was assaulted early this morning by a party of ruffians; he was severely beaten about the head and face. All the roughs escaped but one, who was locked up for examination. The body of an unknown man was found floating in the river. What is to be done under these circumstances? It is to be hoped that the negotiations now pending between the United States and England will be brought to an amicable conclusion. Such an overbearing conduct is not to be tolerated. The new director of the N. Musical Society is spoken of very highly. I do not like to be flattered. He wishes to be remembered to you. I have been advised to embark in this enterprise. Do you think he may be trusted? It has been proved beyond doubt that the evil doings of these fellows were connived at by the police. It is greatly to be regretted that we were deprived of your company at our exhibition, which took place last night.

Redensarten: Do you wish for more money? What do you wish for? I wish for nothing at all. The earth consists of land and water. The United States originally consisted of thirteen States. There is no time more propitious for such an undertaking than the present. There are but few men who are always capable of controlling their temper. There is no rose without thorns. Where there is a will, there is a way. You are to take care of your money. George has no time to play with you; he is to write his lesson. When are we to know your decision? How much did you pay for this cloth? I paid eight dollars a yard for it. Have these goods been paid for? They will be paid on delivery. When you come to New York, you must by no means neglect visiting our Central Park. Would you advise your countrymen to settle in the Southern States? On the contrary, I would advise them by all means to avoid settling in the South. Animals that feed on meat are called carnivorous animals, while those feeding on herbs and vegetables are called herbivorous animals. Some young men will fall in love with a girl at first sight. When I first fell in love I was but seventeen years old. I am very much pleased with your zeal and perseverance. Everybody should mind his own business. You had better mind your own business than always meddle with what you do not understand. It looked like rain this morning; but the weather has cleared up.

Wörter-Verzeichniß.

in der obern Stadt, up-town.
Zeitung, newspaper.
drucken, to print.
betrügen, to cheat.
empfehlen, to recommend.
bieten, to offer.
mir wird geboten, I am offered.
verdienen, to deserve.
auslachen, to laugh at.
ändern, to alter.
in Kenntniß setzen, to inform.
Rath, advice.
er ist schon in Angriff genommen worden, it is building already.
übersetzen, **to translate**.
Redensart, phrase.
einführen bei, to introduce to.
befürchten, **to apprehend**.
binnen Kurzem, **within a short time**.
heimsuchen, **to visit**.

Unruhe, anxiety.
befreien, to relieve.
hintergehen, to deceive.
lieb und werth, near and dear.
Schicksal, fate.
ertragen, to endure.
behaupten, to assert.
modificiren, to modify.
die Linke, the left.
Regierung, government.
ein Uebereinkommen treffen, to arrive at an understanding.
Machtbefugnisse, powers.
gewiß, definite.
fortdauern sollen, are to be continued.
was immer, whatever.
Versammlung, assembly.
zu gestehen, to confess.
die höchste Execution, the chief executive.

unheilbringend, disastrous.
tumultuös, riotous.
Verhandlungen, proceedings.
Kammer, chamber.
gehalten werden für, to be taken as.
Ausbrüche, ebullitions.
leicht erregbar, excitable.
Neu-Seeland, New-Zealand.
vor Kurzem, recently.
Verbindung, connection.
Postdampfer, mail steamship.

Uebungs-Aufgabe 2.

Mein Onkel baut ein neues Haus in der obern Stadt. Das neue Haus, das du gesehen hast, wird von meinem Onkel gebaut. Ich lese jeden Morgen beim Frühstück die englische Zeitung. Die englische Zeitung wird jeden Morgen von mir gelesen. In den Vereinigten Staaten werden mehr Zeitungen gedruckt, als in irgend einem Lande der Welt. Er fragte mich, ob es wahr sei, daß ich mein Geschäft verkauft hätte. Ich wurde von ihm gefragt, ob es wahr sei, daß ich mein Geschäft verkauft hätte. Diese Leute haben uns betrogen. Wir sind von ihnen betrogen worden; wir werden aber nie wieder von ihnen betrogen werden. Dieser junge Mensch ist mir von seinem Onkel empfohlen worden. Wie viel ist Ihnen für Ihr Haus geboten worden? Es sind mir 10,000 Dollars geboten worden; ich würde aber verdienen ausgelacht zu werden, wenn ich es für einen solchen Preis verkaufte. Was ist unter diesen Umständen zu thun; an der Sache läßt sich nicht viel ändern. Wenn ich früher von deinem Vorhaben in Kenntniß gesetzt worden wäre, so hätte ich dir manchen guten Rath geben können. Wann wird der neue Viaduct in New-York gebaut werden? Er ist schon in Angriff genommen worden. Wie ist das Wort "comfortable" zu übersetzen? Es gibt manche Wörter und Redensarten, die schwer zu übersetzen sind, und einige lassen sich gar nicht übertragen. Haben Sie Lust bei meinem Freunde B. eingeführt zu werden? Ich würde mich sehr freuen, mit ihm bekannt zu werden. Es ist sehr zu befürchten, daß wir binnen Kurzem von der Cholera heimgesucht werden. Was ist von einem Menschen zu erwarten, der nie sein Wort hält? Ich würde schon längst von meiner Unruhe befreit worden sein, wenn du früher gekommen wärest. Hintergangen zu werden von denen, die uns lieb und werth sind, ist ein Schicksal, das schwer zu ertragen ist. Es wird behauptet daß Mons. Rivet's Proposition von der Regierung modificirt worden ist. Es ist zwischen der Linken und der Regierung ein Uebereinkommen getroffen worden, nach welchem die Machtbefugnisse des Hrn. Thiers noch eine gewisse Zeit fortdauern solle. Was auch immer gesagt werden mag von dem Rechte der Versammlung, ihn zum Präsidenten zu machen, so muß doch zugestanden werden, daß ein Wechsel in der höchsten Executivgewalt jetzt unheilbringend für Frankreich sein würde. Die tumultuösen Verhandlungen in der Kammer jedoch müssen für nichts anderes gehalten werden, als für harmlose Ausbrüche der leicht erregbaren Franzosen. Neu=Seeland ist vor Kurzem durch eine Linie von Postdampfern in direkte Verbindung mit diesem Lande gebracht worden.

Lesestück 1.

THE PINE-TREE SHILLINGS. (Die Fichten=Schillinge.)

1. Captain John Hull was the mint-master[1] of Massachusetts, and coined[2] all the money that was made there. This was a new line[3] of business; for, in the earlier days of the colony, the current coinage[4] consisted of gold and silver money of England, Portugal, and Spain. These coins[5] being scarce,[6] the people were often forced to barter[7] their commodities instead of selling them.

2. For instance,[8] if a man wanted to buy a coat, he perhaps exchanged[9] a bear-skin for it. If he wished for a barrel of molasses, he might purchase[10] it with a pile[11] of pine-boards.[12] Musket-bullets[13] were used instead of farthings.[14] The Indians had a sort of money, called wampum, which was made of clam-shells;[15] and this strange sort[16] of specie[17] was likewise taken in payment of debts by the English settlers. Bank-bills[18] had never been heard of.[19] There was not money enough of any kind, in many parts of the country, to pay the salaries of the ministers; so that

they sometimes had to take quintals [20] of fish, bushels [21] of corn, or cords [22] of wood, instead of silver or gold.

3. As the people grew more numerous, and their trade, one with another, increased, the want [23] of current money was still more sensibly felt.[24] To supply the demand,[25] the General Court passed a law for establishing a coinage of shillings, sixpences and threepences. Captain John Hull was appointed [26] to manufacture[27] this money, and was to have[28] about one shilling out of every twenty to pay him for the trouble of making them.

4. Hereupon all the old silver in the colony was handed over to Captain John Hull. The battered [29] silver cans and tankards,[30] I suppose, and silver buckles,[31] and broken spoons, and silver buttons of worn-out [32] coats, and silver hilts [33] of swords that had figured [34] at court,—all such curious old articles were doubtless [35] thrown into the melting-pot [36] together. But by far the greater part of the silver consisted of bullion[37] from the mines of South America, which the English buccaneers [38]—who were little better [39] than pirates [40]—had taken from the Spaniards, and brought to Massachusetts.

5. All this old and new silver being melted down and coined, the result was an immense [41] amount [42] of splendid shillings, sixpences and threepences. Each had the date, 1652, on the one side, and the figure of a pine-tree on the other. Hence [43] they were called pine-tree shillings. And for every twenty shillings that he coined, you will remember, Captain John Hull was entitled [44] to put one shilling into his own pocket.

6. The magistrates [45] soon began to suspect [46] the mint-master would have the best of the bargain.[47] They offered him a large sum of money, if he would but give up that twentieth shilling which he was continually [48] dropping[49] into his own pocket. But Captain Hull declared himself perfectly satisfied with the shilling.

7. And well he might be;⁵⁰ for so diligently did he labor that, in a few years, his pockets, his money-bags, and his strong-box³¹ were overflowing with pine-tree shillings. This was probably the case when he came into possession³² of grandfather's chair; and as he had worked so hard at the mint, it was certainly proper⁵³ that he should have a comfortable chair to rest himself in.

¹ Münzmeister, ² prägte, ³ Art, ⁴ Courantgeld, ⁵ Münzen, ⁶ selten, ⁷ tauschen, ⁸ zum Beispiel, ⁹ gab in Tausch, ¹⁰ kaufen, ¹¹ Haufen, ¹² Jahrenbretter, ¹³ Kugeln, ¹⁴ Heller, ¹⁵ Muschelschalen, ¹⁶ merkwürdige Art, ¹⁷ Hartgeld, ¹⁸ Banknoten, ¹⁹ waren etwas Unerhörtes, ²⁰ Centner (112 Pfund), ²¹ Scheffel, ²² Faden, ²³ Mangel, ²⁴ wurde noch fühlbarer, ²⁵ um der Nachfrage zu genügen, ²⁶ ernannt, ²⁷ machen, ²⁸ und sollte haben, ²⁹ voller Beulen, ³⁰ Deckelkrüge, ³¹ Schnallen, ³² abgetragen, ³³ Griffe, ³⁴ die eine Rolle gespielt hatten, ³⁵ zweifelsohne, ³⁶ Schmelztiegel, ³⁷ ungemünztes Gold und Silber, ³⁸ Abenteurer, ³⁹ die nicht viel besser waren als, ⁴⁰ Seeräuber, ⁴¹ ungeheuer, ⁴² Summen, ⁴³ daher, ⁴⁴ berechtigt, ⁴⁵ Behörden, ⁴⁶ argwöhnen, ⁴⁷ den größten Vortheil davon haben würde, ⁴⁸ beständig, ⁴⁹ fallen ließ, ⁵⁰ und das konnte er auch wohl sein, ⁵¹ Geldtruhe, ⁵² Besitz, ⁵³ in der Ordnung.

Lesestück 2.

THE PINE-TREE SHILLINGS. (Schluß.)

1. When the mint-master had grown very rich, a young man, Samuel Sewell by name, came a-courting¹ to his only daughter. His daughter—whose name I do not know, but we will call her Betsey—was a fine, hearty² damsel,³ by no means⁴ so slender⁵ as some young ladies of our own days. On the contrary,⁶ having always fed heartily⁷ on pumpkin pies,⁸ doughnuts,⁹ Indian puddings, and other Puritan dainties,¹⁰ she was as round and plump¹¹ as a pudding herself.

2. With this round, rosy Miss Betsey did Samuel Sewell fall in love.¹² As he was a young man of good character, industrious in his business, and a member¹³ of the church, the mint-master very readily¹⁴ gave his consent.¹⁵ "Yes, you may take her," said he, in his rough¹⁶ way; "and you'll find her a heavy burden enough!"

3. On the wedding day,[17] we may suppose that honest John Hull dressed himself in a plum-colored[18] coat, all the buttons of which were made of pine-tree shillings. The buttons of his waistcoat[19] were sixpences; and the knees of his small-clothes[20] were buttoned[21] with silver threepences. Thus attired,[22] he sat with great dignity[23] in grandfather's chair; and, being a portly[24] old gentleman, he completely filled it from elbow[25] to elbow. On the opposite side of the room, between her bridemaids,[26] sat Miss Betsey. She was blushing[27] with all her might,[28] and looked like a full-blown[29] peony[30] or a great red apple.

4. There, too, was the bridegroom, dressed in a fine purple coat and gold lace[31] waistcoat, with as much other finery[32] as the Puritan laws and customs would allow him to put on. His hair was cropped[33] close[34] to his head, because Governor Endicott had forbidden any man to wear it below the ears. But he was a very personable[35] young man; and so thought the bridemaids and Miss Betsey herself.

5. The mint-master also was pleased with his new son-in-law,[36] especially[37] as he had courted Miss Betsey out of pure love, and had said nothing at all about her portion.[38] So, when the marriage ceremony was over, Captain Hull whispered[39] a word to two to his man-servants, who immediately went out, and soon returned, lugging in[40] a large pair of scales.[41] They were such a pair as wholesale merchants use for weighing[42] bulky commodities;[43] and quite a bulky commodity was now to be weighed in them.

6. "Daughter Betsey," said the mint-master, "get into one side of these scales."

Miss Betsey—or Mrs. Sewell, as we must now call her—did as she was bid,[44] like a dutiful[45] child, without any question of the why and wherefore. But what her father could mean, unless to make her husband pay for her by the pound (in which case she would have been a dear bargain), she had not the least idea.

7. "And now," said honest John Hull to the servants, "bring that box hither."[46] The box to which the mint-master pointed, was a huge,[47] square,[48] iron-bound,[49] oaken chest;[50] it was big enough, my children, for all four of you to play at hide-and-seek in.[51] The servants tugged[52] with might and main,[53] but could not lift[54] this enormous receptacle,[55] and were finally obliged to drag[56] it across the floor.

8. Captain Hull then took a key from his girdle, unlocked the chest, and lifted its ponderous[57] lid.[58] Behold,[59] it was full to the brim[60] of bright pine-tree shillings, fresh from the mint; and Samuel Sewell began to think that his father-in-law[61] had got possession[62] of all the money in the Massachusetts treasury.[63] But it was only the mint-master's honest share[64] of the coinage.

9. Then the servants, at Captain Hull's command,[65] heaped[66] double handfuls of shillings into one side of the scales, while Betsey remained in the other. Jingle, jingle,[67] went the shillings, as handful after handful was thrown in, till, plump and ponderous as she was, they fairly weighed[68] the young lady from the floor.

10. "There, son Sewell!" cried the honest mint-master, resuming[69] his seat in grandfather's chair, "take these shillings for my daughter's portion. Use[70] her kindly, and thank Heaven for her. It is not every wife that's worth her weight in silver!"

HAWTHORNE.

---

[1] zu freien um, [2] kräftig, [3] junges Mädchen, [4] durchaus nicht, [5] hager, [6] im Gegentheil, [7] da sie stets gut gefüttert worden war, [8] Kürbiskuchen (ein Lieblingsgericht in den Neu-England Staaten), [9] ein kleiner Kuchen aus Mehl, Eier und Zucker, in Milch getunkt und in Schmalz gekocht, [10] Leckerbissen, [11] fett, [12] verliebte sich, [13] Glied, [14] bereitwillig, [15] Zustimmung, [16] herb, [17] Hochzeitstag, [18] pflaumfarbig, [19] Weste, [20] Hosen, [21] zuaknöpft, [22] angezogen, [23] Würde, [24] corpulent, [25] Lehne, [26] Brautjungfern, [27] errothete, [28] mit aller Macht (b. i. bis über die Ohren), [29] in voller Blüthe, [30] Päonie, [31] Spitzen, [32] und so viel sonstigen Schmuck, [33] geschnitten, [34] kurz, [35] stattlich, [36] Schwiegersohn, [37] besonders, [38] Mitgift, [39] sagte ins Ohr, [40] hereinschleppend, [41] Wage, [42] zum Wagen von, [43] Waaren von großem Umfang, [44] wie man ihr hieß, [45] gehorsam, [46] hierher, [47] kolossal, [48] viereckig, [49] eisenbeschlagen, [50] eichene

Kiste, ⁵¹ Verstecken, ⁵² legen, ⁵³ aus Leibeskräften, ⁵⁴ heben, ⁵⁵ Behälter, ⁵⁶ schleifsten, ⁵⁷ gewichtig, ⁵⁸ Deckel, ⁵⁹ sieh da! ⁶⁰ bis an den Rand, ⁶¹ Schwiegervater, ⁶² in den Besitz gekommen sei, ⁶³ Schatzamt, ⁶⁴ Antheil, ⁶⁵ Geheiß, ⁶⁶ häuften, ⁶⁷ kling, kling, ⁶⁸ ordentlich wegen, ⁶⁹ wieder einnehmend, ⁷⁰ behandle.

Lestion XXXI.

Die Hülfszeitwörter des Modus. (AUXILIARIES OF MODE.) Redensarten.

Can, may, must, need, ought, dare, could, might, should, would.

Wörter-Verzeichniß.

much ado about nothing, viel Lärmen um Nichts.
to settle, abmachen.
easy circumstances, gute Verhältnisse.
to touch, anrühren.
to accommodate, dienen.
prevented, verhindert.
previous, früher.
drudgery, Plage.
to lock, abschließen.
to bolt, verriegeln.
damaged, beschädigt.
is said to be, soll sein.
to deny, leugnen.
to act, handeln.
otherwise, sonst.
to comply with, genügen.
request, Bitte.
forcibly, kräftig.
if you were to, wenn du solltest.
to prefer, vorziehen.
well-off, gutgestellt.
to forego, verzichten auf.
impaired, geschwächt.
stocks, Aktien.

Redensarten.

to apply for, sich bewerben um.
application, Gesuch.
two weeks ago, vor zwei Wochen.
to agree with, übereinstimmen mit.
to allow ourselves to be carried away, uns hinreißen lassen.
to govern, beherrschen.
to disagree, verschiedener Meinung sein.
provoked, gereizt.
agreed, zugegeben.
justified, gerechtfertigt.
abusive, schmähend; beleidigend.

to be called to account, zur Rechenschaft gezogen werden.
cord, Bindfaden.
parcel, Packet.
will this do? paßt dies?
that will answer, das ist recht.
to keep in view, im Auge halten.
to embark in, sich einlassen auf.
enterprise, Unternehmen.
to afford, vermögen; vertragen.
to advance, vorstrecken.
to make allowance for, Rechnung tragen.
fallibility, Fehlbarkeit.
frailty, Schwachheit.
get along! fort!
to be ashamed, sich schämen.
to attend, besuchen.
to be aware, wissen.
time-table, Stundenplan.
to be anxious, begierig sein.
in honor, zu Ehren.
were in attendance, waren zugegen.

Uebungs-Aufgabe 1.

Can you speak English? I cannot speak, but I can understand it when spoken. If this be the case, you will soon be able to speak. I cannot understand why you make so much ado about nothing. Would you be so kind as to lend me ten dollars? I would if I could. If you wanted him to settle this business for you, you should have told him. This may be true or not. May I ask you, when you can come, and finish the work on my house. He might have been in easy circumstances, if he had been more careful with his money. You must not touch any flowers in this garden. We must all die. The ship had to change her course for fear she might strike a rock. You need not trouble yourself about me, I shall soon be all right again. I dare say you are right. I should be greatly obliged to you, if you would do me this favor. I should be happy to accommodate you, if I were not prevented by a previous engagement. You ought to get up earlier. What ought I to do in such a case? We ought to be kind towards everybody. The study of a foreign language ought to be a pleasure instead of being a drudgery. I know very well what I ought to have answered him. You ought to have locked and bolted the door. How will this have to be expressed in English? What is to be done with these damaged goods? They are to be sold at auction. I am to leave for Europe by the next steamer. What are you going to do with these boys? I am going to punish them. This man is said to be very rich; he is said to be worth one and a half million. He dare not deny that. It might be doubted whether he could have acted otherwise under the circumstances. If he could have complied with your request, he would certainly have done so. You might have been more careful with your words. This could not have been expressed more forcibly, although it might have been expressed more elegantly. If you were to choose between living in Europe or in America, which of the two would you prefer? I should certainly prefer living in Europe, if I were well-off. I am sorry to say that I shall have to forego the pleasure of your company this evening. I should have advised him to go to the country, had I known that his health was impaired. Would you advise me to take stocks in this company? I would not.

Redensarten.—When did you apply for this position? I made application two weeks ago. I fully agree with you that it is far easier to allow ourselves to be carried away by our passions than to govern them. As it seems impossible for us to agree on this point, let us agree to disagree. He was provoked; agreed; but it by no means follows that he was justified in using such abusive language; he is old enough to be called to account for his actions. Please to give me a piece of cord for tying up this parcel. Will this do? Yes, sir, that will answer. If I had kept in view the necessary consequences, I should never have embarked in such an enterprise. It is at once christianlike and wise to forgive an enemy. How great a sum can you afford to advance me? I cannot afford to loan you more than two thousand dollars. No one can afford to lose the good opinion of respectable people. In judging the acts of other people we should always make allowance for human fallibility and frailty. Get along with you! I am ashamed of you. Where do you attend church? I attended a meeting last night at Cooper Institute. Are you aware that the railroad company have changed their time-table? I am very anxious to know what has become of your brother. A banquet was given last night in honor of Prof. Morse, the inventor of the telegraph. More than one hundred people were in attendance.

Wörter-Verzeichniß.

um zu, in order to.
das Abschreiben, copying.
aufhören, to discontinue.
mündlich, oral.
schreiten, to proceed.
anbieten, to offer.
meinen, to think.
überreden, to persuade.
im Begriff, about.
Kunst, art.
erlernen, to acquire.
dabei, about it.
bestehlen, to rob.
vor allen Dingen, above all.

zu Herzen nehmen, to take to heart.
sich schämen, to be ashamed.
Erlaubniß, permission.
bitten um, to ask for.
sich beziehen auf, to refer to.
vermuthen, to presume.
Mittag, noon.
wie man mir sagt, as I am told.
veranstalten, to arrange.
großartig, grand.
Schauspiel, spectacle.
der Art, of the kind.

Uebungs-Aufgabe 2.

Können Sie Englisch? Ich kann es verstehen, wenn es gesprochen wird, ich kann aber nur wenig sprechen. Wann werden wir Englisch sprechen können? Um Englisch sprechen zu können, müssen Sie erst es verstehen lernen, wenn es gesprochen wird. Können Sie diesen Satz übersetzen? Darf ich jetzt mit meinem Abschreiben aufhören? Sie können jetzt aufhören mit Schreiben; wir wollen zum mündlichen Unterricht schreiten. Darf ich Ihnen einen Stuhl anbieten? Ich danke Ihnen, ich mag jetzt nicht sitzen; ich bin nicht müde.

Meinen Sie, daß wir ihn überreden könnten, mit uns auszugehen? Wir waren gerade im Begriff nach dem Central Park zu gehen, als es anfing zu regnen. Wenn ich mit dir zufrieden sein soll, so mußt du fleißiger werden. Die Musik ist eine Kunst, die ein Jeder erlernen sollte, der Talent dazu hat. Kannst du mir sagen, was ich dabei thun soll? Ich bin vorige Nacht bestohlen worden; die Diebe haben mir all mein Geld gestohlen. Was ist dabei zu thun, daß ich es wiederkriege? Vor allen Dingen müssen Sie sich die Sache nicht zu sehr zu Herzen nehmen. Wollen Sie mit mir zu meinem Freunde B. gehen? er soll sehr krank sein. Wer soll diesen Brief schreiben? Sie sollten sich schämen, so etwas zu sagen. Ich habe ihn um Erlaubniß gebeten, mich auf ihn beziehen zu dürfen. Wann werden wir Wilhelm bei uns erwarten können? Ich vermuthe wir werden ihn morgen gegen Mittag erwarten können. Er soll sehr reich geworden sein, wie man mir sagt. Wir waren gestern ausgegangen, um die große Prozession zu sehen, die die Deutschen veranstaltet hatten; wir mußten über eine Stunde warten, ehe sie herankam. Es soll das großartigste Schauspiel der Art gewesen sein, das Neu-York je gesehen hat.

Lesestück 1.

NATIONAL MONUMENT TO WASHINGTON. (1848.)

1. Fellow-citizens[1] of the United States: We are assembled to take the first step towards the fulfilment of a long-deferred[2] obligation. In this eight-and-fortieth year since his death, we have come together to lay the corner-stone of a national monument to Washington.

2. Other monuments to this illustrious[3] person, have, long ago, been erected.[4] By not a few of the great States of our Union, by not a few of the great cities of our States, the chiseled[5] statue, or the lofty[6] column[7] has been set up in his honor.[8] The highest art of the Old World—of France, of Italy, and of England, successively[9]—has been put in requisition[10] for the pur-

pose. Houdon for Virginia, Canova for North Carolina, Sir Francis Chantrey for Massachusetts, have severally[11] signalized [12] their genius by portraying and perpetuating [13] the form and features [14] of the Father of his Country.

3. One tribute to his memory is left[15] to be rendered.[16] One monument remains to be reared[17]—a monument which shall bespeak [18] the gratitude, not of states, or of cities, or of governments; not of separate[19] communities,[20] or of official bodies,[21] but of the people, the whole people of the nation,—a National Monument erected by the citizens of the United States of America.

4. Of such a monument we have come to lay the corner-stone, here and now. On this day, on this spot, in this presence, and at this precise [22] epoch [23] in the history of our country and of the world, we are about[24] to commence this crowning work of commemoration.[25]

5. Yes, to-day, fellow-citizens, at this very moment when the extension[26] of our boundaries,[27] and the multiplication[28] of our territories[29] are producing,[30] directly and indirectly, among the different members[31] of our political system, so many marked[32] and mourned[33] centrifugal tendencies,[34]—let us seize[35] the occasion[36] to renew[37] to each other our vows[38] of allegiance[39] and devotion[40] to the American Union; and let us recognize,[41] in our common title[42] to the name and the fame[43] of Washington, and in our common veneration[44] for his example and his advice, the all-sufficient[45] centripetal power, which shall hold the thick clustering[46] stars of our confederacy[47] in one glorious[48] constellation[49] forever![50]

6. Let the column which we are about to construct be at once[51] a pledge[52] and an emblem[53] of perpetual[54] union! Let the foundations[55] be laid, let the superstructure[56] be built up and cemented,[57] let each stone be raised[58] and riveted[59] in a spirit of national brotherhood![60] And may the earliest ray[61] of the rising sun

—till that sun shall set to rise no more—draw forth [62] from it daily, as from the fabled [63] statue of antiquity, [64] a strain [65] of national harmony, which shall strike [66] a responsive [67] chord [68] in every heart throughout the republic! [69]

7. Proceed, [70] then, fellow-citizens, with the work for which you have assembled. Lay the corner-stone of a monument which shall adequately [71] bespeak the gratitude of the whole American people to the illustrious Father of his Country! Build it to the skies: [72] you cannot outreach [73] the loftiness [74] of his principles! Found [75] it upon the massive and eternal rock: you cannot make it more enduring [76] than his fame! Construct it of the peerless [77] Parian marble: [78] you cannot make it purer than his life! Exhaust [79] upon it the rules and principles of ancient [80] and of modern art: you cannot make it more proportionate [81] than his character!

8. But let not your homage [82] to his memory end here. Think not to transfer [83] to a tablet or a column the tribute which is due from yourselves. [84] Just honor to Washington can only be rendered by observing [85] his precepts, and imitating [86] his example. He has built his own monument. We, and those who come after us, are its appointed [87] and privileged [88] guardians. [89] The wide-spread [90] Republic is the true monument to Washington. Maintain [91] its independence. Uphold [92] its constitution. Preserve [93] its union. Defend its liberty. Let it stand before the world in all its original [94] strength and beauty, securing [95] peace, order, equality, and freedom to all within its boundaries, and shedding [96] light, and hope, and joy upon the pathway [97] of human liberty throughout the world;—and Washington needs no other monument. Other structures [98] may fitly [99] testify our veneration for him; this, this alone can adequately illustrate [100] his services to mankind. [101]

9. Nor does he need even this. [102] The Republic may perish; [103] the wide arch [104] of our ranged Union may

fall; star by star its glories,[105] may expire;[106] stone by stone its columns and capital[107] may moulder[108] and crumble;[109] all other names which adorn[110] its annals[111] may be forgotten; but as long as human hearts shall anywhere pant,[112] or human tongues shall anywhere plead,[113] for a true, rational, constitutional liberty, those hearts shall enshrine[114] the memory, and those tongues prolong[115] the fame, of *George Washington!*

WINTHROP.

[1] Mitbürger, [2] aufgeschoben, [3] hehr, erhaben, [4] errichtet, [5] gemeißelt, [6] hoch, [7] Säule, [8] ihm zu Ehren, [9] nacheinander, [10] ist aufgeboten worden, [11] jeder für sich, [12] bekundet, [13] verewigen, [14] Züge, [15] übrig, [16] gezollt zu werden, [17] errichtet, [18] bezeugen, [19] einzeln, [20] Communen, [21] öffentliche Behörden, [22] genau, [23] Zeitpunkt, [24] im Begriff, [25] Andenken, [26] Erweiterung, [27] Grenzen, [28] Vervielfältigung, [29] Gebiet, [30] hervorbringen, [31] Glieder, [32] deutlich hervortretend, [33] beklagenswerth, [34] Tendenzen, Richtungen, [35] ergreifen, [36] Gelegenheit, [37] erneuern, [38] Gelübde, [39] Treue, [40] Hingebung, [41] anerkennen, [42] Unrecht, [43] Ruhm, [44] Verehrung, [45] allgenugsam, [46] dichtgedrängt, [47] Confederation, [48] herrlich, [49] Sternbild, [50] auf ewig, [51] zu gleicher Zeit, [52] Pfand, [53] Sinnbild, [54] ewig, [55] Fundament, [56] der Bau, [57] fest verbunden, [58] emporgehoben, [59] fest gemacht, [60] Brüderlichkeit, [61] Strahl, [62] hervorrufen, entlocken, [63] melodiehaft, [64] Alterthum, [65] Lied, [66] anschlagen, [67] wiederhallend, [68] Saite, [69] durch die ganze Republik, [70] fahret fort, [71] hinreichend, [72] Himmel, Wolken, [73] übertragen, [74] Erhabenheit, [75] leget den Grund, [76] dauernder, [77] unvergleichlich, [78] Parischer Marmor, [79] verschwendet darauf, [80] alt, [81] von größerem Ebenmaß, [82] Verehrung, [83] übertragen, [84] den ihr schuldig seid, [85] dadurch, daß ihr beobachtet, [86] nachahmt, [87] auserlesen, [88] bevorzugt, [89] Beschützer, [90] weit ausgebreitet, [91] erhaltet, [92] erhaltet aufrecht, [93] bewahret, [94] ursprünglich, [95] sicherstellend, [96] verbreitend, [97] Pfad, [98] Bauten, [99] auf passende Weise, [100] in's Licht stellen, [101] Menschheit, [102] und selbst dessen bedarf er nicht, [103] untergehen, [104] Bogen, [105] Glanz, [106] erlöschen, [107] Capital, [108] vermodern, [109] zerbröckeln, [110] zieren, [111] Geschichtsbücher, [112] seufzen, [113] sprechen für, [114] bewahren, [115] verewigen.

Lesestück 2.

LIBERTY AND UNION. (Freiheit und Vereinigung.)

1. Mr. President: I have thus stated[1] the reasons of my dissent[2] to the doctrines[3] which have been advanced[4] and maintained.[5] I am conscious[6] of having detained[7] you and the Senate much too long. I was drawn into the debate,[8] with no previous[9] deliberation,[10] such as is suited[11] to the discussion of so grave[12]

and important a subject.¹³ But it is a subject of which my heart is full, and I have not been willing to suppress¹⁴ the utterance¹⁵ of its spontaneous¹⁶ sentiments.¹⁷

2. I cannot, even now, persuade myself to relinquish¹⁸ it, without expressing, once more, my deep conviction,¹⁹ that, since it respects²⁰ nothing less than the Union of the States, it is of most vital²¹ and essential²² importance to the public happiness. I profess,²³ sir, in my career²⁴ hitherto,²⁵ to have kept steadily in view²⁶ the prosperity and honor of the whole country, and the preservation²⁷ of our Federal Union. It is to that Union we owe our safety at home and our consideration and dignity abroad. It is to that Union that we are chiefly²⁸ indebted for whatever²⁹ makes us most proud of our country. That Union we reached only by the discipline³⁰ of our virtues in the severe³¹ school of adversity.³²

3. It had its origin³³ in the necessities³⁴ of disordered³⁵ finance, prostrate³⁶ commerce, and ruined credit. Under its benign³⁷ influences, these great interests immediately awoke, as from the dead, and sprang forth³⁸ with newness of life.³⁹ Every year of its duration⁴⁰ has teemed⁴¹ with fresh proofs⁴² of its utility⁴³ and its blessings;⁴⁴ and, although our territory has stretched out wider and wider, and our population spread farther and farther, they have not outrun⁴⁵ its protection or its benefits. It has been to us all a copious⁴⁶ fountain of national, social, personal happiness.

4. I have not allowed myself, sir, to look beyond the Union, to see what might lie hidden in the dark recess⁴⁷ behind. I have not coolly weighed⁴⁸ the chances⁴⁹ of preserving liberty, when the bonds⁵⁰ that unite us together shall be broken asunder.⁵¹ I have not accustomed⁵² myself to hang over the precipice⁵³ of disunion,⁵⁴ to see whether, with my short sight,⁵⁵ I can fathom⁵⁶ the depth of the abyss⁵⁷ below; nor could I regard⁵⁸ him as a safe counsellor⁵⁹ in the affairs of this

government, whose thoughts should be mainly[60] bent on[61] considering, not how the Union might be best preserved, but how tolerable might be the condition of the people when it shall be broken up and destroyed.

5. While the Union lasts,[62] we have high, exciting,[63] gratifying[64] prospects spread out before us, for us and our children. Beyond that I seek not to penetrate[65] the veil.[66] God grant[67] that, in my day at least, that curtain[68] may not rise! God grant that on my vision[69] never may be opened what lies behind! When my eyes shall be turned to behold,[70] for the last time, the sun in heaven, may I not see him shining on the broken and dishonored[71] fragments[72] of a once glorious Union; on States dissevered,[73] discordant,[74] belligerent;[75] on a land rent with[76] civil feuds,[77] or drenched,[78] it may be, in fraternal blood!

6. Let their last feeble and lingering[79] glance,[80] rather, behold the gorgeous[81] ensign[82] of the Republic, now known and honored throughout the earth, still full high advanced, its arms and trophies streaming[83] in their original lustre,[84] not a stripe erased[85] or polluted,[86] nor a single star obscured[87]—bearing for its motto, no such miserable interrogatory[88] as, "What is all this worth?" nor those other words of delusion[89] and folly,[90] "Liberty first, and Union afterwards,"— but everywhere, spread all over in characters[91] of living light, blazing[92] on its ample[93] folds,[94] as they fold over the sea and over the land, and in every wind under the whole heavens, that other sentiment,[95] dear to every true American heart,—LIBERTY AND UNION, *now and forever*, ONE AND INSEPARABLE!

DANIEL WEBSTER.

---

[1] dargelegt, [2] Opposition (abweichende Meinung), [3] Lehren, [4] vorgebracht, [5] vertheidigt, [6] ich bin mir bewußt, [7] aufgehalten zu haben, [8] Debatte, [9] vorhergehend, [10] Ueberlegung, [11] wie sich gehörte für, [12] ernst, [13] Gegenstand, [14] unterdrücken, [15] Aeußerung, [16] unwillkürlich, [17] Gefühle, [18] darauf zu verzichten, [19] Ueberzeugung, [20] betrifft, [21] unumgänglich nothwendig, [22] wesentlich, [23] ich bekenne, [24] Laufbahn, [25] bisher, [26] beständig im Auge behalten zu haben, [27] Erhaltung, [28] hauptsächlich, [29] für Alles was, [30] Zucht, Ausübung, [31] schwer, [32] Unglück, [33] Ursprung, [34] schwierige Lage, [35] zerrüttet,

³⁶ darniederliegend, ³⁷ segensreich, ³⁸ traten hervor, ³⁹ mit neuem Leben, ⁴⁰ Dauer, ⁴¹ ist voll gewesen von, ⁴² Beweise, ⁴³ Nützlichkeit, ⁴⁴ Segnungen, ⁴⁵ entronnen, ⁴⁶ reich, ⁴⁷ Hintergrund, ⁴⁸ abgewogen, ⁴⁹ Gelegenheiten, ⁵⁰ Bande, ⁵¹ auseinander, in Stücken, ⁵² daran gewöhnt, ⁵³ Abgrund, ⁵⁴ Zwietracht, ⁵⁵ Kurzsichtigkeit, ⁵⁶ ergründen, ⁵⁷ Abgrund, ⁵⁸ betrachten, ⁵⁹ Rathgeber, ⁶⁰ hauptsächlich, ⁶¹ sich beschäftigen mit, ⁶² dauert, ⁶³ anregend, ⁶⁴ erfreulich, ⁶⁵ zu durchdringen, ⁶⁶ Schleier, ⁶⁷ Gott gebe, ⁶⁸ Vorhang, ⁶⁹ meinem Blicke, ⁷⁰ anzuschauen, ⁷¹ entehrt, ⁷² Scherben, ⁷³ zertrennt, ⁷⁴ in Zwiespalt, ⁷⁵ kampfbereit, ⁷⁶ zerrissen von, ⁷⁷ Fehde, ⁷⁸ gebadet, befleckt, ⁷⁹ zögernd, ⁸⁰ Blick, ⁸¹ prächtig, ⁸² Banner, ⁸³ flatternd, ⁸⁴ Glanz, ⁸⁵ ausgewischt, ⁸⁶ befleckt, ⁸⁷ verdunkelt, ⁸⁸ Frage, ⁸⁹ Wahn, ⁹⁰ Thorheit, ⁹¹ Buchstaben, ⁹² leuchtend, ⁹³ weit, ⁹⁴ Falten, ⁹⁵ Gesinnung.

Lektion XXXII.

Die progressive Form (PROGRESSIVE FORMS). Redensarten.

Wörter-Verzeichniß.

rapidly, schnell.
counsel, Anwalt.
to plead, plaidiren.
dexterity, Gewandtheit.
apparent, augenscheinlich.
non-concern, Gleichgültigkeit.
pursuer, Verfolger.
trap, Falle, Hinterhalt.
tenements, Familienkasernen.
riot, Aufruhr.
to cause, verursachen.
remains, Ueberreste.
indication, Anzeichen.
review, Heerschau.
to look forward to, aussehen nach.
to come off, stattfinden.
continuous, fortwährend.
to level, dem Boden gleichmachen.
to rage, wüthen.
underneath, unter.
property, Grundstück.
to dissolve, auflösen.
partnership, Geschäftsverbindung.
to settle accounts, Abrechnung halten.
to remit, überwachen.
to deliberate, überlegen.
to extricate, herausziehen.
to occur, eintreten.
ravages, Verwüstungen.
copy, Exemplar.
to argue, begründen.
obvious, offenbar.

to carry (a point), durchsetzen.
to refute, widerlegen.
recent, neulich.
dry-goods, Manufakturwaaren.
regrets, Bedauern.
to heed, beachten.
    Redensarten.
a judge of, ein Kenner von.
to judge, richten, halten für.
expert, geschickt.
sentenced, verurtheilt.
in store, in Bereitschaft.
sole heir, Universalerbe.

to mind one's own business, sich um seine eigene Angelegenheiten kümmern.
to catch cold, sich erkälten.
to chance to meet, zufällig begegnen.
to change, wechseln.
to commit to memory, auswendig lernen.
all's well that ends well, Ende gut, Alles gut.
I cannot help, ich kann nicht dafür.

Uebungs-Aufgabe 1.

The United States are growing very rapidly. How do you sell this cloth a yard? Five dollars a yard; we are selling a great deal of this cloth. While the counsel for the prisoner was pleading his client's case with great dexterity, the latter was looking about himself with apparent non-concern. In trying to escape from the hands of his pursuers he fell into a trap. The neighborhood of Twenty-sixth Street and Seventh Avenue is one of the worst in the city, being surrounded by tenements, many of them containing such characters as those who began the riot on Wednesday, the 12th of July, and caused the death of those, to honor whose remains the regiment was assembling. There was no indication of a confict, and a passage having been cleared, the reserve which had been dispatched there, returned. The review to which all Paris has been looking forward for the past three weeks and more, came off at Longchamps on June the 29th. All the morning there was a continuous stream of troops pouring out to the Bois de Boulogne. At the Porte Dauphine leading into the Bois de Boulogne the workmen are still busy leveling what remains of the gate, and making the road look as much as possible the same as it did about ten months ago. One of the most remarkable fires is said to be raging, underneath property of considerable value, almost in the center of the town of Sheffield, England. It must have been raging for a long period, possibly for some years. Having dissolved the partnership heretofore existing between us, we are now settling our accounts, and request all our friends to remit the amounts they are owing us on or before the first of September next. While we were deliberating as to the best mode of extricating ourselves from this dilemma, a circumstance occurred which at once settled all our difficulties. What have you been doing all this morning? I have been looking for you everywhere this last hour. What is the dog barking at? He is barking at a cat. Reports of the ravages of the recent storm are coming in fast. I was just thinking of you, when you entered the room. While you were sleeping I finished two letters. I was going to request you to send me a few copies of your book. He had not been arguing his point more than ten minutes, when it was obvious that he would carry it; and he did carry it despite all the efforts that were making by the other party to refute him. The house that was building in Broadway, was blown down in the recent storm. Dry-goods are selling at much lower prices than they did during the war. This business being accomplished I bid them good-bye. I cannot take leave of you without expressing my sincere regrets at the course you have been taking in this matter. Having duly notified you of the difficulties which you would necessarily encounter in such an undertaking, you can not blame any one but yourself for not heeding my timely warning.

Redensarten: Are you a judge of wine? I am no judge of wine. Judge not, that you be not judged. How old do you take me? I should judge you to be about forty. I shall judge you by your own words. I have a little sister who is quite an expert in all sorts of needle-work. The criminal who was sentenced yes-

terday to be hung was the greatest expert in lying you
ever saw. I have some good news in store for you;
your uncle who died in California last week has made
you sole heir of all his wealth. Is that any of your
business? I think everybody ought to mind his own
business. 'Tis none of your business. If you go out
without an overcoat at this late hour, you will be sure
to catch cold. I caught cold last night in consequence
of the windows of my bedroom being open. Where
did you chance to meet him? I chanced to meet him
in New York. Can you change a ten-dollar bill? I
do not think I can change a ten-dollar bill. You will
find it profitable to commit these words to memory.
I was greatly disappointed in not finding you at home
when I called on you yesterday. All's well that ends
well. Will you favor me with a call? I shall do my
best to suit you. I could not help laughing at this
idea.

Wörter-Verzeichniß.

ſtudiren, to study.
nach Hauſe, home.
ausgezeichnet, splendid.
Zug, train.
abgefahren, started.
Bahnhof, railroad depot.
ankommen, to reach.
ſich berathen, to deliberate.
was wir thun ſollten, what to do.
man ſagte uns, we were told.
abgeben, to leave.
ſtark wären, numbered.
Inſtitut, institution.
Waiſenkind, orphan.
zweifelhaft, questionable.
Ruf, repute.
bemerken, to discover.

Bürger, citizen.
etwa, about.
langſam, slowly.
ſeines Wegs, along.
Bewegung, motion.
behindert, impeded.
mit einer Kette befeſtigt an, chained to.
nähere Nachforſchung, inquiry.
brachte heraus, elicited.
Deſerteur, runaway.
Klotz, clog.
auf die beſchriebene Weiſe, in the manner described.
herumtragen, to carry about.
ertrinken, to be drowned.
Dock, pier.
Fähre, ferry.

Uebungs-Aufgabe 2.

Fritz, was machst du da? Ich studire meine Lektion. Das Erste, was ich thue, wenn ich aus der Schule nach Hause komme ist, daß ich meine Lektion studire. Ich rauche hier eine ausgezeichnete Havannah. Wollen Sie eine? Ich danke, ich rauche nicht. Ich rauche jeden Abend nach dem Abendessen eine Pfeife. Der Zug war soeben abgefahren, als wir auf dem Bahnhofe ankamen; wir waren dabei uns zu berathen, was wir unter diesen Umständen thun sollten, als man uns sagte, daß der nächste Zug eine Stunde später abgehen würde. Meine Schwägerin ist gestern von Hamburg angekommen. Wir haben sie schon die ganze Woche erwartet. Was haben Sie soeben gesagt? ich habe Sie nicht verstanden. Ich sagte, daß die Deutschen in den Vereinigten Staaten mehr als fünf Millionen stark wären. Das "Susquehanna Valley Home," ein Institut für Waisenkinder in Binghamton, N. Y., ist in einen zweifelhaften Ruf gebracht worden. Am vorigen Dienstag bemerkte Elijah Castle, ein Bürger von Binghamton, N. Y., einen etwa neun Jahre alten Knaben in Oak Straße, wie er langsam seines Weges ging, indem seine Bewegungen durch ein schweres Stück Holz behindert waren, welches mit einer Kette an seinem Halse befestigt war. Nähere Nachforschung brachte aus dem Knaben heraus, daß er ein Deserteur von dem "Home" sei, wo er den Klotz auf die beschriebene Weise vier Wochen lang herumgetragen hatte. Ein Knabe ertrank gestern, während er auf dem Dock an der Fähre spielte.

Lesestück 1.

SUPPOSED SPEECH OF REGULUS TO THE CARTHAGINIANS

(Fingirte Rede des Regulus an die Carthagenienser.)

1. The beams[1] of the rising sun had gilded the lofty[2] domes of Carthage, and given, with its rich[3] and mellow[4] light, a tinge[5] of beauty even to the frowning[6] ramparts[7] of the outer harbor. Sheltered[8] by the

verdant[9] shores a hundred triremes[10] were riding[11] proudly at their anchors, their brazen[12] beaks[13] glittering in the sun, their streamers[14] dancing[15] in the morning breeze, while many a shattered[16] plank and timber gave evidence[17] of desperate conflict with the fleets of Rome.

2. No murmur[18] of business or of revelry[19] arose from the city. The artisan[20] had forsaken[21] his shop, the judge his tribunal, the priest the sanctuary,[22] and even the stern[23] stoic[24] had come forth from his retirement[25] to mingle with the crowd that, anxious and agitated,[26] were rushing[27] toward the senate house, startled[28] by the report that Regulus had returned to Carthage.

3. Onward, still onward, trampling each other underfoot, they rushed, furious with anger[29] and eager for revenge.[30] Fathers were there, whose sons were groaning[31] in fetters;[32] maidens, whose lovers, weak and wounded, were dying in the dungeons[33] of Rome, and gray-haired men and matrons, whom the Roman sword had left childless.

4. But when the stern features[34] of Regulus were seen, and his colossal form towering[35] above the ambassadors who had returned with him from Rome; when the news passed from lip to lip that the dreaded[36] warrior, so far from advising[37] the Roman senate to consent[38] to an exchange[39] of prisoners, had urged[40] them to pursue, with exterminating[41] vengeance, Carthage and Carthaginians,—the multitude[42] swayed[43] to and fro like a forest beneath a tempest,[44] and the rage[45] and hate of that tumultuous[46] throng vented itself[47] in groans,[48] and curses,[49] and yells of vengeance.[50] But calm,[51] cold, and immovable as the marble walls around him, stood the Roman; and he stretched out his hand over that frenzied[52] crowd, with gesture[53] as proudly commanding[54] as though he still stood at the head of the gleaming[55] cohorts[56] of Rome.

5. The tumult ceased; the curse, half muttered,[57] died upon the lip; and so intense[58] was the silence, that the clanking[59] of the brazen manacles[60] upon the

wrist[61] of the captive fell[62] sharp and full upon every ear[62] in that vast[63] assembly, as he thus addressed them:—

6. "Ye doubtless thought—for ye judge of Roman virtue by your own—that I would break my plighted oath,[64] rather than, returning. brook[65] your vengeance. I might give reasons for this, in Punic comprehension,[66] most foolish act of mine. I might speak of those eternal principles which make death for one's country a pleasure, not a pain. But, by great Jupiter! methinks I should debase[67] myself to talk of such high things to you; to you, expert[68] in womanly inventions; to you, well-skilled to drive a treacherous[69] trade with simple Africans for ivory[70] and gold! If the bright[71] blood that fills my veins,[72] transmitted free[73] from god-like ancestry,[74] were like that slimy[75] ooze[76] which stagnates[77] in your arteries,[78] I had remained at home, and broke my plighted oath to save my life.

7. "I am a Roman citizen; therefore have I returned, that ye might work your will[79] upon this mass of flesh and bones, that I esteem no higher than the rags that cover them. Here, in your capital, do I defy[80] you. Have I not conquered[81] your armies, fired[82] your towns, and dragged[83] your generals at my chariot[84] wheels, since first my youthful arms could wield[85] a spear? And do you think to see me crouch[86] and cower[87] before a tamed[88] and shattered[89] senate? The tearing of flesh and rending[90] of sinews[91] is but pastime[92] compared with the mental[93] agony[94] that heaves my frame.[95]

8. "The moon has scarce yet waned[96] since the proudest of Rome's proud matrons, the mother upon whose breast I slept, and whose fair brow[97] so oft had bent over me before the noise of battle had stirred[98] my blood, or the fierce toil of war[99] nerved my sinews, did with fondest memory[100] of bygone[101] hours entreat me to remain. I have seen her who, when my country called me to the field, did buckle on[102] my harness[103] with trembling hands, while the tears fell thick and fast

down the hard corselet scales,[101]—I have seen her tear her gray locks, and beat her aged breast, as on her knees she begged me not to return to Carthage; and all the assembled senate of Rome, grave[105] and reverend[106] men, proffered[107] the same request. The puny[108] torments which ye have in store[109] to welcome me withal,[110] shall be, to what I have endured, even as the murmur of a summer's brook to the fierce roar of angry surges[111] in a rocky beach.[112]

9. "Last night, as I lay fettered[113] in my dungeon, I heard a strange, ominous[114] sound; it seemed like the distant march of some vast army, their harness clanging[115] as they marched, when suddenly there stood by me, Xanthippus, the Spartan general, by whose aid you conquered me, and, with a voice low as when the solemn[116] wind moans[117] through the leafless forest, he thus addressed me: 'Roman, I come to bid thee curse, with thy dying breath, this fated[118] city; know that in an evil moment, the Carthaginian generals, furious with rage that I had conquered thee, their conqueror, did basely[119] murder me. And then they thought to stain[120] my brightest honor. But, for this foul deed,[121] the wrath[122] of Jove shall rest upon them here and hereafter.' And then he vanished.[123]

10. "And now, go bring your sharpest torments. The woes[124] I see impending[125] over this guilty realm[126] shall be enough to sweeten death, though every nerve and artery were a shooting pang.[127] I die! but my death shall prove a proud triumph; and, for every drop of blood ye from my veins do draw, your own shall flow in rivers. Woe[128] to thee, Carthage! woe to the proud city of the waters! I see thy nobles wailing[129] at the feet of Roman senators! thy citizens in terror! thy ships in flames! I hear the victorious shouts of Rome! I see her eagles glittering on thy ramparts. Proud city, thou art doomed![130] The curse[131] of God is on thee—a clinging,[132] wasting[133] curse. It shall not leave thy gates till hungry flames shall lick the fretted

gold[131] from off thy proud palaces, and every brook runs crimson[133] to the sea."

E. KELLOG.

[1] Strahlen, [2] ragend, [3] prächtig, [4] mild, [5] Schein, Anflug, [6] finster drohend, [7] Brustwehre, [8] geschützt, [9] grün, [10] Dreiruderer (ein Boot mit Dreiruderfitzen auf jeder Seite), [11] lagen stolz vor Anker, [12] messingen, [13] Schnäbel, [14] Wimpel, [15] flatternd, [16] zersplittert, [17] Zeugniß, [18] Geräusch, [19] Festgelage, [20] Handwerker, [21] verlassen, [22] Heiligthum, [23] ernst, [24] Stoiker (ein Philosoph der stoischen Schule), [25] Zurückgezogenheit, [26] aufgeregt, [27] strömte, [28] aufgescheucht, [29] wüthend vor Zorn, [30] begierig nach Rache, [31] schmachteten, [32] Fesseln, [33] Kerker, [34] Gesichtszüge, [35] überragend, [36] gefürchtet, [37] weit entfernt zu rathen, [38] seine Zustimmung zu geben, [39] Auswechselung, [40] in sie gedrungen, [41] vertilgend, [42] Menschenmenge, [43] wogte, [44] Sturm, [45] Wuth, [46] lärmend, [47] machte sich Luft, [48] grollendes Gebeul, [49] Flüche, [50] Rachegeheul, [51] ruhig, [52] rasend, [53] Bewegung, [54] gebieterisch, [55] glänzend, [56] Cohorten (Heerschaaren), [57] genturmelt, [58] tief, [59] das Klirren, [60] Handschellen, [61] Handgelenke, [62] klar und deutlich das Ohr eines Jeden traf, [63] ungeheuer, [64] meinen geleisteten Schwur, [65] ertragen, [66] nach Punischen (Carthagenienfischen) Begriffen, [67] erniedrigen, [68] geschickt, [69] verrätherisch, [70] Elfenbein, [71] klar, [72] Adern, [73] frei vererbt, [74] Vorfahren, [75] schleimig, [76] träge fließende Flüssigkeit, [77] fault, [78] Adern, [79] daß ihr euren Muth kühlen mögt, [80] trotze, [81] besiegt, [82] eingeäschert, [83] geschleift, [84] Kampfwagen, [85] schwingen, [86] kriechen, [87] krümmen, [88] unterwürfig, [89] haltlose, [90] zerreißen, [91] Sehnen, [92] Spielerei, [93] geistig, [94] Schmerz, [95] der in meiner Brust wühlt, [96] abgenommen, [97] Stirn, Antlitz, [98] mein Blut hatte wallen gemacht, [99] die wilde Kriegsarbeit, [100] mit zärtlicher Erinnerung an, [101] vergangen, [102] umgürtete, [103] Waffenrüstung, [104] Panzerschuppen, [105] ernst, [106] ehrwürdig, [107] stellten, [108] verächtlich, [109] Bereitschaft, [110] auch, gleichzeitig, [111] Brandung, [112] Felsbucht, [113] gefesselt, [114] bedeutungsvoll, [115] klirrend, [116] feierlich, [117] seufzt, [118] verflucht, [119] niederträchtiger Weise, [120] beflecken, [121] Schandthat, [122] Zorn, [123] verschwand, [124] Unheil, [125] schwebend, [126] Reich, [127] reißender Schmerz, [128] Wehe dir! [129] wehklagend, [130] dein Schicksal ist besiegelt, [131] Fluch, [132] bleibend, [133] vernichtend, [134] Goldverzierungen von erhabener Arbeit, [135] blutroth.

Lesestück 2.

THE ENGLISH LANGUAGE.

Give me of every language, first my vigorous[1] English
Stored[2] with imported wealth, rich in its natural mines—
Grand in its rhythmical[3] cadence,[4] simple for household employment—
Worthy the poet's song, fit for the speech of a man.

Not from one metal alone the perfectest mirror⁵ is shapen,⁶
Not from one color is built the rainbow's aërial⁷ bridge,
Instruments blending together⁸ yield⁹ the divinest¹⁰ of music,
Out of a myriad flowers sweetest of honey is drawn.

So unto thy close¹¹ strength is welded¹² and beaten together
Iron dug¹³ from the North, ductile¹⁴ gold from the South;
So unto thy broad stream the ice-torrents¹⁵ born in the mountains
Rush,¹⁶ and the rivers pour brimming with sun¹⁷ from the plains.

Thou hast the sharp clean edge¹⁸ and the downright¹⁹ blow²⁰ of the Saxon,
Thou the majestical march and the stately pomp of the Latin,
Thou the euphonious²¹ swell,²² the rhythmical roll²³ of the Greek;
Thine is the elegant suavity²⁴ caught from sonorous²⁵ Italian,
Thine the chivalric²⁶ obeisance,²⁷ the courteous²⁸ grace²⁹ of the Norman—
Thine the Teutonic German's inborn³⁰ guttural strength.

Raftered³¹ by firm-laid consonants, windowed³² by opening vowels,
Thou securely art built, free to the sun and the air;
Over thy feudal³³ battlements³⁴ trail³⁵ the wild tendrils³⁶ of fancy,
Where in the early morn warbled³⁷ our earliest birds;

Science looks out from thy watch-tower, love whispers
 in at thy lattice,³⁸
While o'er thy bastions wit flashes³⁹ its glittering⁴⁰
 sword.

Not by corruption rotted nor slowly by ages⁴¹ de-
 graded,⁴²
Have the sharp consonants gone crumbling⁴³ away
 from our words;
Virgin⁴⁴ and clean is their edge like granite blocks
 chiseled⁴⁵ by Egypt;
Just as when Shakespeare and Milton laid them in
 glorious verse.

Fitted for every use like a great majestical river,
Blending thy various streams, stately thou flowest
 along,
Bearing the white-winged ship of Poesy over thy
 bosom,
Laden with spices⁴⁶ that come out of the tropical
 isles,⁴⁷
Fancy's pleasuring yacht⁴⁸ with its bright and flutter-
 ing pennons,⁴⁹
Logic's⁵⁰ frigates of war and the toil-worn⁵¹ barges⁵²
 of trade.

How art thou freely obedient unto the poet or speaker
When, in a happy hour, thought into speech he trans-
 lates;
Caught on the word's sharp angles flash the bright
 hues⁵³ of his fancy—
Grandly the thought rides the words, as a good horse-
 man his steed.⁵⁴

Now, clear, pure, hard, bright, and one by one, like to
 hail-stones,
Short words fall from his lips fast as the first of a
 shower—

Now in a twofold column,⁵⁵ Spondee,⁵⁶ Iamb,⁵⁷ and Trochee,⁵⁸
Unbroke, firm-set,⁵⁹ advance, retreat, trampling along—
Now with a sprightlier springiness⁶⁰ bounding in⁶¹ triplicate⁶² syllables,
Dance the elastic Dactylics⁶³ in musical cadences on,
Now their voluminous⁶⁴ coil⁶⁵ intertangling⁶⁶ like huge anacondas,
Roll overwhelmingly⁶⁷ onward the sesquipedalian⁶⁸ words.

Flexile⁶⁹ and free in thy gait⁷⁰ and simple in all thy construction,
Yielding to every turn thou bearest thy rider along;
Now like our hackney⁷¹ or draught-horse⁷² serving our commonest uses,
Now bearing grandly the Poet Pegasus-like to the sky.

Thou art not prisoned in fixed rules, thou art no slave to a grammar,
Thou art an eagle uncaged,⁷³ scorning⁷⁴ the perch⁷⁵ and the chain;
Hadst thou been fettered and formalized,⁷⁶ thou hadst been tamer and weaker.
How could the poor slave walk with thy grand freedom of gait?
Let, then, grammarians rail,⁷⁷ and let foreigners sigh for thy sign-posts,⁷⁸
Wandering lost in thy maze,⁷⁹ the wilds⁸⁰ of magnificent growth.

Call thee incongruous,⁸¹ wild, of rule and of reason defiant;⁸²
I in thy wildness a grand freedom of character find.
So with irregular outline⁸³ tower up⁸⁴ thy sky-piercing mountains,

Rearing[85] o'er yawning[86] chasms[87] lofty precipitous[88] steeps.[89]
Spreading o'er ledges[90] unclimbable, meadows and slopes[91] of green smoothness,[92]
Bearing the flowers in their clefts, losing their peaks in the clouds.

Therefore it is that I praise thee, and never can cease from rejoicing,
Thinking that good stout English is mine and my ancestors'[93] tongue;
Give me its varying music, the flow of its free modulation—
I will not covet[94] the full roll of the glorious Greek,—
Luscious[95] and feeble Italian, Latin so formal and stately,
French with its nasal lisp[96] nor German inverted[97] and harsh—
Not while our organ[98] can speak with its many and wonderful voices—
Play on the soft flute of love, blow the loud trumpet of war,
Sing with the high sesquialtro,[99] or drawing its full diapason[100]
Shake all the air with the grand storm of its pedals and stops.

WILLIAM W. STORY.

[1] kräftig, [2] versehen, reich an, [3] rythmisch, [4] Tonfall, [5] Spiegel, [6] geformt, [7] luftig, [8] zusammenklingend, [9] bringen hervor, [10] göttlichst, [11] gedrungen, [12] geschmiedet, [13] ausgegraben, [14] dehnbar, [15] die eiligen Gießbäche, [16] strömen, [17] voll von Sonne, d. i. sonnenhell, [18] Schneide, [19] aufrichtig, natürlich, [20] Bucht, [21] wohlklingend, [22] Kraft (kräftigen Wohllaut), [23] Schlag, [24] Weichheit, [25] volltönend, [26] ritterlich, [27] Ergebenheit, [28] höflich, [29] Anmuth, [30] angeboren, [31] das Gerüst, gebaut, [32] mit Fenstern versehen, [33] mittelalterlich, [34] Brustwehren, [35] laufen, [36] Schlingpflanzen, [37] trillerten, [38] Gitterfenster, Kammerfenster, [39] blitzen läßt, [40] glänzend, [41] Jahrhunderte, [42] entartet, [43] verwitternd, [44] jungfräulich, [45] gemeißelt, [46] Gewürze, [47] Inseln, [48] Lustschiff, [49] Wimpel, [50] Logik, [51] von anstrengender Arbeit hart mitgenommen, [52] Lastschiffe, [53] Farben, [54] Roß, [55] Heeressäule, [56] Spondäus (— —), [57] Jambus

Die progressive Form.

($\smile$ —), ⁵⁸ Trochäus (— $\smile$), ⁵ festgefügt, ⁶⁰ Elasticität, ⁶¹ springend, ⁶² dreifach, ⁶³ Daktolen (— $\smile$ $\smile$), ⁶⁴ ungeheuer, ⁶⁵ Ringe, ⁶⁶ ineinanderschlingend, ⁶⁷ überwältigend, ⁶⁸ ellenlang (eigentlich 1½ Fuß), ⁶⁹ biegsam, ⁷⁰ Gang, ⁷¹ Miethgaul, ⁷² Lastgaul, ⁷³ ungefesselt, ⁷⁴ verachtend, ⁷⁵ Sitz, ⁷⁶ zugestutzt, ⁷⁷ spotten, ⁷⁸ Meilenzeiger, ⁷⁹ Labyrinth, ⁸⁰ Urwald, ⁸¹ inconsequent, ⁸² trotzend, ⁸³ Umrissen, ⁸⁴ ragen empor, ⁸⁵ bauend, ⁸⁶ gähnend, ⁸⁷ Schlünde, ⁸⁸ jäh, ⁸⁹ Abhänge, ⁹⁰ Feldrücken, ⁹¹ Abhänge, ⁹² von weichem Grün, ⁹³ Vorfahren, ⁹⁴ begierig sein nach, ⁹⁵ süß, saftig, ⁹⁶ mit näselndem Lispeln, ⁹⁷ verdreht, ⁹⁸ Orgel, Organ, ⁹⁹ Sesquialtro, eine Stimme an der Orgel, die drei Reihen Pfeifen hat, ¹⁰⁰ Diapason, eine andere Stimme.

SIMONNÉ'S MANUAL OF FRENCH VERBS.

Comprising the formation of Persons, Tenses, and Moods of the Regular and Irregular Verbs; a Practical Method to trace the Infinitive of a Verb out of any of its Inflections; Models of Sentences in their different Forms; and a Series of the most useful Idiomatical Phrases. By T. SIMONNÉ. 12mo. 108 pages. Price, 75 cents.

The title of this volume, given in full above, shows its scope and character. The conjugation of the verbs, regular as well as irregular, is the great difficulty that the French student has to encounter; and, to aid him in surmounting it, M. Simonné has applied his long experience as a teacher of the language.

SPIERS AND SURENNE'S

French - and - English and English-and-French Pronouncing Dictionary. Edited by G. P. Quackenbos, A. M. One large vol., 8vo, of 1,316 pp., neat type, and fine paper. Half Mor., $6.

The publishers claim for this work,

1. That it is a revision and combination of (Spiers's) the best defining and (Surenne's) the most accurate pronouncing dictionary extant.
2. That in this work the numerous errors in Spiers's dictionary have been carefully and faithfully corrected.
3. That some three thousand new definitions have been added.
4. That numerous definitions and constructions are elucidated by grammatical remarks and illustrative clauses and sentences.
5. That several thousand new phrases and idioms are embodied.
6. That upward of twelve hundred synonymous terms are explained, by pointing out their distinctive shades of meaning.
7. That the parts of all the irregular verbs are inserted in alphabetical order, so that one reference gives the mood, tense, person, and number.
8. That some four thousand new French words, connected with science, art, and literature, have been added.
9. That every French word is accompanied by as exact a pronunciation as can be represented by corresponding English sounds, and vice versa.
10. That it contains a full vocabulary of the names of persons and places, mythological and classical, ancient and modern.
11. That the arrangement is the most convenient for reference that can be adopted.
12. That it is the most complete, accurate, and reliable dictionary of these languages published.

VOLTAIRE'S HISTORY OF CHARLES XII.

Carefully revised by GABRIEL SURENNE. 16mo. 202 pages. Price, 75 cents.

This is a neat edition of Voltaire's valuable and popular History of Charles XII., King of Sweden, published under the supervision of a distinguished scholar, and well adapted to the use of schools in this country.

WINKELMAN'S FRENCH SYNTAX;

being a course of Exercises in all parts of French Syntax, methodically arranged after Poitevin's "Syntaxe Française;" to which are added Ten Appendices, designed for the use of Academies, Colleges, and Private Learners. By FREDERICK J. WINKELMAN, A. M., PH. D., Professor of Latin, French, and German, in the Packer Collegiate Institute. 12mo. 366 pages. $1.25.

This work is intended for students who already have a partial acquaintance with the French language, but wish to acquire a more thorough knowledge of its Syntax than can be obtained through the text-books in general use. It is arranged in the same manner as the practical part of Poitevin's "Syntaxe Française." The examples of Syntax are mainly translations of passages from the best French authors. The Appendices—of which there are ten—illustrate various difficult points in French grammar.

THE MASTERY SERIES FOR Learning Languages on New Principles. By THOMAS PRENDERGAST, Author of "The Mastery of Languages, or the Art of Speaking Foreign Tongues Idiomatically." This method offers a solution of the problem, How to obtain facility in speaking foreign languages grammatically, without using the Grammar in the first stage. It adopts and systematizes that process by which many couriers and explorers have become expert practical linguists.

HAND-BOOK TO THE MASTERY SERIES, being an Introductory Treatise. Price, 50 cents.

THE MASTERY SERIES, GERMAN. Price, 50 cents.

German.

ADLER'S GERMAN-AND-English, and English-and-German Pronouncing Dictionary. By G. J. ADLER, A. M., Professor of the German Language and Literature in the University of New York. One elegant large 8vo vol. 1,400 pages. Price, $6.

The aim of the distinguished author of this work has been to embody all the valuable results of the most recent investigations in a German Lexicon, which might become not only a reliable guide for the practical acquisition of the language, but one which would not forsake the student in the higher walks of his pursuits, to which its treasures would invite him.

In the preparation of the German and English Part, the basis adopted has been the work of Flügel, compiled in reality by Heimann, Feiling, and Oxenford. This was the most complete and judiciously-prepared manual of the kind in England.

The present work contains the accentuation of every German word, several hundred synonymes, together with a classification and alphabetical list of the irregular verbs, and a dictionary of German abbreviations.

The foreign words, likewise, which have not been completely Germanized, and which often differ in pronunciation and inflection from such as are purely native, have been designated by particular marks.

The vocabulary of foreign words, which now act so important a part, not only in scientific works, but in the best classics, reviews, journals, newspapers, and even in conversation, has been copiously supplied from the most complete and correct sources. It is believed that in the terminology of chemistry, mineralogy, the practical arts, commerce, navigation, rhetoric, grammar, mythology, philosophy, etc., scarcely a word will be found to be wanting.

The Second (or German-English) Part of this volume has been chiefly reprinted from the work of Flügel. The attention which has been paid in Germany to the preparation of English dictionaries for the German student has been such as to render these works very complete. The student, therefore, will scarcely find any thing deficient in this Second Part.

AN ABRIDGMENT OF THE ABOVE. 12mo. 844 pages. Price, $2.50.

With a view of offering to the student of German such a portion of his larger work as would embody the most general and important lexicographical elements of the language in the smallest possible compass, the author has gone over the entire ground of the larger work—revising, condensing, or adding, as the case might require. All provincialisms, synonymes, and strictly scientific terms, have been excluded from these pages, and every thing that might prove unnecessary or embarrassing to beginners, or to travellers, and others for whom a smaller volume is better adapted.

From C. C. FELTON, Prof. of Greek, Harvard Univ.

"The careful manner in which Prof. Adler has investigated the language as employed by the great body of recent German writers, and the accuracy with which the best usage is explained in his definitions, make the work peculiarly valuable for English and American students."

ADLER'S HAND-BOOK OF GERMAN LITERATURE.

Containing Schiller's Maid of Orleans, Goethe's Iphigenia in Tauris, Tieck's Puss in Boots, The Xenia, by Goethe and Schiller. With Critical Introductions and Explanatory Notes; to which is added an Appendix of Specimens of German Prose, from the middle of the Sixteenth to the middle of the Nineteenth Century. By G. J. ADLER. 12mo. 550 pages. Price, $1.50.

For classes that have made some proficiency in the German language, and desire an acquaintance with specimens of its dramatic literature, no more charming selection than this can be found. Sufficient aid is given, in the form of introductions and notes, to enable the student to understand thoroughly what he reads. The progress of the language is graphically illustrated by specimens of the literature at different eras, collated in an Appendix.

ADLER'S PROGRESSIVE GERMAN READER.

By G. J. ADLER, Professor of the German Language and Literature in the University of the City of New York. 12mo. 308 pages. Price, $1.50.

The plan of this German Reader is as follows:

1. The pieces are both prose and poetry, selected from the best authors, and present sufficient variety to keep alive the interest of the scholar.
2. It is progressive in its nature, the pieces being at first very short and easy, and increasing in difficulty and length as the learner advances.
3. At the bottom of the page constant references to the Grammar are made, the difficult passages are explained and rendered. To encourage the first attempt of the learner as much as possible, the twenty-one pieces of the first section are analyzed, and all the necessary words given at the bottom of the page. The notes, which at first are very abundant, diminish as the learner advances.

4. It contains *five* sections. The *first* contains easy pieces, chiefly in prose, with all the words necessary for translating them; the *second*, short pieces in prose and poetry alternately, with copious notes and renderings; the *third*, short popular tales of Grimm and others; the *fourth*, select ballads and other poems from Bürger, Goethe, Schiller, Uhland, Schwab, Chamisso, etc.; the *fifth*, prose extracts from the first classics.

5. At the end is added a vocabulary of all the words occurring in the book.

The pieces have been selected and the notes prepared with great taste and judgment, so much so as to render the book a general favorite with German teachers.

A NEW, PRACTICAL, AND Easy Method of Learning the German Language.

By F. AHN, Doctor of Philosophy, and Professor of the College of Neuss. 12mo. Price, $1.

EICHHORN'S PRACTICAL GERMAN GRAMMAR.

By CHARLES EICHHORN. 12mo. 287 pages. Price, $1.50.

Those who have used Eichhorn's Grammar commend it in the highest terms for the excellence of its arrangement, the simplicity of its rules, and the tact with which abstruse points of grammar are illustrated by means of written exercises. It is the work of a practical teacher, who has learned by experience what the difficulties of the pupil are and how to remove them.

ROEMER'S POLYGLOTT READER IN GERMAN.

Being a Translation of the English Selection. Translated by Dr. SOLGER. 12mo. $1.50.

WORMAN'S GERMAN GRAMMAR.

1 vol., 12mo. 500 pages. Price, $2.00.

The Elementary work by the same author has met with great success, having been introduced into a large number of schools and colleges.

OLLENDORFF'S NEW METH-OD of Learning to Read, Write, and Speak the German Language. By GEORGE J. ADLER, A. M. 12mo. 610 pages. Price, $1.25.

KEY TO EXERCISES. Separate volume. Price, $1.

Few books have maintained their popularity in the schools for so long a period as the Ollendorff series. The verdict pronounced in their favor, on their first appearance in Europe, has been signally confirmed in America. The publishers have received the strongest testimonials in relation to their merits from the press, from State and county school officers, from principals of academies, and teachers of public and private schools in all sections of the United States.

Grammars for Teaching English to Germans.

OLLENDORFF'S NEW METH-OD for Germans to Learn to Read, Write, and Speak the English Language. Arranged and Adapted to Schools and Private Academies. By P. GANDS. 12mo. 599 pages. Price, $1.50.

KEY TO THE EXERCISES. Separate volume. Price, $1.

BRYAN'S GRAMMAR FOR Germans to learn English. Edited by Professor SCHMIEDER. 12mo. 189 pages. Price, $1.25.

The publishers have got out these volumes in view of the great number of Germans residing in and constantly emigrating to the United States, with whom the speedy acquisition of English is a highly desirable object. To aid them in this, the services of competent and experienced teachers have been procured, and the admirable Grammars named above are the results of their labors.

The Ollendorff Grammar embraces a full and complete synopsis of English Grammar, applied at every step to practical exercises. It is constructed according to the "New Method" which has so generally approved itself to public favor. A month's study of this volume will supply the learner with such current idioms that he can comprehend ordinary conversation, and in turn make himself understood.

Bryan's Course is briefer, and better adapted for primary classes and those whose time of study is limited. It presents the cardinal principles of the language, well arranged and clearly illustrated. The anomalies of English syntax are handled in a masterly manner, and the general treatment of the subject such as to remove from it all difficulties by the way.

ELEMENTARY GERMAN READER. By Rev. L. W. HEYDENREICH, Professor of Languages at Bethlehem, Pa. Price, $1.00.

This is an excellent volume for beginners, combining the advantages of Grammar and Reader. It has received strong and cordial commendations from the best German scholars in the country; among whom are Prof. Schmidt, of Columbia College, N. Y.; William M. Reynolds, late Pres. of Capitol Univ., Columbus, Ohio; Edward H. Reichel, Principal of Nazareth Hall; W. D. Whitney, Prof. of Sanscrit and German in Yale College, etc., etc.

Italian.

MEADOWS'S ITALIAN-AND-ENGLISH DICTIONARY. In Two Parts. I. Italian-and-English; II. English-and-Italian. Comprehending, in the First Part, all the Old Words, Contractions, and Licences used by the ancient Italian Poets and Prose Writers; in the Second Part, all the various Meanings of English Verbs. With a new and concise Grammar, to render easy the acquirement of the Italian Language; exhibiting the Pronunciation by Corresponding Sounds, the Parts of Speech, Gender of Italian Nouns, New Conjugation of Regular and Irregular Verbs, Accent on Italian and English Words, List of usual Christian and Proper Names, Names of Countries and Nations. By F. C. MEADOWS, M. A. 1 vol., 16mo. $2.

ELEMENTARY GRAMMAR

OF THE ITALIAN LANGUAGE. Progressively Arranged for the use of Schools and Colleges. By G. B. FONTANA. 12mo. 236 pp. $1.50.

The object of this work is to present the language as spoken to-day, in its simplest garb, both theoretically and practically. The Grammar is divided into two parts, embracing Sixty Lessons and Sixty Exercises. The first part is exclusively given to rules indispensable to a general idea of the language; the second is framed for those who are desirous of having an insight into its theory, and consists of synonyms, maxims, idioms, and figurative expressions. The Exercises of both parts are very regularly progressive,—and those of the second part are of course the most difficult. Some of them contain extracts from celebrated poems translated into plain prose, so that the pupil may compare his Italian translation with the original, which has been inserted for that purpose at the end of the book. Others are biographical sketches of the most prominent among the Italian writers; by which means the pupil, whilst acquiring the language, may become familiar with the life and works of some of the classic Italian authors, such as Manzoni, Alfieri, Tasso, Petrarch, and the father of Italian language and literature, Dante Alighieri.

FORESTI'S ITALIAN

READER: A Collection of Pieces in Italian Prose, designed as a Reading-Book for Students of the Italian Language. By E. FELIX FORESTI, LL. D. 12mo. 293 pages. Price, $1.50.

In making selections for this volume, Prof. Foresti has had recourse to the modern writers of Italy rather than to the old school of novelists, historians, and poets; his object being to present a picture of the Italian language as it is written and spoken at the present day. The literary taste of the compiler and his judgment as an instructor have been brought to bear with the happiest results in this valuable Reader.

From the Savannah Republican.

"The selections are from popular authors, such as Botta, Manzoni, Machiavelli, Villani, and others.

They are so made as not to constitute mere exercises, but contain distinct relations so complete as to gratify the reader and engage his attention while they instruct. This is a marked improvement on that old system which exacted much labor without enlisting the sympathies of the student. The idioms that occur in the selections are explained by a glossary appended to each. The Italian Reader can with confidence be recommended to students in the language as a safe and sure guide. After mastering it, the Italian poets and other classicists may be approached with confidence."

MILLHOUSE'S NEW ENG-

lish-and-Italian and Italian-and-English Dictionary. With the Pronunciation of the Italian. With many additions, by FERDINAND BRACCIFORTI. 2 vols., 8vo. Half bound, $6.00.

This Italian Dictionary is considered the best which has yet been published. It was prepared by the late John Millhouse, and is acknowledged, by those who have made themselves familiar with the Italian, to excel all that have yet appeared.

ROEMER'S POLYGLOTT

Reader, in the Italian Language; being a Translation of the English Book under that title. 1 vol., 12mo. $1.50.

Ollendorff's Italian Grammars.

PRIMARY LESSONS IN

Learning to Read, Write, and Speak the Italian Language. Introductory to the Larger Grammar. By G. W. GREENE. 18mo. 238 pages. Price, 75 cts.

OLLENDORFF'S NEW METH-

OD of Learning to Read, Write, and Speak the Italian Language. With Additions and Corrections. By E. FELIX FORESTI. LL. D. 12mo. 533 pages. Price, $1.50.

KEY. Separate volume. Price, $1.

In Ollendorff's grammars is for the first time presented a system by which the student can acquire a conversational knowledge of Italian. This will recommend them to practical students; while, at the same time, there is no lack of rules and principles for those who would pursue a systematic grammatical course with the view of translating and writing the language.

Prof. Greene's Introduction should be taken up by youthful classes, for whom it is specially designed, the more difficult parts of the course being left for the larger volume.

The advanced work has been carefully revised by Prof. Foresti, who has made such emendations and additions as the wants of the country required. In many sections the services of an Italian teacher cannot be obtained; the Ollendorff Course and Key will there supply the want of a master in the most satisfactory manner.

From the United States Gazette.

"The system of learning and teaching the living languages by Ollendorff is so superior to all other modes, that in England and on the Continent of Europe, scarcely any other is in use. In well-directed academies and other institutions of learning. To those who feel disposed to cultivate an acquaintance with Italian literature, this work will prove invaluable, abridging, by an immense deal, the period commonly employed in studying the language."

Spanish.

AHN'S SPANISH GRAMMAR;

being a New, Practical, and Easy Method of Learning the Spanish Language; after the System of A. F. Ahn, Doctor of Philosophy, and Professor at the College of Neuss. First American edition, revised and enlarged. 12mo. 149 pages. $1.

KEY. **25 cents.**

Prof. Ahn's method is one of peculiar excellence, and has met with great success. It has been happily described in his own words: "Learn a foreign language as you learned your mother tongue"—in the same simple manner, and with the same natural gradations. This method of the distinguished German Doctor has been applied in the present instance to the Spanish Language, upon the basis of the excellent Grammars of Lespada and Martinez, and it is hoped that its simplicity and utility will procure for it the favor that its German, French, and Italian prototypes have already found in the Schools and Colleges of Europe.

(DE BELEM) THE SPANISH

PHRASE-BOOK; or, Key to Spanish Conversation. Containing the chief Idioms of the Spanish Language, with the Conjugations of the Auxiliary and the Regular Verbs, on the plan of the late Abbé Bossut. By E. M. DE BELEM. 1 vol., 18mo. 87 cents.

DE VERE'S GRAMMAR OF

THE SPANISH LANGUAGE. With a History of the Language and Practical Exercises. By M. SCHELE DE VERE. 12mo. 273 pages. Price, $1.50.

In this volume are embodied the results of many years' experience on the part of the author, as Professor of Spanish in the University of Virginia. It aims to impart a critical knowledge of the language by a systematic course of grammar, illustrated with appropriate exercises. The author has availed himself of the labors of recent grammarians and critics; and by condensing his rules and principles, and rejecting a burdensome superfluity of detail, he has brought the whole within a comparatively small compass. By pursuing this simple course, the language may be easily and quickly mastered, not only for conversational purposes, but for reading it fluently and writing it with elegance.

From the Philadelphia Daily News.

"No student of the Castilian dialect should be without this Grammar. It is at once concise and comprehensive—*multum in parvo*—containing nothing that is redundant, yet omitting nothing that is essential to the learner. The conjugations are so admirably arranged as no longer to present that stumbling-block which has frightened so many from the study of one of the richest and most majestic of languages."

BUTLER'S SPANISH TEACH-er and Colloquial Phrase-Book: An Easy and Agreeable Method of Acquiring a Speaking Knowledge of the Spanish Language. By Professor BUTLER. 18mo. 293 pages. Price, 60 cts.

The object of the author is to make the Spanish language a living, speaking tongue to the learner; and the method he adopts is that of nature. He begins with the simplest elements, and progressively advances, applying all former acquisitions as he proceeds, until the learner has mastered one of the most perfect languages of modern times.

From the N. Y. Journal of Commerce.
"This is a good book, and well fitted for the purposes for which it is designed. The Spanish language is one of great simplicity, and more easily acquired than any other modern tongue. For a beginner, we recommend this little book, which is small, and designed to be carried in the pocket."

MEADOWS'S SPANISH-AND-ENGLISH DICTIONARY. In Two Parts. I. Spanish-and-English; II. English-and-Spanish. The First Part comprehends all the Spanish Words, with their appropriate Accents, and every Noun with its Gender. The Second Part, with the addition of many new Words, contains all the various Meanings of English Verbs, in Alphabetical Order, all expressed by their correspondent Spanish, in a simple and definite sense. At the end of both Parts is affixed a list of usual Christian and Proper Names, Names of Countries, Nations, etc. By F. C. MEADOWS, M. A. 1 vol., 16mo. $2.

MERCANTILE DICTIONARY: A Complete Vocabulary of the Technicalities of Commercial Correspondence, Names of Articles of Trade, and Marine Terms in English, Spanish, and French. With Geographical Names, Business Letters, and Tables of Abbreviations in Common Use in the three languages. By J. DE VIETELLE. 1 vol., 12mo. $2.

Ollendorff's Grammar for Teaching French to Spaniards.

GRAMATICA FRANCESA: Un Método para Aprender á Leer, Escribir y Hablar el Frances, segun el Verdadero Sistema de Ollendorff. Ordenado en Lecciones Progresivas, consistiendo de Ejercicios Orales y Escritos; enriquecido de la Pronunciacion Figurada como se estila en la Conversacion; y de un Apendice, abrazando las Reglas de la Sintaxis, la Formacion de los Verbos Regulares, y la Conjugacion de los Irregulares. Por TEODORO SIMONNE. 12mo. 341 pages. Price, $2.

KEY TO EXERCISES. Separate volume. Price, $1.

M. Simonne has done a good work in bringing the French language within the reach of Spaniards by this application of the Ollendorff system. A few weeks' study of his "Gramática Francesa" will impart a knowledge of the more common conversational idioms, and a thorough mastery of it will insure as perfect an acquaintance with French as can be desired. With the aid of the KEY the study can be pursued without a master; for the illustrative exercises at once show whether the grammatical rules and principles successively laid down are properly understood.

ROEMER'S POLYGLOTT READER (IN SPANISH). Translated by SIMON CAMACHO. 1 vol., 12mo. Half bound, $1.50.

KEY TO SAME (IN ENGLISH). 1 vol., 12mo. $1.50.

MORALES'S PROGRESSIVE SPANISH READER. With an Analytical Study of the Spanish Language. By AGUSTIN JOSÉ MORALES, A. M., H. M., Professor of the Spanish Language and Literature in the New York Free Academy. 12mo. 336 pages. Price, $1.50.

The prose extracts in this volume are preceded by an historical account of the origin and progress of the Spanish Language, and a condensed, scholarlike treatise on its grammar; the poetical selections are introduced with an essay on Spanish versification. Prepared in either case by the preliminary matter thus furnished, bearing directly on his work, the pupil enters intelligently on his task of translating. The extracts are brief, spirited, and entertaining; drawn mainly from writers of the present day, they are a faithful representation of the language as it is now written and spoken. The arrangement is progressive, specimens of a more difficult character being presented as the student becomes able to cope with them.

NEW SPANISH READER. Consisting of Extracts from the Works of the most approved Authors in Prose and Verse, arranged in Progressive Order. With Notes explanatory of the Idioms and most difficult constructions, and a copious Vocabulary. By M. VELAZQUEZ DE LA CADENA. 12mo. 351 pages. Price, $1.50.

This book, being particularly intended for the use of beginners, has been prepared with three objects in view: first, to furnish learners with pleasing and easy lessons, progressively developing the beauties and difficulties of the Spanish language; secondly, to enrich their minds with valuable knowledge; and thirdly, to form their character, by instilling correct principles into their hearts. In order, therefore, to obtain the desired effects, the extracts have been carefully selected from those classic Spanish writers, both ancient and modern, whose style is generally admitted to be a pattern of elegance, combined with idiomatic purity and sound morality.

OLLENDORFF'S SPANISH GRAMMAR; A New Method of Learning to Read, Write, and Speak the Spanish Language. With Practical Rules for Spanish Pronunciation, and Models of Social and Commercial Correspondence. By M. VELAZQUEZ and T. SIMONNE. 12mo. 560 pages. Price, $1.5).

KEY TO THE SAME. Separate volume. Price, $1.

The admirable system introduced by Ollendorff is applied in this volume to the Spanish language. Having received, from the two distinguished editors to whom its supervision was intrusted, corrections, emendations, and additions, which specially adapt it to the youth of this country, it is believed to embrace every possible advantage for imparting a thorough and practical knowledge of Spanish. A course of systematic grammar underlies the whole; but its development is so gradual and inductive as not to weary the learner. Numerous examples of regular and irregular verbs are presented; and nothing that can expedite the pupil's progress, in the way of explanation and illustration, is omitted.

From the Republic.

"It contains the best rules we have ever yet seen for learning a living language. It leads the student on, by almost imperceptible steps, from the simplest principles to the most recondite and complex combinations of grammatical constructions; and the parts are so arranged as to render every thing subservient to that which should be the chief point of view, the great object of ambition, viz., use, speech, conversation. Every part of speech, every simple and compound sentence, is so analyzed, so illustrated by explanatory dialogues, that it is impossible to open the book at any page without acquiring some valuable information capable of advancing the student in his progress as a linguist."

From the N. Y. Courier and Enquirer.

"The editors of this work are widely known as accomplished scholars and distinguished teachers, and the book derives still higher authority from their connection with it. We commend it with great confidence to all who desire to become acquainted with the Castilian tongue."

www.ingramcontent.com/pod-product-compliance
Lightning Source LLC
Chambersburg PA
CBHW022025240426
43667CB00042B/1176